Advances in Experimental Philosophy of Action

Advances in Experimental Philosophy

Series Editor:
Justin Sytsma, Lecturer in Philosophy, Victoria University of Wellington, New Zealand

Editorial Board:
Joshua Knobe, Yale University, USA
Edouard Machery, University of Pittsburgh, USA
Thomas Nadelhoffer, College of Charleston, UK
Eddy Nahmias, Neuroscience Institute at Georgia State University, USA
Jennifer Nagel, University of Toronto, Canada
Joshua Alexander, Siena College, USA

Empirical and experimental philosophy is generating tremendous excitement, producing unexpected results that are challenging traditional philosophical methods. *Advances in Experimental Philosophy* responds to this trend, bringing together some of the most exciting voices in the field to understand the approach and measure its impact in contemporary philosophy. The result is a series that captures past and present developments and anticipates future research directions.

To provide in-depth examinations, each volume links experimental philosophy to a key philosophical area. They provide historical overviews alongside case studies, reviews of current problems and discussions of new directions. For upper-level undergraduates, postgraduates and professionals actively pursuing research in experimental philosophy these are essential resources.

Titles in the series include:
Advances in Experimental Epistemology, edited by James R. Beebe
Advances in Experimental Moral Psychology, edited by Hagop Sarkissian and Jennifer Cole Wright
Advances in Experimental Philosophy and Philosophical Methodology, edited by Jennifer Nado
Advances in Experimental Philosophy of Aesthetics, edited by Florian Cova and Sébastien Réhault
Advances in Experimental Philosophy of Language, edited by Jussi Haukioja
Advances in Experimental Philosophy of Logic and Mathematics, edited by Andrew Aberdein and Matthew Inglis
Advances in Experimental Philosophy of Mind, edited by Justin Sytsma
Advances in Religion, Cognitive Science, and Experimental Philosophy, edited by Helen De Cruz and Ryan Nichols
Experimental Metaphysics, edited by David Rose
Methodological Advances in Experimental Philosophy, edited by Eugen Fischer and Mark Curtis
Advances in Experimental Philosophy of Free Will and Responsibility, edited by Thomas Nadelhoffer and Andrew Monroe
Advances in Experimental Philosophy of Causation, edited by Alex Wiegmann and Pascale Willemsen
Experimental Philosophy of Identity and the Self, edited by Kevin Tobia

Advances in Experimental Philosophy of Action

Edited by
Paul Henne and Samuel Murray

BLOOMSBURY ACADEMIC
LONDON • NEW YORK • OXFORD • NEW DELHI • SYDNEY

BLOOMSBURY ACADEMIC
Bloomsbury Publishing Plc
50 Bedford Square, London, WC1B 3DP, UK
1385 Broadway, New York, NY 10018, USA
29 Earlsfort Terrace, Dublin 2, Ireland

BLOOMSBURY, BLOOMSBURY ACADEMIC and the Diana logo are trademarks of Bloomsbury Publishing Plc

First published in Great Britain 2023
This paperback edition published 2024

Copyright © Paul Henne, Samuel Murray, and Contributors, 2023

Paul Henne and Samuel Murray have asserted their right under the Copyright, Designs and Patents Act, 1988, to be identified as Editors of this work.

Series design by Catherine Wood
Cover image © Dieter Leistner / GallerystockCover

All rights reserved. No part of this publication may be reproduced or transmitted in any form or by any means, electronic or mechanical, including photocopying, recording, or any information storage or retrieval system, without prior permission in writing from the publishers.

Bloomsbury Publishing Plc does not have any control over, or responsibility for, any third-party websites referred to or in this book. All internet addresses given in this book were correct at the time of going to press. The author and publisher regret any inconvenience caused if addresses have changed or sites have ceased to exist, but can accept no responsibility for any such changes.

A catalogue record for this book is available from the British Library.

A catalog record for this book is available from the Library of Congress.

ISBN: HB: 978-1-3502-6632-2
PB: 978-1-3502-6636-0
ePDF: 978-1-3502-6633-9
eBook: 978-1-3502-6634-6

Series: Advances in Experimental Philosophy

Typeset by Deanta Global Publishing Services, Chennai, India

To find out more about our authors and books visit www.bloomsbury.com and sign up for our newsletters.

*Dedicated to Walter Sinnott-Armstrong
and Felipe De Brigard*

Contents

List of Figures		viii
List of Contributors		ix
	Introduction to *Advances in Experimental Philosophy of Action*	
	Samuel Murray and Paul Henne	1
1	Consciousness, Phenomenal Consciousness, and Free Will	
	Justin Sytsma and Melissa Snater	13
2	Skilled Action and Metacognitive Control Myrto Mylopoulos	33
3	Bringing Self-control into the Future Samuel Murray	51
4	Who Is Responsible?: Split Brains, Dissociative Identity Disorder, and Implicit Attitudes Walter Sinnott-Armstrong	73
5	The Everyday Irrationality of Monothematic Delusion Paul Noordhof and Ema Sullivan-Bissett	87
6	Truth, Perspective, and Norms of Assertion: New Findings and Theoretical Advances John Turri	113
7	The Distinct Functions of Belief and Desire in Intentional Action Explanation Joanna Korman	135
8	Free Enough: Human Cognition (And Cultural Interests) Warrant Responsibility Cory J. Clark, Heather M. Maranges, Brian B. Boutwell, and Roy F. Baumeister	151
9	Beyond the Courtroom: Agency and the Perception of Free Will Edouard Machery, Markus Kneer, Pascale Willemsen, and Albert Newen	171
10	Do Rape Cases Sit in a Moral Blindspot? The Dual-Process Theory of Moral Judgment and Rape Katrina L. Sifferd	191
11	How People Think about Moral Excellence: The Role of Counterfactual Thoughts in Reasoning about Morally Good Actions Shane Timmons and Ruth M. J. Byrne	209
12	Why Idealized Agency Gets Animal (and Human) Agency Wrong Caroline T. Arruda and Daniel J. Povinelli	229
Index		253

Figures

1.1	Study results by condition and dendrogram for hierarchical cluster analysis	26
6.1	Rates of attribution and visualization of generalized linear mixed model for Experiment 1	120
6.2	Rates of attribution and visualization of generalized linear mixed model for Experiment 2	124
6.3	Visualization of generalized linear model predicting evaluations of assertion in Experiment 2	127
7.1	Belief-desire explanations and various puzzles of social explanation	138
9.1	Two versions of the Agency Model	174
9.2	Visualization of video stimuli used in Experiment	175
9.3	Mean ratings across Agency (agent v. object) split by Valence (help v. hinder)	179
9.4	Mean ratings across Valence split by Agency	179
9.5	Mediation analysis for the impact of agency on free will attribution	180
9.6	Mediation analysis for the impact of valence on free will attribution	180
11.1	Types of counterfactuals created by participants	215
11.2	Judgments that an action should have been takne	219

Contributors

Caroline T. Arruda is an associate professor in the Department of Philosophy at Tulane University.

Roy F. Baumeister is a professor of psychology in the School of Psychology at the University of Queensland in Australia. He is also president-elect of the International Positive Psychology Association.

Brian Boutwell is an associate professor of criminal justice and legal studies at the University of Mississippi.

Ruth M. J. Byrne is a professor of cognitive science in the School of Psychology and the Institute of Neuroscience at Trinity College Dublin, Ireland.

Cory J. Clark is the director of the Adversarial Collaboration Project and a visiting scholar at the University of Pennsylvania.

Paul Henne is an assistant professor of Philosophy and Neuroscience at Lake Forest College.

Marcus Kneer is a research associate at the University of Zurich, Switzerland.

Joanna Korman is an assistant professor of psychology in the Department of Natural and Applied Sciences at Bentley University.

Edouard Machery is a distinguished professor in the Department of History and Philosophy of Science at the University of Pittsburgh. He is also the director of the Center for Philosophy of Science at the University of Pittsburgh.

Heather M. Maranges is the co-director of research at the Program for Leadership and Character and research associate in the Department of Psychology at Wake Forest University.

Samuel Murray is an assistant professor in the Department of Philosophy and the Neuroscience Program at Providence College.

Myrto Mylopoulos is an associate professor of philosophy and cognitive science at Carleton University in Ottawa, Canada.

Albert Newen is professor of philosophy at the Ruhr University Bochum, Germany.

Paul Noordhof is the Anniversary Professor of Philosophy in the Department of Philosophy at the University of York, United Kingdom.

Daniel J. Povinelli is a professor of biology at the University of Louisiana at Lafayette.

Katrina L. Sifferd is a professor in the Department of Philosophy and holds the Genevieve Staudt Endowed Chair at Elmhurst University.

Walter Sinnott-Armstrong is Chauncey Stillman Professor of Practical Ethics in the Department of Philosophy and the Kenan Institute for Ethics at Duke University. He is core faculty in the Duke Center for Cognitive Neuroscience and has an appointment with the Duke Law School.

Melissa Snater is a graduate student at the Victoria University of Wellington.

Ema Sullivan-Bissett is a reader in philosophy in the School of Philosophy, Theology and Religion at the University of Birmingham, United Kingdom.

Justin Sytsma is an associate professor in the Philosophy Programme in the School of History, Philosophy, Political Science and International Relations at Victoria University of Wellington, New Zealand.

Shane Timmons is a research officer with the Behavioural Research Unit at the Economic and Social Research Institute in Dublin, Ireland.

John Turri is the Canada Research Chair in Philosophy and Cognitive Science at the University of Waterloo, Canada.

Pascale Willemsen is an SNSF Ambizione Research Fellow and the principal investigator of the "Investigating Thick Ethical Concepts" group located at the University of Zurich, Switzerland.

Introduction to *Advances in Experimental Philosophy of Action*

Samuel Murray and Paul Henne

Action theory—or the philosophy of action—aims to explain the difference between a wink and a blink (Juarrero 2002). Blinks are complex movements, involving coordination between different muscle groups. But complex and coordinated movement is insufficient for action; instead, there is some special feature that transforms blinks into winks, movements into actions.[1]

Action theorists debate what this feature is—and whether there is just one. Some philosophers speculated about whether causation was the key feature that distinguished movements and actions. Davidson, for instance, argued that actions have a distinctive causal connection to an agent's psychology (Davidson 1963). Specifically, actions are events caused by a desire and a belief about how to satisfy that desire. While blinks happen whether you want them to or not, you wink when you *want* to do it. On this view, your wanting to wink and your belief about how to satisfy that desire jointly caused you to wink, so it is an action. Blinks lack a direct causal connection to your desires and beliefs, so they are mere movements.

In contrast, Anscombe held that agents have a special kind of self-knowledge in acting that they lack in merely moving (Anscombe 1958). When acting, an agent knows what they are doing without making any inferences from observing their own behavior. This self-knowledge allows people to state authoritatively what they are doing when they are acting. For example, you understand better than anybody else whether or not you are winking. When merely moving, however, an agent lacks knowledge about what they are doing unless they make inferences from observing their own behavior. Blinking, for example, can happen without any awareness of that movement at all.

Importantly for Anscombe's view, self-knowledge does not *cause* actions. In contrast to the Davidsonian view, the Anscombean view does not require a causal connection between psychological states and behaviors for those behaviors to count as action. It is not the case that self-awareness of the wink, for example, causes the wink; rather, this self-knowledge simply distinguishes actions from movements—winks from blinks. While the Anscombean account is extensively discussed in recent philosophy of action (Paul 2009) and has been revived recently (Ford 2018; Schwenkler 2019), the causalist view outlined by Davidson remains the predominant view among action theorists working in the Anglo-American analytic tradition.

There are, nonetheless, difficulties for causalism. One major problem is that some counterexamples suggest that the causal relation between mental states and behaviors seems insufficient for action: some events have the right kind of causal connection to an agent's psychology but do not count as actions. For example, consider the following case proposed by Davidson himself:

> A climber might want to rid himself of the weight and danger of holding another man on a rope, and he might know that by loosening his hold on the rope he could rid himself of the weight and danger. This belief and want might so unnerve him as to cause him to loosen his hold. (Davidson 1980: 79)

The climber wants to injure his companion and believes the best way to do this is to let the rope slip. Ultimately, this belief as well as desire causes the climber to let the rope slip. In this case, the causal influence of the mental states is indirect—or *deviant*: they cause the climber to be nervous, thereby putting him in a state where he nervously drops the rope. The mental states cause the event (without them, the climber would have held the rope tightly), yet the event—letting the rope slip—is not an action. Many action theorists through the 1970s and 1980s debated and proposed solutions to this *problem of causal deviance* (Bishop 1989; Brand 1984; Davidson 1974; Goldman 1971; Mele 2003b; Peacocke 1979; Schlosser 2007; Thalberg 1984; Velleman 1992).

Many philosophers eventually agreed that instances of causal deviance are not actions because the agent's movements do not unfold according to a plan (Bishop 1989; Brand 1984; Mele 2003a; Thalberg 1984).[2] When actions unfold according to a plan, the content of the intention guides behavior over time. Accordingly, action theorists amended the causalist proposal to say that actions are events that are initiated and guided by relevant mental states (Adams and Mele 1989; Frankfurt 1978). For the most part, action theorists held that the relevant mental states were intentions, a sui generis attitude grounded in, but not reducible to, beliefs and desires (Bratman 1987; Mele 1992). Intentions have special desire-like properties—such as a mind-to-world direction of fit (Humberstone 1992)—that explain their role in initiating action (Bratman 1987). They also have belief-like properties—such as representational content—that guide action over time (Brand 1984). This amendment dove-tailed nicely with a separate line of argument developed in Bratman (1987), which showed that intentions provide a distinctive kind of volitional commitment to acting that cannot be explained merely in terms of an individual's beliefs and desires. On this view, the special feature that transforms mere movement into action is an intention.

This brief overview does not do justice to the complexity and nuance of the philosophy of action. But the story of action theory today is, to a considerable degree, the story of intentions. Today, there are lively debates about the causal properties of intentions, the representational content of intentions, the scope of intentions, and the physical implementation of intentions at the psychological and neural levels. Based on these central concerns, researchers have explored a range of issues. Philosophers have argued about issues of intentional omissions (Sartorio 2009; Shepherd 2014), the nature of agency (Shepherd 2021), the nature of free will (Mele 2017; Sartorio 2016), guidance and acting over time (Buehler 2022; Irving 2016), the individuation of action (Goldman 1971), animal agency (Steward 2012), practical reasoning and action (Audi 2006), the nature of skill in agency (Cath 2020; Pavese 2021), the possibility and function of partial intentions (Holton 2009), the nature of joint action (Bratman 2013), and much more (Paul 2020). But, despite disagreements over how best to characterize intentions, a significant amount of action theory presumes something like the amended causalist account that takes intentions to be the key feature that distinguishes movements and actions.

Some of the themes of this volume involve discussions about the role of intentions in action. To see this, consider two related issues. First, much of the work on intentions is really a way of thinking about how activities of the mind can endow physical happenings with a special ontological status. Here, we should note familiar questions about mental causation, including questions about the possibility of mental causation within a naturalist worldview (Kim 1990).

But while we can question how intentions interact with the body, we can also question how intentions operate within the broader psychology of agency. People acquire intentions through conscious mental processes like deliberating and deciding, which means that consciousness and higher-order mental processes, broadly construed, cause action–albeit indirectly. This model informs a commonsense picture of agency that assigns a central role to consciousness. We make conscious decisions about what to do and, because of these decisions, act accordingly. However, this commonsense picture seems to clash with the seemingly notable role of unconscious processes and situational factors in decision-making (Doris 2021). Action and higher-order cognition—including consciousness—seem tightly interconnected due to the central role of intentions in producing actions.

Second, some actions are morally significant, and they often serve as the basis for attributions of blame, praise, punishment, and credit. And actions have this moral significance because they bear a special relationship to intentions (Malle, Guglielmo, and Monroe 2014; Scanlon 2010). Recall that intentions mark a special kind of commitment toward acting. People acquire intentions by deliberating and making decisions. And intentions guide behavior over time. Thus, intentions unify the outer world and the inner life of an agent. Intentions reflect what an individual values, wants, and is committed to doing (Hieronymi 2004). For this reason, intentional actions provide distinctive evidence about moral evaluation. For instance, how people evaluate unintentional actions seems to differ from how people evaluate intentional actions (Irving et al. 2020; Malle, Guglielmo, and Monroe 2014; Murray et al. n.d.). Recent metaphors between action and conversation are understandable in this framework: actions, much like words, have *expressive significance* because they are based on what an agent wants and is committed to (McKenna 2012; Tognazzini 2015; Watson 2004). Any study of the expressive significance of actions must situate this significance within the rudiments of intentional psychology.

Any reader of this introduction might now understand that while there is agreement about what studying the nature of action requires, the boundaries of action theory are fuzzy (Paul 2020). There is a wide overlap with different areas of philosophy, including metaphysics, philosophy of mind, ethics, epistemology, and even philosophy of language. The pervasiveness of the philosophy of action reflects, as we have argued earlier, the many faces of intention and the questions surrounding their ontological status and moral significance.

In all this, then, one might wonder what the *experimental* approach adds to the philosophy of action. In recent years, experimental philosophers have taken on some issues in the philosophy of action. They have explored intentionality (Buckwalter, Rose, and Turri 2021; Knobe 2003; Nadelhoffer 2004; Uttich and Lombrozo 2010), the relationship between causal judgment and intentionality (Quillien and German 2021), the relationship between knowledge and action (Beebe and Buckwalter 2010), the nature of skill in agency (Bermúdez 2021; Carter, Pritchard, and Shepherd 2019; Nadelhoffer 2005), the nature of joint action (Gomez-Lavin and Rachar 2019), free will (May 2014; Nahmias et al. 2005; Nichols 2011; Nichols and Knobe 2007; Roskies 2006), responsible agency (Murray et al. 2019), attributions of obligations and ability (Henne et al. 2016; Semler and Henne 2019), causation by omission (Clarke et al. 2015; Henne, Pinillos, and De Brigard 2017, 2019; Willemsen 2018; Willemsen and Reuter 2016), and much more (Nadelhoffer 2011). There are, to be sure, general benefits of embedding experimental methodologies in any philosophical sub-field. Experimentation can play an important role in diagnosing the referents of theoretical terms such as "cause" or "know" (Vargas 2017). But experimental methods can also diagnose idiosyncratic or parochial reactions to intuition pumps, which play indispensable roles in philosophical theorizing (Machery 2017; Rose et al. 2019). Unchecked, we risk spinning out theories of phenomena that make no contact with people's ordinary experiences and psychological categories (Dennett 2006).

Beyond these general benefits, however, we think the experimental approach is distinctively useful for advancing our understanding of action. Conceptions of action and intention play a role in moral judgment and decision-making. As the chapters in this volume indicate, peculiar features of our moral reasoning can be understood better when we see how people reason about action. Moreover, people are familiar with key concepts in the philosophy of action. Unlike technical concepts in metaphysics or epistemology, action-theoretic categories organize domains of everyday experience. Thus, while there is some question as to whether there is a folk notion of metaphysical composition, our practical need for thinking about action suggests that there are real psychological categories to explore here.

This volume includes some empirical approaches to the philosophy of action that are not strictly *experimental*. That is, some chapters neither report new empirical results nor systematize different experimental results into an overarching framework. We include these perspectives in part because we think that research in action theory could benefit from greater sensitivity to advances in the cognitive and social sciences. While a significant amount of work has been dedicated to the psychology and neuroscience of free will and moral responsibility, considerably less has examined other issues in action theory. We hope that, by including discussions of overarching empirical frameworks, philosophers and cognitive scientists can begin to widen their approach to action beyond the domain of free will and moral responsibility to assess different dimensions of action experimentally.

As such, this volume includes articles from authors who are advancing the issues in the philosophy of action by using experimental methods or by relying on empirical findings to inform the philosophy of action. These chapters advance both the areas of the philosophy of action that have been explored in the literature and the methods that experimental philosophers of action have used previously. We hope that this volume encourages young philosophers to explore further applications of experimental methods to core issues in the philosophy of action.

In Chapter 1, Sytsma and Snater investigate the relationship between phenomenal consciousness, agency, and free will. Some work found that people employ a concept of phenomenal consciousness when attributing mental states (Knobe and Prinz 2008), and some philosophers argue that consciousness is required for free will attributions (Shepherd 2015). Sytsma's earlier work, however, suggests that nonphilosophers do not employ a concept of phenomenal consciousness when making judgments about mental states (Sytsma and Machery 2010). Noting the importance of these findings for the philosophy of action and free will, Sytsma and Snater ran a new study. In this exploratory study using hierarchical cluster analysis, Sytsma and Snater find that people's concept of free will is more related to their concept of non-phenomenal consciousness than to states traditionally assumed to involve phenomenal consciousness. Beyond these interesting results, this chapter makes a compelling case for using qualitative methods to study the structure of different action-theoretic concepts (Chartrand 2022).

In Chapter 2, Mylopoulos discusses what kind of control is necessary for skilled action. After reviewing the work in epistemology and cognitive science on skill and know-how, she argues for a form of cognitivism about skill, under which cognitive control is necessary for skilled action. Uniquely, she argues that cognitivist views are incomplete without metacognition. She then describes how metacognition plays a role in the phenomenology of skilled action. Mylopoulos's chapter not only provides a unique, empirically oriented philosophical argument about skilled action but also expands the domain of what experimental philosophers of action who are interested in skill ought to attend to in their work.

In Chapter 3, Murray argues against the view that the function of self-control is to resist impulses or temptation. Drawing on recent computational and neurobiological work on cognitive control, Murray claims that the function of self-control is to manage interference that arises from overlapping information-processing pathways. In Murray's view, exercises of self-control manifest an agent's being vigilant. This account has three benefits. It provides a biologically plausible motivational account of self-control limitations that locates the source of these limitations in representational, rather than metabolic or structural, limitations. It also makes sense of the role that personal-level construal plays in self-control insofar as construal alters processes of control allocation. And it explains why self-control is essential for planning agents who engage in complex, temporally extended action.

In Chapter 4, Sinnott-Armstrong raises some questions about how identity and moral responsibility are related. Relying on the critical, new discussions and arguments from Schechter (2018), he focuses on split-brain patients and people with dissociative identity disorder that raise questions about how many agents can be located in one body and the relationship between sub-personal and personal mental processes. Sinnott-Armstrong uses these cases to shed light on how people might be responsible for behavior motivated by implicit attitudes. This discussion exemplifies how empirical details about brains and behavior can bear on metaphysical and moral questions regarding action.

In Chapter 5, Noordhof and Sullivan-Bissett tackle the complicated subject of irrationality in delusional experience. It seems obvious that delusions are characterized by some kind of irrationality. While some claim that delusions reflect the most severe form of irrationality, Noordhof and Sullivan-Bissett carefully argue that delusional experiences manifest common forms of irrationality, such as wishful thinking or self-deception. Because of this, they argue against the view that philosophers and clinicians must invoke a special form of clinical irrationality to explain delusion. This chapter makes a forceful case for extending action theory into clinical domains to better understand action in both clinical and nonclinical contexts.

In Chapter 6, Turri provides new evidence that answers recent criticisms of his work on the norms of assertion. He provides experimental evidence that there are at least two norms: truths and blamelessness. He provides some evidence that different vocabulary about norms will be more or less apt for expressing these norms. He has a detailed discussion of the related literature and how his results relate to other recent findings. His chapter advances the recent discussion about norms of assertion in experimental philosophy. Furthermore, insofar as these norms inform our sense of rationality and permissibility, they are importantly related to normative dimensions of action.

In Chapter 7, Korman examines a puzzling phenomenon in action explanation. Drawing on intentional systems theory, Korman claims that explanations aim to rationalize what someone is doing in light of their beliefs and desires. However, our explanations rarely mention both mental states. Instead, people cite either what people believe or what they want. Korman provides evidence for her hypothesis that belief-based and desire-based explanations have different pragmatic implications. She shows that people tend to produce more belief-based explanations when confronted with Means-End puzzles, or behavior that seems inconsistent with achieving one's goal. And people tend to produce more desire-based explanations when confronted with Goal-Blocking puzzles, or behavior that is inconsistent with achieving one's overall set of goals. Korman discusses several implications for what these results show about the difference between desire-based and belief-based action explanations.

In Chapter 8, Clark and colleagues review recent, exciting work in the experimental philosophy of free will. They argue that free will is best understood in terms of a capacity to deliberate about perceived alternatives. They suggest that the ability to deliberate depends on the capacity for counterfactual thinking and mental simulation, which enables complex and flexible decision-making. Moreover, Clark and colleagues claim that the widespread belief in free will reflects a cultural adaptation: formal and informal institutions of punishment function better when people believe that they are responsible for their decisions. Ultimately, they suggest that while people may not have a coherent view of free will, the belief in free will and responsibility for one's actions may promote moral decision-making.

In Chapter 9, Machery and colleagues advance a novel view of free will in experimental philosophy and a new experimental paradigm for studying the psychology of free will. Much of the work in the experimental philosophy of free will has focused on people reasoning about vignette-based stimuli and making a judgment. But Machery and colleagues suggest that people also perceive free will. The authors then propose a new model under this perceptual approach—the agency model, whereby perceptual cues that prompt attributions of agency affect people's experience of free will. The authors introduce a perception-based paradigm to test this novel view of free will attribution. Using this new paradigm, the authors present new experimental evidence that supports their account. Not only do the authors provide a novel view about free will but they also present a new experimental paradigm for philosophers of action.

In Chapter 10, Sifferd explains why moral judgments about wrongdoing that lack publicly observable harms are subject to pernicious biases. She begins with some puzzling moral luck cases, or situations where individuals are judged more or less harshly depending on the outcomes of their actions, even though these outcomes are not under their control. Sifferd, following (Kumar 2019), argues that there are consequentialist grounds for basing our moral judgments on results rather than on intentions. However, for some wrongs, there are no results on which to base our judgments. Sifferd uses the example of rape to illustrate how moral judgments are susceptible to different biases when there are no observable harms to guide judgment. To borrow Sifferd's phrase, wrongs that lack publicly observable harms sit in a "moral blindspot." Sifferd's chapter advances recent work on moral luck and moral judgment in the experimental philosophy of action.

In Chapter 11, Timmons and Byrne build on their previous work (Timmons et al. 2021; Timmons and Byrne 2019) and investigate an issue at the intersection of moral cognition, philosophy of action, and counterfactual thinking. In contrast to much of moral psychology, they explore how people think about *morally good* actions. This new body of work shows that when people think about morally good actions, they think about these much differently than how they think about morally bad actions. When people think of a good action that leads to a bad outcome, they tend to think of alternatives where something better happened by adding some new action. But when people think of a good action that leads to a good outcome, they imagine a world in which something worse happened by removing something from the situation. The authors discuss how this affects people's intention formation and how future work can explore these issues.

In Chapter 12, Arruda and Povinelli discuss a core issue in comparative psychology that is relevant to the philosophy of action. Oftentimes, researchers presume that nonhuman animal behavior reflects simplified forms of analogous human behavior. Researchers treat nonhuman animal behavior as a model system that explains human behavior. Arruda and Povinelli, however, argue against the assumption that nonhuman animal behavior is always less complex than corresponding human behavior. Their key point is that this assumption is credible only if we accept that human behavior always reflects idealized forms of agency. But—they argue—we have no reason to suppose that humans are ideal agents relative to nonhumans. In the end, Arruda and Povinelli defend *species-specific* models of explanation. Their chapter illustrates how the experimental philosophy of action might usefully extend beyond the study of human action.

This volume includes some critical advances in the experimental philosophy of action. This work pushes the field to explore new experimental paradigms and to continue challenging and expanding the issues at hand. But the implications of this volume are much wider. Experimental philosophers have recently begun working more systematically on issues in bioethics (Earp et al. 2020) and jurisprudence (Kneer and Bourgeois-Gironde 2017; Sommers 2019, 2021; Tobia 2020). This volume includes methodological and philosophical advances in the experimental philosophy of action that we believe could prove valuable to the continuing development of this new work. We hope that experimental philosophers continue to integrate work both within philosophical subdisciplines and across traditional disciplinary boundaries.

Notes

1 Philosophers of action have been mostly concerned with two broad issues: the individuation of—or the ontology of—action (Goldman 1971) and the explanation of action (Mele 1997). The issue of explanation involves questions about what produces, causes, or explains the action. For instance, do reasons to act—or mental states about some action—explain the action? We focus here on the ontology of action: what makes some event an action rather than not? Another dimension of the individuation issue concerns what distinguishes one action from others (Bennett 1998). For example, when I wave my hand to signal a turn, have I performed one action (signaling) or two (waving and signaling)? Recent work has turned toward the relationship between action and nothingness. What, for instance, distinguishes an action from an inaction? What distinguishes omissions and absences (Bernstein 2015; Clarke 2014)?

2 This summary elides a number of interesting distinctions in the literature on causal deviance, such as the distinction between basic, consequential, and heteromesial deviance. Properly accounting for the role of intentions in action is insufficient to defuse these different worries about deviance, though intentions do play a major part in those discussions. Interested readers should consider the papers collected in Aguilar, Buckareff, and Frankish (2010).

References

Adams, F. and A. Mele (1989), "The Role of Intention in Intentional Action," *Canadian Journal of Philosophy*, 19 (4): 511–31.

Aguilar, J., A. Buckareff, and K. Frankish (2010), *New Waves in Philosophy of Action*, New York: Springer.

Anscombe, G. E. M. (1958), "Modern Moral Philosophy," *Philosophy*, 33 (124): 1–19.

Audi, R. (2006), *Practical Reasoning and Ethical Decision*, London: Routledge.

Beebe, J. R. and W. Buckwalter (2010), "The Epistemic Side-Effect Effect," *Mind & Language*, 25 (4): 474–98.

Bennett, J. (1998), *The Act Itself*, New York: Oxford University Press.

Bermúdez, J. P. (2021), "The Skill of Self-Control," *Synthese*, 199 (3): 6251–73.

Bernstein, S. (2015), "The Metaphysics of Omissions," *Philosophy Compass*, 10 (3): 208–18. https://doi.org/10.1111/phc3.12206.

Bishop, J. C. (1989), *Natural Agency: An Essay on the Causal Theory of Action*, Cambridge: Cambridge University Press.

Brand, M. (1984), *Intending and Acting: Toward a Naturalized Action Theory*, Cambridge, MA: MIT Press.
Bratman, M. (1987), *Intention, Plans, and Practical Reason*, Cambridge, MA: Harvard University Press.
Bratman, M. (2013), *Shared Agency: A Planning Theory of Acting Together*, New York: Oxford University Press.
Buckwalter, W., D. Rose, and J. Turri (2021), "Impossible Intentions," *American Philosophical Quarterly*, 58 (4): 319–32.
Buehler, D. (2022), "Agential Capacities: A Capacity to Guide," *Philosophical Studies*, 179 (1): 21–47.
Carter, J. A., D. Pritchard, and J. Shepherd (2019), "Knowledge-How, Understanding-Why and Epistemic Luck: An Experimental Study," *Review of Philosophy and Psychology*, 10 (4): 701–34.
Cath, Y. (2020), "Know How and Skill: The Puzzles of Priority and Equivalence," in Ellen Fridland and Carlotta Pavese (eds.), *The Routledge Handbook of Philosophy of Skill and Expertise*, 157–67, London: Routledge.
Chartrand, L. (2022), "Modeling and Corpus Methods in Experimental Philosophy," *Philosophy Compass*, 17 (6): e12837.
Clarke, R. (2014), *Omissions: Agency, Metaphysics, and Responsibility*, New York: Oxford University Press.
Clarke, R., J. Shepherd, J. Stigall, R. R. Waller, and C. Zarpentine (2015), "Causation, Norms, and Omissions: A Study of Causal Judgments," *Philosophical Psychology*, 28 (2): 279–93. https://doi.org/10.1080/09515089.2013.815099.
Davidson, D. (1963), "Actions, Reasons, and Causes," *Journal of Philosophy*, 60 (23): 685–700.
Davidson, D. (1974), "Psychology as Philosophy," in S.C. Brown (ed.), *Philosophy of Psychology*, 41–52, London: Springer.
Davidson, D. (1980). *Essays on Actions and Events: Philosophical Essays Volume 1*. New York: Oxford University Press.
Dennett, D. C. (2006), "Higher-Order Truths About Chmess," *Topoi*, 25 (1): 39–41.
Doris, J. M. (2021), *Character Trouble: Undisciplined Essays on Moral Agency and Personality*, New York: Oxford University Press.
Earp, B. D., J. Demaree-Cotton, M. Dunn, V. Dranseika, J. A. Everett, A. Feltz, G. Geller, I. R. Hannikainen, L. A. Jansen, and J. Knobe (2020), "Experimental Philosophical Bioethics," *AJOB Empirical Bioethics*, 11 (1): 30–3.
Ford, A. (2018), "The Progress of the Deed," *Process, Action, and Experience*, 168: 168–84.
Frankfurt, H. G. (1978), "The Problem of Action," *American Philosophical Quarterly*, 15 (2): 157–62.
Goldman, A. I. (1971), "The Individuation of Action," *Journal of Philosophy*, 68 (21): 761–74.
Gomez-Lavin, J. and M. Rachar (2019), "Normativity in Joint Action," *Mind & Language*, 34 (1): 97–120. https://doi.org/10.1111/mila.12195.
Henne, P., V. Chituc, F. De Brigard, and W. Sinnott-Armstrong (2016), "An Empirical Refutation of 'Ought' Implies 'Can,'" *Analysis*, 76 (3): 283–90.
Henne, P., L. Niemi, Á. Pinillos, F. De Brigard, and J. Knobe (2019), "A Counterfactual Explanation for the Action Effect in Causal Judgment," *Cognition*, 190: 157–64. https://doi.org/10.1016/j.cognition.2019.05.006.
Henne, P., Á. Pinillos, and F. De Brigard (2017), "Cause by Omission and Norm: Not Watering Plants," *Australasian Journal of Philosophy*, 95 (2): 270–83. https://doi.org/10.1080/00048402.2016.1182567.

Hieronymi, P. (2004), "The Force and Fairness of Blame," *Philosophical Perspectives*, 18 (1): 115–48.
Holton, R. (2009), *Willing, Wanting, Waiting*, New York: Oxford University Press.
Humberstone, I. L. (1992), "Direction of Fit," *Mind*, 101 (401): 59–83.
Irving, Z. (2016), "Mind-Wandering is Unguided Attention: Accounting for the 'Purposeful' Wanderer," *Philosophical Studies*, 173 (2): 547–71.
Irving, Z., S. Murray, A. Glasser, and K. Krasich (2020), *The Catch-22 of Forgetfulness: Responsibility for Mental Mistakes*. https://www.researchgate.net/publication/360381810_The_Catch-22_Of_Forgetfulness_Responsibility_for_Mental_Mistakes.
Juarrero, A. (2002), *Dynamics in Action*, Cambridge, MA: MIT Press.
Kim, J. (1990), "Supervenience as a Philosophical Concept," *Metaphilosophy*, 21 (1/2): 1–27.
Kneer, M. and S. Bourgeois-Gironde (2017), "Mens Rea Ascription, Expertise and Outcome Effects: Professional Judges Surveyed," *Cognition*, 169: 139–46.
Knobe, J. (2003), "Intentional Action and Side Effects in Ordinary Language," *Analysis*, 63 (3): 190–4.
Knobe, J. and J. Prinz (2008), "Intuitions About Consciousness: Experimental Studies," *Phenomenology and the Cognitive Sciences*, 7 (1): 67–83.
Kumar, V. (2019), "Empirical Vindication of Moral Luck," *Nous*, 53 (4): 987–1007.
Machery, E. (2017), *Philosophy Within Its Proper Bounds*, New York: Oxford University Press.
Malle, B. F., S. Guglielmo, and A. E. Monroe (2014), "A Theory of Blame," *Psychological Inquiry*, 25 (2): 147–86.
May, J. (2014), "On the Very Concept of Free Will," *Synthese*, 191 (12): 2849–66.
McKenna, M. (2012), *Conversation & Responsibility*, New York: Oxford University Press.
Mele, A. R. (1992), "Recent Work on Intentional Action," *American Philosophical Quarterly*, 29 (3): 199–217.
Mele, A. R., ed. (1997), *The Philosophy of Action*, 1st edn, New York: Oxford University Press.
Mele, A. R. (2003a), "Intentional Action: Controversies, Data, and Core Hypotheses," *Philosophical Psychology*, 16 (2): 325–40.
Mele, A. R. (2003b), *Motivation and Agency*, New York: Oxford University Press.
Mele, A. R. (2017), *Aspects of Agency: Decisions, Abilities, Explanations, and Free Will*, New York: Oxford University Press.
Murray, S., K. Krasich, Z. C. Irving, T. Nadelhoffer, and F. De Brigard (n.d.), "Mental Control and Attributions of Blame for Negligent Wrongdoing," *Journal of Experimental Psychology: General*.
Murray, S., E. D. Murray, G. Stewart, W. Sinnott-Armstrong, and F. De Brigard (2019), "Responsibility for Forgetting," *Philosophical Studies*, 176 (5): 1177–201.
Nadelhoffer, T. (2004), "The Butler Problem Revisited," *Analysis*, 64 (3): 277–84.
Nadelhoffer, T. (2005), "Skill, Luck, Control, and Intentional Action," *Philosophical Psychology*, 18 (3): 341–52.
Nadelhoffer, T. (2011), "Experimental Philosophy of Action," in Jesús H. Aguilar, Andrei A. Buckareff, and Keith Frankish (eds.), *New Waves in Philosophy of Action*, 50–77, New York: Springer.
Nahmias, E., S. Morris, T. Nadelhoffer, and J. Turner (2005), "Surveying Freedom: Folk Intuitions About Free Will and Moral Responsibility," *Philosophical Psychology*, 18 (5): 561–84.
Nichols, S. (2011), "Experimental Philosophy and the Problem of Free Will," *Science*, 331 (6023): 1401–3.

Nichols, S. and J. Knobe (2007), "Moral Responsibility and Determinism: The Cognitive Science of Folk Intuitions," *Nous*, 41 (4): 663–85.
Paul, S. (2009), "How We Know What We're Doing," *Philosopher's Imprint*, 9 (11): 1–24.
Paul, S. (2020), *Philosophy of Action*, 1st edn, London: Routledge.
Pavese, C. (2021), "Know-How, Action, and Luck," *Synthese*, 198 (7): 1595–617.
Peacocke, C. (1979), Holistic Explanation: Action, Space, *Interpretation*, New York: Oxford University Press.
Quillien, T. and T. C. German (2021), "A Simple Definition of 'Intentionally,'" *Cognition*, 214: 104806.
Rose, D., E. Machery, S. Stich, M. Alai, A. Angelucci, R. Berniūnas, E. E. Buchtel, A. Chatterjee, H. Cheon, and I.-R. Cho (2019), "Nothing at Stake in Knowledge," *Noûs*, 53 (1): 224–47.
Roskies, A. (2006), "Neuroscientific Challenges to Free Will and Responsibility," *Trends in Cognitive Sciences*, 10 (9): 419–23.
Sartorio, C. (2009), "Omissions and Causalism," *Noûs*, 43 (3): 513–30.
Sartorio, C. (2016), *Causation and Free Will*, New York: Oxford University Press.
Scanlon, T. M. (2010), *Moral Dimensions: Permissibility, Meaning, Blame*, Cambridge, MA: Harvard University Press.
Schechter, E. (2018), *Self-Consciousness and "Split" Brains: The Minds' I*, New York: Oxford University Press.
Schlosser, M. E. (2007), "Basic Deviance Reconsidered," *Analysis*, 67 (3): 186–94.
Schwenkler, J. (2019), *Anscombe's Intention: A Guide*, New York: Oxford University Press.
Semler, J. and P. Henne (2019), "Recent Experimental Work on 'Ought' Implies 'Can,'" *Philosophy Compass*, 14 (9). https://doi.org/10.1111/phc3.12619.
Shepherd, J. (2014), "Causalism and Intentional Omission," *American Philosophical Quarterly*, 51 (1): 15–26.
Shepherd, J. (2015), "Consciousness, Free Will, and Moral Responsibility: Taking the Folk Seriously," *Philosophical Psychology*, 28 (7): 929–46.
Shepherd, J. (2021), *The Shape of Agency: Control, Action, Skill, Knowledge*, New York: Oxford University Press.
Sommers, R. (2019), "Commonsense Consent," *Yale Law Journal*, 129: 2232.
Sommers, R. (2021), "Experimental Jurisprudence," *Science*, 373 (6553): 394–5.
Steward, H. (2012), *A Metaphysics for Freedom*, New York: Oxford University Press.
Sytsma, J. and E. Machery (2010), "Two Conceptions of Subjective Experience," *Philosophical Studies*, 151 (2): 299–327.
Thalberg, I. (1984), "Do Our Intentions Cause Our Intentional Actions?," *American Philosophical Quarterly*, 21 (3): 249–60.
Timmons, S. and R. M. J. Byrne (2019), "Moral Fatigue: The Effects of Cognitive Fatigue on Moral Reasoning," *Quarterly Journal of Experimental Psychology*, 72 (4): 943–54.
Timmons, S., E. Gubbins, T. Almeida, and R. M. J. Byrne (2021), "Imagined Alternatives to Episodic Memories of Morally Good Acts," *Journal of Positive Psychology*, 16 (2): 178–97.
Tobia, K. P. (2020), "Testing Ordinary Meaning," *Harvard Law Review*, 134: 726.
Tognazzini, N. A. (2015), "The Strains of Involvement," in R. Clarke (ed.), *Nature of Moral Responsibility*, 19–44, New York: Oxford University Press.
Uttich, K. and T. Lombrozo (2010), "Norms Inform Mental State Ascriptions: A Rational Explanation for the Side-Effect Effect," *Cognition*, 116 (1): 87–100.
Vargas, M. R. (2017), "Contested Terms and Philosophical Debates," *Philosophical Studies*, 174 (10): 2499–510.

Velleman, J. D. (1992), "What Happens When Someone Acts?," *Mind*, 101 (403): 461–81.
Watson, G. (2004), *Agency and Answerability: Selected Essays*, Clarendon Press.
Willemsen, P. (2018), "Omissions and Expectations: A New Approach to the Things We Failed to Do," *Synthese*, 195 (4): 1587–614.
Willemsen, P. and K. Reuter (2016), "Is There Really an Omission Effect?," *Philosophical Psychology*, 29 (8): 1142–59. https://doi.org/10.1080/09515089.2016.1225194.

1

Consciousness, Phenomenal Consciousness, and Free Will

Justin Sytsma and Melissa Snater

There is a tension between some recent work in experimental philosophy concerning how nonphilosophers conceptualize mental states and work on the relationship between attributions of consciousness and free will. While researchers are not in complete agreement about how "phenomenal consciousness" should be understood, the standard idea is that a mental state is phenomenally conscious just in case there is "something it is like" (Nagel 1974) to be in that state, with this being understood in terms of the state having phenomenal qualities. A growing body of evidence, however, suggests that nonphilosophers do not tend to employ this philosophical concept (e.g., Sytsma and Machery 2010; Sytsma and Ozdemir 2019). This work shows that nonphilosophers do not tend to categorize mental states in the way that philosophers do, distinguishing between those states that are phenomenally conscious and those that are not. At the same time, another body of evidence has been taken to indicate that nonphilosophers typically treat the possession of phenomenal consciousness as a necessary condition for freely willed action (e.g., Shepherd 2015; Nahmias, Allen, and Loveall 2020). But if nonphilosophers don't employ the concept of phenomenal consciousness, then they couldn't treat phenomenal consciousness as a necessary condition for free will; and if they do treat it as a necessary condition, then researchers arguing they don't employ such a concept must be mistaken.

In this chapter we explore this tension. We begin in Section 1.1 by noting that terms like "consciousness" are ambiguous, and we distinguish between senses that concern notions like being awake, aware, and exercising control and the sense that philosophers have tended to focus on—phenomenal consciousness—suggesting that the former corresponds with the dominant usages outside of academia. We then survey the empirical evidence indicating that nonphilosophers do not tend to categorize mental states in the way we would expect if they recognize the (supposed) phenomenality of certain mental states. In Section 1.2, we discuss recent studies of free will attribution that suggest a close connection between these attributions and judgments about consciousness, focusing on work that interprets this in terms of phenomenal consciousness and especially phenomenally conscious emotions. We critically examine this research, arguing that the evidence does not clearly support the conclusion. Finally, in Section 1.3, we suggest a different picture in which consciousness and free will are treated as more biologically basic features of living animals. We then report the results of a new study building off Ozdemir's (2022) work on the dimensions of mind perception.

1.1 Concepts of Consciousness

The English word "consciousness" is used in a number of different ways. As Ned Block (1995: 227) famously notes, "the concept of consciousness is a hybrid, or better, a mongrel concept." Similarly, David Chalmers states that "the term 'consciousness' is ambiguous, referring to a number of different phenomena," including that "sometimes it is used synonymously with 'awakeness'" and "sometimes it is closely tied to our ability to focus attention, or to voluntarily control our behavior" (1996: 6). Each of these senses readily suggests a connection to free will, either as a precondition for it (one must be awake to act freely) or more directly (exhibiting voluntary control of behavior presumably being a hallmark of free action). And each sense is suggested by standard dictionary entries. For instance, the full set of definitions for the adjective "conscious" given by Oxford's free English dictionary reads as follows:

1. Aware of and responding to one's surroundings; awake.
1.1 Having knowledge of something; aware.
1.2 (conscious of) Painfully aware of; sensitive to.
1.3 Concerned with or worried about a particular matter.
1.4 (of an action or feeling) deliberate and intentional.
1.5 (of the mind or a thought) directly perceptible to and under the control of the person concerned.[1]

Here, definition **1** corresponds with awakeness, while the focus on awareness (as well as in **1.1** and **1.2**) is suggestive of attention, and "deliberate and intentional" in **1.4** indicates voluntary action. Further, similar definitions are found for related terms like "consciously" (e.g., "in a deliberate and intentional way") and "consciousness" (e.g., "the state of being awake and aware of one's surroundings").[2] And a preliminary corpus investigation is in line with such definitions.[3] Using the word2vec semantic space for nonacademic portions of the Corpus of Contemporary American English built by Sytsma et al. (2019), we find that the nearest neighbor—the term that the model suggests has the closest meaning to "consciousness" based on the contexts in which they are used—is "awareness," while other nearby neighbors include "wakefulness."[4]

While a full and careful analysis of the ordinary use of terms like "consciousness" is beyond the scope of the present chapter, we take the preceding to suggest that the dominant usages relate to being awake, aware, and exercising control. Philosophers of mind, however, have most commonly been concerned with another sense of "consciousness" that does not clearly coincide with the definitions seen earlier—what is typically referred to as "phenomenal consciousness." This is the sense that both Block and Chalmers are concerned with, with each author raising the comparison in part to note the potential for confusion and to urge that we need to be careful in reasoning about consciousness. And, in fact, recent work on psycholinguistic biases indicates that people are prone to make inferences licensed only by the dominant or most common sense of a term even when it is used in a subordinate sense (Fischer and Engelhardt 2017, 2020; Fischer and Sytsma 2021; Fischer, Engelhardt, and Sytsma 2021). So, indeed, caution is warranted.

What is the (supposed) phenomenon of phenomenal consciousness? While phenomenal consciousness has been a focus of fierce debate in contemporary philosophy of mind, researchers are not in complete agreement about how it should be understood. Nonetheless, the standard idea is that a range of mental states have something important in common: there is "something it is like" (Nagel 1974) to undergo these states, with this being understood in terms of their having certain introspectively accessible qualities ("phenomenal qualities" or "qualia" for short), such as the redness we're acquainted with in looking at a ripe tomato. The phrase "phenomenal consciousness" is, thus, generally taken to characterize a diverse range of mental states as having something important in common—each having phenomenal qualities—and this feature is taken to distinguish these mental states from others that lack such qualities. While there is disagreement about exactly what range of states have phenomenal qualities, they are prototypically taken to include perceptual states and bodily sensations and to exclude at least some intentional states. As Chalmers puts it (2018: 7), "it is widely accepted that seeing a bright red square and feeling pain are phenomenally conscious, and that one's ordinary background beliefs (my belief that Paris is in France, say, when I am not thinking about the matter) are not."

1.1.1 Attributions of Consciousness

It is often assumed that while phrases like "phenomenal consciousness" and terms like "qualia" are clearly technical, the underlying concepts are nonetheless widespread among nonphilosophers, and this assumption is made by both skeptics and realists. For instance, Dennett (2005: 27) suggests that belief in qualia is part of our "folk theory of consciousness." On the other end of the spectrum, qualia realists generally take the occurrence of such qualities to be both introspectively obvious and of clear importance. As Chalmers (1995: 207) puts it, qualia are "the most central and manifest aspect of our mental lives." If this is correct, then we would expect the concept of phenomenal consciousness to play a central role in our folk-psychological conception of mind. And, in fact, Chalmers (2018: 13) makes this expectation clear, suggesting that "the central intuitions [about phenomenal consciousness] are widely shared well beyond philosophy" and contending that "it is highly plausible that versions of many of these intuitions can be teased out of ordinary subjects." While Chalmers is focused on what he terms "problem intuitions" here—intuitions reflecting that we take there to be a problem of phenomenal consciousness, including judgments that it is distinctively hard to explain or is nonphysical—such intuitions presuppose a conception of phenomenal consciousness that is suitably close to the philosophical concept.[5]

Further, there is some supporting evidence for such claims about the folk theory of consciousness. Knobe and Prinz (2008) present results suggesting that nonphilosophers employ the concept of phenomenal consciousness. Most notably, in their second study they gave participants a series of ten statements attributing mental states to a corporation—five that they classified as phenomenal and five that they classified as non-phenomenal—and asked them to rate how weird sounding the statements were. Knobe and Prinz found that on average each of the phenomenal statements was judged to sound less natural than each of the non-phenomenal statements.[6] Another body of evidence, however, suggests that nonphilosophers do not tend to employ a concept that is relevantly akin to the philosophical one. Evidence for this was first put forward by Sytsma and Machery (2010), and as detailed later, their contention has since gained further support from a range of follow-up studies, as well as work on beliefs about perception and studies on the dimensions of mind perception.

Sytsma and Machery (2010) argue that if the existence of phenomenal consciousness is pretheoretically obvious and is a central part of our folk-psychological conception of mental life, then we would expect the distinction between phenomenal and non-phenomenal states to be clear in how people categorize mental states. To test this hypothesis, in their first study Sytsma and Machery gave philosophers and nonphilosophers a description of either a simple, non-humanoid robot or an ordinary human performing one of two simple tasks. The tasks were designed to elicit the judgment that the human had underwent a prototypical phenomenal state—either seeing red or feeling pain—and the robot was described as behaving in an analogous manner. Participants were then asked whether the agent had the relevant state.

As expected, philosophers tended to treat the two states similarly, ascribing both to the ordinary human and denying both of the simple robot. In contrast, participants with little to no training in philosophy did not treat them similarly: although they tended to ascribe both states to the ordinary human, they were split with regard to the simple robot, tending to ascribe one prototypical phenomenal state to it (seeing red), while tending to deny the other (feeling pain). These results have subsequently been replicated and expanded upon (Sytsma and Machery 2012; Sytsma 2012; Sytsma and Ozdemir 2019; Cova et al. 2021; Ozdemir 2022). This includes that key results have been found regardless of how reflective the participants are (Sytsma and Machery 2012 responding to Talbot 2012), when using an expanded range of questions to allow participants to distinguish between merely detecting and truly seeing (Sytsma 2013 responding to Fiala, Arico, and Nichols 2013), when using phrasings expected by critics to more clearly indicate phenomenal consciousness ("experience red," "experience pain"; Sytsma and Ozdemir 2019), and on larger cross-cultural samples (Sytsma and Ozdemir 2019; Ozdemir 2022).

1.1.2 Dimensions of Mind Perception

The results reported by Sytsma and Machery (2010), and supported by subsequent follow-up work, suggest that by and large nonphilosophers do not tend to treat two prototypical examples of phenomenal states as having something important in common.

Given standard justifications for taking the supposed phenomenon of phenomenal consciousness seriously in the first place—that it is central and manifest—finding that nonphilosophers do not tend to treat two prototypical examples of supposed phenomenal states similarly in turn suggests that they do not share the philosophical concept of phenomenal consciousness.

This conclusion gains further support from two sources. First, research suggests that nonphilosophers tend to hold a naïve view of both colors and pains, treating these as qualities of extra-cranial objects rather than qualities of mental states (Sytsma 2009, 2010, 2012; Reuter 2011; Reuter, Phillips, and Sytsma 2014; Reuter, Sienhold, and Sytsma 2019; Kim et al. 2016; Sytsma and Reuter 2017; Reuter and Sytsma 2020; Goldberg, Reuter, and Sytsma forthcoming).[7] Since the standard understanding of phenomenal qualities treats them as qualities of mental states, this work suggests that people do not generally think of colors and pains as being phenomenal. But, given that these are two prototypical examples of phenomenal qualities, this raises further doubts about whether they employ such a concept in the first place.

Second, recent work on the dimensions of mind perception suggests that the way nonphilosophers tend to attribute various mental states does not respect the philosophical division between phenomenal and non-phenomenal states (Weisman, Dweck, and Markman 2017; Malle 2019; Ozdemir 2022). This work seeks to uncover the conceptual structures that frame how people conceive of mental life by looking at patterns of similarity and difference in the capacities they attribute to a range of entities. If the concept of phenomenal consciousness is a central part of folk psychology, then we would expect people to treat clear examples of phenomenal states as tending to hang together. For instance, like the philosophers surveyed by Sytsma and Machery (2010), we would expect them to treat simple robots as being incapable of any phenomenal states, while treating ordinary humans as being capable of the full range of typical phenomenal states. But this is not what we find: across a range of studies, prototypical examples of phenomenal states are found to fall across different dimensions.

While the pioneering work on dimensions of mind perception by Gray, Gray, and Wegner (2007) suggests that there are two distinct dimensions, subsequent work often suggests three or more dimensions, although the exact character of these differs somewhat. Weisman, Dweck, and Markman (2017) conducted a series of four studies asking people about whether a range of entities—such as a stapler, robot, beetle, or adult human—were capable of each of forty mental capacities. Across these studies, they found a consistent three-dimensional structure to participants' attributions, which they termed *Body*, *Heart*, and *Mind*. Most importantly for present purposes, while the capacities tested included many that philosophers would typically classify as phenomenal, these were spread across the three dimensions. To illustrate, the Body dimension, which Weisman and colleagues characterize in terms of "physiological sensations related to biological needs, as well as the kinds of self-initiated behavior needed to pursue these needs" (11375), included such "phenomenal" capacities as experiencing pain and experiencing pleasure. The Heart dimension was characterized in terms of "basic and social emotions, as well as the kinds of social-cognitive and self-regulatory abilities required of a social partner and moral agent" (11375), and included feeling embarrassed. And the Mind dimension, characterized in terms of "perceptual-cognitive abilities to detect and use information about the environment" (11375), included sensing temperatures and seeing things. Weisman et al.'s goal here was to use patterns of attributions to the different entities "to infer which mental capacities were seen as related and which were considered independent" (11375). Focusing on phenomenal states, their results then suggest that people tend to consider some prototypical examples as being independent of one another.

Malle (2019) also arrived at and replicated a three-dimensional structure across a series of five studies involving attributions of a different set of capacities to a variety of entities. While the dimensions he found are largely consistent with those identified by Weisman et al., they differ in some details and were given different labels—*Affect* (including such prototypically phenomenal capacities as "feeling pain" and "feeling happy"), *Moral & Social Cognition* (including "feel shame or pride" in Study 1), and *Reality Interaction* (including "seeing and hearing the world"). The key point for present purposes, though, is that we once again find that capacities that philosophers would typically classify as phenomenal fell across different dimensions. Insofar as these dimensions capture "people's folk conception of [how] the mind is organized" (2268), such findings again suggest that nonphilosophers do not tend to divide up the mental world in a way that follows the philosophical concept of phenomenal consciousness.

Finally, Ozdemir (2022) ran two studies exploring the dimensions of mind perception from an angle more in line with philosophical discussions and thought experiments. In similar fashion to the studies on free will from Shepherd (2015) and Nahmias, Allen and, Loveall (2020) that we will discuss later, participants were given a description of a highly sophisticated robot:

Imagine that in the future scientists are able to exactly scan a person's brain at the molecular level. Using the information from the brain scan they can create a perfect computer simulation of the working brain. They can then embed that computer in a robot body to create a robot version of the person.

Imagine that scientists scan your brain and use that information to create a robot version of you. On a scale of 0 (Not at all capable) to 6 (Highly capable), how capable would the robot be of . . .

After reading the description, in Ozdemir's first study, participants were asked to rate the same forty capacities tested by Weisman and colleagues. He found a four-dimensional structure, similar to those seen previously except for separate dimensions for *Negative States* (including experiencing pain and experiencing fear) and *Positive States* (including experiencing pleasure and feeling love). The other two dimensions were *Perception and Cognition* (including seeing things and sensing temperature) and *Consciousness and Agency* (which included no prototypically phenomenal capacities but did include being conscious). The capacities tested by Weisman and colleagues weren't specifically designed with the philosophical distinction between phenomenal and non-phenomenal states in mind, however. As such, it might be worried that some of the items wouldn't clearly suggest phenomenal states even if participants employ such a notion. Most notably "seeing things" might be interpreted in a purely informational sense along the lines of "detecting objects" rather than a phenomenal sense. Because of this, in his second study, Ozdemir used the same vignette as in the previous study but included two statements involving seeing ("the robot would see colours"; "the robot would experience sights and sounds"). Against the worry, and in line with Sytsma and Ozdemir's (2019) extension of Sytsma and Machery's (2010) results, ratings for the "see" and "experience" statements were similar ($M = 6.07, M = 5.75$), while each was significantly different from ratings for the "pain" statement ($M = 3.79$); further, while "see" and "experience" fell under the same dimension (*Perception and Cognition*), "pain" was in a different dimension (*Consciousness and Agency*).

To summarize, we saw earlier that many philosophers hold that the concept of phenomenal consciousness is a central facet of the folk-psychological conception of mind, with the existence of phenomenal consciousness being taken to be pretheoretically obvious and its occurrence of central importance to people, both philosophers and nonphilosophers alike. If this is the case, then we would expect people to tend to treat at least prototypical examples of phenomenal states similarly, tending to deny them of entities that intuitively lack phenomenal consciousness and to ascribe them to entities that intuitively possess phenomenal consciousness. But this is not what the data suggest. Across a range of studies conducted by different researchers and using different materials and methods, we consistently find that prototypical examples of phenomenal states are treated differently; in fact, they seem to fall across different aspects of the folk conceptualization of mental life. This suggests, minimally, that the concept of phenomenal consciousness does not play a central role in the folk-psychological conception of mind. Absent this, however, it is unclear why we should suppose that nonphilosophers possess something like the philosophical concept of phenomenal consciousness in the first place. It of course remains *possible* that they possess such a concept, even if they don't systematically employ it when we would expect them to. Nonetheless, given that nonphilosophers by and large don't seem to carve up the mental world in the way we would expect if they were calling on the concept of phenomenal consciousness, we contend that we have defeasible reason for skepticism about such a concept being part of folk psychology.

1.2 Free Will

While the empirical evidence surveyed in the previous section suggests that the concept of phenomenal consciousness is not part of folk psychology, another prominent body of work in experimental philosophy seems to paint a different picture. A large body of research has sought to understand the ordinary concept of free will, and some of this work suggests that it bears a close relationship to judgments about consciousness, with some interpreting this in terms of phenomenal consciousness (e.g., Shepherd 2012, 2015; Nahmias, Allen, and Loveall 2020). In this section we'll survey this research, arguing that while it does indeed indicate a connection between the ordinary concept of free will and *some* notion of consciousness, it is at best unclear that that notion is phenomenal consciousness.

Consider the work of Shepherd (2012). He reports the results of three studies asking participants about a vignette that states that neuroscientists are convinced either that *conscious* or *unconscious* processes direct people's actions, with the exact wording being varied across the studies. This manipulation had a sizable effect on judgments about free will in each study, with ratings being significantly higher in the conscious conditions than the unconscious conditions. Shepherd concludes from this that "consciousness plays a central role in folk conceptions of free will" (926). It is not clear exactly what sense of "consciousness" he has in mind here, however, and while the discussion highlights awareness it also hints at phenomenal consciousness. For instance, Shepherd states that "the common conception of consciousness involves awareness of the world and ourselves," although he then proceeds to offer illustrations that are typical of discussions of phenomenal consciousness, such as "perceptions of vivid red" and "the feel of anger" (915). The manipulations in the studies are similarly ambiguous, although each emphasizes awareness. Thus, the key notion in the conscious conditions in Studies 1 and 2—"conscious brain events"—is clarified as "brain events within that person's awareness" (917), while Study 3 focuses on "conscious thoughts and events—thoughts and events within an agent's awareness" (924). Given this focus, Shepherd's studies do not allow us to conclude that judgments about *phenomenal* consciousness, specifically, impacted participants' free will judgments.

Shepherd (2015) extends these results, reporting three further studies involving consciousness manipulations, and again concludes that "many laypeople regard consciousness as important to free will" (944). We contend that as with the previous studies, it is unclear how participants understood the manipulations, a point that Shepherd notes in Section 1.5. Thus, while he takes his studies to "emphasize elements of *phenomenal* consciousness," he also notes that they "emphasize elements such as deliberation" (942). We're skeptical that this is the case for Shepherd's first two studies, although it is accurate for his third. In the latter case, however, we worry that despite noting elements that philosophers will tend to interpret as emphasizing phenomenal consciousness, nonphilosophers will nonetheless focus on deliberation.

The key description in Shepherd's first study is that the agent at issue (Jim) is said to have "no conscious awareness of the right side of his visual field" (932), with the relevant manipulation then involving whether Jim punched someone on his left side (such that "Jim was consciously aware that he was there") or on his right side (such that "Jim had no conscious awareness that he was there"). As in the previous studies, this manipulation had a strong effect on free will judgments, with judgments being significantly higher in the conscious conditions. Shepherd's second study was similar, but now Shepherd describes Jim as having "no conscious control over his left hand" and then punching a person with either his left or his right hand. Despite this change, the manipulation had a comparable effect on free will judgments.

In each of Shepherd's first two studies, while the vignettes *involve* an agent acting on visual information, what they *emphasize* is conscious awareness (Study 1) or conscious control (Study 2). In contrast, Shepherd's third study clearly emphasizes elements that philosophers would tend to interpret in terms of phenomenal consciousness. Participants were given a vignette describing a sophisticated robot that was then said to be either conscious or nonconscious:

In the future, humans develop the technology to construct humanoid machines. These machines have very sophisticated computers instead of brains, and very intricate movement-generation systems instead of bones, ligaments and muscles. In fact, they are so sophisticated that they look, talk, and act just like humans, and they integrate into human society with no problem at all. The only way to tell if they are a humanoid machine instead of a human being is to look inside of them (by x-ray, for example).

Conscious: These creations are behaviorally just like human beings, and in addition, these creations possess consciousness. They *actually feel* pain, *experience* emotions, *see* colors, and *consciously* deliberate about what to do.

Nonconscious: These creations are behaviorally just like human beings. But, these creations do not possess consciousness. They do not *actually feel* pain (even when they say "Ouch!"), they do not *experience* emotions, they do not *see* colors, and they do not *consciously* deliberate about what to do.

After this, a particular robot was described as performing either a good or a bad action and participants were asked a series of questions, including whether the robot acted of his own free will. Overall, Shepherd found that while participants tended to attribute free will to the conscious robot (M = 4.98 on a 1–6 scale), judgments about the nonconscious robot were below midpoint (M = 2.97).

As Shepherd suggests, philosophers are likely to read "*actually feel* pain, *experience* emotions, *see* colors" in terms of phenomenal states. This is not the only interpretation available, however. Alternatively, it seems plausible to see this as drawing a distinction between actually undergoing such states and faking it—the robot merely *acting as if* it had those states—which is arguably neutral with regard to phenomenality. Further, as Shepherd notes, the concluding statement that the robot does or does not "*consciously* deliberate about what to do" can be readily understood in terms of another sense of consciousness altogether—one that emphasizes that the action was under the robot's control. Thus, while Shepherd's studies provide further support for the contention that nonphilosophers tend to treat consciousness as a requirement for free will, they do not provide strong evidence that they tend to treat *phenomenal* consciousness as a requirement.[8]

Nahmias, Alle, and Loveall (2020) have recently expanded on Shepherd's work, reporting the results of two studies involving sophisticated robots. Most importantly, in their second study they gave participants a vignette based on the one used in Shepherd's (2015) third study, but with revised descriptions for the consciousness manipulation that excluded the potentially problematic phrasing noted earlier ("*consciously* deliberate"). The revised paragraphs read as follows:

Conscious: Furthermore, the robots are able to behave just like human beings, and they also have components that enable conscious experiences. The robots *actually feel* pain, *see* colors, and *experience* emotions. They do not *just appear* to be conscious when they carry out the same behaviors as humans.

Nonconscious: Furthermore, the robots are able to behave just like human beings even though they do not have conscious experiences. They have components that process information such that they can carry out all the same behaviors as humans in just the same ways, but when they do so, they *just appear* to feel pain, *just appear* to see colors, and *just appear* to experience emotions.

After reading one of the vignettes, participants were asked a series of questions involving items on free will, basic emotions (e.g., that the robot can feel happiness, anger, etc.), Strawsonian emotions (e.g., that the robot can feel guilt, pride, etc.), and conscious sensations, among others, answering each using a 7-point scale where 1 indicates strong disagreement and 7 indicates strong agreement.

Crucially, Nahmias and colleagues found that the consciousness manipulation had a significant effect on free will judgments. While this is in line with what Shepherd found in his third study, the difference in the mean responses was quite notably smaller than Shepherd reports. While Shepherd found a (very) large effect, reporting a partial eta squared of 0.34 for the consciousness manipulation, Nahmias et al. found a small effect, with a partial eta squared of just 0.014. Unlike Shepherd, they found that participants did not tend to ascribe free will to the robot in *either* condition, with the means for their free will scale falling below the neutral point in both the conscious condition ($M=3.84$) and the unconscious condition ($M=3.53$).[9] Finally, Nahmias and colleagues report the results of a multiple mediation analysis indicating that judgments about Strawsonian and basic emotions fully mediate the effect of the consciousness manipulation on free will judgments, while sensations did not play a significant role.

Nahmias et al. take these results to support their contention that there is a "strong intuition among most people . . . that the capacity to have conscious experiences is crucial for free will" (61). Their aim, however, is to go beyond this and offer an indication of *why* people treat phenomenal consciousness as being necessary for free will. Nahmias and colleagues suggest that the reason is that people hold that for an agent to have free will things have to *really* matter to the agent, and that this requires phenomenal consciousness. They then take the results of their mediation analysis to suggest that people take the capacity for phenomenally conscious emotions to be crucial for having things truly matter to an agent.[10]

In our view, the consciousness manipulation used by Nahmias and colleagues is notably clearer than previous attempts, avoiding explicit mention of awareness, deliberation, or control. For a philosophical reader, we have no doubt that the descriptions unambiguously convey that they are talking about phenomenal consciousness. We are less convinced, however, that this will be so clear for nonphilosophers.[11] First, as noted in our discussion of the third study in Shepherd (2015), one potential issue is that the descriptions intended to flag phenomenal consciousness might equally be interpreted as drawing a distinction between actually undergoing such episodes and merely faking it. And the added emphasis on whether the robots "*just appear*" to be conscious in Nahmias et al.'s vignettes would seem to further promote such a reading. Second, unlike in Shepherd's study, Nahmias and colleagues report a quite small difference in free will ratings between the two conditions. Because of this, even if their descriptions worked as intended, we do not find that this result offers strong support for the claim that people *generally* treat phenomenal consciousness as being necessary for free will and believe that caution is warranted at this point.

In fact, re-considering Shepherd's results in light of those reported by Nahmias et al., we find that they cast significant doubt on the hypothesis that Shepherd's results reflect judgments about phenomenal consciousness. While there are a number of differences between the two studies, including the exact phrasing of the vignettes and the questions, Nahmias and colleagues based their materials off of Shepherd's and the phrasing is generally similar. The difference that stands out, however, is that Nahmias et al. only emphasized the "phenomenal elements" in the consciousness paragraphs, excluding the description of whether the robot could or could not consciously deliberate about what to do. Thus, one plausible hypothesis is that the much larger effect found by Shepherd primarily reflects judgments about conscious deliberation, *not* phenomenal consciousness.

1.3 Further Explorations

While the studies discussed earlier provide considerable evidence that nonphilosophers take consciousness *in some sense* to be related to free will, we find it to be far less clear that these findings specifically reflect judgments about *phenomenal* consciousness. Instead, we suspect that participants have tended to interpret the consciousness talk in these studies in ways that concern being awake, aware, and exercising control. We believe that this alternative explanation is quite plausible. First, as noted in Section 1.1, this cluster of concepts bear a clear relation to free action, such that the results are readily explicable on this interpretation. Second, we saw preliminary evidence that this cluster corresponds with the dominant ordinary usages of terms like "consciousness" outside of academia. Third, we saw reason to doubt that nonphilosophers tend to employ the philosophical concept of phenomenal consciousness. Thus, absent strong evidence to the contrary, we believe the *default assumption* should be that people will interpret consciousness talk in terms of being awake, aware, and exercising control rather than phenomenal consciousness. And, fourth, looking across the studies from Shepherd (2015) and Nahmias, Allen, and Loveall (2020) discussed earlier, the effect of the consciousness manipulation on free will judgments was greatly diminished when reference to "conscious deliberation" was excluded.

In the remainder of this chapter, we'll further explore the relationship between consciousness and free will. We begin by returning to the work on the dimensions of mind perception discussed earlier in light of Nahmias et al.'s research, now with a focus on judgments about free will and emotions. We then add to this body of work.

1.3.1 Revisiting the Dimension Studies

In Section 1.1, we discussed recent work on the dimensions of mind perception with a focus on prototypical phenomenal states such as feeling pain and seeing red. Several of these studies also included a question about free will, however, potentially offering insight into how this fits into the folk conception of how the mind is organized.

Perhaps most importantly, Weisman, Dweck, and Markman (2017) found that having free will fell within the Body dimension, not the Heart dimension as Nahmias et al. might plausibly predict. As Weisman et al. put it, "having free will tracked the physiological phenomena of the body more closely than the social-emotional capacities of the heart" (11376). We saw earlier that Nahmias et al.'s basic picture is that one crucial aspect of thinking about an agent having free will is that things can truly matter to the agent, and they suggest that this in turn requires phenomenal consciousness—that the agent can experience the consequences of her actions—focusing especially on the ability to feel emotions. But Weisman et al.'s work doesn't fit cleanly with this picture. As noted earlier, the Body dimension is characterized in terms of bodily sensations and capacities related to meeting biological needs. And while some basic emotions fall under this dimension, they relate especially to biological safety (e.g., experiencing fear, feeling safe). In contrast, most emotions fell under Weisman et al.'s Heart dimension. Recalling that these dimensions reflect the items that tended to be treated as going together across a range of entities, what we take this to suggest is that people tend to treat free will as being a more biologically basic feature of living animals than social emotions.[12]

Interestingly, Weisman et al. also found that being conscious and being self-aware fell under the Body dimensions. This is plausibly in keeping with the analysis of "consciousness" in Section 1.1 and the alternative explanation we offered of the effect of consciousness manipulations on free will judgments. It suggests a basic biological conception of consciousness that is congruent with a focus on being awake, aware, and exercising control. We might think of these as "abilities related to the physical, biological body" of living animals, as Weisman et al. (11375) describe the Body dimension.[13]

While the results for Ozdemir's (2022) dimension studies are largely congruent with Weisman et al.'s findings, they paint a less clear picture with regard to having free will. In his first study, this item did not load especially strongly on any of the dimensions he identified, while the various emotions tested grouped together under either the Negative State or Positive State dimensions. In Ozdemir's second study, however, both having free will and having emotions fell within his broad Consciousness and Agency dimension, as did items like being alive and being aware of oneself. While this is congruent with the picture drawn from Weisman et al., it is also compatible with Nahmias et al.'s contention that free will is more closely tied to feeling emotions. As such, we conclude by expanding upon Ozdemir's second study, reporting the results of a new study based on his materials and employing an analysis aimed at revealing the relations between the items comprising his broad Consciousness and Agency dimension.

1.3.2 Clustering Attributions

To further explore the relationship between the items in Ozdemir's (2022) second study, we tested two variations on his vignette. We then employed bottom-up cluster analyses to help assess the patterns of judgments across the twenty-five capacities he tested.

As detailed earlier, the vignette for Ozdemir's study involved a person's brain being scanned to create a computer simulation that was then embedded in a robot body. We updated this to further emphasize that the resulting being was a *physical* duplicate of the original person, doing so in two different ways. The first variation stuck closely to Ozdemir's original scenario, but specified that both the person's brain *and* body were scanned to build an android duplicate. The second variation went further, replacing the android with a "molecule by molecule" biological duplicate reminiscent of philosophical zombies (Chalmers 1996), and specifying that it was only the physical make-up of the person that was duplicated, such that "if there was any non-physical aspect to the person—such as a non-physical soul or mind—the scientists would not be able to duplicate that aspect of the person." Participants were given one of the two vignettes, then asked whether they agreed or disagreed with each of the twenty-five statements used by Ozdemir (with "duplicate" replacing "robot"), in random order, answering on a 1–7 scale where 1 indicates "Disagree Strongly" and 7 indicates "Agree Strongly." In addition, they were asked a range of demographic and check questions. Participants were recruited globally through advertising for a free personality test on Google Ads, with the ad and questionnaire presented in English. Responses were collected from 886 participants who were at least sixteen years of age and completed the philosophical questions. The full text for both vignettes, as well as extended details about the questions, sample, and analysis are provided in the supplemental materials.[14] For space, we'll focus on giving just a high-level overview of the findings here.[15] Results are shown in Figure 1.1.

To assess differences between the conditions, Welch's t-tests were run for each of the twenty-five items, applying the Holm–Bonferroni correction. Only three showed a significant difference, and even here the effect sizes were small: ratings for [2] *Feel Pain*, [18] *Alive*, and [23] *Deserve Human Rights* were significantly higher for the physical duplicate ($M = 4.88, 4.96, 5.07$) than the android ($M = 4.25, 4.47, 4.46$).[16] To assess general agreement or disagreement with the items, we ran one-sample Student's t-tests with the Holm–Bonferroni correction for each condition. Each item was above and significantly different from the midpoint, with the exception of [12] *Have Dreams during Sleep* for the android. Thus, interestingly, participants tended to treat the android as being alive, although there was disagreement on this score. And the general agreement found for [19] *Conscious* casts further doubt on the claim that "problem intuitions" are widespread (Chalmers 2018), and specifically intuitions that consciousness is nonphysical (see note 7).

For present purposes, though, our primary concern is with the relation between different judgments about the duplicates. To assess this, we began by calculating distance matrices for the items using two distance measures (Euclidean, Spearman). These provide measures of how similar participants' responses were between each pair of items. Euclidean, or straight-line distance, is perhaps the most common in hierarchical clustering and is often treated as the default. This method treats the ratings as having an interval scale, however, and while this is a common assumption for Likert-ratings, it might not hold. The Spearman distance measure, by contrast, is a rank-based

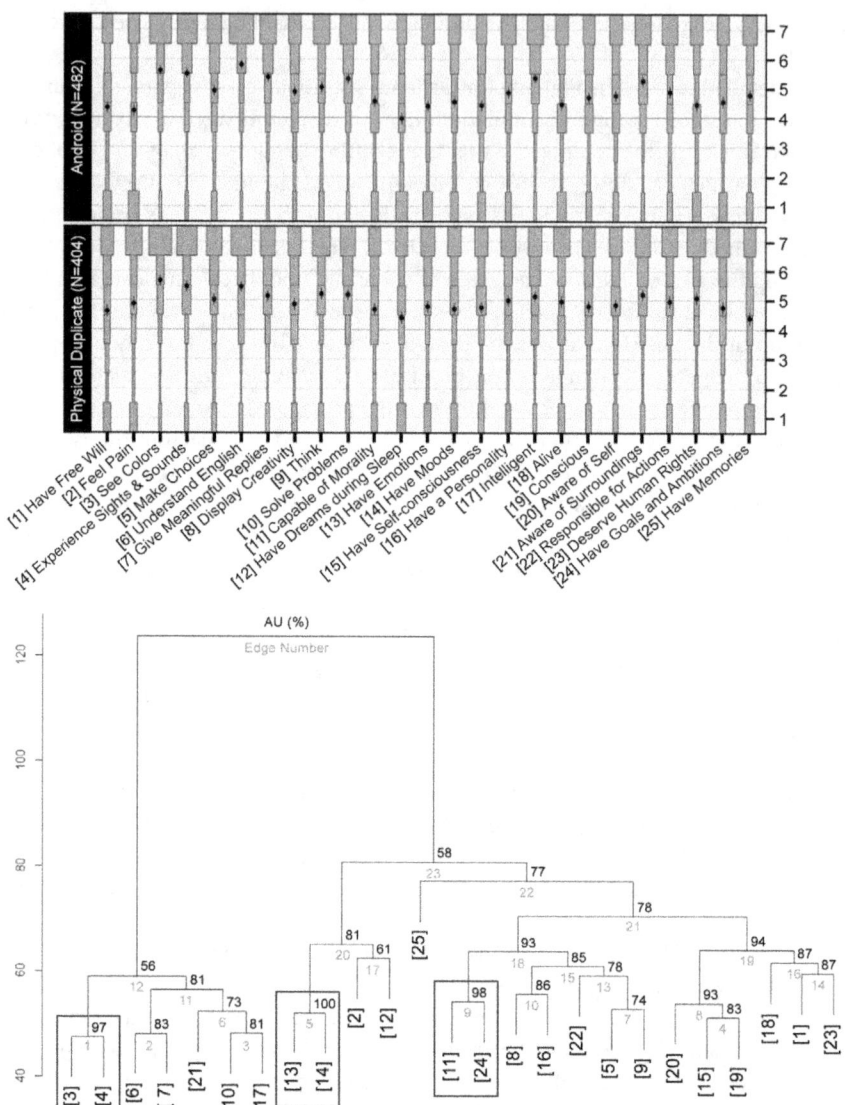

Figure 1.1 (Top) Study results broken down by condition, with the relative percentage of participants selecting each response option shown in gray and the mean and 95 percent confidence interval overlaid in black. (Bottom) Dendrogram for the hierarchical cluster analysis using Ward's method with the Euclidian distance measure. Edge numbers are displayed below (gray) and AU values are displayed above (black). Highest-level clusters occurring in 95 percent or more of the resamples are highlighted. © Justin Sytsma and Melissa Snater.

correlation metric. As detailed in the supplemental materials, the results were similar for each measure. This includes that pairs of items that we expected to be treated similarly were in fact close together on both measures, offering some indication that participants understood the task: [3] *See Colors* was the closest item to [4] *Experience Sights & Sounds* for each, and vice versa, with this being the closest pair overall by Euclidean distance; and likewise for [13] *Have Emotions* and [14] *Have Moods*, which were the closest pair overall by Spearman distance. By contrast, [1] *Have Free Will* was not so notably close to [13] *Have Emotions* on either measure, with [14] *Have Moods*, [15] *Have Self-consciousness*, [16] *Have a Personality*, and [12] *Have Dreams during Sleep* being closer on each (and [23] *Deserve Human Rights*, [9] *Think*, [2] *Feel Pain*, and [11] *Capable of Morality* also being closer using Spearman distance).

To better assess the patterns of similarity between item ratings, we performed a series of agglomerative hierarchical cluster analyses. This works in a bottom-up manner based on the distance matrix, starting with each item being considered as a single-element cluster, then iteratively combining the most "similar" clusters until all items are grouped together. By working in a bottom-up manner, agglomerative clustering tends to do a better job of identifying smaller clusters, making it a good choice for present purposes. The specific clustering produced depends not only on the distance measure but also on the clustering method employed. We tested five clustering methods for each of the two distance measures. These were then assessed with two goals in mind—faithfulness to the distance matrix and the strength of clustering produced. Based on this, we identified the two best methods for each measure. This included what is perhaps the most common combination—Ward's method with Euclidean distance. We'll focus on this clustering here, but the other three analyses paint a similar picture, as detailed in the supplemental materials. To assess the uncertainty of the analyses we used a resampling method with 10,000 iterations to produce approximately unbiased (AU) p-values. This gives the percentage of iterations where the same cluster was found, and we highlight clusters with values of ninety-five or greater in the dendrograms. The dendrogram for Ward's method with Euclidean distance is shown in Figure 1.1.

The first thing to note is that the two high-level clusters in the dendrogram largely correspond with the dimensions found by Ozdemir (with the exception of [5] *Make Choices* and [8] *Display Creativity*), while the lowest-level clusters include the pairs of items discussed earlier that were expected to be similar ([3] *See Colors* and [4] *Experience Sights & Sounds*, [13] *Have Emotions* and [14] *Have Moods*). This offers some validation for the clustering. Further, in line with Ozdemir's findings, we again find that the prototypical examples of phenomenal states—[2] *Feel Pain* and [3] *See Colors*/[4] *Experience Sights & Sounds*—fell across different top-level clusters. This adds to the findings discussed in Section 1.1, lending further support to Sytsma and Machery's (2010) conclusion.

Most importantly for present purposes, looking more closely at the structure produced, we find that [1] *Have Free Will* falls in a mid-level cluster with [18] *Alive*, [23] *Deserve Human Rights*, [19] *Conscious*, [15] *Have Self-consciousness*, and [20] *Aware of Self*. This is in line with the expected connection between free will and consciousness, further suggesting that people treat these as going together. In contrast, while [1] *Have Free Will* falls within the same top-level cluster as [13] *Have Emotions*, they weren't otherwise especially close, with [**13**] *Have Emotions* grouping together with the bodily state of [**2**] *Feel Pain* as well as [**12**] *Have Dreams during Sleep*. This is largely congruent with the picture drawn from Weisman et al.'s work. The structure again suggests that people treat free will as being closely connected to consciousness and self-awareness, with these being tied to being alive and moral patiency. While we consider these results to best be thought of as exploratory, we also find them to be congruent with the picture we've suggested: even focusing on sci-fi examples reminiscent of philosophical thought experiments, we find that judgments about free will, consciousness, and self-awareness are closely connected to judgments about being alive, suggesting that these form a basic cluster in people's thinking that is congruent with thinking about consciousness in terms of being awake, aware, and exercising control.

1.4 Conclusion

A large body of empirical evidence indicates that the judgments of nonphilosophers about consciousness and free will are related. And some have interpreted the former in terms of the philosophical concept of phenomenal consciousness, with Nahmias, Allen and Loveall (2020) suggesting that people treat the capacity for phenomenally conscious emotions as critical for having free will. Several other bodies of research, however, at the very least indicate that caution is warranted with regard to interpreting nonphilosophers' understanding of consciousness in this way. Further, standard dictionary definitions and a preliminary corpus analysis support this conclusion. A critical look at several key empirical studies casts doubt on their providing evidence for there being a close relationship between nonphilosophers' judgments about free will and *phenomenal* consciousness. This skeptical conclusion is further supported by the results of a new exploratory study, which suggests that attributions of free will are not so closely tied to attributions of emotions. Rather we suggest that both free will and consciousness are treated as being more biologically basic than this.

Notes

1. Accessed through Lexico.com, June 3, 2021, using the US dictionary (Oxford University Press, 2021). Similar sets of definitions are found for other online dictionaries, as noted in the supplemental materials.
2. From Lexico.com using the US dictionary, accessed June 3, 2021 (Oxford University Press, 2021).
3. Corpus analysis involves the use of large collections of text for assessing some research question. For instance, the Corpus of Contemporary American English contains over one billion words drawn in a balanced ways from a variety of sources, including spoken English, fiction, popular magazines and newspapers, and academic texts. Terms in the corpus are searchable, including by part of speech and proximity to other terms, and provide the context for utterances of interest. Such a corpus offers a cross-section of "words in the wild," as it were, providing a means of assessing linguistic hypotheses outside of an experimental setting and, hence, free of the potential biases

such a setting might introduce. The full text for the corpus is also available and can be used to develop computational models of word meaning by looking at the relative distribution of words across the corpus, such as the distributional model employed here. For a discussion of the value of corpus analysis for philosophy, see Bluhm (2016) and Caton (2020). And, for an extended discussion of corpus methods, see McEnery and Wilson (2001). For an introduction to distributional semantic models see Erk (2012) and Turney and Pantel (2010).

4 The ten nearest neighbors of "consciousness" in decreasing order of similarity as measured by the cosine of the vectors (in parentheses) are: "awareness" (.69), "unconsciousness" (.65), "wakefulness" (.62), "realization" (.59), "psyche" (.59), "transcendence" (.59), "selfhood" (.59), "subconscious" (.59), "emotion" (.58), and "aliveness" (.58).

5 We'll focus on the prior question of whether nonphilosophers tend to possess such a conception of phenomenal consciousness. If they do not, of course, then it will also follow that they lack further problem intuitions *about* phenomenal consciousness. Nonetheless, assuming for the sake of argument that people do tend to have such a conception, recent empirical work suggests that the majority do not harbor problem intuitions (Peressini 2014; Gottlieb and Lombrozo 2018; Fischer and Sytsma 2021; Diaz 2021; Ozdemir 2022).

6 A number of notable criticisms have been raised against Knobe and Prinz's interpretation of these results, however, including Sytsma and Machery (2009), Arico (2010), and Phelan, Arico, and Nichols (2013). Further evidence for nonphilosophers potentially having a concept of phenomenal consciousness is provided by Peressini (2014), although he holds that "folk phenomenality is importantly different from the philosophical sense in that it is grounded in the *physical* as opposed to the metaphysical nature of the experiencer" (883). See Sytsma (2014) for a discussion of these works and Sytsma (ms) for an extended critique of Peressini's studies.

7 But see Borg et al. (2019), Salomons et al. (2022), and Liu (forthcoming) for responses that suggest a more complicated picture for pains.

8 More recently, Shepherd (2017) finds an effect for consciousness on free will judgments about a person, with the consciousness manipulation emphasizing both control and awareness. And, in a fascinating series of studies, Björnsson and Shepherd (2020) reverse things, showing that whether a "humanoid machine" is described as operating deterministically or indeterministally affects judgments about whether it has a conscious mental life.

9 Thanks to Eddy Nahmias and Corey Allen for providing these numbers.

10 Note that the proposed conceptual connection between consciousness and emotions gains some support from the nearest neighbors analysis in Section 1.1, where "emotion" was one of the ten closest terms to "consciousness" in the semantic space.

11 Arguably in line with this, although it was stipulated that the robot has conscious experiences in the conscious condition, the mean responses for the sensation items—for example, "These robots *experience*, more than just *process*, the sounds in music, the images in art, the smells of food, and the softness of a blanket." (70)—was below the neutral point. Similarly, despite having specified that the robots *actually experience* emotions, mean ratings for both basic emotions and Stawsonian emotions were below the midpoint.

12 Compare, for example, the neutral to positive mean ratings for having free will for a beetle, goat, and elephant to the low mean ratings for feeling embarrassed and experiencing guilt for these animals in Weisman et al.'s Figure 1.

13 Recall that "aliveness" was one of the nearest neighbors for "consciousness" in the analysis earlier. See Arico et al. (2011) for experimental evidence that judgments that something is alive might be a basic cue for a range of mental state attributions.
14 http://philsci-archive.pitt.edu/19556
15 Given the diversity of the sample exploratory tests were run to check for demographic differences. As few notable differences were found, we'll focus on the full sample here.
16 The result for [2] *Feel Pain* is in keeping with previous work indicating that what an agent's body is made of impacts people's pain judgments (Sytsma 2012). Similarly, the results for the other two statements seem readily explicable in terms of difference between a robotic and an organic system.

References

Arico, A. (2010), "Folk Psychology, Consciousness, and Context Effects," *Review of Philosophy and Psychology*, 1 (3): 371–93.

Arico, A., B. Fiala, R. Goldberg, and S. Nichols (2011), "The Folk Psychology of Consciousness," *Mind & Language*, 26 (3): 327–52.

Björnsson, G. and J. Shepherd (2020), "Determinism and Attributions of Consciousness," *Philosophical Psychology*, 33 (4): 549–68.

Block, N. (1995), "On a Confusion About a Function of Consciousness," *Behavioral and Brain Sciences*, 18 (2): 227–87.

Bluhm, R. (2016), "Corpus Analysis in Philosophy," in M. Hinton (ed.), *Evidence, Experiment and Argument in Linguistics and the Philosophy of Language*, 91–109, Frankfurt am Main: Peter Lang Publishing.

Borg, E., R. Harrison, J. Stazicker, and T. Salomons (2019), "Is the Folk Concept of Pain Polyeidic?," *Mind & Language*, 35 (1): 29–47.

Caton, J. (2020), "Using Linguistic Corpora as a Philosophical Tool," *Metaphilosophy*, 51 (1): 51–70.

Chalmers, D. (1995), "Facing Up to the Problem of Consciousness," *Journal of Consciousness Studies*, 2 (3): 200–19.

Chalmers, D. (1996), *The Conscious Mind*, New York: Oxford University Press.

Chalmers, D. (2018), "The Meta-problem of Consciousness," *Journal of Consciousness Studies*, 25 (9–10): 6–61.

Cova, F., B. Strickland, A. Abatista, A. Allard, J. Andow, M. Attie, et al. (2021), "Estimating the Reproducibility of Experimental Philosophy," *Review of Philosophy and Psychology*, 12 (1): 9–44.

Dennett, D. (2005), *Sweet Dreams*, Cambridge, MA: MIT Press.

Diaz, R. (2021), "Do People Think Consciousness Poses a Hard Problem? Empirical Evidence on the Meta-problem of Consciousness," *Journal of Consciousness Studies*, 28 (3–4): 55–75.

Erk, K. (2012), "Vector Space Models of Word Meaning and Phrase Meaning: A Survey," *Language and Linguistics Compass*, 6 (10): 635–53.

Fiala, B., A. Arico, and S. Nichols (2013), "You, Robot," in E. Machery and E. O'Neill (eds.), *Current Controversies in Experimental Philosophy*, 31–47, London: Routledge.

Fischer, E. and P. Engelhardt (2017), "Diagnostic Experimental Philosophy," *Teorema: International Journal of Philosophy*, 36 (3): 117–37.

Fischer, E. and P. Engelhardt (2020), "Lingering Stereotypes: Salience Bias in Philosophical Argument," *Mind & Language*, 35 (4): 415–39.

Fischer, E., P. Engelhardt, and J. Sytsma (2021), "Inappropriate Stereotypical Inferences? An Adversarial Collaboration in Experimental Ordinary Language Philosophy," *Synthese*, 198 (11): 10127–68.

Fischer, E. and J. Sytsma (2021), "Zombie Intuitions," *Cognition*, 215: 104807.

Goldberg, B., K. Reuter, and J. Sytsma (forthcoming), "A Brief History of Pain Concepts," in K. Hens and A. De Block (eds.), *Advances in Experimental Philosophy of Medicine*, London: Bloomsbury.

Gottlieb, S. and T. Lombrozo (2018), "Can Science Explain the Human Mind?, Intuitive Judgments About the Limits of Science," *Psychological Science*, 29 (1): 121–30.

Gray, H., K. Gray, and D. Wegner (2007), "Dimensions of Mind Perception," *Science*, 315 (5812): 619.

Kim, H.-e., N. Poth, K. Reuter, and J. Sytsma (2016), "Where is Your Pain? A Cross-Cultural Comparison of the Concept of Pain in Americans and South Koreans," *Studia Philosophica Estonica*, 9 (1): 136–69.

Knobe, Joshua and Jesse Prinz (2008), "Intuitions about Consciousness: Experimental Studies," *Phenomenology and the Cognitive Sciences*, 7: 67–85.

Liu, M. (forthcoming), "The Polysemy View of Pain," *Mind & Language*.

Malle, B. (2019), "How Many Dimensions of Mind Perception Really Are There?," in A. Goel, C. Seifert, and C. Freska (eds.), Proceedings of the 41st Annual Meeting of the Cognitive Science Society, 2268–74, Montreal, QB: Cognitive Science Society.

McEnery, T. and A. Wilson (2001), *Corpus Linguistics*, 2nd edn, Edinburgh: Edinburgh University Press.

Nagel, T. (1974), "What is it like to be a Bat?" *The Philosophical Review*, 83 (4): 435–50.

Nahmias, E., C. Allen, and B. Loveall (2020), "When Do Robots Have Free Will? Exploring the Relationships Between (Attributions of) Consciousness and Free Will," in B. Feltz, M. Missal, and A. Sims (eds.), *Free Will, Causality, and Neuroscience*, 57–80, Leiden: Brill.

Oxford University Press (2021), Definition of Conscious. Available online: https://www.lexico.com/en/definition/wake (accessed 3 June 2021).

Ozdemir, E. (2022), Empirical Evidence Against Phenomenal Theses [PhD Dissertation], Victoria University of Wellington, Wellington.

Peressini, A. (2014), "Blurring Two Conceptions of Subjective Experience: Folk Versus Philosophical Phenomenality," *Philosophical Psychology*, 27 (6): 862–89.

Phelan, M., A. Arico, and S. Nichols (2013), "Thinking Things and Feeling Things: On an Alleged Discontinuity in the Folk Metaphysics of Mind," *Phenomenology and the Cognitive Sciences*, 12 (4): 703–25.

Reuter, K. (2011), "Distinguishing the Appearance from the Reality of Pain," *Journal of Consciousness Studies*, 18 (9–10): 94–109.

Reuter, K., D. Phillips, and J. Sytsma (2014), "Hallucinating Pain," in J. Sytsma (ed.), *Advances in Experimental Philosophy of Mind*, 75–100, London: Bloomsbury.

Reuter, K., M. Sienhold, and J. Sytsma (2019), "Putting Pain in Its Proper Place," *Analysis*, 79 (1): 72–82.

Reuter, K. and J. Sytsma (2020), "Unfelt Pain," *Synthese*, 197 (4): 1777–801.

Salomons, T., R. Harrison, N. Hansen, J. Stazicker, A. G. Sorensen, P. Thomas, and E. Borg (2022), "Is Pain 'All in Your Mind'? Examining the General Public's Views of Pain," *Review of Philosophy and Psychology*, 13: 683–98.

Shepherd, J. (2012), "Free Will and Consciousness: Experimental Studies," *Consciousness and Cognition*, 21 (2): 915–27.

Shepherd, J. (2015), "Consciousness, Free Will, and Moral Responsibility: Taking the Folk Seriously," *Philosophical Psychology*, 28 (7): 929–46.

Shepherd, J. (2017), "The Folk Psychological Roots of Free Will," in D. Rose (ed.), *Experimental Metaphysics*, 95–115, London: Bloomsbury.

Sytsma, J. (2009), "Phenomenological Obviousness and the New Science of Consciousness," *Philosophy of Science*, 76 (5): 958–69.

Sytsma, J. (2010), "Dennett's Theory of the Folk Theory of Consciousness," *Journal of Consciousness Studies*, 17 (3–4): 107–30.

Sytsma, J. (2012), "Revisiting the Valence Account," *Philosophical Topics*, 40 (2): 197–8.

Sytsma, J. (2013), "The Robots of the Dawn of Experimental Philosophy of Mind," in E. Machery and E. O'Neill (eds.), *Current Controversies in Experimental Philosophy*, 48–64, London: Routledge.

Sytsma, J. (2014), "Attributions of Consciousness," *WIREs Cognitive Science*, 5 (6): 635–48.

Sytsma, J. (ms), "Experiencers and the Ambiguity Objection." http://philsci-archive.pitt.edu/15481/

Sytsma, J., R. Bluhm, P. Willemsen, and K. Reuter (2019), "Causal Attributions and Corpus Analysis," in E. Fischer and M. Curtis (eds.), *Methodological Advances in Experimental Philosophy*, 209–38, London: Bloomsbury.

Sytsma, J. and E. Machery (2009), "How to Study Folk Intuitions About Consciousness," *Philosophical Psychology*, 22 (1): 21–35.

Sytsma, J. and E. Machery (2010), "Two Conceptions of Subjective Experience," *Philosophical Studies*, 151 (2): 299–327.

Sytsma, J. and E. Machery (2012), "On the Relevance of Folk Intuitions: A Reply to Talbot," *Consciousness and Cognition*, 21 (2): 654–60.

Sytsma, J. and E. Ozdemir (2019), "No Problem: Evidence that the Concept of Phenomenal Consciousness is not Widespread," *Journal of Consciousness Studies*, 26 (9–10): 241–56.

Sytsma, J. and K. Reuter (2017), "Experimental Philosophy of Pain," *Journal of Indian Council of Philosophical Research*, 34 (3): 611–28.

Talbot, B. (2012), "The Irrelevance of Folk Intuitions to the 'Hard Problem' of Consciousness," *Consciousness and Cognition*, 21 (2): 644–50.

Turney, P. and P. Pantel (2010), "From Frequency to Meaning: Vector Space Models of Semantics," *Journal of Artificial Intelligence Research*, 37: 141–88.

Weisman, K., C. Dweck, and E. Markman (2017), "Rethinking People's Conceptions of Mental Life," *PNAS*, 114 (43): 11374–9.

2

Skilled Action and Metacognitive Control

Myrto Mylopoulos

2.1 Introduction

A skilled agent exercises a high degree of control in some action domains as the result of extensive practice. A theory of skilled action aims to specify the precise nature of such control. This is the topic of this chapter.

I start by tracing the early stages of skilled action theory, which focused primarily on the nature of the practical knowledge that skilled agents possess, to more recent stages, which look to cognitive science for insights about the control processes underlying skill. I then distinguish between two competing views in the current literature: "automatism," which takes skilled action control to be driven by "mindless" automatic motor control processes with little to no intervention from cognitive control, and "cognitivism," which views thought and cognitive control as being at the heart of skilled action. I motivate cognitivist views and outline some advantages they have over their automatist counterparts. I then highlight an unsatisfied desideratum of such views: a general account of *how* exactly the cognitive control processes to which they appeal, for example, situational awareness, focus, and attention, interact and coordinate with automatic control processes. I propose that in order to answer this question, one must appeal to a certain type of *meta*-control, over *both* automatic and cognitive control processes, that skilled agents possess in the form of metacognition. In the last two sections, I explain the importance of metacognition for skilled action control and how it may account for aspects of the subjective experiences that are characteristic of skill.

2.2 From Epistemology to Cognitive Science

Contemporary theorizing about skilled action began by looking at the phenomenon from a predominantly epistemological lens. Through this lens, skilled performers are agents par excellence in virtue of the practical knowledge, or know how, that they possess with respect to some type of activity. A theory of know how can thereby do double duty as a theory of skill: once we understand what it is to possess and exercise practical knowledge, we understand what sets apart expert performers from mere novices. But how should we understand the nature of know how?

So-called intellectualists argue that practical knowledge is just a type of theoretical knowledge ("knowledge that") and should be understood in terms of an agent's standing in a certain relation to a proposition or set of propositions concerning how to perform some action type. An early opponent of this view was Gilbert Ryle (1949/2009). He argued against what he called the "intellectualist legend," according to which what it is for an agent to know how to Φ is for them to consider the appropriate proposition or rule prior to applying it to their present action, that is, for the agent to exercise suitable theoretical knowledge about the activity of Φ-ing.

According to Ryle, such a view fails for a variety of reasons. First, knowledge how does not seem to be *sufficient* for knowledge that. After all, one might know how to perform some action skillfully without being able to verbally express or articulate the knowledge they possess in propositional form. Second, knowledge how does not seem to be *necessary* for knowledge that. One might know a set of propositions corresponding to the skill of cycling, for example, yet not know how to ride a bicycle. Finally, it would seem that knowledge how must *precede* knowledge that, since applying a rule correctly is itself something one must first know how to do. But if this know how itself requires the appropriate application of a rule, then we are off on an infinite regress.

Ryle's anti-intellectualist arguments remained largely unscathed until the publication of a landmark paper by Stanley and Williamson (2001), which not only criticizes Ryle's main arguments against intellectualism but also mounts a positive case in its favor. Their case relies on observations about the syntax and semantics of ascriptions of knowledge-wh states (e.g., ascriptions of knowledge where, knowledge when, knowledge why) of which knowledge how is a type. In short, they argue that all knowledge-wh ascriptions are ascriptions of knowledge that and this suggests that knowledge how is a species of knowledge that. In Stanley and Williamson's view, knowing how to F is equivalent to knowing in what way to F, and this is a form of propositional knowledge, that is, knowing of some way w of F-ing, *that w is a way to F*, under a practical mode of presentation (the nature of which remains to be elucidated, see Pavese 2015).

One of the main lines of criticism against Stanley and Williamson's position is that the methodology it pursues in order to establish that knowledge how is a species of knowledge that is problematic. Thus, Noë (2005) advances skepticism regarding the relevance of technical linguistic analysis to the debate on the grounds that what is at issue is not how *attributions* of knowledge how and knowledge that work but the very nature of knowledge how and knowledge that. Similarly, Devitt (2011) argues that Stanley and Williamson's methodology of constructing a theory of knowledge how on the basis of a linguistic theory of ascriptions without looking at the science of knowledge how is deeply misguided. Likewise, in a recent paper Levy (2017) urges that whether knowledge how can be reduced to propositional knowledge is partly an empirical issue, arguing ultimately that the relevant science indicates that knowledge how has a nonpropositional component.

Theorizing about skilled action control, including in later work by Stanley (Stanley and Krakauer 2013; Stanley 2011), has since taken what might be called a *cognitive scientific turn*, with insights garnered from work in cognitive neuroscience, cognitive psychology, computer science, and cognitive ethology (see Schwartz and Drayson 2019 for discussion of this shift in methodology). Some of this work still focuses on the relationship between theoretical and practical knowledge. Thus, Devitt argues that the folk's theoretical and practical knowledge should be viewed as equivalent to the psychologists' declarative and procedural knowledge and that the empirical evidence that the two dissociate strongly suggests that they are distinct. And both Devitt and Noë argue in favor of anti-intellectualism on the grounds that cognitive science has by and large characterized practical knowledge in nonrepresentational terms (i.e., as involving embodied capacities), while Roth and Cummins (2011) argue that even where cognitive scientists treat practical knowledge as involving representations, they are not considered to be propositional in format.

The cognitive scientific turn has expanded the scope of theorizing about skill in a way that has taken it beyond concerns about the relationship between practical and theoretical knowledge and the nature of each. The emphasis, instead, has come to be on the nature of the *control* that underlies skilled action. In general, we may say that what it is for an agent to possess control is to possess the capacity to bring about mental or physical activity in accordance with their goals. When it comes to skilled action control, the question concerns the extent to which such control is subserved by psychological processes associated with higher-level cognition and propositional representations versus those psychological processes that proceed automatically, and are associated with the motor system and nonpropositional representations. In light of this broader focus, characterizing the debate as being one between intellectualists versus anti-intellectualists seems no longer apt, since all parties agree (see, e.g., Stanley and Krakauer 2013; Pavese 2019) that skilled action control is not exhausted by propositional knowledge. Rather, the debate is now better construed as holding between what we might call *automatism*—the view that skilled action control, under optimal circumstances, is largely driven by automatic motor processes—and *cognitivism*—the view that skilled action control, under optimal circumstances—essentially involves significant contributions from cognitive control.

The two competing views may be characterized more precisely as follows:

Automatism: Under optimal circumstances (i.e., not novel or otherwise unpredictable), skilled action is primarily driven by automatic motor control processes that are characterized by a lack of (i) conscious reflection about what the agent is doing, (ii) explicit intention guiding one's behavior each step of the way, (iii) monitoring and attention directed toward what the agent is doing, or (iv) deliberation or reasoning about what the agent is doing.

Cognitivism: Under optimal circumstances (i.e., not novel or otherwise unpredictable), skilled action control is primarily driven by cognitive control processes that are characterized by the presence of (i) conscious reflection on what the agent is doing, (ii) sustained focus on the agent's intention, (iii) monitoring and attention directed toward what the agent is doing, or (iv) deliberation and reasoning about what the agent is doing.

In the next section, I look more closely at the debate between these two views and motivate a form of cognitivism.

2.3 Automatism versus Cognitivism about Skill

According to automatism about skill, skill acquisition is characterized by an increase in automaticity and reduced involvement of cognitive control at advanced levels (Anderson 1982; Fitts and Posner 1967; Dreyfus and Dreyfus 1986). In such a view, novices start out learning a skill by following step-by-step rules or procedures and explicitly thinking about what they are doing. But once they have advanced to higher levels of skill by automatizing the motor routines involved in various tasks through extensive practice, there is no longer any need for them to direct cognitive control—in the form of conscious attention and monitoring—toward their performance. These and other forms of cognitive control (e.g., focus, reflection) might be required in novel or unpredictable circumstances, such as when an experienced driver is trying to navigate an unfamiliar route during poor road conditions, but under normal or typical circumstances, skilled performance unfolds without them.

A standard argument in favor of automatism appeals to a phenomenon known as "the yips." Expert performers who suffer from the yips repeatedly perform below their own baseline level in high-pressure situations, despite the absence of any physical injury. Importantly, the yips typically interfere with heavily automatized, routine behaviors that experts can normally perform without any difficulty, such as throwing the ball to a teammate in baseball.

According to one prominent theory, known as "explicit monitoring theory," in cases of the yips, performances are hurt because the agent's anxiety, triggered by the high-stakes scenario within which they find themselves, causes them to turn their attention inward, thus self-consciously monitoring motor routines that would normally proceed automatically. On this view, it is the agent's monitoring of and attention toward their own activity that interferes with their ability to perform, rather than their anxiety per se (Baumeister 1984; Masters, Polman, and Hammond 1993; Wulf and Prinz 2001; Beilock and Carr 2001).

Support for explicit monitoring theory comes from a range of empirical studies that use what is known as the "varied focus" paradigm (e.g., Beilock and DeCaro 2007; Ford, Hodges, and Williams 2005; Gray 2004). Here participants are divided into two groups: the highly skilled group and the novice group. Both groups are asked to perform the same task (e.g., dribbling a soccer ball) under three conditions: (i) normal, that is, perform the main task on its own ("single-task/control condition"), (ii) while directing attention to some aspect of their performance (e.g., what side of their foot last touched the ball when an auditory tone occurred) ("skill-related supplemental task condition"), and (iii) while engaging in an extraneous task (e.g., counting backward by twos) ("skill-unrelated supplemental task condition"). Participants in the highly skilled group perform significantly worse (vs. the normal/control condition) in the skill-related supplemental task condition, but only negligibly worse in the skill-unrelated supplemental task condition. Novices show the reverse pattern, performing significantly worse in the skill-unrelated supplemental task condition (vs. the control condition) and marginally better in the skill-related supplemental task condition (vs. the control condition)

One explanation for why highly skilled participants perform only negligibly worse in the skill-unrelated supplemental task condition accords with automatism. In light of their ability to perform the primary task automatically, highly skilled participants have conscious monitoring and attentional resources to spare. These can be used for the skill-unrelated supplemental task, but they should not be directed toward movements that have already been automatized and typically proceed in the absence of monitoring and attention. By contrast, novices do not have extra cognitive resources left for supplemental tasks—they must direct attention to their bodily movements to ensure they are proceeding smoothly. According to some, these "findings clearly show that if experienced individuals direct their attention to the details of skill execution, the result is almost certainly a decrement in performance" (Wulf 2007: 23).

From these empirical considerations, proponents of automatism argue that a central prediction of the view, that is, that conscious attention and monitoring is disruptive to expert performance, is borne out, thus lending it significant support.

But in recent years, several theorists have pushed back on this line of reasoning. In particular, some have argued that we can allow that conscious monitoring and attention to the implementation of automatized motor routines is detrimental to performance, while maintaining that (other varieties) of cognitive control are essential to skill even under normal or optimal conditions. For instance Papineau (2015) argues that focusing on one's present goal and "keeping one's mind right" are crucial for successful skilled performance, while agreeing that attending to the details of one's motor routines—what he calls the components of basic actions—will result in disaster. Similarly, Bermúdez (2017) argues that certain forms of reflection are essential to skill, since such states are required for appropriately structuring one's attention to relevant aspects of the situation of action, while allowing that the yips are caused by attending to the detailed components of our actions. And Christensen, Sutton, and McIlwayn (2016) emphasize the importance of "situational awareness," which involves the moment-by-moment perception of task-relevant features in the environment in a way that enables the agent to anticipate what will happen next, thus adequately preparing them to respond.

The recent interest in the various roles that cognitive control plays in skill, which are not restricted to conscious monitoring and attention of one's bodily movements, has resulted in theorists seeking to develop cognitivist accounts of skilled action control that reserve substantive roles in skilled performance for *both* cognitive control processes and automatic forms of control, even under optimal conditions (Christensen, Sutton, and McIlwayn 2016; Fridland 2014, 2017; Levy 2017; Montero 2016; Papineau 2013, 2015; Shepherd 2019; Toner and Moran 2020; Bicknell 2021). The central commitment of such views is that automatization "frees up" cognitive resources that are then reinvested such that they continue to contribute to performance even at advanced levels of skill. Further, such views take on a more nuanced understanding of automatic motor control processes according to which they are not merely brute, rigid, reflex-like responses, but flexible and intelligent in their own ways (see, esp., Fridland 2014, 2017). Importantly, cognitivist accounts treat both cognitive and automatic control processes as richly integrated, coordinating to help the skilled agent smoothly satisfy their goals. As such, these views are required to articulate how it is that cognitive and automatic control processes interact.

Cognitivist views of skill have much going for them. For one, they are well-motivated by considerations pertaining to the variability of circumstances under which skilled agents perform. When selecting what action to perform in a given context, skilled agents must be finely attuned to a wide range of situational features. For instance, in tennis, the choice of the type of shot and how to make it will depend on factors such as wind conditions, court surface, the opponent one is playing, their positioning, and so on (Nadal and Carlin 2011: 6). A second motivating consideration, emphasized by Christensen, Sutton, and McIlwayn (2016), is that a *familiar* task is not necessarily an *easy* one. This means that even if an expert has performed a certain type of action countless times, some actions may be so difficult and challenging that they can never be fully automatized.

In attempts to flesh out versions of cognitivism, theorists argue for the role of different aspects of cognitive control in skill that go beyond explicit monitoring and thought (Montero 2015, 2016) such as top-down, selective attention (Bermúdez 2017), focus and concentration (Papineau 2015), situational awareness (Christensen, Sutton, and McIlwayn 2016), and strategic control (Fridland 2014).

This is all well and good. Certainly an overly narrow emphasis on explicit monitoring is problematic if one wants to give a comprehensive account of the range of cognitive control processes underlying skilled action. But while we can (and should) grant that cognitive control that goes beyond explicit monitoring of bodily movements is crucial to skill, one might nonetheless allow, as many cognitivist theorists do, that in many scenarios and skill domains, explicit monitoring and attention to the implementational details of one's action is detrimental. If this is right, as I think it is, then we are left with an important question that requires an answer: how does a skilled agent ensure that the implementational details of their performance unfold smoothly if not via explicit monitoring and attention? Furthermore, how is it that the agent can flexibly *integrate* cognitive and automatic control processes, knowing when and how much of each is needed at any given moment?

It seems to me that in order to answer these questions, we must appeal to an overarching type of meta-control process that is directed toward *both* cognitive and automatic control and helps to integrate them. I submit that skilled agents differ from novices due significantly to their enhanced metacognitive capacities. Metacognition may play a number of roles in skilled performance, but here I will emphasize its role in regulating automatic motor control processes, as well as its role in guiding the interplay between cognitive and automatic control processes. Thus, metacognition may be seen as a form of meta-control that no skilled performance goes without. I will also argue that an appeal to metacognition can help us better understand aspects of the distinctive phenomenology of skill. Before turning to these issues, I next offer a brief account of metacognition.

2.4 What Is Metacognition?

2.4.1 Metacognition as Meta-control, Not Metarepresentation

Metacognition is often characterized as a capacity for self-knowledge that is acquired when the mind turns in on itself. Thus, Flavell (1976) writes, "[m]etacognition refers to one's knowledge concerning one's own cognitive processes or anything related to them" (232).

Some who subscribe to this general view supplement it with the further claim that this capacity for self-knowledge relies on the same mechanisms that enable us to acquire knowledge of *other* minds, that is, our so-called "mindreading capacities" or "theory of mind" (Premack and Woodruff 1978). In this picture, our third-person theory of mind capacities is *metarepresentational*: when I attribute a belief that it is raining to John, I do so by way of metarepresenting him as being in a mental state with that representational content. Metacognition, understood in this way, is simply one's theory of mind applied to oneself, and is thus seen as a form of first-person metarepresentation (Carruthers 2009: 121).

While popular, this way of thinking about metacognition falls short in that it fails to emphasize that the main function of metacognition is the *control* of one's cognition and behavior, not *merely the* acquisition of self-knowledge. This is why, for example, the bare act of introspecting on one's thoughts in the stream of consciousness without any subsequent use of the knowledge gained for the purposes of control, is not properly construed as an instance of metacognition. In addition to the mere monitoring of some cognitive process or a feature thereof, there is an evaluative component regarding the success of that process, and this feeds into a control component that is sensitive to this evaluation in deciding what to do

As a paradigmatic case of metacognition understood as such, consider that which results in judgments of learning. These are characterized as judgments that occur during or after the acquisition of some target information (e.g., word pairs) and pertain to the likelihood of success in the future retrieval of the target information. Here, the monitoring aspect of metacognition is directed toward the acquisition process itself, the evaluative aspect is directed toward its success relative to future retrieval, and the control aspect is directed toward actions being taken as a result of the outputs of monitoring and evaluation, for example, allocating a longer amount of study time or terminating study (see Nelson and Narens 1990). Given this central control function of metacognition, the definition that I favor is as follows:

Metacognition: The capacity to monitor and evaluate one's own psychological processes for the purposes of control.

And since the psychological processes that metacognition targets are themselves control processes, that is, directed toward some goal, at its core, metacognition is a form of meta-control.

2.4.2 Metacognition as Directed toward Control Processes, Not Representation

The second feature of metacognition to emphasize is that it makes use of metacognitive representations, which are representations of a feature or set of features of a psychological process (Shea et al. 2014: 187). Note, crucially, that I do not say that metacognitive representations are representations of features of *representations*, but representations of features of *processes*. This stipulation is a departure from the characterization of metacognition as metarepresentational. In my view, this characterization is inaccurate, as metacognitive representations are not, strictly speaking, about features of first-order representations, but rather features of first-order psychological processes that tend to yield representations as outputs.

Why insist on this understanding? First, if we look at paradigm cases of metacognition in the psychological literature, including judgments of learning that were just discussed, it is pretty clear that it is *primarily* directed at the likelihood that a given psychological process has resulted or will result in an accurate or successful outcome rather than the outcome itself. For instance, metacognitive judgments of learning reflect one's confidence that one has accurately understood some target material (Nelson and Narens 1990). Likewise, the feeling of knowing judgments in metamemory tasks reflect one's confidence that one will be able to successfully recall some currently nonrecallable item in the future, for example, on a retention test (Nelson and Narens 1990). And metacognitive confidence judgments in perceptual decision tasks reflect one's confidence that one has accurately detected some target stimulus or discriminated one of its features (Fleming and Daw 2017). In none of these paradigm cases of metacognition does the metacognitive representation refer to the representation that is the output of a psychological process—it refers to features of the process itself.

Looking to paradigm cases of metacognition also indicates that metacognitive representations do not *themselves* result in the *attribution or awareness* of a psychological state that is the output of a psychological process. The best illustration of this comes from the feeling of knowing judgments. Such judgments do not make one aware of the psychological state that will or will not be the future output of the retrieval process—one does not yet have access to this state. They pertain to the retrieval process itself.

To be clear: I am not claiming that metacognition cannot be directed toward a process that outputs a representation of which one comes to be aware. This often happens. For instance, in a perceptual decision task, one is typically aware of the perceptual state that gives rise to the decision. Nonetheless, metacognition (in the form of confidence judgments) is here primarily directed toward the reliability of the perceptual process that gives rise to the conscious perceptual state, and not the perceptual state itself.

2.4.3 Two Levels of Metacognition

Many theorists have found it fruitful to think of metacognition as operating at two different levels, each involving a different structure, functional role, and type of representations (e.g., Arango-Muñez 2011; Proust 2013). I will adopt the same framework here. In such a model, two types of metacognitive capacity are differentiated.

At what I will call "low-level" metacognition, the metacognitive representations deployed in the monitoring and evaluation of first-order psychological processes are nonconceptual "feelings," that is, states with qualitative character for which there is something to be like when they are conscious. Metacognitive feelings do not require the possession or deployment of concepts corresponding to the psychological processes that they are about in order to be tokened. They belong to the same family as other representations that have nonconceptual qualitative characters such as emotions, pains, and visual sensations. These metacognitive feelings, when tokened, constitute a metacognitive evaluation that is primarily sensitive to the *fluency* of the psychological processes toward which they are directed. Fluency can be understood as a function of the ease with which some psychological process is carried out. What this amounts to depends on the type of psychological process in question. In the case of perception, it is taken to mean a lower signal-to-noise ratio (Whittlesea and Williams 2001). In the case of memory or learning, it is often taken to correspond to self-paced processing time (Undorf and Erdfelder 2015). Since these feelings reliably carry information about the success of psychological processes, they can be used by the subject to directly guide subsequent decisions and behavior, and in the absence of explicit thought or reflection.

The main motivation for positing this basic, lower-level form of metacognition is a body of empirical work that suggests that nonhuman animals (e.g., rhesus macaques) possess metacognitive capacities, as measured by their performance on metacognitive tasks, but fail false belief tasks[1]. For instance, when both bottlenose dolphins and rhesus macaques are offered the opportunity to "opt out" from perceptual decision or memory retrieval tasks, they show a similar pattern of responses to human subjects presented with the same tasks (Hampton 2001; Smith 2009). If this is correct, then it suggests that the metacognitive representations they employ for the purposes of those tasks are not conceptually encoded, but rather nonconceptual, qualitative states.

The second type of metacognition, which I will call "high-level" metacognition, operates by way of verbally expressible, conceptual representations with propositional format and is thought to be unavailable to creatures that do not possess the relevant concepts. This is the type of metacognition that is often assimilated to self-knowledge, as it was discussed earlier, though we will not lose sight of the control function it is meant to serve. The metacognitive representations it uses deploy concepts that correspond to the psychological processes toward which they are directed, such as remembering, perceiving, and learning. It is common to view higher-level metacognition as requiring mind reading capacities or theory of mind for extracting the standards of evaluation of a given psychological process (Arango-Muñez 2011; Carruthers 2009). The evaluation such states express tracks their success or accuracy by way of sensitivity to various cues, external and internal, including metacognitive feelings themselves.

There is dispute about how exactly these two posited systems interact. But all agree that, at the very least, the outputs of low-level metacognition are available to be used as inputs by the higher level. For instance, a feeling of perceptual fluency is available as input to the higher-level metacognition that gives rise to a perceptual decision. And a feeling of knowing is available as input to high-level metacognition that gives rise to the feeling of knowing judgments. This is not to say that the outputs of low-level metacognition must be used as input by the higher level. Indeed, an agent can override their influence in cases where metacognitive feelings may be leading them astray. The point is that they are available to be used as cues by high-level metacognition.

With this conceptual framework in place, I go on in the next section to explain how it is that metacognition is crucial to the meta-control that skilled agents exhibit.

2.5 Metacognition and Skill

In this section, I will argue that metacognition is crucial to the control that skilled experts deploy in that it makes available a form of action monitoring and evaluation for the implementation of intentions that does not disrupt performance and allows them to balance the interplay between cognitive and automatic control.

First, a brief word about control. Any system capable of adaptively controlling its behavior must be capable of setting a goal or an aim, predicting the effects of the action that is selected as a means toward satisfying that goal, and comparing the actual effects with those predicted, making adjustments as necessary. The motor system is no different.

Second, a concern to address: some would balk at the suggestion that metacognition can be directed toward agency tout court, insisting that it is specific to mental or cognitive forms of agency. For instance, Proust (2010) argues that bodily actions are constitutively governed by an instrumental norm, such that what it is to act with one's body is to aim to change the world in a certain way and to pursue the means sufficient for bringing about changes in accordance with that aim. Metacognitive processes directed toward bodily action would thus have the function of evaluating the success of an action by comparing its sensory outcomes with the guiding intention. But in addition to any instrumental norms, according to Proust, mental actions involve "epistemic requirements." And it is sensitivity to different epistemic requirements associated with different mental action types (e.g., correctness, exhaustiveness, relevance, informativeness) that metacognition is specialized for, not simply the success of an action relative to one's aim or intention.

Proust's characterization of bodily agency and the instrumental norm it is governed by is likely true of many everyday action types that simply aim toward satisfying some intention. But what we are interested in here is skilled action, that is, action par excellence, and not just basic everyday activity. And in this context, it is clear that a broader set of norms applies in that an agent need not merely satisfy a certain goal or intention, but do so *well*, and this requires adhering to standards such as efficiency, smoothness, accuracy, and so on. It is here that metacognition can (and I think does) play a role that is analogous to that which it plays in mental agency in that it can monitor and evaluate various context-sensitive cues, both internal to external to action control mechanisms, that carry information about the extent to which those norms are met and inform control processes directed toward ensuring that they are. This form of metacognition pertains to performance as a whole, and not just the extent to which individual goals are satisfied.

In fact, the very limited discussion of metacognition in the skill literature lends support to this picture. In a series of qualitative studies examining expert/novice differences in the use of metacognitive processes in endurance runners, Brick et al. (2015) interviewed ten elite-level endurance runners. They then analyzed their interview data with an eye to determining the extent to which they used metacognitive processes in order to regulate their online performance. One form of metacognition that elite runners reported using was monitoring during running, which included the monitoring of internal sensory events, for example, bodily sensations of muscular fatigue, breathing, overall feelings of effort or difficulty, and exertional pain. They reported using these cues to inform their choices of further strategies to deploy for enhancing their overall performance, for example, the use of an active self-regulatory strategy versus the use of a distraction strategy. In a follow-up study focused on recreational instead of elite runners, Brick et al., found that participants used significantly fewer metacognitive strategies than experts and deployed them less effectively and flexibly.

The type of metacognition just described corresponds to what we earlier characterized as higher-level metacognition and is of a variety that the agent explicitly intends to engage in. Here the outputs of metacognition are judgments pertaining to aspects of the skilled performance and are based on a conceptual understanding of the type of action in question and on factors that contribute to its going well. We can call the judgments in question judgments of performance. Importantly, the monitored cues (e.g., exertional pain) that such judgments are based on can include elements external to the motor control processes responsible for bringing about the relevant action outcomes. What is important is that these cues carry information about the extent to which the performance is going well, which includes information about how much effort is being exerted and the extent to which overall task demands are being met. The judgments of performance that the agent forms on their basis can then help dictate what aspects of the performance might need to be adjusted or regulated as well as how—in particular, which aspects of the performance might benefit from additional forms of cognitive control.

But not all forms of action-related metacognition are carried out in this explicit manner. I propose that it is implicit, low-level metacognition in the form of feelings of dis/fluency that regulate the motor control processes that implement an agent's goals, analogously to how they regulate mental processes such as remembering, learning, or perceiving.

A range of studies provides evidence that one of the main cues to which metacognitive feelings of fluency are sensitive in the context of motor control is the *ease or smoothness* of action selection, that is, the degree of response conflict or competition that is present on a given task. In general, these studies use subliminal priming of actions to manipulate the ease of action selection in simple response-selection tasks (Chambon and Haggard 2012; Chambon et al. 2014; Sidarus, Vuorre and, Haggard 2017; Wenke, Fleming, and Haggard 2010). In one such study, participants were asked to press left or right keys corresponding to left or right pointing target arrows, that is, to perform a left-key press in response to a left-pointing arrow and a right-key press in response to a right-pointing arrow. Prior to the appearance of the target arrows, they were presented with *subliminal* arrow primes that were either compatible or incompatible with the target arrow. After they gave their response, and with variable delays, they were presented with disks, the color of which depended on whether the primes were compatible or incompatible with the correct response. At the end of each block, participants were then asked to rank-order how much control they experienced for each color that appeared, that is, to make judgments of control.

Unsurprisingly, participants' reaction times were faster for compatible primes versus incompatible primes. But what is interesting for our purposes is that participants also gave higher *control* ratings for colors following action-compatible primes versus colors following action-incompatible primes. This finding suggests that their judgments of control were based on feelings of fluency pertaining to the ease of the action selection process. In other words, the easier their actions were to perform in terms of not conflicting with a primed alternate response, the more they judged themselves to be in control over the effects of that action.

It is important to note that the judgments of control solicited in these types of studies may be sensitive to a range of cues pertaining to motor control that goes beyond feelings of dis/fluency. Indeed, in a recent attempt to isolate the respective contributions of action selection fluency and action-outcome monitoring to judgments of control, Sidarus, Vuorre, and Haggard (2017) conducted a multi-study analysis of seven experimental studies investigating judgments of control under various conditions. In particular, the authors examined three cues: congruency between primes and action—that is, the ease of action selection—the temporal interval between the action and its outcome—andthe action-outcome itself—that is, the color of the disk, dependent on the congruency between prime and action.

Interestingly, the authors found that the relative contribution of the two retrospective cues (action-outcome interval and outcome identity) to judgments of control was modulated by contextual information, including what the participants were instructed to attend to. What this finding suggests is that the agent's ongoing attention to various situational factors contributes to their judgments of control, a finding which fits well with a view of these judgments as forms of metacognitive monitoring and evaluation that are based on attending to certain cues that carry information about the success of one's control processes.

What all this suggests is that (i) skilled agents can use metacognitive judgments of performance to determine when to exert more cognitive control over aspects of their performance and (ii) even when agents are not consciously monitoring their actions, or engaged in explicit metacognition, a significant degree of implicit metacognitive monitoring is nonetheless taking place. This constitutes an important form of online control in skilled performance and helps to explain how it is that skilled agents monitor what they are doing in ways that do not result in the yips or other detriments to performance.

2.6 Metacognition and Flow

Central to the phenomenology of skill is a subjective experience that is known as "flow." This experience has been characterized in numerous ways, but it can be understood generally as "the subjective experience of engaging just-manageable challenges by tackling a series of goals, continuously processing feedback about progress, and adjusting action based on this feedback" (Nakamura and Csikszentmihalyi 2009, p. 90). The phenomenology of flow is multifaceted. As Shepherd (2021) recently discusses, researchers have identified at least nine dissociable components of flow, and there are several ways to think about how exactly they all hang together—the verdict still largely out about what is the best one.

Here I will focus on three of the most commonly discussed components of flow experience: (i) a sense of effortlessness accompanying one's actions, (ii) a merging of action and awareness, and (iii) the subjective balance between abilities and task demands (also known as feelings of "being in the zone"). All three, I conjecture, can be fruitfully understood as forms of metacognition.

Start with the sense of effortlessness. I suggest that this is underpinned by implicit metacognitive feelings of fluency as an action unfolds, and is also related to judgments of control. The more fluent action selection is, the more predictable are action outcomes, and the better able a skilled agent is to exert and feel control over their situation. Moreover, the type of implicit metacognitive monitoring underlying feelings of fluency can also be appealed to in order to account for "the merging of action and awareness" that is characteristic of flow, which is described as follows by Csizksentmihalyi (2014):

> A person in flow does not operate with a dualistic perspective: one is very aware of one's actions, but not of the awareness itself. [...] The moment awareness is split so as to perceive the activity from "outside," the flow is interrupted. (138)

This merging of action and awareness can be readily explained if the monitoring in question is not carried out by the agent explicitly or deliberately and involves processes that are internal to action control itself, as I am suggesting here.

Higher degrees of fluency likely also contribute to higher levels of confidence with respect to one's overall performance, as reflected in the following testimony by a golfer experiencing a series of positive outcomes within a performance:

> "I was just confident in pretty much everything. . . . It was kind of a feeling like "well there's not really too much in my way right now, everything's going my way," and I just felt like I can shoot the lights out. . . . My swing was beginning to feel good and . . . I liked the holes coming up, I knew I could play well." (Swann et al. 2016: 17)

And this confidence, in turn, may contribute to the type of performance control that Swann et al., (2016) have termed "letting it happen," which involves the agent letting their actions unfold largely automatically and with little intervention from cognitive control, including explicit metacognition. Finally, when it comes to the sense of being "in the zone," I suggest that this is the result of explicit metacognitive judgments of performance. Recent experimental work supports this proposal. The results of a study by Vuorre and Metcalfe (2016) indicate that judgments of being in the zone show a different pattern of task sensitivity than judgments of control. Judgments of control are highest when a task is easy and decrease linearly as the task becomes more difficult. Judgments of "being in the zone," by contrast, increase as the task becomes more difficult and peak at middle values of difficulty when an agent's skills and task demands are balanced.

But what appears to be important here is not that an agent's skills and task demands *are* balanced, but that the agent perceives them to be. Thus, Kennedy et al. (2014) have tested out what they call the "balance-plus-hypothesis," according to which "in the zone" judgments are highest when the balance between task demand and ability is accompanied by a metacognitive evaluation of one's own performance. In particular, they hypothesized that "higher levels of zone may be experienced when perceived performance on a particular trial is high compared to when it is low" (p. 50), and this is indeed what the results of their study suggested.

Just as implicit metacognitive monitoring underlying the sense of effortlessness is plausibly associated with "letting things happen," I suggest that the explicit form of metacognition underlying the sense of being in the zone is associated with the type of control that Swann et al. (2016) call "making things happen," which often occurs in the context of so-called "clutch" performances. Toner and Moran (2020) offer a useful characterization of this phenomenon as "an intentional process involving a conscious decision to increase the attentional resources that one devotes to performance. During this state, task execution continues to unfold in an automatic manner but the performer devotes additional cognitive resources to strategic control." This is precisely the type of shift in the interplay between cognitive and automatic control that metacognition is ideally suited guide.

An understanding of when to let things happen and when to make things happen is obviously essential to skilled action. I hope to have shown here how a focus on metacognition can help us see how this is achieved, and shed some light on aspects of the phenomenology of skilled action to boot (see Pacherie and Mylopoulos 2021 for further discussion and Bicknell 2021 for an additional take on the role of metacognition in skill).

2.7 Conclusion

In this chapter, I suggested that recent theorizing about skill is best understood as having taken a cognitive scientific turn, where the main debate concerns the extent to which cognitive control versus automatic motor control processes contribute to skilled action control. I then motivated a cognitivist view of skilled action, according to which cognitive control plays a crucial role in skilled performance, alongside automatic motor routines. Finally, I argued that no cognitivist account is complete without considering the role of metacognition in skill, as it provides a form of meta-control that is essential to navigating the interplay between cognitive and automatic control, as well as an implicit form of monitoring over motor control processes that does not disrupt performance. I closed with some empirically motivated conjectures regarding the relationship between metacognitive processes and the phenomenology of skill.

Note

1 Whether it is ultimately correct to claim that nonhuman primates are incapable of passing false belief tasks is a matter of debate, which for present purposes I must bracket. But see, for example, Lewis and Krupenye 2021 for an overview.

References

Anderson, J. R. (1982), "Acquisition of a Cognitive Skill," *Psychological Review*, 89 (4): 369–406.

Arango-Muñoz, S. (2011), "Two Levels of Metacognition," *Philosophia*, 39 (1): 71–82.

Baumeister, R. F. (1984), "Choking Under Pressure: Self-Consciousness and Paradoxical Effects of Incentives on Skillful Performance," *Journal of Personality and Social Psychology*, 46 (3): 610–20.

Beilock, S. and M. DeCaro (2007), "From Poor Performance to Success Under Stress: Working Memory, Strategy Selection, and Mathematical Problem Solving Under Pressure," *Journal of Experimental Psychology: Learning, Memory, and Cognition*, 33 (6): 983–98.

Beilock, S. L. and T. H. Carr (2001), "On the Fragility of Skilled Performance: What Governs Choking Under Pressure?," *Journal of Experimental Psychology: General*, 130 (4): 701–25.

Bermúdez, J. P. (2017), "Do We Reflect While Performing Skillful Actions? Automaticity, Control, and the Perils of Distraction," *Philosophical Psychology*, 30 (7): 896–924.

Bicknell, K. (2021), "Embodied Intelligence and Self-Regulation in Skilled Performance: Or, Two Anxious Moments on the Static Trapeze," *Review of Philosophy & Psychology*, 12 (3): 595–614.

Brick, N., T. MacIntyre, and M. Campbell (2015), "Metacognitive Processes in the Self-Regulation of Performance in Elite Endurance Runners," *Psychology of Sport and Exercise*, 19: 1–9.

Carruthers, P. (2009), "How We Know Our Own Minds: The Relationship Between Mindreading and Metacognition," *Behavioral and Brain Sciences*, 32 (2): 164–82.

Chambon, V., E. Filevich, and P. Haggard (2014), "What is the Human Sense of Agency, and is it Metacognitive?," in S. M. Fleming, and C. D. Frith (eds.), *The Cognitive Neuroscience of Metacognition*, 321–42, Berlin, Heidelberg: Springer.

Chambon, V. and P. Haggard (2012), "Sense of Control Depends on Fluency of Action Selection, not Motor Performance," *Cognition*, 125 (3): 441–51.

Christensen, W., J. Sutton, and D. McIlwayn (2016), "Cognition in Skilled Action: Meshed Control and the Varieties of Skill Experience," *Mind & Language*, 31 (1): 37–66.

Csikszentmihalyi, M. (2014), "Play and Intrinsic Rewards," in *Flow and the Foundations of Positive Psychology*, 135–54, Berlin, Heidelberg: Springer Dordrecht.

Devitt, M. (2011), "Methodology and the Nature of Knowing How," *Journal of Philosophy*, 108 (4): 205–18.

Dreyfus, H. and S. Dreyfus (1986), *Mind over Machine*, New York: The Free Press.

Fitts, P. M. and M. I. Posner (1967), *Human Performance*, Belmont, CA: Brooks/Cole.

Flavell, J. H. (1976), "Metacognitive Aspects of Problem Solving," in L. B. Resnick (ed.), *The Nature of Intelligence*, 231–5, Hillsdale, NJ: Lawrence Erlbaum.

Fleming, S. M. and N. D. Daw (2017), "Self-Evaluation of Decision Performance: A General Bayesian Framework for Metacognitive Computation," *Psychological Review*, 124 (1): 91–114.

Ford, P., N. J. Hodges, and A. M. Williams (2005), "Online Attentional-Focus Manipulations in a Soccer-Dribbling Task: Implications for the Proceduralization of Motor Skills," *Journal of Motor Behavior*, 37 (5): 386–94.

Fridland, E. (2014), "They've Lost Control: Reflections on Skill," *Synthese*, 91 (12): 2729–50.
Fridland, E. (2017), "Skill and Motor Control: Intelligence all the Way Down," *Philosophical Studies*, 174 (6): 1539–60.
Gray, R. (2004), "Attending to the Execution of a Complex Sensorimotor Skill: Expertise, Differences, Choking, and Slumps," *Journal of Experimental Psychology: Applied*, 10 (1): 42–54.
Hampton, R. R. (2001), "Rhesus Monkeys Know When They Remember," *Proceedings of the National Academy of Sciences of the United States of America*, 98 (9): 5359–62.
Kennedy, P., D. B. Miele, and J. Metcalfe (2014), "The Cognitive Antecedents and Motivational Consequences of the Feeling of Being In the Zone," *Consciousness and Cognition*, 30: 48–61.
Levy, N. (2017), "Embodied Savoir-Faire: Knowledge-How Requires Motor Representations," *Synthese*, 194 (2): 511–30.
Lewis, L. S. and C. Krupenye (in press), "Theory of Mind in Nonhuman Primates," in B. L. Schwartz and M. J. Beran (eds.), *Primate Cognitive Studies*, Cambridge University Press.
Masters, R. S. W., R. C. J. Polman, and N. V. Hammond (1993), "Reinvestment: A Dimension of Personality Implicated in Skill Breakdown Under Pressure," *Personality and Individual Differences*, 14 (5): 655–66.
Montero, B. (2015), "Is Monitoring One's Actions Causally Relevant to Choking Under Pressure?" *Phenomenology and the Cognitive Sciences*, 14: 379–95.
Montero, B. (2016), *Thought in Action: Expertise and the Conscious Mind*, New York: Oxford University Press.
Nadal, R. and J. Carlin (2011), *Rafa: My Story*, New York, NY: Hyperion.
Nakamura, J. and M. Csikszentmihalyi (2009), "Flow Theory and Research," in C. R. Snyder and S. J. Lopez (eds.), *Handbook of Positive Psychology*, 195–206, New York: Oxford University Press.
Nelson, T. O. and L. Narens (1990), "Metamemory: A Theoretical Framework and New Findings," in G. H. Bower (ed.), *The Psychology of Learning and Motivation*, 1–45, New York, NY: Academic Press.
Noe, A. (2005), "Against Intellectualism," *Analysis*, 65 (4): 278–90.
Pacherie, E. and M. Mylopoulos (2021), "Beyond Automaticity: The Psychological Complexity of Skill," *Topoi*, 40: 649–62.
Papineau, D. (2013), "In the Zone," *Royal Institute of Philosophy Supplement*, 73: 175–96.
Papineau, D. (2015), "Choking and the Yips," *Phenomenology and the Cognitive Sciences*, 14 (2): 295–308.
Pavese, C. (2015), "Practical Senses," *Philosophers' Imprint*, 15 (29): 1–25.
Pavese, C. (2019), "The Psychological Reality of Practical Representation," *Philosophical Psychology*, 32 (5): 784–821.
Premack, D., and G. Woodruff (1978), "Does the Chimpanzee Have a Theory of Mind?," *Behavioral and Brain Sciences*, 1 (4): 515–26.
Proust, J. (2010), "Metacognition," *Philosophy Compass*, 5 (11): 989–98.
Proust, J. (2013), *The Philosophy of Metacognition: Mental Agency and Self-Awareness*, New York: Oxford University Press.
Roth, M. and R. Cummins (2011), "Intellectualism as Cognitive Science," in A. Newen, A. Bartels, and E.-M. Jung (eds.), *Knowledge and Representation*, 23–39, Palo Alto, CA: CSLI Publications.

Ryle, G. (1949), *The Concept of Mind*, Chicago, IL: The University of Chicago Press (reprinted as 60th Anniversary Edition, Routledge, London, 2009).

Schwartz, A. and Z. Drayson (2019), "Intellectualism and the Argument from Cognitive Science," *Philosophical Psychology*, 32 (5), Online First.

Shea, N., A. Boldt, D. Bang, N. Yeung, C. Heyes, and C. D. Frith (2014), "Supra-personal Cognitive Control and Metacognition," *Trends in Cognitive Sciences*, 18 (4): 186–93. https://doi.org/10.1016/j.tics.2014.01.006.

Shepherd, J. (2019), "Skilled Action and the Double Life of Intention," *Philosophy and Phenomenological Research*, 98 (2): 286–305.

Shepherd, J. (2021), "Flow and the Dynamics of Conscious Thought," *Phenomenology and the Cognitive Sciences*, 21: 969–88.

Sidarus, N., M. Vuorre, and P. Haggard (2017), "Integrating Prospective and Retrospective Cues to the Sense of Agency: A Multi-Study Investigation," *Neuroscience of Consciousness*, 2017 (1): nix012.

Smith, J. D. (2009), "The Study of Animal Metacognition," *Trends in Cognitive Sciences*, 13 (9): 389–96.

Stanley, J. (2011), *Know How*, New York: Oxford University Press.

Stanley, J. and J. W. Krakauer (2013), "Motor Skill Depends on Knowledge of Facts," *Frontiers in Human Neuroscience*, 7 (503): 1–11.

Stanley, J. and T. Williamson (2001), "Knowing How," *Journal of Philosophy*, 98 (8): 411–44.

Swann, C., R. Keegan, L. Crust, and D. Piggott (2016), "Psychological States Underlying Excellent Performance in Professional Golfers: 'Letting it Happen' vs. 'Making it Happen,'" *Psychology of Sport and Exercise*, 23: 101–13.

Toner, J. and A. Moran (2020), "Exploring the Orthogonal Relationship Between Controlled and Automated Processes in Skilled Action," *Review of Philosophy and Psychology* [Advance online publication].

Undorf, M. and E. Erdfelder (2015), "The Relatedness Effect on Judgments of Learning: A Closer Look at the Contribution of Processing Fluency," *Memory and Cognition*, 43 (4): 647–58.

Vuorre, M. and J. Metcalfe (2016), "The Relation Between the Sense of Agency and the Experience of Flow," *Consciousness and Cognition*, 43: 133–42.

Wenke, D., S. M. Fleming, and P. Haggard (2010), "Subliminal Priming of Actions Influences Sense of Control over Effects of Action," *Cognition*, 115 (1): 26–38.

Whittlesea, B. W. A. and L. D. Williams (2001), "The Discrepancy-Attribution Hypothesis: I. The Heuristic Basis of Feelings and Familiarity," *Journal of Experimental Psychology: Learning, Memory, and Cognition*, 27 (1): 3–13.

Wulf, G. and W. Prinz (2001), "Directing Attention to Movement Effects Enhances Learning: A Review," *Psychonomic Bulletin and Review*, 8 (4): 648–60.

Wulf, G. and J. Su (2007), "An External Focus of Attention Enhances Golf Shot Accuracy in Beginners and Experts," *Research Quarterly for Exercise and Sport*, 78 (4): 384.

3

Bringing Self-control into the Future

Samuel Murray

Introduction

The standard story about self-control centers on three claims. First, many think that self-control is limited. Exercising self-control at one moment makes it more difficult to exercise self-control thereafter in the absence of a recovery period. There are a variety of explanations for these limitations, ranging from consumption of limited resources (Baumeister et al. 1998) to structural and functional limitations of processes supporting self-control (Edin et al. 2009; Ma and Huang 2009; Miller 1956; Oberauer and Kliegel 2006; Usher et al. 2001). Second, exercising self-control requires effort and is, for that reason, aversive (Kool et al. 2010; Kurzban 2016; Inzlicht, Shenhav, and Olivola 2018). Finally, the function of self-control is to resist temptation or suppress impulses (Ainslie and Haslam 1992; Bargh and Chartrand 1999; Holton 2009; Joosten et al. 2015; Mischel, Shoda, and Rodriguez1989; Muraven and Baumeister 2000; Myrseth and Fishbach 2009; Soutschek et al. 2016; Watson 1977).

Discussions of self-control are historically tied to explanations of weakness of will (Mele 2011). Framed in this way, the standard story of self-control makes sense. In such a case, the agent must employ self-control to avoid succumbing to temptation (functional claim). Because of the temptation, the agent must use self-control to resist something she currently desires (aversion claim). Lastly, if the individual does not remove herself from the tempting scenario, then she eventually gives in because her self-control is depleted (limitation claim). It's a nice package. And it's incorrect.

We can challenge the standard story from the bottom up. While self-control is sometimes employed to resist temptation or suppress impulses, this certainly does not exhaust the range of applications for self-control. To see this, consider the following example:

Hot Car. Kate normally dropped her daughter Sam off at daycare before working from home. But one summer morning, Kate had an early meeting and her daughter was sleeping in. This meant Brad—Kate's husband—had to take Sam in before heading to work. Unfortunately, Brad forgot to drop his daughter Sam off. By the time he remembered, the little girl had been sitting inside a car, windows closed, on a summer day in Texas for several hours. EMT's declared Sam dead a mere 80 minutes after Brad called 9-1-1.

This, I submit, is a failure of self-control. But where's the temptation? Where's the impulse? You won't find them because they aren't there. This suggests that there is more to self-control than the motivational dimension encapsulated in the functional claim of the standard story.

Self-control is not exclusively aversive. Theorists typically infer aversion from the fact that exercising self-control requires effort. But neither self-control nor effort is necessarily aversive. Consider the fact that learning a new language, or a new instrument, requires lots of self-control and effort, but neither experience is aversive (or, at least, not always aversive). The aversion claim ignores a general truth, namely that some of the enjoyable experiences in life *also* require lots of effort.[1]

Discussions of limitations on self-control are complicated, and we should distinguish the target of the discussion. There is the phenomenon of self-control limits and the candidate's explanations of those limits. Let's consider first the phenomenon of self-control limitations. In a standard study on self-control limits, participants in the experimental condition perform two tasks, both of which require self-control. The control group performs a non-control task in the first block and a self-control task in the second block. These tasks range from Stroop tasks to emotion suppression tasks. Participants in the experimental condition typically perform worse on the second task (or tasks following an initial self-control task) across a variety of dimensions relative to the control group (Schmeichel 2007; see Hagger et al. 2010 for a meta-analysis of depletion effects in self-control studies). Some of the findings include lower inhibition after performing a controlled task (Vohs and Faber 2007), stronger bias toward behaviors that require only automatic processing (Schmeichel, Vohs, and Baumeister 2003), higher rates and intensity of prejudicial judgments (Muraven 2003), and diminished performance on tasks that require a speed/accuracy tradeoff (DeWall et al. 2011).

These depletion effects have shown up in hundreds of independent studies (see Baumeister and Vohs 2016: 75–93 for a summary of findings). A meta-analysis showed that effects from these various studies were both robust and significant (Hagger et al. 2010). However, some challenge whether this meta-analysis appropriately accounted for possible publication and small-study biases (Carter and McCullough 2014). Following up on this possibility, a later meta-analysis found a corrected effect that is effectively zero (Carter et al. 2015). And, though a subsequent preregistered, multi-lab replication effort found significant effects (Sripada, Kessler, and Jonides 2016), a meta-analysis of the results found an ego-depletion effect close to zero (Hagger et al. 2016), and Bayesian analyses of the results supported this null finding (Etherton et al. 2018). Additionally, attempts to replicate some of the training effects on ego depletion found in the original Hagger et al. (2010) meta-analysis failed when correcting for timescale and task type (Miles et al. 2016). When participants performed controlled tasks that lasted over longer timescales (i.e., tasks with higher ecological validity), Wenzel et al. (2019) found a reversed ego-depletion effect.

What this means is that ego-depletion effects are more complicated than the original two-task experimental conditions suggested. While there is some evidence that ego-depletion effects do not exist, it seems more probable that ego-depletion effects are highly sensitive to contextual factors. This would explain the highly variable findings. In fact, in what is becoming a near-weekly tradition, yet *another* meta-analysis of ego-depletion studies found significant overall effects of depletion across nine different task types (Dang 2018). Hence, it seems safe to say that ego-depletion effects are real, so we need some explanation for them.

One explanation is that exercising self-control consumes a limited resource. Hence, an exercise of self-control depletes the agent's resources. When this occurs, a central governing mechanism registers that the agent is consuming resources at an unsustainable rate, thus causing the brain to reduce exertion and conserve energy (see Evans, Boggero, and Segerstrom 2016). This framework construes self-control as analogous to a muscle and willpower as analogous to physical strength and posits that the limited resource is metabolic (see Baumeister and Vohs 2016).

There are two problems with this view. The first is that the strength theory has difficulty explaining the variety of contextual factors that modulate ego-depletion effects (see Kurzban et al. 2013). The second is that there appears to be no plausible metabolic substrate that supports self-control. The original proposal for the metabolic substrate was glucose (Gailliot and Baumeister 2007 and Gailliot et al. 2007). This proposal has not fared well over time. Later studies found that exerting self-control sometimes *raised* blood glucose levels over time (Baumeister and Vohs 2016). A meta-analysis of various glucose-related results found no significant effects (Dang 2018). The proposal is also highly counterintuitive. Brain processing consumes a minuscule amount of glucose relative to the rest of the body. Exercising self-control raises glucose consumption by a minuscule fraction. If such small increases in glucose consumption are sufficient to trigger depletion effects, then self-control would be much too volatile to support temporally extended agency (Wenzel et al. 2019).[2]

In the wake of suspicion surrounding the strength theory, several alternative theories about the nature of self-control have emerged. Many of these alternatives cite motivation and attention as essential components of self-control (e.g., Botvinick and Braver 2015; Eastwood et al. 2012; Inzlicht, Schmeichel, and Macrae 2014; Hockey 2011; Inzlicht, Shenhav, and Olivola 2018; Kool and Botvinick 2014; Kurzban et al. 2013; Shenhav et al. 2017). There are some important differences between these theories, but the central thread connecting them is that ego-depletion effects result from shifts in motivation (thereby causing shifts in attention). For example, Inzlicht, Schmeichel, and Macrae (2014) explain that one explanation of ego-depletion effects in laboratory studies is that participants are motivated to think about other things, like what they'll be eating for dinner later or what they'll do with their friends over the weekend. This also explains why shifting incentives mitigates the ego-depletion effect. Limitations of self-control, then, reflect our fleeting motivations to carry out any single task (and, perhaps, our underlying propensity to shift attention from tasks we must do to tasks we want to do).

While the motivational theory avoids the problems that plague the strength theory, the view is also unintuitive in some respects. Consider, again, the *Hot Car* case. There, we identified a self-control failure, but it's not clear that there's a shift in motivation that explains the self-control failure. In fact, we can press this point and say that it's *wildly implausible* that parents in these kinds of scenarios have changed their preferences or shifted motivation. That would imply that the parent has come to value getting to work on time over the life of their child. We see this inadequacy when we extrapolate out to other performance breakdowns. For example, forgetful cooks do not suddenly lose motivation to have their kitchen not be engulfed in flames. And forgetting a birthday or an anniversary does not reflect an individual's devaluation of a relationship.

Both major theoretical approaches to self-control turn out to be inadequate. Thus, we need some approach that explains apparent limitations on self-control (and suggests some principled explanation of the influence of contextual factors on these limitations) in an empirically tractable way that maps onto the various dimensions of self-control. Additionally, it would be nice for the theory to explain the connection between effort and self-control in a way that avoids construing self-control as necessarily aversive *and* to explain where temptation resistance fits into the scheme of self-control. Finally, we want our resulting theory of self-control to explain what's going wrong in the *Hot Car* case.

In this chapter, I propose a theory of *self-control as vigilance*. In Section 3.1, I explain why we should expect vigilance and self-control to be related. In Section 3.2, I propose an alternative way to understand limitations on control that grounds self-control limits in efficient cognitive network architecture. Section 3.3 discusses the computational principles that govern control allocation. With this in hand, in Section 3.4 I outline the maintenance dimension of vigilance and discuss two modes of maintenance, portrayal and recovery, and the relationship between these modes and the computational account of control allocation from Section 3.3. Finally, Section 3.5 ties together various threads, discussing the connection between self-control and effort, the kind of self-control that temptation resistance requires, and the explanation of various ego-depletion effects.

3.1 Self-control as Vigilance (I)

To see the reasons for connecting self-control to vigilance, let's step back and consider what the purpose of self-control is. If we reject the claim that the function of self-control is just to resist temptation or impulse, then why do creatures like us have self-control at all?

Agents like us pursue a variety of goals and commit to a wide range of projects. Living a meaningful life requires heterogeneity of pursuits. However, these goals cannot be simultaneously realized or even simultaneously pursued. Thus, multiplicity of goals, combined with limits on cognitive and bodily resources, generates the need for a goal maintenance mechanism (Murray 2020). Vigilance regulates goal-relevant information and the implementation of goal-relevant information in mind that facilitates goal-directed action (Murray and Vargas 2020). A perfectly virtuous creature with heterogeneous pursuits and certain cognitive limitations that experiences no temptations and is subject to no impulses would still require vigilance for effective goal maintenance. Further, it seems intuitive to think of part of the function of self-control as goal maintenance. Self-control, then, amounts to the pursuit of multiple goals in an effective and efficient manner.

One benefit of this account is that it classifies obsessions as failures of self-control. This is not possible on the standard story of self-control. The obsessed individual does not succumb to temptation or impulse; rather, she focuses too much on one thing at the expense of everything else. Obsession, then, manifests lack of efficiency and, hence, lack of self-control to some degree.

Given the overlap between the functional description of vigilance and the functional description of self-control, it makes intuitive sense to consider the claim that self-control is a species of vigilance.[3]

3.2 The Limits of Control

Why is it that an Apple Watch—with four circuits—can calculate two two-digit math problems simultaneously, but the human brain—with over 20 billion cortical neurons—*cannot*? As the question suggests, control limitations derive neither from metabolic limitations (extra sugar won't help) nor from structural/functional limitations (as a structurally and functionally limited computational device can do things the human brain cannot).

The Stroop task provides another example on the limits of control. Try as hard as you might, you cannot engage in color identification and word naming simultaneously (if you could, incongruent Stroop tasks wouldn't be harder and take longer than their congruent counterparts). You cannot imagine what it's like to be in Berlin *and* what it's like to be Bogotá simultaneously. The examples are endless. But, again, it does not seem like these limitations are ultimately reducible to structural or functional limitations. The human brain has an enormous number of resources that it *could* devote to controlled processing. So, even if structural or functional limitations are part of the explanation for limited controlled processing, it seems that something else is fundamentally explanatory.

But, if we're not going to appeal to metabolic, structural, or functional limitations, then what might explain these strict limitations on control? To get to the answer, consider an example. We utilize task representations to guide goal-directed behavior. So, we store task representations that correspond to crossing the street, whisking the eggs, and watering the garden. However, you wouldn't want a unique representation for *every* unique task you can perform. For example, you don't need a separate street-crossing task representation for every street you happen to cross. A single, generalized "street-crossing" task representation will do (see Rougier et al. 2005).

This is true in general. Representations that can be utilized for multiple tasks are more efficient than highly specialized representations. Drawing from a basic stock of generalized representations that can be flexibly deployed across various task types is known as *multiplexing*. Allport, Antonis, and Reynolds (1972) were the first to suggest that the brain multiplexes. Multiplexing, however, introduces the possibility of channel crosstalk. If you have a variety of available input-output task mappings subserved by the same representation, then these tasks might potentially interfere with each other

(Forbus, Gettner, and Law 1995; Hinton, McClelland, and Rumelhart 1986). The Stroop task provides a simple example. The input-output mappings that correspond to word naming and color identification both utilize the same representation. Hence, the processes that subserve these two tasks cannot be activated simultaneously, and activating one implies performance deficits for the other. Thus, multiplexing correlates negatively with the capacity to multitask, as the more multiplexing occurs, the greater the possibility of crosstalk, which reduces the capacity to multitask without the possibility of interference (see Feng et al. 2014 for a computational model of the absolute limits of multiplexing on multitasking in an optimal control network independent of network size and number of control nodes).

Dramatic limitations on control reflect the brain's preference for efficient coding through multiplexing. We can infer the brain's preference for multiplexing over multitasking from the fact that we can perform so few controlled tasks simultaneously. This, however, generates a problem of interference. A high degree of pathway overlap implies several potential sites of interference between task mappings. To solve this problem of interference, you need a control manager. Thus, Jon Cohen claims: "These [shared resource] models suggest that constraints on the simultaneous execution of multiple tasks can be viewed as the *purpose* of control, rather than a limitation in its ability" (2017: 5, emphasis original).

The function of the manager unit, as Cohen suggests, is to adjudicate conflicts between overlapping pathways and bias lower-level information processing in ways that support goal-directed behavior (Botvinick et al. 2001). Biasing is accomplished by allocating control to unique pathways to alter the threshold for a neuronal population to fire. Hence, conflict management requires allocation of control (Section 3.3 discusses the computational principles of control allocation).

One natural question is why the brain (or the evolutionary principles that govern brain development) did not generate unique control units for every site of potential crosstalk. However, the addition of extra control units (beyond the optimal convergence point) generates performance *deficits* (see Feng et al. 2014: Fig. S5). Both error rate and expected reward attainment decrease in proportion to additional control units. Feng and colleagues do not offer a computational story for the performance deficits, but the effect makes intuitive sense. Efficiency declines when there are too many cooks. There might also be adaptive value in having fewer control units. With fewer control units, local and global reconfigurations of task mappings in response to task acquisition can occur more easily. This is because a system that utilizes minimal control units requires a simpler network architecture. Over time, this might represent a metabolic advantage over massively modular architectures (Anderson 2014: 38).

This framework provides a new way to think about limitations on self-control. Multiplexing, combined with a small number of control nodes, constrains the capacity to multitask. This computational account of control limitations is more empirically tractable than the metabolic account and explains the structural and functional limits on controlled processing. Return to the Apple Watch. The watch doesn't multiplex, instead utilizing discrete informational units for each calculation. This is fine for the watch because it doesn't do much and so can afford to prefer multitasking. We, however, have the advantage of being able to do innumerable things. The price for this is that we multiplex for the sake of efficiency. This generates pathway overlap that decreases the capacity to multitask. However, we can solve this interference problem with control nodes that manage channel interference. This generates a new question: what are the computational principles that dictate the allocation of control across these various channels?

3.3 The Expected Value of Control

One cornerstone of cognitive architecture research is that cognitive efficiency is built on a speed/accuracy tradeoff (Bogacz et al. 2006). There are benefits associated with a system of heuristics and defaults (e.g., fast processing speed), but there are also costs (e.g., error and inflexibility) (Miller and Cohen 2001). There are benefits associated with a deliberative system that assesses available actions relative to an internal causal model of the environment (e.g., accuracy and flexibility), and there are costs (e.g., slow processing speed).

The computational principles that govern control allocation should, then, solve for an optimal balance between speed and accuracy. A background presumption is that the network is configured for long-term maximization of reward. Thus, the optimal balance between speed and accuracy reflects an aim toward maximizing reward. But, given the discussion from Section 3.2, the optimal balance must be measured relative to the bounded computational powers of a control network that utilizes shared representations. One engineering principle that seems intuitive is that the network should rely on a system of default settings, with control units intervening only when necessary. This is plausible because optimal network design would suggest that you use the fast/computationally cheap system as much as possible and correct for errors (with the slower/computationally expensive system) when necessary. Control units, then, would monitor for conflicts among lower-level information-processing units. When conflict is detected, the control unit would calculate the costs and benefits of engaging control to resolve conflict.

Recent computational models of control allocation provide a framework for thinking about these issues at the psychological level. That is, if we understand the computational principles that govern control allocation at the neurobiological level, we will gain a foothold for understanding how those principles manifest at the psychological level. One popular model is the Expected Value of Control (EVC) model articulated by Jonathan Cohen (see Shenhav, Botvinick, and Cohen 2013 for an early statement of the computational and mechanistic aspects of the view). The mechanistic aspects of the EVC are not important here, so I will focus only on the computational elements. The following three computations represent the core of this evaluation (these equations are taken directly from Shenhav, Botvinick, and Cohen 2013: 221):

Equation 1:
  $\text{EVC(signal, state)} = [\, \Sigma_i \, Pr(\text{outcome}_i | \text{signal, state}) \cdot \text{Value}(\text{outcome}_i)] - \text{Cost(signal)}$

Equation 2:
   Value(outcome) = ImmediateReward(outcome) + $\gamma max_i[EVC(signal_i, outcome)]$

Equation 3:
   signal* ← $max_i[EVC(signal_i, state)]$

The computational principle of the EVC calculates the value of a particular control signal based on three components. The first component represents the probability of achieving a particular outcome given that a control signal is sent in a particular environment ($Pr(outcome_i|signal, state)$). The second component is the value of the outcome (Value($outcome_i$)), and the third component represents the intrinsic cost of the signal (Cost(signal)).

Currently, there are no widely accepted theories of which mechanisms compute values for the probability of achieving an outcome given transmission of a control signal nor what computational principles govern these mechanisms. Some suggest that certain mechanisms simulate controlled behavior to rapidly generate estimates (Pezzulo, Rigoli, and Chersi 2013). Others suggest that model-free learning mechanisms update estimates of probabilities for the system without the use of simulation (Gershman, Horvitz, and Tenenbaum 2015; Braem 2017). Others find evidence for the use of heuristics to estimate probabilities without assessing task-specific demands (Dunn, Lutes, and Risko 2016). At this point, not enough is known about task representation acquisition and updating to know *how* this process is carried out. But the point remains that the computations underlying control allocation are sensitive to the probability of achieving the outcome. When the probability of success diminishes, control decreases (Kool, Gershman, and Cushman 2017).

The representation of value has two parts. The first concerns the immediate expected reward upon achieving the outcome. Part of the cost-benefit analysis associated with determining control allocation should be sensitive to the potential *benefits* of achieving the outcome. However, the EVC model includes a temporal component to value representation. Outcome value representation reflects the kinds of action-reward sets that will be available from the achieved outcome state ($\gamma max_i[EVC(signal_i, outcome)]$). Thus, a highly immediately rewarding outcome will diminish in overall value if there are no desirable action-reward sets available from the state in which one has attained the outcome.

This aspect of the value representation reflects part of the cost of control (but not the intrinsic cost represented in the third component). Consider two possible outcomes, O_1 and O_2. Suppose that the immediate reward associated with these outcomes is such that $O_1 > O_2$. But, achieving O_1 would put you in a position where you could not pursue other rewards without some "rest" (the quotes suggest resisting an interpretation of limited resource consumption; the issue of limitations is discussed as follows). Achieving O_2, on the other hand, puts you in a better relative position to achieve further rewards. Of course, the value of O_1 might greatly exceed O_2, thereby nullifying these costs. The point is simply that the computation is sensitive not just to the value of available outcomes but about future deployments of control.

Finally, there is the cost of the signal. Recently, there has been debate about how to interpret the cost of control. Roughly, this represents the *intrinsic* costs of control.

Recall that our cognitive network architecture is designed so that only one (or a very small number) of controlled tasks can be pursued at any one time. When we utilize control, we intervene on the "default" settings of lower-level information-processing pathways, thereby configuring the system to support goal-directed behavior in the circumstances. However, this configuration means that any number of available configurations are not available, meaning that the rewards associated with pursuing other actions are missed. Hence, we can understand the intrinsic costs of control in terms of the opportunity costs associated with not pursuing other goals.

It is worth noting that there are two separate cost values computed. The first is part of the outcome value representation. This cost reflects "depleted" resources that result from using control. This depletion, however, is metaphoric. The real cost consists in task-switching costs associated with reconfiguring the system either toward another goal or back to a default (unconfigured) state. This also implies diminished behavioral flexibility relative to non-goal-related activities, thereby increasing switching costs. The intrinsic cost, on the other hand, reflects the opportunity cost of thinking and pursuing one goal at the exclusion of others or at the exclusion of plural (unconfigured) goal pursuit.

The EVC model assigns a unique value to a particular control signal as a function of the probability of achieving an outcome given the transmission of a control signal, the value of the outcome, and the cost of that signal. To see how the model works, consider an idealized, non-iterated incongruent Stroop task condition. Here, one is presented with a word (e.g., "green") filled in with a different color (e.g., RED) and told to identify the color. When the word is presented, there is a conflict among lower-level information-processing units associated with word naming and color identification (since both utilize the same representation). The EVC model describes the calculations that control units compute to determine whether to allocate control. Because the scenario is idealized, we can assume that the probability of achieving the outcome given the signal = 1, while the probability of achieving the outcome without the signal = 0. The value of the outcome-given-signal is high (as it conforms to experimenter instructions), so we can assign it a value of 1, whereas the value of outcome-without-signal is 0. The cost of the signal drops out here, as the Stroop task in this case is not repeated. Hence, relative to the experimental condition, there is no need to calculate values relative to the state where one has achieved the outcome. The expected value of the control signal outweighs both its costs *and* the alternative based on not signaling. With the computation complete, the control unit signals to bias the network toward goal-relevant processing. Of course, the computations get more complicated as probabilities are added, tasks become temporally extended, and the value of other control signals must be weighed. But the idealized example shows what the various components are meant to represent.

The EVC model is one of many available models of the cost-benefit analysis associated with control allocation. So why go on at length about the components and implications of this one model? There are good reasons to prefer this model to others. For one, the EVC model has plausible neurobiological realizers and provides an integrative framework for thinking about various neurobiological mechanisms (Shenhav et al. 2017). Recent work seems to show that we can map EVC computations to various functionally localized neural mechanisms (Shenhav, Botvinick, and Cohen 2013 for a review). Also, experimental work supports the EVC model, especially in reinforcement-learning paradigms, where the EVC makes divergent predictions from other control allocation algorithms (e.g., Kool, Shenhav, and Botvinick 2017). Finally, the model connects with recent theoretical advances in artificial intelligence research and machine learning applications. For example, the EVC model mirrors theoretical frameworks that model rational metareasoning and algorithm selection in artificial intelligence systems (Lieder et al. 2018) and implementing the EVC model has produced advances in machine learning (LeCun, Bengio, and Hinton 2015). In addition, the EVC model seems compatible with other computational models of control allocation (Musslick and Cohen 2021), but that argument lies outside the scope of the present chapter. Should the EVC model turn out incorrect, it is likely that whatever the correct model is will be close enough to the EVC that the applications to vigilance remain apt.

3.4 The Maintenance Dimension of Vigilance

In this section, I will outline the connections between the EVC model and vigilance. The maintenance dimension of vigilance maps most directly onto the various components of the EVC model (though I'll also argue that implementation corresponds to the EVC, too, so that the EVC model provides a fully computational account of vigilance). This will then give us a template for discussing various failures of vigilance. In the next section, I'll discuss the relationship between EVC, vigilance, and self-control.

First, I will briefly outline an account of vigilance I have defended elsewhere (Murray 2017, 2020; Murray and Vargas 2020; Murray and De Brigard 2021). Being vigilant is realized in virtue of three mental events that facilitate plan-directed awareness: (1) monitoring for circumstantial and task-relevant information that, when perceived (2) triggers implementing task-appropriate representations that are (3) maintained through the completion of the task (or task-segment) or until the agent revises their intention. Being vigilant is realized whenever these operations aim to produce task-congruent temporally extended action. These operations correspond to two different dimensions of vigilance: monitoring and maintenance.[4]

These dimensions reflect distinctive kinds of performance breakdowns whenever some operation fails to occur. There are failures to recall a task set, failures to preserve a task set, failures to coordinate two tasks, and failures to coordinate tasks with known information. In the former two types of failures, the agent fails to apprehend a presently available consideration that is relevant given some previously adopted plan. In the latter two types of failures, there is a failure to coordinate between one's present and future self. In other words, there is a failure to apprehend that some future consideration is relevant to one's current planning and task-set acquisition. Thus, in the former cases the agent fails to apprehend that a *present* consideration is relevant given *prior* planning, whereas in the latter cases the agent fails to apprehend that a *future* consideration is relevant to one's *current* planning. All share the common feature of exhibiting a failure to move from an adopted plan to relevant features of an action context.

Each failure has a different temporal orientation (past or future). Both dimensions of vigilance have temporally variegated deployments. Thus, the four kinds of failures correspond to the four different aspects of vigilance (present monitoring/maintenance and future monitoring/maintenance). Here, I want to focus on the maintenance dimension of vigilance. I call the future-directed aspect of maintenance *portrayal*, while the present-directed aspect of maintenance is called *recovery*. To get a sense of these different aspects, let's again look at what happens when they break down.

In the Hot Car example, the parent plans to drop the kid off at school before heading to work but ends up going straight to work. This is a present-directed case of maintenance failure (hence, a failure of recovery). The parent fails to adequately respond to goal threats and goal substitution. What happens is that, in general, favoring task sets that minimize the cost of control leads to reliance on habitual routines. The parent, when putting the kid in the backseat, fails to accurately assess the need for engaging in controlled processing for goal maintenance. In one sense, this is understandable. As we saw in the previous section, there is a tendency toward minimizing the use of control. Given the past record of success when relying on habits, there seems to be no need to deliberate about the use of control, much less initiate an actual deployment of control. From the parent's perspective, both the likelihood of failure and the task demands are so low that there seems to be no need to think very hard about the task of dropping the kid off.

This can be represented in terms borrowed from the EVC model. Recall that there are three representational components to the model: the probability of achieving an outcome given a signal, the value of the outcome, and the cost of the signal. Misrepresentations could occur at each point. The parent might misrepresent the probability of achieving the outcome in the absence of a control signal, she might misrepresent some aspect of the value of the outcome (though this is unlikely), or she might misrepresent the cost of the control signal. As the case is described here, it seems that the parent misrepresents the cost of control. Rather than move from a default to controlled configuration, the parent instead sees no need to pay the cost of control.

This might seem fishy. You might think: "Wait, the *parent* is misrepresenting? Surely people don't perform these computations at the personal level. These *misrepresentations* are sub-personal glitches, not anything you can pin on the agent." The answer to this objection, however, provides a bridge between the agent and the computational principles outlined in the previous sections. Roughly, the computational failure can be attributed, in failure of vigilance cases, to the agent's failure to construe her tasks appropriately (in other words, the agent fails to structure her plans appropriately, leaving those plans susceptible to goal threat or substitution).

The way that an agent construes her goals is important. Literature on implementation intentions suggests that concretely structured plans are less likely to be abandoned prematurely (Gollwitzer 1999). Similarly, task construal can have an impact on how attractive some tempting item seems (Fujita et al. 2006). Task construal bears on plan structure, as task construal typically implies a certain plan structure (Ho et al. 2022). For instance, there's an enormous difference between forming a plan to exercise as "I'll workout when I have the time" and "I'll only take a rest if I've worked out the previous two days" (Fujita 2011). Similarly, recovering alcoholics who adopt a narrower, more present-directed focus of their circumstances (low-level construal) tend to relapse at higher rates than recovering alcoholics who adopt a more global perspective (high-level construal) (Keough, Zimbardo, and Boyd 1999).[5]

This might make it seem like all failures of vigilance are just failures of construal, thereby implying that there is just one kind of failure of vigilance, not four. With the EVC in hand, we can outline more precisely the four different kinds of vigilance failure. This account depends on the functional distinctness of maintenance and monitoring.

One speculative difference between monitoring and maintenance concerns the calculation of probability. Recall, from Section 3.3, that separate mechanisms calculate probability estimates for achieving an outcome. Perhaps the mechanism of monitoring consists in these probability calculators, whereas the mechanism of maintenance consists in cost calculators (value representations would be subserved by valuative—possibly reinforcement-learning—mechanisms). Hence, the aim of monitoring at the information-processing level is probability calculation, while the aim of maintenance at the same level is cost calculation.

This connection to the EVC suggests the following taxonomy of vigilance failures. We can distinguish broadly between two kinds of failures: maintenance failures and monitoring failures. Within each type, there can be either present-directed or future-directed failures. These four failures can be characterized in psychological terms. A present-directed maintenance failure consists in failing to preserve a task set over time. A future-directed maintenance failure consists in a failure to coordinate multiple task sets over time. A present-directed monitoring failure consists in a failure to recall a task set at the appropriate time. And a future-directed monitoring failure consists in "double booking," or committing to practically incompatible tasks. While each of these failures can be characterized at the psychological level, each failure can also be characterized at the computational level based on elements of the EVC. A present-directed maintenance failure consists in inaccurately representing the cost of a control signal. A future-directed maintenance failure, on the other hand, consists in inaccurately representing the *future* costs of some present course of action. A present-directed monitoring failure consists in an incomplete representation of the decision space, while a future-directed monitoring failure consists in inaccurately representing the probability of success contingent on sending a control signal.

The case of present-directed monitoring failures requires some discussion. Part of the activity of monitoring is to accurately represent features of the action context relevant to one's planning. At the computational level, this amounts to accurately entering values for the various arguments in the EVC function. For example, suppose I'm telling a funny story around you that recounts your doing something embarrassing. I don't even recognize that you're getting upset and I continue telling the story. Here, I've misinterpreted the situation such that certain values (like your taking offense at the anecdote) are not even represented in my decision procedure to continue telling the story. This seems to be a failure of monitoring, but on a slightly different order than other kinds of failures of vigilance.

Note that each aspect of vigilance maps to a component of the EVC. This strengthens the claim made earlier that the EVC provides a fully computational account of vigilance. Additionally, the EVC model leaves room for the importance of task construal. The representation of plan structure might play an important role at the computational level. The foregoing at least suggests that failures of monitoring and maintenance are distinct, even though they both share a common constituent, namely task construal. This also demonstrates the dynamic interactions between the different dimensions of vigilance. For instance, the representation of cost might be sensitive to representations of probability and vice versa (consider the Hot Car case; perhaps the representation of probabilities affects the representation of current costs of control. Not enough is currently known about the relations between these different aspects of the computations, so nothing definitive can be stated about dependence or fundamentality of one relative to the other).

The EVC model provides a computational underpinning for the functional account of vigilance. The reason for connecting these two constructs is not to reduce vigilance to the EVC model. Of course, an individual who realized a psychology that failed to be accurately described by either the computational or representational theory of mind might have vigilance. The point of tying the vigilance account to the EVC model is that it provides a computationally tractable way of thinking about the activity of vigilance. When tied to a sufficient mechanistic model of vigilance, EVC enables predictions about when and where vigilance will break down and how we might improve the exercise of vigilance.

3.5 Self-control as Vigilance (II)

What remains is to determine whether the account of vigilance and cognitive control adequately captures certain features of the self-control construct. In this section, I'll show how vigilance explains the activity of various processes typically associated with self-control. Additionally, I'll consider two potential problems with the self-control as vigilance theory, namely that there are empirical reasons to dissociate cognitive control and self-control and that the function of self-control is exhausted by temptation resistance.

There are three foundational components typically associated with models of self-control: inhibition, task updating, and task-switching (Davisson and Hoyle 2017). Additionally, there are four components typically associated with cognitive control: working memory, response selection, response inhibition, and task-set switching (e.g., Sabb et al. 2008). The EVC model makes explicit connection between cognitive control and vigilance. To connect this to components of self-control, consider that vigilance structures the flow of information into working memory. The activity of monitoring aims to bring plan-relevant information to mind at the appropriate time, while filtering out information when it is no longer relevant. Bringing information to mind here amounts to bringing the information into working memory (Baddeley 2012). This shows that updating is a component of vigilance and, by extension, that cognitive control is partly constitutive of self-control. As for inhibition and switching, these components fall under the maintenance dimensions of vigilance. Sending a control signal (which is constitutive of the activity of vigilance) is constitutively relevant to inhibiting some response for the sake of selecting some other response.[6] Similarly, when the cost of some ongoing controlled activity becomes too great (relative to other goals that one could pursue), then the agent shifts. Again, this is just the function of the maintenance dimension of vigilance in its present-directed aspect. Thus, it seems possible to map both cognitive control and self-control onto the functional account of vigilance, thereby linking all three constructs.

One worry about this account is that it seems to make self-control back into mere impulse control/temptation resistance. After all, if conflict monitoring is part of the maintenance dimension of vigilance (which dimension, recall, is the one associated with self-control), then isn't self-control still just a form of conflict management? But the objection gets the view wrong. Conflict monitoring *may* involve the detection of distractions, temptations, or impulses toward short-term rewards. However, note that "conflict" applies to a much wider range of phenomena than this. Any creature with a heterogeneous set of goals that cannot be simultaneously pursued will need self-control. And the conflicts that get monitored might simply be conflicts between pursuing one or another goal at any particular time. Hence, there is a need for conflict monitoring even in the absence of being distracted or tempted.[7]

One final objection to consider concerns empirical evidence that self-control and cognitive control are distinct constructs. In a recent study, Scherbaum et al. (2018) proposed that self-control and cognitive control recruit distinct processes and are, therefore, distinct constructs. They hypothesized that if cognitive control and self-control rely on the same set of processes, then "experimental manipulations that cause control adjustments in one task should also increase controlled behavior in the other task" (2018: 195). The experimental design used two tasks, a cognitive control task (Simon task) and a self-control task (intertemporal value decision). Each trial pair consisted of the cognitive control task followed by the self-control task. Participants had two seconds to perform the Simon task before immediately moving to the self-control task. Every participant completed 576 trial pairs. The results showed that there is "no difference in the probability of [choices exhibiting high self-control] for decisions following conflict Simon trials . . . and decisions following non-conflict Simon trials" (2018: 196). Hence, they conclude that self-control and cognitive control recruit distinct processes.

There are two problems with this, however. The first is a small point with experimental design. There is some evidence that when individuals perform a control-demanding task, they exhibit a tendency to continue performing the same task despite being cued to switch. This is known as the "task-set inertia" effect (Allport, Styles, and Hsieh1994; Yeung 2010). The experimental design, however, did not rule out the possibility of task-set inertia effects. Hence, participants might have directed control resources toward the Simon task, relying on more habitual/default routines to complete the self-control task. The short time scale over which participants completed trials does not compensate for potential inertia effects.

The second problem concerns the hypothesis, namely that if cognitive control and self-control share similar processes, then tasks that activate cognitive control processes should elicit higher degrees of self-control in subsequent tasks. This, however, does not hold true even in cases where the two tasks are cognitive control tasks. For instance,

Yeung et al. (2006) found that participants perform a cognitive control task more slowly and less accurately following the performance of a different cognitive control task when compared to the performance of the same cognitive control task (there were also small "restart" costs observed on same-same cognitive control task blocks). Hence, there is no reason to expect the claim that if two constructs share similar processes, then performing one kind of task will boost the performance of the other kind of task. For these reasons, we can dismiss the supposed evidence in favor of the distinction between cognitive control and self-control.

With this model in hand, we can explain some phenomena connected with traditional studies of self-control. The first concerns the relationship between self-control and effort. The underlying neurological basis of self-control, on this view, is the cognitive control system implicated in maintaining task sets. Allocations of control, on this view, are determined by cost-benefit analyses and so are partly sensitive to the costs of control. This provides a naturalistically plausible framework for thinking about the feeling of effort. Effort is the subjective correlate or phenomenological component associated with the costs of control, specifically the opportunity costs associated with allocating control in a particular way (Cohen 2017; Kool, Shenhav, and Botvinick 2017; Kurzban et al. 2013; Shenhav et al. 2017). However, this experience of effort need not always be aversive. This is because sometimes the lost opportunity costs are not valued more than the goals pursued in allocating control. When control is aversive, this might be due to diminished *motivation* or willingness to pay the costs of control (see Botvinick and Braver 2015; Winecoff and Huettel 2017). This would then incorporate a motivational element into the "self-control as vigilance theory" (or, vigilance theory), thereby explaining the appeal of purely motivational views of self-control posited before.

Second, the view shows how impulse control/temptation resistance falls under the purview of self-control. Succumbing to temptation or giving into impulse is a kind of recovery failure. Typically, impulses and temptations have pull in virtue of being goal-relevant (though these goals might be maximally coarse-grained, like "experience pleasure"; see Levy 2011: 143). Hence, being in the presence of a temptation or under the pull of an impulse threatens to shift goal pursuit. Self-control is needed to recover from the initial pull of temptations and impulses. This recovery consists in reallocating control to manage conflicts between the goals activated by temptations/impulses and the goals one was originally pursuing.[8]

Ego-depletion effects also make sense on the vigilance view. In general, the vigilance theory predicts that in a traditional two-task paradigm (like those used in original ego-depletion studies) agents lose motivation to perform the task rather than run out of metabolic resources. In other words, the opportunity costs associated with allocating control to task performance become too high and agents shift either to focused thinking about something else or to mind wandering (Murray et al. 2020). This connects to an old interpretation of the vigilance decrement (the deficit in performance associated with continued performance of a vigilance task), namely that as the stimuli associated with task performance lose novelty, the subject begins to think of other things (Broadbent 1958). In other words, when agents get bored, they shift to other tasks and therefore perform worse.

This also answers some criticisms addressed to attention/motivation theories of self-control. For instance, Baumeister and Vohs (2016: 100) offer two criticisms:

> [Some suggest] that fatigue in general has nothing to do with low energy but is instead a signal to interrupt one's activities, reflecting opportunity and regulatory costs of perseverance. But what are those regulatory costs if not expenditure of energy?
>
> ....The opportunity cost argument has difficulty explaining the multi-task paradigm findings. If fatigue were merely a signal that it is generally a good idea to switch tasks (as opposed to being a signal that one's energy has been somewhat depleted), why would it transfer so that fatigue from the first task is still felt during the unrelated second task (and indeed impairs performance on it?).

Consider these criticisms in reverse order. The second criticism we already considered by suggesting that subjects get bored and shift attention. The reason why this effect carries over between tasks is that subjects lose their motivation to perform in-lab activities (Nicholls et al. 2015). This also explains why increasing incentives on task performance between tasks in the ego-depletion paradigm eliminates the depleting effect entirely (Muraven and Slessareva 2003). When an agent sufficiently values performance on the second task, the opportunity costs reset and the agent performs close to ceiling (there are also reports of limited feelings of mental effort in these cases; see Boksem and Tops 2008; Lorist, Boksem, and Ridderinkhof 2005).

The first criticism is simply a demand to understand what grounds the cost of control if not depletion of a metabolic resource. Recall from Section 3.2 that the ground of opportunity costs is the shared representational resources used in the brain (i.e., multiplexing). Because of the limited representational resources available for use in cognition, there are costs associated with allocating control (devoting representational resources to one processing pathway over another) that give rise to opportunity costs. Hence, the theory of self-control offered here can answer the criticisms raised against similar views.

3.6 Conclusion

This chapter showed three things. The first is that the standard story of self-control is incorrect. When we reorient our understanding of self-control around trying to understand limitations associated with control that derive from representational resources (rather than metabolic resources or brute structural limitations), a biologically plausible view of self-control emerges based on cost-benefit analyses of allocating control to a single task.

We also saw how this theory of self-control connects to vigilance. As vigilance manages goal maintenance, and self-control consists in allocating control to maintain goal pursuit, self-control is a species of vigilance (the two are not equivalent, as monitoring is not reducible to maintenance or self-control functions). There is a way to translate self-control functions into the language of vigilance when we characterize self-control functions in terms of maintenance. This also suggested a way to connect the sub-personal computational story about the allocation of control to personal-level properties. In particular, a crucial aspect of maintenance is task construal, and the representation of certain task sets at the computational level is sensitive to personal-level construal. Hence, vigilance (or the self-control aspect of vigilance) is not just a matter of sub-personal computations.

Finally, we saw how the vigilance theory of self-control explains several phenomena related to self-control such as effort and ego depletion. Additionally, the vigilance theory can supply answers to criticisms normally leveled against motivation/attention views of attention.

Acting over time is different from concatenated sequences of actions at a time. This shows that many elements of planning psychology are temporally modulated (or have future-directed aspects). From this perspective, one issue with the standard story of self-control is that it centers on the needs of agents acting *at a time*. Even discussions of resolutions and temporally extended wills are all about preparing to act at a time. A planning agent needs something different. This account of self-control takes acting *in time* as fundamental to self-control. This is reflected in the EVC computation containing an essential future-oriented component. This is part of a mechanism for future-directed self-control and, hence, fits the needs of a planning agent.

Notes

1 Spinoza captures this point eloquently: "How would it be possible, if salvation were ready to our hand, and could without great labour be found, that it should be by almost all men neglected? But all things excellent are as difficult as they are rare" (*Ethics* Vp52 s).
2 Feng et al. (2014) point out that self-control processes depend on prefrontal cortex. However, other cognitive and perceptual processes (like vision) engage the prefrontal cortex for sustained periods of time without any depletion effects on the scale observed in self-control studies.
3 Self-control is just a species of vigilance, not equivalent to it. This is because some exercises of vigilance might not consist in a manifestation of self-control. Again, this will be a point of discussion in Section 3.4.
4 Monitoring encompasses implementation operations because monitoring aims to bring about implementation in the right context. Therefore, there are two dimensions of vigilance rather than three.
5 There is some evidence that low-level construal sometimes benefits self-control (see Schmeichel, Cohs, and Duke 2011).
6 See the discussion of constitutive relevance in Craver (2007).
7 This contradicts Gary Watson's assessment of the role that the virtue of self-control plays within the moral life: "Self-control is a virtue only for beings who are susceptible to motivation which is in potential conflict with their judgments of what is good to pursue" (1977: 322). Self-control, as a component of vigilance, is a virtue only for planning agents that must manage pursuit of heterogeneous goods across time.

8 There is some question as to what distinguishes temptations and impulses from ordinary conflicts that arise from plural goal pursuit. This, I think, is not a question that falls on the vigilance theory to answer, but I suspect the answer has something to do with agential autonomy. That is, something is a temptation or impulse in virtue of the fact that the goal pursuit activated by the temptation or impulse is either counter-resolutional (as in Holton 2009) *or* that the agent does not identify or endorse the goal pursuit (as in cases of addiction relapse). This, however, has more to do with the metaphysics of autonomy and the psychology of commitments than with self-control.

References

Ainslie, G. and N. Haslam (1992), "Self-Control," in G. Loewensten and J. Elster (eds.), *Choice over Time*, 177–209, New York: Russell Sage Foundation.

Allport, A., B. Antonis, and P. Reynolds (1972), "On the Division of Attention: A Disproof of the Single Channel Hypothesis," *Quarterly Journal of Experimental Psychology*, 24 (2): 225–35.

Allport, A., E. A. Styles, and S. Hsieh (1994), "Shifting Intentional Set: Exploring the Dynamic Control of Tasks," in C. Umiltà and M. Moscovitch (eds.), *Attention and Performance XV: Conscious and Nonconscious Information Processing*, 421–52, Cambridge, MA: MIT Press.

Anderson, M. (2014), *After Phrenology*, Cambridge, MA: MIT Press.

Baddeley, A. (2012), "Working Memory: Theories, Models, and Controversies," *Annual Review of Psychology*, 63: 1–29.

Bargh, J. A. and T. L. Chartrand (1999), "The Unbearable Automaticity of Being," *American Psychologist*, 54 (7): 462–79.

Baumeister, R. F. and K. D. Vohs (2016), "Strength Model of Self-Regulation as Limited Resource: Assessment, Controversies, Update," *Advances in Experimental Social Psychology*, 54: 67–127.

Baumeister, R. G., E. Bratslavsky, M. Muraven, and D. M. Tice (1998), "Ego Depletion: Is the Active Self a Limited Resource?," *Journal of Personality and Social Psychology*, 74 (5): 1252–65.

Bogacz, R., E. T. Brown, J. Moehlis, P. Hu, P. Holmes, and J. D. Cohen (2006), "The Physics of Optimal Decision Making: A Formal Analysis of Models of Performance in Two-Alternative Forced Choice Tasks," *Psychological Review*, 113 (4): 700–65.

Boksem, M. A. S. and M. Tops (2008), "Mental Fatigue: Costs and Benefits," *Brain Research Reviews*, 59 (1): 125–39.

Botvinick, M. M. and T. S. Braver (2015), "Motivation and Cognitive Control: From Behavior to Neural Mechanism," *Annual Review of Psychology*, 3 (66): 83–113.

Botvinick, M. M., T. S. Braver, C. S. Carter, D. M. Barch, and J. D. Cohen (2001), "Conflict Monitoring and Cognitive Control," *Psychological Review*, 108 (3): 624–52.

Braem, S. (2017), "Conditioning Task Switching Behavior," *Cognition*, 166: 272–76.

Broadbent, D. E. (1958), *Perception and Communication*, Elmsford, NY: Pergamon Press.

Carter, E. C., L. M. Kofler, D. E. Forster, and M. E. McCullough (2015), "A Series of Meta-analytic Tests of the Depletion Effect: Self-Control Does Not Seem to Rely on a Limited Resource," *Journal of Experimental Psychology: General*, 144 (4): 768–815.

Carter, E. C. and M. E. McCullough (2014), "Publication Bias and the Limited Strength Model of Self-Control: Has the Evidence for Ego Depletion Been Overestimated?," *Frontiers in Psychology*, 5: 823.

Cohen, J. D. (2017), "Cognitive Control: Core Constructs and Current Considerations," in T. Egner (ed.), *Wiley Handbook of Cognitive Control*, 3–28, London: Wiley.

Craver, C. (2007), *Explaining the Brain*, New York: Oxford University Press.

Dang, J. (2018), "An Updated Meta-analysis of the Ego Depletion Effect," *Psychological Research*, 82 (4): 645–51.

Davisson, E. K. and R. H. Hoyle (2017), "The Social-Psychological Perspective on Self-Regulation," in T. Egner (ed.), *Wiley Handbook of Cognitive Control*, 440–54, London: Wiley.

DeWall, C. N., R. F. Baumeister, N. L. Mead, and K. D. Vohs (2011), "How Leaders Self-Regulate Their Task Performance: Evidence that Power Promotes Diligence, Depletion, and Disdain," *Journal of Personality and Social Psychology*, 100 (1): 47–65.

Dunn, T. L., D. J. C. Lutes, and E. F. Risko (2016), "Metacognitive Evaluation in the Avoidance of Demand," *Journal of Experimental Psychology: Human Perception and Performance*, 42 (9): 1372–87.

Eastwood, J. D., A. Frischen, M. J. Fenske, and D. Smilek (2012), "The Unengaged Mind: Defining Boredom in Terms of Attention," *Perspectives in Psychological Science*, 7 (5): 482–95.

Edin, F., T. Klingberg, P. Johansson, F. McNab, J. Tegner, and A. Compte (2009), "Mechanism for Top-Down Control of Working Memory Capacity," *Proceedings of the National Academy of Sciences of the United States of America*, 106 (16): 6802–7.

Etherton, J. L., R. Osborne, K. Stephenson, M. Grace, C. Jones, and A. S. De Nadai (2018), "Bayesian Analysis of Multimethod Ego-Depletion Studies Favours the Null Hypothesis," *British Journal of Social Psychology*, 57 (2): 367–85.

Evans, D., I. Boggero, and S. Sergerstrom (2016), "'The Nature of Self-Regulatory Fatigue and "Ego Depletion': Lessons from Physical Fatigue," *Personality and Social Psychology Review*, 20 (4): 291–310.

Feng, S. F., M. Schwemmer, S. J. Gershman, and J. D. Cohen (2014), "Multitasking vs. Multiplexing: Toward a Normative Account of Limitations in the Simultaneous Execution of Control-Demanding Behaviors," *Cognitive, Affective and Behavioral Neuroscience*, 14 (1): 129–46.

Forbus, K. D., D. Gentner, and K. Law (1995), "MAC/FAC: A Model of Similarity-Based Retrieval," *Cognitive Science*, 19 (2): 141–205.

Fujita, K. (2011), "On Conceptualizing Self-Control as More than the Effortful Inhibition of Impulses," *Personality and Social Psychology Review*, 15 (4): 352–66.

Fujita, K., Y. Trope, N. Liberman, and M. Levin-Sagi (2006), "Construal Levels and Self-Control," *Journal of Personality and Social Psychology*, 90 (3): 351–67.

Gailliot, M. and R. F. Baumeister (2007), "The Physiology of Willpower: Linking Blood Glucose to Self-Control," *Personality and Social Psychology Review*, 11 (4): 303–27.

Gailliot, M., R. F. Baumeister, C. N. DeWall, J. K. Maner, E. A. Plant, D. M. Tice, L. E. Brewer, and B. Schmeichel (2007), "Self-Control Relies on Glucose as a Limited Energy Source: Willpower is More than a Metaphor," *Journal of Personality and Social Psychology*, 92 (2): 325–36.

Gershman, S. J., E. J. Horvitz, and T. B. Tenenbaum (2015), "Computational Rationality: A Converging Paradigm for Intelligence in Brains, Minds, and Machines," *Science*, 349 (6245): 273–8.

Gollwitzer, P. (1999), "Implementation Intentions: Strong Effects of Simple Plans," *American Psychologist*, 54 (7): 493–503.

Hagger, M. S., N. L. D. Chatzisarantis, H. Alberts, C. O. Anggono, C. Batailler, A. R. Birt, et al. (2016), "A Multilab Preregistered Replication of the Ego-Depletion Effect," *Perspectives in Psychological Science*, 11 (4): 546–73.

Hagger, M. S., C. Wood, C. Stiff, and N. L. Chatzisarantis (2010), "Ego Depletion and the Strength Model of Self-Control: A Meta-analysis," *Psychological Bulletin*, 136 (4): 495–525.

Hinton, G. E., J. L. McClelland, and D. E. Rumelhart (1986), *Parallel Distributed Processing. Volume I: Foundations*, Cambridge, MA: MIT Press.

Ho, M. K., D. Abel, C. G. Correa, M. L. Littman, J. D. Cohen, and T. L. Griffiths (2022), "People Construct Simplified Mental Representations to Plan," *Nature*, 606 (7912): 129–36.

Hockey, G. R. J. (2011), "A Motivational Control Theory of Cognitive Fatigue," in P. L. Ackerman (ed.), *Cognitive Fatigue: Multidisciplinary Perspectives on Current Research and Future Applications*, 167–88, Washington, DC: American Psychological Association.

Holton, R. (2009), *Willing, Wanting, Waiting*, New York: Oxford University Press.

Inzlicht, M., B. J. Schmeichel, and C. N. Macrae (2014), "Why Self-Control Seems (but may not be) Limited," *Trends in Cognitive Sciences*, 18 (3): 127–33.

Inzlicht, M., A. Shenhav, and C. Y. Olivola (2018), "The Effort Paradox: Effort is Both Costly and Valued," *Trends in Cognitive Sciences*, 22 (4): 337–49.

Joosten, A., M. van Dijke, A. Van Hiel, and D. De Cremer (2015), "Out of Control!? How Loss of Self-Control Influences Prosocial Behavior: The Role of Power and Moral Values," *PLoS One*, 10 (5): e0126377.

Keough, K. A., P. G. Zimbardo, and J. N. Boyd (1999), "Who's Smoking, Drinking and Using Drugs? Time Perspective as a Predictor of Substance Use," *Basic and Applied Social Psychology*, 21 (2): 149–64.

Kool, W. and M. M. Botvinick (2014), "A Labor/Leisure Trade-Off in Cognitive Control," *Journal of Experimental Psychology: General*, 143 (1): 131–41.

Kool, W., S. J. Gershman, and F. A. Cushman (2017), "Cost-Benefit Arbitration Between Multiple Reinforcement-Learning Systems," *Psychological Science*, 28 (9): 1321–33.

Kool, W., J. T. McGuire, Z. B. Rosen, and M. M. Botvinick (2010), "Decision Making and the Avoidance of Cognitive Demand," *Journal of Experimental Psychology*, 139 (4): 665–82.

Kool, W., A. Shenhav, and M. M. Botvinick (2017), "Cognitive Control as Cost-Benefit Decision Making," in T. Egner (ed.), *Wiley Handbook of Cognitive Control*, 167–89, London: Wiley.

Kurzban, R. (2016), "The Sense of Effort," *Current Opinion in Psychology*, 7: 67–70.

Kurzban, R., A. Duckworth, J. W. Kable, and J. Myers (2013), "An Opportunity Cost Model of Subjective Effort and Task Performance," *Behavioral and Brain Sciences*, 36 (6): 661–79.

LeCun, Y., Y. Bengio, and G. Hinton (2015), "Deep Learning," *Nature*, 521 (7553): 436–44.

Levy, N. (2011), "Resisting 'Weakness of the Will,'" *Philosophy and Phenomenological Research*, 82 (1): 134–55.

Lieder, F., A. Shenhav, S. Musslick, and T. L. Griffiths (2018), "Rational Metareasoning and the Plasticity of Cognitive Control," *PLoS Computational Biology*, 14 (4): 31006043.

Lorist, M. M., M. A. Boksem, and K. R. Ridderinkhof (2005), "Impaired Cognitive Control and Reduced Cingulate Activity During Mental Fatigue," *Cognitive Brain Research*, 24 (2): 199–205.

Ma, W. J. and W. Huang (2009), "No Capacity Limit in Attentional Tracking: Evidence for Probabilistic Inference Under a Resource Constraint," *Journal of Vision*, 9 (11): 1–30.
Mele, A. (2011), "Self-Control in Action," in S. Gallagher (ed.), *The Oxford Handbook of the Self*, 465–86, New York: Oxford University Press.
Miles, E., P. Sheeran, H. Baird, I. Macdonald, T. Webb, and P. Harris (2016), "Does Self-Control Improve with Practice? Evidence from a 6-Week Training Program," *Journal of Experimental Psychology: General*, 145 (8): 1075–91.
Miller, E. K. and J. D. Cohen (2001), "An Integrative Theory of Prefrontal Cortex Function," *Annual Review of Neuroscience*, 24: 167–202.
Miller, G. A. (1956), "The Magical Number Seven, Plus or Minus Two: Some Limits on Our Capacity for Processing Information," *Psychological Review*, 63 (2): 81–97.
Mischel, W., Y. Shoda, and M. I. Rodriguez (1989), "Delay of Gratification in Children," *Science*, 244 (4907): 933–8.
Muraven, M. (2003), "Prejudice as Self-Control Failure," *Journal of Applied Social Psychology*, 38: 314–33.
Muraven, M. and R. F. Baumeister (2000), "Self-Regulation and Depletion of Limited Resources: Does Self-Control Resemble a Muscle?," *Psychological Bulletin*, 126 (2): 247–59.
Muraven, M. and E. Slessareva (2003), "Mechanisms of Self-Control Failure: Motivation and Limited Resources," *Personality and Social Psychology Bulletin*, 29 (7): 894–906.
Murray, S. (2017), "Responsibility and Vigilance," *Philosophical Studies*, 174 (2): 507–27.
Murray, S. (2020), "The Place of the Trace: Negligence and Responsibility," *Review of Philosophy and Psychology*, 11 (1): 39–52.
Murray, S. and F. De Brigard (2021), "The Neurocognitive Mechanisms of Responsibility: A Framework for Normatively Relevant Neuroscience," in M. Hevia (ed.), *Developments in Neuroethics and Bioethics*, vol. 4, 19–40, New York: Academic Press.
Murray, S., K. Krasich, J. W. Schooler, and P. Seli (2020), "What's in a Task? Complications in the Study of the Task-Unrelated-Thought Variety of Mind Wandering," *Perspectives on Psychological Science*, 15 (3): 572–88.
Murray, S. and M. Vargas (2020), "Vigilance and Control," *Philosophical Studies*, 177 (3): 825–43.
Musslick, S. and J. D. Cohen (2021), "Rationalizing Constraints on the Capacity for Cognitive Control," *Trends in Cognitive Sciences*, 25 (9): 757–75.
Myrseth, K. O. R. and A. Fishbach (2009), "Self-Control: A Function of Knowing When and How to Exercise Restraint," *Current Directions in Psychological Science*, 18 (4): 247–52.
Nicholls, M. E. R., K. M. Loveless, N. A. Thomas, T. Loetscher, and O. Churches (2015), "Some Participants May Be Better than Others: Sustained Attention and Motivation Are Higher Early in Semester," *Quarterly Journal of Experimental Psychology*, 68 (1): 10–8.
Oberauer, K. and R. Kliegel (2006), "A Formal Model of Capacity Limits in Working Memory," *Journal of Memory and Language*, 55 (4): 601–26.
Pezzulo, G., F. Rigoli, and F. Chersi (2013), "The Mixed Instrumental Controller: Using Value of Information to Combine Habitual Choice and Mental Simulation," *Frontiers in Psychology*, 4: 92.
Rougier, N. P., D. C. Noelle, T. S. Braver, J. D. Cohen, and R. C. O'Reilly (2005), "Prefrontal Cortex and the Flexibility of Cognitive Control: Rules Without Symbols," *Proceedings of the National Academy of the United States of America*, 102 (20): 7338–43.

Sabb, F. W., C. E. Bearden, D. C. Glahn, D. S. Parker, N. Freimer, and R. M. Bilder (2008), "A Collaborative Knowledge Base for Cognitive Phenomics," *Molecular Psychiatry*, 13 (4): 350–60.

Scherbaum, S., S. Frisch, A.-M. Holfert, D. O'Hora, and M. Dshemuchadse (2018), "No Evidence for Common Processes of Cognitive Control and Self-Control," *Acta Psychologica*, 182: 194–99.

Schmeichel, B. (2007), "Attention Control, Memory Updating, and Emotion Regulation Temporarily Reduce the Capacity for Executive Control," *Journal of Experimental Psychology*, 136 (2): 241–55.

Schmeichel, B., K. D. Cohs, and S. C. Duke (2011), "Self-Control at High and Low Levels of Mental Construal," *Social Psychological and Personality Science*, 2 (2): 182–9.

Schmeichel, B., K. D. Vohs, and R. F. Baumeister (2003), "Intellectual Performance and Ego Depletion: Role of the Self in Logical Reasoning and Other Information Processing," *Journal of Personality and Social Psychology*, 85 (1): 33–46.

Shenhav, A., M. M. Botvinick, and J. D. Cohen (2013), "The Expected Value of Control: An Integrative Theory of Anterior Cingulate Cortex Function," *Neuron*, 79 (2): 217–40.

Shenhav, A., S. Musslick, F. Lieder, W. Kool, T. L. Griffiths, J. D. Cohen, and M. M. Botvinick (2017), "Toward a Rational and Mechanistic Account of Mental Effort," *Annual Reviews of Neuroscience*, 40: 99–124.

Soutschek, A., C. C. Ruff, T. Strombach, T. Kalenscher, and P. N. Tobler (2016), "Brain Stimulation Reveals Crucial Role of Overcoming Self-Centeredness in Self-Control," *Science Advances*, 2 (10): e1600992.

Sripada, C., D. Kessler, and J. Jonides (2016), "Sifting Signal from Noise with Replication Science," *Perspectives on Psychological Science*, 11 (4): 576–78.

Usher, M., J. D. Cohen, H. Haarmann, and D. Horn (2001), "Neural Mechanism for the Magical Number 4: Competitive Interactions and Nonlinear Oscillation," *Behavioral and Brain Sciences*, 24 (1): 151–52.

Vohs, K. D. and R. Faber (2007), "Spent Resources: Self-Regulatory Resource Availability Affects Impulse Buying," *Journal of Consumer Research*, 33 (4): 537–47.

Watson, G. (1977), "Skepticism About Weakness of Will," *Philosophical Review*, 85 (3): 316–39.

Wenzel, M., M. Lind, Z. Rowland, D. Zahn, and T. Kubiak (2019), "The Limits of Ego Depletion: A Crossover Study on the Robustness of Performance Deterioration in Consecutive Tasks," *Social Psychology*, 50 (5–6): 292–304.

Winecoff, A. A. and S. A. Huettel (2017), "Cognitive Control and Neuroeconomics," in T. Egner (ed.), *Wiley Handbook of Cognitive Control*, 408–21, London: Wiley.

Yeung, N. (2010), "Bottom-Up Influences on Voluntary Task Switching: The Elusive Homunculus Escapes," *Journal of Experimental Psychology: Learning, Memory, and Cognition*, 36 (2): 348–62.

Yeung, N., L. E. Nystrom, J. A. Aronson, and J. D. Cohen (2006), "Between-Task Competition and Cognitive Control in Task Switching," *Journal of Neuroscience*, 26 (5): 1429–38.

4

Who Is Responsible?

Split Brains, Dissociative Identity Disorder, and Implicit Attitudes

Walter Sinnott-Armstrong

Most discussions of moral and legal responsibility focus on whether the act in question was free, voluntary, intentional, conscious, reckless, or negligent. A more basic question that is often taken for granted is whether the agent who is being judged as responsible or not is the one who did the act.

This question is crucial if one person is not responsible for what another person does, as many assume. Of course, sometimes an agent is responsible for failing to stop someone else from doing wrong. In this case, however, they are responsible for their own failure to prevent the wrongful act instead of for the other person's wrongful act or for doing that wrongful act themselves. Failing to stop someone else from killing or stealing is distinct from killing or stealing.

The identity of the wrongdoer is at stake whenever criminal defendants provide alibis, which are supposed to show that the defendant is not the person who committed the crime. Philosophers, however, have rarely discussed alibis except in the context of epistemology, when the issue is whether to believe the witness who provides the alibi.

Different kinds of issues arise in special cases, including split brains, dissociative identity disorder, and others that I will discuss. Epistemology is relevant to these cases insofar as we often do not know exactly what is happening in the minds or brains of people with these conditions. However, I will not focus on epistemic issues here. Instead, I will focus on questions of metaphysics and ethics. These special cases raise metaphysical questions about whether a single body includes two agents or only one. They also raise ethical questions about whom we should hold morally or legally responsible for what agents with these conditions do.

These metaphysical and ethical issues cannot be resolved adequately without a great deal of empirical information. We need to know precisely how one part relates to the other part in people with split brains, dissociated identities, and related conditions as well as how they actually make decisions and perform actions. Then we need to figure out how this scientific knowledge bears on and interacts with epistemology, metaphysics, and ethics.

As a path into this complex maze, I will start with split brains, depending heavily on Elizabeth Schechter's masterpiece, *Self-Consciousness and "Split" Brains: The Minds' I* (2018). Along the way, I will compare and contrast split brains with Tourette's syndrome, anarchic hands, married couples, conjoined twins, dissociated identities, and implicit attitudes. My goal is not to settle any of these complicated and controversial issues but only to make a few tentative suggestions about how to begin to approach some of them.

4.1 Individual versus Group Agents

Surgeons split brains as a last resort only when they cannot stop severe epilepsy in any other way. The full operation involves severing both the entire corpus callosum and the anterior commissure, which are white matter bundles running between the hemispheres of the brain. This procedure stops epileptic seizures from spreading from one hemisphere to the other, but it also prevents normal, direct transfer of information from one hemisphere to the other.

After these operations, patients usually behave normally, but some patients report unusual behaviors and experiences. For example, one patient described this incident: "I open the door. I know what I want to wear. As I reach for something with my right hand, my left comes up and takes something different" (Schechter 2018: 71–2). The left hand is controlled by the right hemisphere, and the right hand is controlled by the left hemisphere, so here it seems that the right hemisphere is trying to do something other than what the left hemisphere wants, intends, and decides to do. Similarly, there are reports of the right and left sides of a patient whose brain was split pursuing different alternatives when getting eggs versus cheese and taking a bath versus going to toilet (Schechter 2018: 77).

To discuss these cases, we have to settle on what to call the different parts of the brain and mind. I will refer to the left hemisphere and the right hemisphere of the brain. This crude terminology overlooks residual connections between the hemispheres, which Schechter describes in detail (2018: 221–58), but it suffices for our purposes here. In addition to the physical brain, we will need to consider mental states, including thoughts, beliefs, desires, intentions, and emotions. I will call the group of mental states associated with the left hemisphere "Lefty" and the group of mental states associated with the right hemisphere "Righty." I do not assume that either Lefty or Righty is reducible or not to its associated hemisphere. This terminology is intended only to signal whether I am talking about mental or physical properties.

Based on patient reports like those earlier, Schechter argues for several theses about split-brain patients:

(1) Lefty is an individual intentional agent.
(2) Righty is an individual intentional agent.
(3) Lefty and Righty are not the same individual intentional agent.
(4) Lefty and Righty are a group intentional agent.

One could formulate parallel theses about the left and right hemispheres, but we will focus on Lefty and Righty for now, since intentions are mental states.

To understand these theses, we first have to define what an intentional agent is. Schechter's answers are fairly standard. Most simply and abstractly, an intentional agent is anything with the ability to initiate choices or actions (Schechter 2018: 61). But then what are the actions that agents initiate? Schechter answers that actions are "behaviors motivated by goals and intentions" (2018: 51). But then what are the intentions that motivate actions? She says that intentions are plans about how to achieve a goal (2018: 52). Like Schechter, I will accept and assume these common accounts of agents, actions, and intentions.

Intentional actions are thus distinguished from behaviors resulting solely from sub-personal processes (Schechter 2018: 53–5). Some sub-personal processes are bilateral, including those in Tourette's syndrome that cause tics, such as sudden and involuntary head jerking or shouting obscenities. Other sub-personal processes are unilateral, including those in alien or anarchic hand syndrome, in one example of which a woman's left hand moved without her knowledge and stroked her face and hair (Panikkath et al. 2014). Despite appearances, tics and anarchic hand movements are not intentional actions, because they are not guided by a goal, intention, or plan, so they are not signs of an intentional agent.

Anarchic hand movements do resemble some movements of the left hand of a Split, as in cases described earlier and later. These left-hand movements are caused by activity in the right side of the brain, but are they intentional or not? Schechter argues forcefully that they are intentional, because "damage to the corpus callosum alone leaves intact the systems responsible for intentional agency in each hemisphere, though impeding communication between them" (Schechter 2018: 54). Those systems responsible for intentional agency are not intact in anarchic hand syndrome, so anarchic hands and Splits' left-hand movements have different sources, even when they look the same. Moreover, Splits' left-hand movements are not truly anarchic if they are aimed at a goal, as they seem to be, at least sometimes (see cases earlier and later). That is why Schechter sees these Split's left-hand movements as intentional actions, while anarchic hand movements are not.

This argument does not yet tell us whether the intentional agent associated with Righty is the same intentional agent as the intentional agent associated with Lefty. To settle that issue, Schechter lays out an explicit criterion of individuation: "What distinguishes *individual intentional agents* from *group intentional agents* is that for agents of the former sort, intention integration can occur prior to any action" (Schechter 2018: 57). She later clarifies that the relevant kind of intention integration is direct instead of being based indirectly on external sources of information, such as conversation or observation of behavior (Schechter 2022: 195).

Lefty and Righty do not pass this test. As Schechter says, "right-hemisphere associated intentions are *not integrated* with left-hemisphere associated intentions in the way that is *necessary* for them to all be intentions of an *individual intentional agent*" (Schechter 2018: 50). Lefty and Righty can sometimes discover indirectly (such as by observation) what the other is doing or wants to do (Schechter 2018: 95–9), and then they can adjust their own intentions according to what is possible given the other's intentions, but this is not the kind of direct intention integration that defines an individual agent. This is her main argument for thesis (3).

To understand intention integration, imagine first a normal agent with conflicting desires. Jenn, who is in London, wants to go to Mardi Gras in New Orleans, and she also wants to go to Carnival in Rio de Janeiro. She wants to go to each festival this year, and not wait until next year, but they occur at the same time or close enough that she cannot go to both. Jenn knows that she has both desires and cannot satisfy both, but that does not make her irrational. Conflicting desires are neither uncommon nor irrational. Nonetheless, Jenn still does need eventually to integrate her desires into an overall preference and make a decision. She would have to be irrational to think, "I decide and intend to go to Mardi Gras in New Orleans, and I also decide and intend to go to Carnival in Rio de Janeiro, though I know that I cannot do both." In order to form a final plan about what to do, she needs to integrate her intentions. Assuming that she has normal mental capacities, she is able to do this in time. She can weigh her desires in deliberation or simply choose intuitively or arbitrarily so that she does not intend to take both of the incompatible trips at the time when she steps on the plane to her chosen destination. It would be irrational for her to intend to go to New Orleans today while she knowingly boards a plane to Rio, but it is not irrational for her to continue to desire or want to go to New Orleans today while she boards the plane to Rio, if she still wishes that she could take both trips. Thus, in order to avoid irrationality, her choices and intentions need to be integrated in a way that her desires need not be integrated.

Contrast a couple who have been married happily for forty-five years. They usually want the same thing, but it is possible for one to desire, prefer, and decide to go to Mardi Gras in New Orleans, while the other desires, prefers, and decides to go to Carnival in Rio de Janeiro on the same day, while both know the other's desire, preference, and decision. Neither might be irrational, despite their conflicting choices. Even if each would prefer to go to their festival of choice together instead of alone, they can still prefer to go to their festival of choice alone instead of the other festival together. They do not always have to form a preference, intention, or choice together or make a decision together in order to be rational, because they are separate intentional agents. In Schechter's words, despite their history, shared values, and desire to be together, they do not share a single "deliberative standpoint" (59), since they can and sometimes do deliberate and choose separately. That is why they are not a single individual agent.

Are they a group agent? Only sometimes. The two individual agents that make up the married couple do not act as a group agent on occasions when they go their separate ways—one to New Orleans and the other to Rio—or when one coerces or forces the other to go where they do not want to go. Nonetheless, they still can act as a group agent when they voluntarily choose together to go to one location instead of the other.

The same analysis applies to conjoined twins, who are obviously also distinct individual agents. One famous pair are Abigail and Brittany Hensel, who were born in 1990 and are still alive today. They have completely separate heads, and each of them controls one arm and one leg (as Lefty and Righty do), but they can type with two hands, play softball, drive a car, and so on. Still, sometimes they perform different acts simultaneously. One can read a book, while the other reads a different book. Then they have distinct intentions, and neither agent could fulfill both intentions at once. Indeed, like the married couple, Abigail might intend to go to Mardi Gras in New Orleans, while Brittany intends to go to Carnival in Rio de Janeiro on the same day. Of course, one of them will have to give in eventually, since they cannot go their separate ways, as the married couple can. Nonetheless, they can still form conflicting intentions without being irrational, if they plan later to convince the other to go along with what they intend or if they do not yet know what the other intends. Moreover, they cannot know what the other intends without asking or observing how the other behaves. They do not have direct access into each other's minds. That shows that they cannot integrate their intentions directly in the same way as an individual intentional agent, so they are not an individual agent. Nonetheless, they can still act as a group agent when they compromise and cooperate.

The crucial question, then, is whether Righty and Lefty in a Split are more like Abigail and Brittany—in which case they are two distinct individual agents—or instead more like Jenn—in which case they are together only one individual agent. The answer to this question clearly depends on empirical facts.

4.2 Evidence for Distinct Agents

Schechter argues that a Split is more like the group agent than the individual agent. To support this claim, she cites many cases, including those described earlier as well as this one:

> Several split-brain subjects complained that after surgery, their left hands wouldn't "let" them read any more but would push the book or paper down over and over again . . . ; indeed, over the long term, split-brain subjects typically stop reading for pleasure. (Schechter 2018: 61–2)

As Schechter comments, it might be "relevant that the right hemisphere can't read" (Schechter 2018: 62). Similar cases of inter-manual prevention have been observed in smoking, buttoning a shirt, pulling trousers up, opening a door, and slapping to prevent oversleeping (Schechter 2018: 61, 66, 68).

These examples occur in everyday life, but others happen in experimental contexts:

> In one test, the split-brain subject L.B. was given several block letters on each trial to feel with his left hand—from which only the RH receives tactile sensation—and asked to rearrange them into words without looking at them. The left hand (R) went to work, while L.B.—or anyway L—complained immediately and without ceasing that the task was impossible because he couldn't feel the letters. [R was six for six before] L.B. refused to participate further. (Schechter 2018: 64)

Here Lefty interferes with what Righty is trying to do, whereas in other cases Righty interferes with what Lefty is trying to do.

When such conflicts arise, it is important to consider how Lefty and Righty interact and view each other. Schechter comments,

> Lack of mutual recognition means that R and L do not relate to each other by discussing reasons. When R repeatedly pushes books away and throws magazines on the ground, L never asks, "What's the matter with you? Don't you like reading? Don't you at least think it's important?" Nor does L ever attempt to persuade R or negotiate with R. Instead, L either gives up and stops reading (the way one might give up on an outing if one's child won't stop crying) or physically restrains R's left-handed responses (the way one might physically restrain a dog from jumping up on guests). (Schechter 2018: 195)

Roughly, Lefty views Righty like a dog instead of a person. However, even if Lefty and Righty do not view each other as distinct persons, they still might be distinct persons. If so, their tendency not to recognize the other as a person might be "an understandable but awful mistake" (Schechter 2018: 181).

Besides, it is not completely clear that Lefty and Righty do not view each other as persons who can recognize and react to reasons. Another interpretation of why Lefty and Righty do not discuss reasons or try to persuade or negotiate with each other is simply that they cannot communicate after the brain is split. When a hacker corrupts my computer, if I know that I cannot communicate with them, then I do not try to reason or negotiate with them. I just get frustrated and try to stop them. Still, I do not deny their personhood.

Moreover, Lefty and Righty are not totally unable to communicate. They sometimes do seem to communicate in indirect ways, for example, by using hand movements to show the other what they want (Schechter 2018: 95-9). The point is instead only that they seem to be unable to know what the other is thinking directly without any inference from behavior in the way that an individual agent like Jenn can know each of her conflicting desires, at least in the most common view. That inability to interact directly suggests that Lefty and Righty are not the same individual agent.

This evidence (and Schechter provides much more) convinces me that at least some Splits should be understood not as one individual agent but instead as including two separate individual agents who form a group agent, at least when Lefty and Righty act in concert, which is most of the time. When Lefty and Righty interfere with each other's attempts to perform an action, they seem to have conflicting intentions and make conflicting choices. They do not simply have conflicting desires, since one makes a choice and tries to act before the other interferes. These conflicts are unusual, so people with split brains usually seem completely normal in their daily lives. Still, in these few observed cases they seem unable to work together toward a shared intention or choice. Here, then, they seem unable to integrate their intentions prior to action in the very way that Schechter argued is necessary for them to be an individual intentional agent.

Admittedly, observation of behaviors outside of controlled experimental contexts is always subject to different interpretations. Even so-called controlled experiments do not control for all possible confounds, and the experiments here have not been replicated, since very few subjects are available. Thus, we cannot be completely sure what is going on. Nonetheless, these observations and experiments provide significant evidence that some Splits should be understood to include two separate individual agents who form a group agent when they act together. Then Lefty and Righty are more like Abigail and Brittany than like Jenn, the single individual agent with conflicting desires.

4.3 Brain and Behavior

This conclusion is based on behavior, so it is worth asking how much the details of split-brain surgeries matter to the issue of one versus two agents. As we saw earlier, Schechter does cite neural details in order to distinguish Splits from patients with anarchic hand syndrome, but the fact that a patient's brain is split still might not be necessary for one body to realize two agents.

Imagine that Sara's brain is not split, and she does not have Tourette's or anarchic hand syndrome. Sara is neurotypical and just has a habit of reading a lot. She enjoys reading, but she reads so much that this activity leaves her with less time for other interests that she also wants to pursue; so Sara develops a desire to read less (and maybe also a second-order desire not to desire to read so much). When Sara reads a book, she usually holds it in her right hand, since she is right-handed. After she has the desire to read less, sometimes her free left hand knocks the book down. Would such behavior alone be enough to show that Sara includes two separate agents? Or is a split or damaged brain necessary for two individual agents to inhabit the same body?

As Schechter has pointed out in response to such cases (2022: 188–9), Sara's left hand might be the one that usually knocks the book down only because she is right-handed. If she happened to hold the book in her left hand one day, then she might knock the book down with her right hand instead. In this case, Sara's situation is very different from that of a Split. In reported cases of Splits, it is always the left hand that stopped the reading. As Schechter said, this might be because the left hand is controlled by the right hemisphere, and "the right hemisphere can't read" (2018: 62).

To remove this difference between the cases, let's imagine instead that it is always Sara's left hand that stops the reading. If she happened to hold the book in her left hand one day, then she would never knock the book down with her right hand. She would just drop it with her left hand. This addition to the example suggests that Sara's desire to read is somehow associated with her left hemisphere, which controls her right hand, and her desire to read less (or not to read now) is somehow associated with her right hemisphere, which controls her left hand. It also suggests that Sara is not able to integrate her intentions before action, since her left hand stops her right hand from holding the book. If she were able to integrate her intentions, then she might decide at some point to stop reading, but then her right hand would simply put the book down gently without her left hand knocking it down. In this extreme case, we might conclude that Sara includes two agents instead of just one, even though her brain is not split, as far as we can tell.

This conclusion implies that having a split brain is not strictly necessary for a single body to house two individual agents. However, this case is pure fiction. Nothing like

Sara has ever been reported, to my knowledge. Moreover, if there were a real person who acted this way, then it would be reasonable to suspect some brain abnormality, even if we cannot pinpoint what kind of abnormality it is or where it is located. And, even if a split brain is not necessary for two agents in a single body, the fact that someone's brain is split could still provide additional support for the hypothesis of two agents, if only because we would understand why and how a single body houses multiple agents in a Split, whereas this occurrence would be inexplicable in Sara. Thus, the neural evidence would be relevant and important even if not strictly necessary to establish dual agency within a body.

4.4 Dissociative Identity Disorder

Sara might seem farfetched, but some real cases raise similar issues. Dissociative identity disorder (DID) was formerly known as multiple personality disorder (MPD). Though some have questioned whether anyone actually has DID and even whether DID is a legitimate psychological category, here we will assume for the sake of argument that some cases of DID are real (Sinnott-Armstrong and Behnke 2000).

One actual example of DID is Grimsley, whose primary alter or personality is named Robin and who also has another alter or personality named Jennifer. Robin describes Jennifer as impulsive, angry, fearful, and anxious and as having a drinking problem—very different from Robin. Moreover, when Jennifer is in control, Robin is not aware of what is going on and cannot control Jennifer's actions, according to Robin. On one occasion, Grimsley drove after drinking, and she was charged with driving under the influence of alcohol. Robin claimed that Jennifer was driving and that Robin was unaware and could not control what was happening. Still, Grimsley was found guilty on the grounds that Jennifer was in control at the time and had no excuse for drunk driving (*State v. Grimsley*).

Such cases of DID are different from Splits in many respects, but one that matters here concerns whether the two entities interact directly. As Schechter pointed out (2022: 194), sometimes one alter in a case of DID is aware of the other's thoughts, desires, and feelings without using any indirect means like an inference from observations of how their shared body moves when the first alter did not will the motion. In such cases of direct awareness, the alters do seem able to integrate their intentions in a way that Lefty and Righty cannot, so the case for two distinct agents is weaker (or at least has to be made on different grounds). Robin and Jennifer Grimsley might fit this model if Robin was aware at the time when Jennifer was driving drunk.

The story becomes more complicated if the alters engage in conversations with each other that they use to infer what the other desires and intends (Schechter 2022: 194). That indirect inference from what is said does not count as direct knowledge of the others' mental states. If this is Robin's only way to know what Jennifer is like, then Robin and Jennifer would not count as one individual agent on Schechter's criteria.

Further, suppose Robin is never directly aware of Jennifer and never has any conversations with her but only indirectly infers her existence from reports by others of what Jennifer did and of what Grimsley called herself at times when Robin was blacked out. In that case, the alters seem unable to integrate their intentions in much the same way as Lefty and Righty. If so, then they are two individual agents instead of non-agential parts of one individual agent.

It does not matter that Grimsley's brain is not split. We know very little about the neural basis for DID, and Grimsley's brain has never been studied as far as I know, so we cannot point to any brain abnormalities to explain or understand Grimsley's behavior, though there must be some brain abnormality. Still, Robin and Jennifer's behaviors plus Robin's claimed lack of awareness of Jennifer's actions suggest that Robin cannot integrate her intentions with Jennifer's intentions in the way that characterizes an individual agent. Thus, this behavior seems to be enough without any detected brain abnormality to show that Robin and Jennifer should be considered not as a single individual agent but instead as two individual agents (though they still might not be separate persons; see Sinnott-Armstrong and Behnke 2000).

4.5 Implicit Attitudes

DID is a clinical condition of a small minority, but a much larger number of everyday people with no mental illness also show some signs of including multiple individual agents. The signs are not simply temporary moods or conflicting desires (as in Jenn discussed earlier) but instead a long-lasting dual system that includes both implicit and explicit attitudes that conflict. In particular, some people hold strong explicit beliefs against racism and sexism, so they sincerely speak out against racism and sexism, and they decide to take action against these social scourges. Nonetheless, they still can have implicit racist and sexist attitudes that are supposed to affect their behavior (Banaji and Greenwald 2016). For example, people who vehemently oppose racism still might tend to feel fear and maybe also believe they are in danger when a Black man approaches them in the dark, and this might make them change the direction in which they were walking. Similarly, they might be less likely to speak with Black guests at a social gathering and more likely to disfavor Black job applicants. Sometimes they do not realize what they are doing or why they are doing it, and sometimes they cannot (directly) control either their implicit attitudes or the resulting behaviors.

Many such claims about implicit attitudes have been criticized (e.g., Machery 2016), and some of these claims do seem unjustified or false. However, the point here is only to ask whether these two "systems" of implicit versus explicit attitudes could ever count as distinct individual agents. To address that issue, I will assume for the sake of argument much of the story told by proponents of implicit attitudes.

When implicit attitudes are unconscious and uncontrollable (at least in the moment) and conflict with explicit beliefs, people do not seem to be able to integrate their intentions related to their explicit attitudes (such as fighting racism) with their intentions related to their implicit attitudes (such as preferring and hiring the White job candidate instead of an equally or better qualified Black job candidate). They cannot integrate these intentions either because they are not aware of their own implicit attitudes (as the term "implicit" suggests) or because, even when they do become aware of their implicit attitudes and consciously deliberate about what they prefer to do in light of all of their attitudes, they are still unable to prevent the effects of their rejected implicit attitudes on their behavior. If they cannot integrate their intentions for either reason, then these everyday people might not seem to meet Schechter's criteria for an individual intentional agent. They might even be seen as two separate individual intentional agents—one associated with explicit attitudes and another associated with implicit attitudes. If so, the phenomenon of multiple intentional agents within a single body is not restricted to clinical cases like Splits and DID. It is common for many of us.

Against this suggestion, Schechter (2022: 187) points out that sometimes the implicit attitude causes an explicit attitude, such as when a racist implicit attitude causes someone to believe explicitly that a White candidate is better. However, that does not remove the conflict, because the explicit anti-racist attitude would cause the person to believe explicitly that the White candidate is not better when there is no reason other than the implicit racist attitude to prefer the White candidate. Moreover, this causal connection does not lead to *direct* awareness of the kind that characterizes an individual agent and is lacking in Righty and Lefty (as well as Robin and Jennifer, as described earlier). The explicit attitudes can become aware of the implicit attitudes only indirectly by observing what the body does (or maybe feels), according to proponents of implicit attitudes.

Schechter also suggests that implicit attitudes cannot count as a separate mind or agent unless they are rich enough to be "capable of perceiving, believing, valuing, decision-making, and forming intentions" (Schechter 2018: 187). I agree that it is not clear that people's implicit attitudes are this complex, but it is also not clear that they are not. Some people might have isolated implicit attitudes that affect them only by creating fear of large Black men in the dark. But others are supposed to have a large system of implicit attitudes that also affect whom they hire or talk with, where they sit, whose parties they attend, which movies they like and attend, and so on. In such cases, it is not obvious why we should not say that the implicit side of someone's mind is capable of perceiving danger, believing a candidate is better, valuing a movie, deciding to sit in a certain place, and forming an intention to talk (or not to talk) with a particular person. If so, then the implicit attitudes might sometimes meet Schechter's requirements (quoted earlier) for a separate mind or agent.

Nonetheless, I share Schechter's doubts about whether implicit attitudes usually (or ever?) are rich, unconscious, and uncontrollable enough to constitute a separate agent (cf. Machery 2016). I would not exclude this possibility, but whether implicit attitudes and explicit attitudes actually meet the conditions for distinct individual agents can be settled only by more targeted scientific research.

4.6 Responsibility

What difference does it make whether or not Lefty and Righty—or Abigail and Brittany or Robin and Jennifer or implicit and explicit attitudes—count as the same individual agent? Two agents or one—so what?

One answer lies in responsibility. As I said at the beginning, I am responsible for my own decisions, but I am not responsible for acts done by other agents—at least not directly. I can become responsible when my business partner embezzles from our clients if I know that he is embezzling, and I can stop him, yet I do nothing. But if I have no way of knowing that my business partner is embezzling, then I am not responsible for what my partner does (though I still might have to pay back our clients).

The same basic principle applies to two kinds of responsibility (Watson 2004). An agent has the kind of responsibility called *accountability* when they do an act that makes them liable to anger, guilt, and sometimes public sanctions, including punishment. In contrast, an agent has the kind of responsibility called *attributability* when they do an act that justifies attributing to them a vice or some lasting character defect (or a virtue in the positive case). In the case of the embezzling partner, if I had no way to know about it or to stop my partner, then it would not be appropriate either to attribute dishonesty to me because of my partner's act (so I lack attributability) or to be angry at me or punish me for what my partner did (so I lack accountability).

How do these standards apply to Righty and Lefty in a Split? Imagine that a Split is driving safely down the road when suddenly Righty uses the left hand to steer a car into pedestrians. No case like this has ever been observed or would ever be expected from any real Split. Nonetheless, it can be instructive to ask who would be responsible for the harm to pedestrians if this did happen.

If Lefty and Righty are parts of a single individual intentional agent, then the answer is easy: Lefty and the whole Split are responsible for what Righty does. If an individual agent has conflicting desires, they can be responsible for acting on one desire even if their action frustrates their other desire. If Jenn promised to meet a friend at Mardi Gras in New Orleans but instead acted on her desire to go to Carnival in Rio de Janeiro, then Jenn cannot defend her action by saying, "I did want to meet you as I promised, but my other desire took over and led me to Rio." Her friend will still be justified in being angry and applying sanctions (so Jenn has accountability) and in concluding that Jenn is untrustworthy and maybe not a good friend (so Jenn has attributability).

The situation is more complex if Lefty and Righty are separate individual intentional agents. Then Lefty and Righty would seem analogous to conjoined twins Abigail and Brittany Hensel. Abigail controls the right arm, and Brittany controls the left arm. They can drive safely together, but imagine that Brittany suddenly uses the left arm to steer their car into pedestrians, while Abigail had no way of knowing that Brittany was going to do anything like this, and Abigail could not stop it. Then Abigail would not have responsibility of either kind in this imagined situation. What Brittany did would show that Brittany is an untrustworthy driver and malicious or at least careless, but Brittany's act would not provide any reason to attribute any character trait to Abigail. Victims and others (including Abigail) would be justified in being angry at Brittany but not in being angry at Abigail, and Brittany but not Abigail would be liable to punishment (though it is not clear how one could be punished without the other).

The same holds for Lefty and Righty in the analogous case if they are separate individual agents. If Lefty cannot know or stop Righty's quick action because communication between them was prevented by surgery, then Lefty does not seem responsible for the harm caused by Righty. This holds for both kinds of responsibility: attributability and accountability. It would not be appropriate to attribute bad driving or maliciousness to Lefty on the basis of what Righty did. It would also not be appropriate to hold Lefty accountable by becoming angry at Lefty or by punishing Lefty for what Righty did.

It matters in this example that the action is quick and unexpected. If Lefty knew Righty's intentions in advance (perhaps because Righty somehow signaled to Lefty that Righty was planning to turn into the pedestrians), and if Lefty was able to stop Righty from turning the car (perhaps by pushing the brakes with the right foot), but Lefty did nothing to stop Righty, then Lefty would be responsible for the harm to the pedestrians. Lefty would not be responsible for Righty's act but would instead be responsible for Lefty's own failure to stop Righty's act. In my example, however, Lefty cannot foresee or prevent Righty's quick action, so Lefty is not responsible for anything.

What about the Split as a whole? Even if Lefty is not responsible, Righty is responsible, so one might think that the Split has at least partial responsibility of some kind. After all, we do sometimes hold group agents responsible for what one individual in the group did, such as when we hold a country or government responsible for what an elected president, unelected ambassador, or other official does on behalf of the government. However, a group normally has neither accountability nor attributability for what one of its members does alone unless that member was acting with authorization on behalf of the group. Such actions by representatives of the group are very different from our case. Righty is neither authorized by nor acting on behalf of either Lefty or the Split as a whole. As a result, it is hard to see why the Split as a whole has responsibility of either kind in our case, at least on the assumption that Lefty and Righty are separate individual agents.

4.7 Conclusions

For these reasons, I conclude that Lefty and Righty are distinct individual agents, more like conjoined twins (Abigail and Brittany) than like a single agent with conflicting desires (Jenn). As a result, Lefty is not responsible (either attributable or accountable) for what Righty does unless Lefty knows in advance and can prevent what Righty does.

Some qualifications to these conclusions are needed, since Lefty might be responsible for what Righty does if there is no conflict between their intentions, because Lefty has the same intention and makes the same decision as Righty. Moreover, my conclusions could be undermined by further empirical discoveries, such as that Lefty is or can be directly aware of Righty's intentions, though it is not clear how direct awareness could be established. Thus, my conclusions are not and are not intended to be the last word on this topic.

Nonetheless, even if qualified, my arguments and conclusions are intended mainly to stimulate others to think more deeply about the relatively neglected issues of agent identity and responsibility in these fascinating cases. We have a lot more to learn in this area.[1]

Acknowledgments

I am grateful to Paul Henne, Sam Murray, and Lizzie Schechter for helpful comments on earlier versions of this chapter.

Note

1 This chapter includes many passages from Sinnott-Armstrong (2022). The point of reusing this material is to begin to sketch my own answers to the questions that I asked Schechter in my comment on her book.

References

Banaji, Mahzarin R., and Anthony G. Greenwald (2016), *Blindspot: Hidden Biases of Good People*, London: Bantam Press.

Machery, E. (2016), "DeFreuding Implicit Attitudes," in Michael Brownstein and Jennifer Saul (eds.), *Implicit Bias and Philosophy, Vol. 1: Metaphysics and Epistemology*, 104–29, New York: Oxford University Press.

Panikkath, R., D. Panikkath, D. Mojumder, and K. Nugent (2014), "The Alien Hand Syndrome," *Proceedings (Baylor University, Medical Center)*, 27 (3): 219–20.

Schechter, E. (2018), *Self-Consciousness and "Split" Brains: The Minds' I*, New York: Oxford University Press.

Schechter, E. (2022), "Reply to Commentators," *Journal of Consciousness Studies*, 29 (1–2): 179–203.

Sinnott-Armstrong, W. (2022), "Which Agent? Questions for Schechter," *Journal of Consciousness Studies*, 29 (1–2): 170–8.

Sinnott-Armstrong, W. and S. Behnke (2000), "Responsibility in Cases of Multiple Personality Disorder," *Philosophical Perspectives*, 14: 301–23.

State v. Grimsley, 444 N.E.2d 1071, 1076 (Ohio App. 1982).

Watson, G. (2004), *Agency and Answerability: Selected Essays*, Oxford: Clarendon Press.

5

The Everyday Irrationality of Monothematic Delusion

Paul Noordhof and Ema Sullivan-Bissett

Irrationality comes in hot and cold varieties. The hot involves the influence of motivation, or emotion more generally; the cold does not. Under which category does delusion lie, or can it come in both varieties? Empiricist accounts of monothematic delusion (those delusions concerning a single theme) claim that anomalous experiences are explanatorily relevant to the formation of distinctive delusional beliefs. So far, no irrationality has been identified. But many philosophers and psychologists have argued that, in addition, there is a special clinically significant irrationality involved in delusion formation, understood as the manifestation of some cognitive deficit, bias, or performance error. All of these are cold varieties of irrationality with the possible exception of some kinds of performance error. Those who propose such irrationality note that not all people with anomalous experiences develop delusions, and so, the thought goes, we should explain why some subjects develop delusions off the back of anomalous experiences by identifying some clinically significant irrationality at work.

We have argued that it is a mistake to argue from variation in response to experience to the presence of some clinical irrationality in folk who form delusions (Noordhof and Sullivan-Bissett 2021). Individual differences of various kinds explain why some subjects have delusional beliefs and others do not. Actually, we do not think that all cases of delusion involve irrationality but we set aside that possibility here. Where delusions are the result of irrationality, the irrationality involved is quite every day. In this chapter we argue for this claim in two ways. First, an examination of nonclinical paranormal beliefs shows that it is a mistake to think that monothematic delusional belief usually involves a kind of irrationality distinct from everyday kinds. Crucially, in these nonclinical cases, we have beliefs with bizarre contents, often based on strange experiences that are also had by subjects who do not form paranormal beliefs. Nevertheless, researchers interested in their genesis have not sought to identify clinically significant irrationality. By reflecting on the structure of nonclinical cases of paranormal belief, we show that the appeal to clinically significant irrationality to explain delusion formation is unmotivated. These everyday irrationalities may be "cold"—that is, not the result of motivation—but they are still mundane.

Second, there are various kinds of motivated irrationality in everyday life with which we are familiar, for example, wishful thinking and self-deception. It wouldn't be surprising if some cases of delusion involved these forms of irrationality and, as we shall see, there is evidence that they do. But, here again, the situation is rather different from what might reasonably be called the orthodoxy. Delusions are often seen as the most serious form of irrationality, at the extreme end of self-deception or involving a further, more substantial form of irrationality. This is a mistake. Motivated irrationalities are more substantially irrational than the cold cases of delusion and when delusions run hot, they typically involve fewer motivational features than everyday motivated irrationality. Overall, then, we conclude that not only do we need not appeal to any clinical irrationality to explain monothematic delusion formation but that, in addition, the reputation of delusions as the most serious form of irrationality is unmerited. Throughout the chapter, we remain neutral on the question of whether monothematic delusions more often come in cold or hot varieties.

5.1 Monothematic Delusion Formation

Delusions tend to be characterized in terms of their epistemic failings, with the most recent *Diagnostic and Statistical Manual of Mental Disorders* calling them "fixed beliefs[1] that are not amenable to change in light of conflicting evidence" (American Psychiatric Association 2013: 87). The characterization is unhelpful because it ignores the controversies concerning the role of anomalous experience in giving rise to a delusional belief, so we offer some examples to get our target phenomenon in sight. Subjects with Capgras delusion believe that someone familiar to them (often a spouse or close family member) has been replaced by an imposter. Subjects with Cotard delusion believe that they are dead or that they do not exist. Subjects with anosognosia believe that they are not disabled in some way, a typical manifestation which we discuss is that they deny a paralysis or weakness in their left side (a left hemiplegia) and believe that they have full use of their limbs (Section 5.4.2). Our examples are all *monothematic*, that is, to recall, delusions concerning a single theme and ones which "can present in isolation in people whose beliefs are otherwise unremarkable" (Coltheart, Langdon, and McKay 2007: 642). Subjects with these delusions tend not to display more general delusional belief formation and present a challenge to those convinced that there is a substantial, clinically significant, irrationality at work to explain why its effects are so localized (as we shall go into more detail later).

Subjects with monothematic delusions often undergo some highly anomalous experiences. For example, a subject with perceptual delusional bicephaly (the delusion that one has a second head) may hallucinate a second head on her shoulder (Ames 1984). Not all anomalous experiences associated with kinds of delusion are hallucinatory in this way (i.e., they do not all falsely present objects and properties in the world). In Capgras, the experience has been understood as one of *absence* of something expected, the subject has reduced affective response to familiar faces traceable to ventromedial prefrontal cortex damage (Tranel, Damasio, and Damasio 1995; Coltheart 2007), or right lateral temporal lesions and dorsolateral prefrontal cortex damage (Wilkinson 2015; Corlett 2019). In the case of Cotard, similar damage is present and it has been suggested that these subjects have no emotional feelings regarding their environment (Young et al. 1992: 800). Empiricists about delusion formation claim that such experiences play an explanatory role in the formation of delusions. Within empiricism, the current orthodoxy insists on an additional clinical irrationality at the level of belief formation or evaluation, on the grounds that not every subject who has the relevant anomalous experience has the associated delusional belief. There must, then, be some additional abnormality which explains why some people become delusional based on some anomalous experience and others do not (see, e.g., Chapman and Chapman 1988: 174; Garety 1991: 15; Garety, Hemsley, and Wessely 1991: 194–5; Davies and Coltheart 2000: 11–12; Davies et al. 2001: 144; Young and de Pauw 2002: 56; Davies et al. 2005: 224–5; Coltheart 2015: 23).

We turn briefly to give a handful of examples of the clinical irrationalities proposed to be active in delusion formation. These are irrationalities claimed to be either not present in nonclinical populations, or if they are found here, they are systematically present to a lesser degree. The putative irrationalities, or the degree to which they present, are taken to be unique to folk with delusions, and explanatorily relevant to the project of explaining *delusional* belief in particular.

Bias theorists seek to characterize the kind of irrationality involved. Philippa Garety and Daniel Freeman have argued for a data-gathering bias, specifically, people with delusions *jump to conclusions* (Garety and Freeman 1999; see also Huq et al. 1988; Garety, Hemsley, and Wessely 1991; cf. Dudley et al. 2015; Ross et al. 2015). Tony Stone and Andrew W. Young opt for a tendency to privilege observational data over minimizing adjustments to one's beliefs (1997: 349–50). Martin Davies and colleagues locate the clinical abnormality in the belief maintenance process, understanding it as a failure to inhibit a prepotent doxastic response (Davies et al. 2001: 153). Although they give no further characterization of the kind of irrationality involved, they offer a causal explanation of the hypothesized deficit. Thus, Max Coltheart (2005) has developed this view, tracing the putative abnormality to damage to the right lateral prefrontal cortex found in many subjects with monothematic delusions. Others, like Philip Gerrans (2001), have argued for neither a bias nor a deficit but instead, more circumspectly, for a *performance failure*, whereby a subject has the competence to properly form or maintain beliefs but fails to put it to practice.

Elsewhere we argue that these cognitive processes thought to be clinical abnormalities are no such things after all, either because the evidence fails to show that they are indeed contributory, or that they are clinically significant, or that they offer appropriate coverage and explanatory adequacy of the posited abnormality (Noordhof and Sullivan-Bissett 2021). Rather, we argue, the default position ought to be that the anomalous experiences subjects with delusions undergo are the only clinically significant contribution to the formation of delusional beliefs with nonclinical individual differences accounting for why some subjects form monothematic delusions and others do not. Here we move away from a critical analysis of the empirical support for clinical irrationality and take a different approach to establishing the status of the cognitive contributions to delusion formation. We argue for the following two claims: (1) such contributions should not be understood as constituting clinically significant irrationality and (2) the irrationality involved in delusion formation is not—as has often been thought—of the most serious kind. To establish (1) we discuss paranormal beliefs and the motivated irrationalities of everyday life, and to establish (2) we discuss some of the specific features involved in a particular form of motivated irrationality: self-deception.

5.2 Paranormal Belief

We take paranormal beliefs to be beliefs in phenomena that meet the following two conditions. First, they are, in principle, not explicable in terms of the natural sciences (either by the entities they currently postulate or by entities that resemble those they currently postulate that might be postulated in the future as the sciences develop). Second, the effects of the phenomena are often of a type explained by the natural sciences but, when the result of these "paranormal" phenomena, the effects conflict with the predictions of the natural sciences concerning them. In brief, the paranormal seems inexplicable in a certain way and miraculous. Without the second condition, any nonphysical entity would be categorized as paranormal. Without the first condition, any candidate miracle would have the implication that the preceding cause was paranormal no matter how mundane it is.

To see how these conditions work, consider the case of telekinesis. Suppose, by the power of our minds, we move a chair slightly to the left. Such movements aren't out of the ordinary in themselves. What is paranormal is that, as far as the forces identified by the natural sciences are concerned, there should be no movement. This is the miraculous element. If our mental power were possible to characterize by the natural sciences, we would be contemplating adjusting our account of the character of the laws that applied to the entities so characterized. Again, there would be nothing paranormal involved. It is the combination of these two features that makes something paranormal.

The characterization avoids some of the difficulties that afflict characterizations of the paranormal such as the idea that they are "physical, biological, or psychological phenomena that feature fundamental or core ontological properties of another ontological category" (Lindeman and Aarnio 2006: 586–7).[2] We may believe that psychological phenomena may have physical or biological properties without being committed to the paranormal. Paranormal beliefs include but are not limited to beliefs in extrasensory perception (ESP) including telepathy and clairvoyance, ghosts, witches, astrology, psychokinesis, and alien abduction.[3] The last category—that of alien abduction—need not involve the paranormal in our sense. Aliens may abduct and experiment upon us without this being in any way inexplicable to the natural sciences or, for that matter, involving a misattribution of the property of one ontological category to another. It depends upon the nature of what is envisaged in alien abduction hypotheses (e.g., levitation). Religious beliefs involve another complexity since they may well fall under any characterization of the paranormal. In any event, we think that paranormal beliefs of the standard sort are an instructive case when thinking about delusion formation. That is for two reasons: (1) they share two important features with delusions, namely they have *bizarre contents* and are *supported by strange experiences*, and (2) the research program of those interested in their genesis does not seek clinically significant irrationality to explain them. Let us take these points in turn.

5.2.1 Bizarre Contents

Paranormal beliefs are, almost by definition, ones with bizarre contents. Fans of the paranormal may believe that they can transmit thoughts to others through the power of the mind alone, or that they can speak to dead people, or move objects with their minds. They may also believe that the movements and positions of celestial objects can give us information about human lives and that witchcraft is not a mistaken relic of yesteryear but alive and well today. We take it that these beliefs are pretty bizarre. Insofar as we could measure it though, it might naturally be thought that paranormal beliefs are less bizarre than some delusions (belief in astrology might be less bizarre than believing that one's partner has been replaced by an almost-identical looking imposter as in Capgras delusion). That said, a case can be made for the converse, perhaps believing that one can move physical objects with one's mind (telekinesis) is more bizarre than believing that one's partner has been replaced by an imposter (which is highly improbable but need not involve inexplicability) and certainly believing that one's ex-partner remains faithful (as in the case of Reverse Othello delusion), which is not bizarre however remote it may be from the character of human relationships. It certainly isn't clear that monothematic delusions are systematically more bizarre than paranormal beliefs and certainly not so much more bizarre that we should expect an entirely different treatment to be necessary for this reason.

5.2.2 Anomalous Experience

Experiences (ostensibly) of the paranormal play a key role in the formation and maintenance of paranormal beliefs (Dagnall et al. 2020). Indeed, such experiences have become an important topic of investigation for a burgeoning field of study, anomalistic psychology, which attempts to explain paranormal beliefs and experiences in terms of psychological and physical factors observed in the more general healthy population. It turns out that these strange experiences occur in the healthy population at rates significantly higher than previously thought (Beyerstein 2007: 317–18). People with paranormal beliefs commonly give as the reason for them some personal paranormal experience (Dagnall et al. 2020: 6, see also Blackmore 1984; Clarke 1990, and Rattet and Burski 2001), and it has been found that there is a positive correlation between the number of such experiences and the strength of paranormal belief (Glicksohn 1990; Misch and Ehrenberg 2002).[4]

To give some examples: those subjects who believe in alternate planes of reality or that they possess psychic powers report vivid mental imagery which seems to come to them unbidden from an external force and is accompanied by a high degree of emotional content (Beyerstein 2007: 314). Such images "can have all the vividness and tangibility of percepts generated by any real event that actually transpired in our presence . . . [and] . . . [t]he emotional significance of such events can seem profound"

(Beyerstein 2007: 316). Subjects who believe that they have been abducted by aliens report nighttime paralysis, seeing aliens, and levitation (see McNally and Clancy 2005 for case studies). Mildly anomalous sensations (e.g., sudden temperature changes or dizziness) might also be interpreted as involving the paranormal (French and Wilson 2007: 13).

All of these experiences are—just as with experiences associated with delusions—amenable to naturalistic explanations. The vivid mental imagery reported by occultists can be explained as a by-product of brain processes involved in conscious awareness and behavior control. One suggestion is that thoughts or emotions may seem unwilled by a subject when inputs from unconscious modules bypass executive functions of self-awareness (Beyerstein 2007: 315–16). Alien abduction experiences have been explained by appeal to the combined effects of awareness during sleep paralysis (ASP) and hypnogic (sleep onset) and hypnopompic (sleep offset) hallucinations (McNally and Clancy 2005). At the same time, the intensity of such experiences may make naturalistic explanations seem less plausible to some subjects. Susan Blackmore had an experience of this kind in the laboratory, undergoing magnetic brain stimulation, where weak magnetic pulses were delivered to her temporal lobe. This intervention resulted in her feeling as though she were being grabbed by the shoulders, yanked around, that her leg was being pulled, and as though she "had been stretched half way up to the ceiling" (Beyerstein 2007: 329). This was followed by intense feelings of anger and then fear. Of this experience she says:

> Of course, I knew that it was all caused by the magnetic field changes but what, I wondered, would I feel if such things happened spontaneously. What if I woke in the middle of the night with all those feelings? I knew I would want, above all, to find an explanation, to find out who had been doing it to me. To have such powerful feelings and no reason for them is horrible. You feel as if you are going mad. If someone told me an alien was responsible and invited me to join an abductees' support group, I might well prefer to believe the idea; rather than accept I was going mad. (Beyerstein 2007: 329)

There is an important point here. Blackmore underwent an anomalous experience in an artificial environment and retained insight into what was happening to her. But she could reflect on how that might have felt in a different context, outside of an artificial environment and without the insight. The explanatory gap left open by these "powerful feelings" is described as "horrible," thus one might think it is hardly surprising that people who have such experiences form beliefs which seem to explain them.

5.2.3 Explaining Paranormal Belief

Despite these similarities with clinical delusions, theorists interested in the etiology of paranormal belief have taken a markedly different approach. In particular, the research has proceeded not by seeking to identify kinds of clinical irrationality to explain how such beliefs arise, but rather by seeking to identify which normal range cognitive styles might play such an explanatory role.⁵ This trend is especially interesting given that these theorists recognize that strange experiences are not sufficient for paranormal belief (recall that it is a parallel fact which has motivated a search for clinical abnormality in the case of delusion). For example, as Lindeman notes, hearing the voice of a deceased person may foster the belief that that person spoke to you, but it may also foster the belief that you had a hallucination (Lindeman 2017: 3). Both cases occur. But researchers of paranormal beliefs are not *thus* moved to search for a clinical abnormality of belief formation or evaluation to explain why some folk believe that dead people are communicating with them.

So what of these normal range cognitive styles then? A tremendous amount of research has sought to identify which styles or biases may play a role in the genesis of beliefs in the paranormal. We give a snapshot of it here to highlight the variety in hypothesized contributions (see French and Wilson 2007 and Irwin, Dagnall, and Drinkwater 2012 for more thorough overviews).

Some researchers have looked at intuitive and analytical thinking. The former is understood to be "implicit, nonverbalizable, associative and automatic and regards personal experience as the main tool by which information is assessed," while the latter is understood as "explicit, verbalizable and conscious reasoning that is based on conceptual thinking, logic and evidence" (Lindeman and Aarnio 2006: 587–8). High intuitive thinking and low analytical thinking have been shown to predict paranormal belief (Lindeman and Aarnio 2006).⁶

There is some evidence, although mixed, that poor syllogistic reasoning is correlated with paranormal belief. One study by Michael Wierzbicki had participants complete W. H. Jones and colleagues' (1977) Belief in the Paranormal Scale and a reasoning task containing sixteen syllogisms. He found a significant relationship between scores on the paranormal belief scale and errors in the reasoning task (1985: 492). Overall, Chris French and Krissy Wilson describe the evidence for a correlation here as "fairly robust" noting that only two published studies have failed to find this effect (2007: 8).

A third possible contributor to paranormal belief is probability misjudgment. Susan Blackmore and Emily Troscianko had participants in their study answer questions on their experience of precognitive dreams and telepathy, and their belief in ESP. These questions generated a belief score, and they found that those with lower scores were better at tasks involving judgments about probabilities (1985: 461–2). However, this effect was not replicated in a larger scale study of 6,238 people (Blackmore 1997), and while it was replicated in Jochen Musch and Katja Ehrenberg's study (2002), it did not survive controlling for cognitive ability. Overall, French and Wilson suggest that the role of probability misjudgment in paranormal belief enjoys only modest support (2007: 11).

Finally, there is good evidence for the role of some perceptual biases in the formation of paranormal belief, specifically, for seeing patterns and meaning in noisy or random stimuli (French and Wilson 2007: 12–13). For example, Peter Brugger and colleagues showed participants random dot patterns and told them that the experiment was set up to investigate subliminal perception and that half of the presented stimuli would contain meaningful information. They found a significant difference in the reporting of seeing "something meaningful," with believers in ESP reporting this more often than nonbelievers (Brugger et al. 1993, see also Blackmore and Moore 1994).

Aside from the foregoing, there is also some evidence for the role of the following on the formation of paranormal beliefs: confirmation bias (Irwin, Dagnall, and Drinkwater 2012), metacognitive beliefs (Irwin, Dagnall, and Drinkwater 2012), and fantasy proneness (Irwin 1990, 1991; Wilson and Barber 1983; Beyerstein 2007), and there is mixed evidence for the role of critical thinking (French and Wilson 2007: 5).

5.3 Lessons Learned

We make two main points about the foregoing, and what it can teach us about the research focus of those interested in monothematic delusion formation. First, none of the previously discussed cognitive contributions have been characterized as marking clinical deviation from normal range psychology. All have been taken to be representative of different positions along the normal range of belief formation and maintenance. This is despite the fact that it is recognized that the experiences reported by believers are also had by nonbelievers. That such experiences can prompt different beliefs is of course what one would expect from those experiences interacting with the variety of cognitive styles found among healthy subjects. In the case of delusion, those keen to identify clinical irrationality have appealed to cases of anomalous experience without the corresponding delusion, suggesting that we need a clinical abnormality to distinguish those who become delusional from those who do not. The research orientation of theorists working on the etiology of paranormal beliefs teaches us that that is a mistake. Instead, we say, for those interested in a full causal analysis of delusion formation, normal range cognitive biases and styles ought to be of interest, as Lamont notes, "such errors are by no means the monopoly of believers in the paranormal" (2007: 29).

The second point relates to what French and Wilson say following their summary of normal range cognitive contributions to paranormal belief:

> It is a mistake to conceive of paranormal belief as a unidimensional entity. Different cognitive biases are likely to be correlated with different aspects of paranormal belief and experience. (French and Wilson 2007: 4, see also Irwin 1993: 4)

The same goes for delusions. It is a mistake to search for a particular abnormality which would—whatever the background psychology—result in delusional belief when coupled with an anomalous experience. Not only is the search for clinical irrationality unmotivated, the search for a particular kind of clinical irrationality shared among an otherwise disparate set of beliefs is unwise. The variety in cognitive styles as they contribute to belief formation and maintenance is vast, once placed in the context of anomalous experience we might well expect some of these styles, perhaps interacting, to tip subjects into delusional belief. The search for a single contribution of this kind is one which underestimates the heterogeneity of human cognition and restricts our explanatory power.

The case of paranormal beliefs reveals that bizarre beliefs can result from strange experiences and a range of normal range cognitive styles not constitutive of clinical irrationality. The case shares with delusion the fact that not all instances of experience are given a nonnaturalistic interpretation. The research approach employed when investigating the genesis and maintenance of paranormal beliefs ought to be taken seriously in the case of delusional belief.

Let us consider three differences between paranormal belief and delusional belief which might put pressure on our claim that the research methodology when it comes to investigating the genesis and maintenance of the former has much to say for that of the latter: (1) neurological damage, (2) testimonial transmission or background beliefs, and (3) the social currency of paranormal beliefs.

(1) As mentioned in Section 5.1, damage to the right lateral prefrontal cortex found in many subjects with monothematic delusion has been identified as responsible for a clinical irrationality in belief maintenance (Coltheart 2005: 154). There is no evidence that such damage is present in paranormal believers, and so it might be thought that lessons learned from this case cannot be generalized to delusion. However, establishing a neurological abnormality in the delusional population is not to establish an abnormality amounting to clinical irrationality. Of course, this damage might make some folk more susceptible to delusional belief, but that could be by placing them at a different point in the normal range. It is only if the damage introduces clinical irrationality that it is problematic for our argument. To be clear: our view is not that it's clinically normal to have damage to the right lateral prefrontal cortex, but only that that fact does not establish clinical irrationality (for more on this see §6 of Noordhof and Sullivan-Bissett 2021).

(2) There is evidence that paranormal beliefs can be adopted from other people, for example, a subject's friends or family may transmit these beliefs (Lindeman 2017: 3). Putting aside relatively rare cases of folie à deux where a similar mechanism *might* be involved, this isn't usually the case for delusional belief. Another difference is the role of background beliefs in paranormal belief formation and how these might lead to particular interpretations of experience. In general, paranormal belief is associated with a "subjective world view," understood as for example, the belief that humans are more than mere physical or biological structures (Irwin 1993: 14). In the case of hypnopompic imagery, a subject who has a preexisting belief in the possibility of ESP may thus be disposed to interpret such imagery in paranormal terms (Glicksohn 1990: 676). In the case of alien abduction, some studies have shown that abductees tend to have New Age beliefs (e.g., astral projection), which might have disposed them to interpret certain experiences in abduction terms (McNally and Clancy 2005: 120), and Irwin and colleagues (2012) suggested that paranormal beliefs may be found within folk with New Age beliefs. Again, there is a difference here—subjects with Capgras delusion might not begin with a high subjective probability in the possibilities of imposters.[7] Overall, the testimonial transmission of paranormal beliefs and the role of background beliefs in interpreting paranormal experience might make belief formation stories in the two cases look very different. It might be thought that these differences

threaten to block any generalization we want to make regarding how research on the genesis and maintenance of delusion should proceed.

To this concern we say the following: we do not deny that these differences may exist,[8] but that they do does not undermine our key point. We are not claiming that paranormal beliefs and delusional beliefs are formed and maintained *in the same way*, and so it is fine by us if the cases involve different cognitive contributions. Rather our claim is that the normal range cognitive contributions present in paranormal beliefs are enough to tip a subject into a belief of that kind (often, though not always, following an anomalous experience). We say that this structure may well be present in the case of delusion. There are all sorts of ways that a subject can find herself in the normal range of cognitive contributions to belief formation and maintenance, with her position along that range helping to explain the move from strange experience to bizarre belief. It is this similarity to which we draw attention, and which we argue undermines the search for clinically significant irrationality in the case of delusions. We are not in the business of claiming that there are *particular* normal range cognitive contributions shared between the cases. Rather, our point is that the case of paranormal belief formation teaches us that whichever cognitive contributions are present in the formation of bizarre belief formation, we need not suppose that they are constitutive of clinical irrationality.

(3) Paranormal beliefs have a certain social currency. Many people have such beliefs. By contrast, the beliefs of subjects with delusions are generally thought to be bizarre. So it might thus be thought legitimate to appeal to a particular kind of clinical irrationality to explain the delusional beliefs.[9] We note two things in response. First, subjects with delusions have striking and repeated anomalous experiences to compensate for the absence of the social support for their beliefs. In particular, these anomalous experiences make up for the absence of testimonial support in favor of paranormal beliefs from all those who take the content of such beliefs seriously. But, by the same token, the fact that anomalous experiences are more persistent in the case of monothematic delusion shows that postulating a clinical irrationality is unnecessary. Second, while paranormal beliefs may have a certain social currency, they are genuinely bizarre beliefs. We suspect that when psychologists studying subjects with delusions become convinced that there needs to be a second factor involving clinical irrationality, they don't keep in firm view just how bizarre the beliefs of subjects in the normal range are, which are formed on the basis of less profound anomalous experiences with socially supported paranormal interpretation. If clinical irrationality is not required here, then it is not required for delusional beliefs.

5.4 Motivated Irrationality

As we noted at the beginning, delusions are usually seen as a more extreme form of irrationality than the typical motivated irrationalities of everyday life. The definition of delusion expressed in *DSM-IV* may well reflect this:

> A false belief based on incorrect inference about external reality that is firmly sustained despite what almost everybody else believes and despite what constitutes *incontrovertible and obvious proof or evidence to the contrary.* (American Psychiatric Association 2000: 821)

Motivated irrationalities are usually seen as susceptible to incontrovertible and obvious proof or evidence to the contrary. Alfred Mele expresses the standard view as follows.

> If what produces the Capgras delusion is a weird experience together with the removal or disabling of a cognitive mechanism that, in special cases inhibits the kind of default transition from experience to the corresponding belief, *the delusion seems to lie well beyond the sphere of self-deception.* (Mele 2009: 64)

Similarly, William Hirstein claims (using the term "clinical confabulator" for those with monothematic delusions):

> Confabulation patients, especially those exhibiting denial of illness, seem to be engaged in a form of dense and completely successful self-deception.... All of this suggests a continuum on which these syndromes and their degrees of tension can be placed:
> Clinical confabulator
> Sociopath
> Self-deceived normal person without tension
> Normal confabulator
> Neutral normal person
> Self-deceived normal person with tension
> Lying normal person
> Obsessive-compulsive normal person
> Clinical OCD sufferer
> At the top end of the continuum, confabulators experience no tension at all when they make their ill-grounded claims. (Hirstein 2006: 214–15)

Hirstein's continuum is in terms of the kind of tension the subject is under rather than an explicit concern about the significance of the irrationality involved. However, the degrees of absence of tension at the top of the continuum are taken to correspond to the extent to which the irrationality the subject displays is substantial as indicated by the talk of "completely successful self-deception." Similarly, Ken C. Winters and John M. Neale take delusions to differ from self-deception in degree of conviction. Bearing in mind that the degree of conviction is supposed to be inappropriate given the evidence, it follows that they take delusion to involve greater irrationality than self-deception (Winters and Neale 1983: 229). There may well be a theoretical notion of delusion that occupies the extreme position and, in earlier work, one of us sought to characterize what this might be like involving the adoption of different principles of evidential reasoning or failing to accept the application of standard evidential principles without the kind of explanation in terms of anomalous experience described in what follows (Noordhof 2009: 69). The interesting thing about the monothematic delusions we come across in clinical settings is that they do not have this character, contrary to the claims that are made.

The impression that delusions are the results of particularly serious lapses of rationality probably has three sources. First, their contents often have an exotic character, which, for a subject not prey to them, suggests that the subject with delusions is in some way divorced from reality. Thus, delusions, as opposed to more mundane cases of motivated irrationality, "disrupt functioning" (cf. McKay, Langdon, and Coltheart 2009: 173). Second, delusions tend to be rather resistant to the standard ways in which we alter somebody's beliefs: persuasion and presenting counter-evidence (see Noordhof and Sullivan-Bissett 2021 and cited literature for discussion on this point). Third, for this reason, the psychology of the subject with a delusion seems inaccessible to us. By contrast, the standard cases of motivated irrationality—wishful thinking and self-deception—are recognizable everyday phenomena, and subjects who suffer from either seem susceptible to the standard ways in which we seek to alter people's beliefs or their resistance seems psychologically comprehensible given the motivation we take to be at work.

Things look rather different when we remind ourselves of the features of everyday irrationality that we discussed earlier, and their potential overlap with monothematic delusions. What the various everyday cases of irrationality discussed share with monothematic delusion is a root in anomalous experience. We saw that some of the background beliefs that helped to support paranormal beliefs are derived from the testimony of other people and these background beliefs have wide currency, especially in certain communities. But many of the cases of monothematic delusion have a subject matter which also has currency. For example, in general terms, the idea of somebody being replaced by an imposter (Capgras), being followed by people you know in disguised form (Fregoli), and, for that matter, somebody being in love with you from a fleeting meeting and yet denying it (Erotomania) are all ideas that have some currency in the stories we tell. We also noted the prevalence of certain thinking styles such as the contrast between intuitive and analytical thinking and looking for meaning in what we perceive. It is plausible that different thinking styles will have an influence upon how people respond to the distinctive anomalous experiences of monothematic delusions. These features may well account for the exotic character and general resistance to evidence that are observed. Subjects with monothematic delusions have, in their anomalous experiences, a particular form of evidence whose weight is hard to quantify for those who do not have the experiences. All of this shows why the cold cases of monothematic delusion do not differ extensively from everyday irrationalities in either kind or degree. Subjects with monothematic delusions have dispositions to respond to experiences taken individually or together which do not differ from those of some subjects who do not show up in clinical settings at all and yet because of the anomalous character of the experiences they undergo, they end up with delusional beliefs. And, as we said, there is no reason to suppose that there may not be hot cases as well, and it is our contention that these hot cases do not support the view that monothematic delusions involve a particularly substantial form of clinical irrationality.

Discussion of this issue is hampered a little because the characterization of various motivated irrationalities is contested. One natural division is between non-agential and agential-motivated irrationalities. On the non-agential side, we have wishful thinking and weak self-deception. The main difference between these two is that wishful thinking involves the production of a belief that *p* by a desire that *p* is true; weak self-deception adds the requirement that *p* is false (see, e.g., Barnes 1997: 118; Mele 2001). Some of its proponents also require that the support for the self-deceptively favored belief is anxiety rather than desire but this doesn't cover all cases and we can set it aside here (e.g., Johnston 1988; Barnes 1997; see Noordhof 2003: 86 for discussion). Strong self-deception involves an agent having, as a part, a sub-agent that produces the self-deceptive belief as a result of its agency, or something analogous to this. The existence of strong self-deception is controversial and leads many to take weak self-deception to be the only kind there is (e.g., Barnes 1997: 117; Mele 2001). We shall discuss them in turn.

5.4.1 Wishful Thinking and Weak Self-deception

Wishful thinking and weak self-deception both give a central role to the desire that *p*. The prima facie problem is that it is hard to see how the desire that *p* can be a reason to believe that *p*. Having the attitude of desire to the proposition that *p* does not make *p* the case, or more likely to be true. Equally, desiring that *p*, rather than desiring that *one believe that p*, does not constitute a reason to have that belief. We don't rule out the possibility that there may be a pragmatic reason for believing that *p*—if doing so would serve interests other than the desire to believe the truth, then there may be pragmatic reasons to have the belief. We just deny that the desire that *p* constitutes one.

Often if you desire that *p*, it is also plausible to attribute to you a desire that you believe that *p*. In that case, there may be a basis for an explanation of why the subject forms the belief that *p* that sees it as a result of rational agency. We have allowed that the desire to believe that *p* may constitute a pragmatic reason to believe that *p* although we are skeptical. Appeal to the desire to believe that *p* is not needed, though, to provide an account of how the desire that *p* may influence the formation of our belief that *p*. There are other, indirect, ways in which the desire that *p* may have an influence over the process of belief formation. We can divide these into two. First, there is how the desire that *p* may highlight or help to find epistemic reasons to believe that *p*. Second, there is the way in which the desire that *p* may influence the impact of these epistemic reasons by adjusting the threshold for believing that *p* or believing that not-*p*.

Mele gives a detailed characterization of both of these indirect ways in his account of weak self-deception which we reproduce with some supplementation (Mele 2001: ch. 2; Mele 2009: 56–9; Noordhof 2009: 50). Examples of highlighting or finding epistemic reasons for *p* include the following: first, selective focusing on, or attending to, likely sources of positive evidence for *p* while ignoring evidence for not-*p*; second, interpreting things in a way favorable to *p*; third, selective evidence gathering by making more effort to find evidence for *p*; fourth, evidence for *p* being more vivid; fifth, the evidence for *p* being more readily available, where ready availability is often taken as a proxy for the likelihood of p being true; and finally, confirmation bias where we search for evidence in favor of our hypothesis that p from a desire to be right about our hypothesis.

The role of desire is clear in the last case but it is plausible that our desire that p would make us selectively attend to evidence in its favor, interpret things in a favorable way, make more effort to find evidence for p, and find the information that supports p more vivid and more readily available. In all of these ways, the desire that p highlights or assists in the finding of epistemic reasons.

The second way in which the desire that p plays a role is with regard to the impact of the evidence. If a subject desires that p, the desire has an influence upon the confidence level that is required before you believe that p, by pushing them down, or upon the confidence level that is required before you believe that not-p, by pushing them up. It is not the case that new epistemic reasons are found but rather that the weight of the ones you have, as far as their capacity to produce belief is concerned, are adjusted.

Mele suggests that we have motivated irrationality, and in the case of false belief, self-deception, if the following condition is met:

> S's believe that p is motivatedly irrational if, if D (the evidence readily available to S during the process of acquiring the believe that p) were made readily available to S's impartial cognitive peers who engaged in at least as much reflection on p as S does (and this is at least a moderate amount of reflection), then those who would conclude that p is false would significantly out number those would conclude that p is true.

"Impartial" in the characterization of the condition just given means without the desires that the subject who is motivatedly irrational has related to whether p or not-p (Mele 2009: 60–1). Noordhof has argued that self-deception does not require failure of the impartiality condition if the conditions for strong self-deception are met but we can set this aside for now (Noordhof 2009: 63–4).

The first point to observe about Mele's account is that, although the ways in which a desire that p may have an effect on us are familiar, there is nothing rational about the connection between the desire and our tendency to highlight or find epistemic reasons for p. Indeed, bearing in mind that it is the truth of p that we want, and not merely to believe it, the irrationality into which we have fallen is quite profound. This is also the case with regard to the way in which desire has an effect on the impact of the evidence by adjusting the threshold. It is familiar that when the truth of p is high stakes, then the threshold may be raised. But here the aim is to make additionally sure that we get the answer right. In the present case, it is not getting the answer right that matters but rather a particular answer one favors.

The second point is easiest to make by considering a particular case of monothematic delusion: Capgras. If what we have argued is correct, then the cognitive peers (rather than betters) of Capgras subjects will be those that make the normal range of responses to their experiences. Among the data that cognitive peers must receive will be the anomalous experiences themselves. No amount of information can reproduce what a subject gets from actually experiencing something. In such circumstances, we would expect that the majority of those cognitive peers responding to such anomalous experiences would believe that their loved one has been replaced by an imposter. Notice that this point is neutral between those who posit an irrationality distinct to the deluded and those who do not. For those who do, the cognitive peers of those with Capgras will be those who have the same deficit, bias, or performance failure. In which case, we would expect the majority would have the Capgras defining belief. For those who do not, a range of responses to the anomalous experience is allowed for, but it is plausible that they will hold that most of those subjects who are cognitive peers of a Capgras subject will believe that their partner has been replaced by an imposter. Our observation that the normal range may include some who don't draw that conclusion is not committed to the majority not drawing that conclusion on the basis of their anomalous experience.

It is no surprise that putatively cold cases of monothematic delusion will fail to satisfy the condition for motivated irrationality and, given what we have argued about both normal range responses and the substantial irrationality involved in motivational irrationality, that means that such delusions do not involve a substantial irrationality in their formation. However, as we have already remarked, it is plausible that they may sometimes involve motivated irrationality. In particular, having concluded, for example, that one's partner has been replaced by an imposter, Maher notes that subjects with Capgras delusion may be committed to their hypothesis as a theoretical achievement, and he draws the comparison with scientists developing a theory (Maher 1988: 20–2). As a result, subjects with delusions may display confirmation bias. When they do, there will be an aspect of motivated irrationality in their persisting belief. But note, even here, they will display much less of the influence of the desire that p than subjects who display all the hallmarks of weak self-deception identified by Mele.

There are, of course, circumstances in which more of the features may be present. Psychodynamic theories of Capgras have talked about the subject feeling ambivalent or suspicious of the person they conclude is replaced by an imposter prior to the onset of the delusion (e.g., Todd 1957: 254, 259, 264; Vogel 1974: 323–4; Enoch and Trethowan 1991: 11–17), and even those not tempted by the psychodynamic note that Capgras patients tend to be more suspicious (e.g., Ellis and Young 1990: 241; Ellis et al. 1997: 1086). This was not always found to be the case and that was part of the reason for moving to an approach that centered on the brain damage giving rise to anomalous experiences and potential cognitive deficits (e.g., Alexander, Struss, and Benson 1979: 334, 336–8; Fleminger and Burns 1993 note that there is an inverse relationship between cases with an organic source and the presence of persecutory delusions, 26–8). Nevertheless, if a subject were ambivalent toward or suspicious of their loved one, then other features of weak self-deception may be in play in arriving at the target delusional belief.

So our first conclusion of this section is this. Some monothematic delusions involve less of the features of motivated irrationality than standard cases of wishful thinking or weak self-deception and don't need to, although they may, involve more. They constitute a form of irrationality not at the extreme end of the continuum but rather closer to everyday irrationality with some cases that might be more severe. Those that do involve more of the features of motivational irrationality characteristic of weak self-deception are only more severe due to the extra motivational elements present in more extreme cases of motivational irrationality *in general* rather than delusion in particular.

5.4.2 Strong Self-deception

Strong self-deception involves two elements that have been thought potentially to lead to paradox. The first of these is that the self-deceived both have the target belief which is the product of the self-deception and a belief in the opposite (call this the *origin belief*). So, for example, a self-deceived person believes that their partner is faithful to them and, at the same time, believes that they are unfaithful. The second is that the self-deceptively favored belief is the result of an intention to have the belief as a result of finding the origin belief unacceptable. The problem with the first element is understanding how a subject can have contradictory beliefs. The problem with the second element is how the subject can intend to have the target belief, as a result of finding the origin belief unacceptable, without knowing what they are up to.

In previous work, Noordhof has argued that an essential feature of strong self-deception is an instability that both grounds and extends the idea of strong self-deception (2003: 83–8, 2009: 59–68). It captures when a certain combination of states involves genuine self-deception and extends it by allowing for various types of psychological history giving rise to the production of the self-deceptive belief and for an attribution of something short of the origin belief to initiate the process. So long as the distinctive instability is in place, self-deception is present. However, as we shall shortly see, it also may ground the attribution of the intention or other motivational or emotional state playing a quasi-agentive role, giving rise to the production of the belief (for more on the way emotional states may play this role, see Noordhof 2008: 337–45).

Let us first state the instability and then explain how this has the effects mentioned. The instability involves a certain kind of counterfactual:

(a) The subject, S, fails to attend consciously in a certain way, W, to either the evidence that rationally clashes with p (the content of the self-deceptive belief), which they believe, or some element of the psychological history characteristic of the self-deception behind the belief that p.
(b) If the subject were to attend consciously in way W to both p (the content of their belief) and either the evidence that rationally clashes with it which they believe or the psychological history (whichever applies in (a)), then p would no longer be believed.

The talk of "attend consciously in way W" needs a bit of unpacking. We may be conscious of something without being attentive to it. If we aren't attentive to what we are conscious of, then it is unlikely that it would be enough to make us see the clash between a belief we have and what we are nonattentively conscious of. So the instability needs to be formulated in terms of attentive consciousness. However, even attentive consciousness is not enough. We can attend to something consciously without recognizing it appropriately. That's where "way W" comes in. The subject needs to recognize that not-*p*, or that the evidence favors not-*p*, and recognize it as a content of their belief, or they need to recognize the psychological history that is supporting their belief that *p* for what it is. For example, they must be aware that the belief that *p* is supported by an intention rather than consciously attending to intention but somehow taking it to be evidence.

The instability allows for the extension of strong self-deception to, for example, not believing that not-*p* but believing other propositions that one takes as evidence that not-*p*, because the belief that *p* is extinguished if these propositions believed are attended to. There is no need to suppose that a subject must explicitly believe that not-*p* if other propositions believed generated the self-deceptive strategy, these are threatening to the favored belief, and so on. The subject need not have inferred that not-*p*. Similarly, the psychological history supporting the belief that *p* may not be an intention but if a subject's conscious recognition of it is similarly undermining of the belief, then this history is playing a structurally similar role. For example, you recognize that you believe that you had the novel coronavirus that causes Covid-19 previously because the symptoms were mild and that would mean your immune system is able to handle it, which you'd love to believe, but once you bring this into view you appreciate you probably have only had a cold and abandon the belief you previously had coronavirus.

We've described how the instability extends the states that might be involved in strong self-deception. We turn to the question of how it grounds an attribution of strong self-deception. The key idea is that it may be legitimate to attribute an intention to produce or sustain the belief that *p* in virtue of whether a subject's cognitive or other behavior shows a recognition of the instability. The most obvious kind of behavior would be avoiding situations in which they are reminded of the evidence against *p* but equally all of the various ways in which they may direct their attention, avoid certain discussions and reflections, and so on, would be the basis for the attribution of the intention. The more the behavior seems systematic or planned, the more the attribution of an intention to believe that *p*, or persist in believing that *p*, is plausible. Often the attribution of an intention to do A is taken to involve nonobservational knowledge of what one is doing. However, it is a mistake to suppose that whenever it is legitimate to attribute the intention, there will be nonobservational knowledge about what one is intending. We can know what we are up to, focusing on such and such evidence, not feeling happy about considering the following issues, without recognizing that taking all of this intentional activity together we are intending to believe that *p*. We are responding systematically to the apprehension of an instability—an appreciation of a particular dispositional structure—that concerns a particular proposition that we believe *p*, without knowing that what we are up to is preserving that belief (Noordhof 2009: 58–9).

The irrationality involved in strong self-deception is substantial. First, our agency is involved in the support of a particular belief independent of an appeal to evidence and the threshold that is set for forming the belief in the light of the evidence. Second, the instability suggests that we are holding the belief against principles of belief formation to which we ourselves are committed and which threaten to undermine the belief. This is not present in many cases of delusion.

It might be thought that there is a sense in which the irrationality involved in delusion may be worse. The instability of self-deceptive belief displays a way in which the self-deceived may be more familiar than those subject to delusions. The self-deceived seem, at least to some degree, affected by the same requirements on belief formation that we are in our rational moments. Those suffering from delusions, if these show no instability but are held resiliently, either seem not to recognize the same principles of belief formation or take them not to be applicable (Noordhof 2009: 69–71). If it is the first, then the irrationality involved is in one way significantly different from everyday irrationality although there is a way in which it is also less substantial, namely by the subject's own lights. However, if what we have argued is correct, cases of monothematic delusion either involve everyday irrationalities that are not unstable because quite minor, or failures to recognize that certain principles of belief formation apply because the anomalous experiences are so compelling, other evidence is set aside. In the latter case, the stability that those who suffer from delusions display is not a sign of a more entrenched form of irrationality but rather because the delusional beliefs are supported by the evidence of experience in the way that standard cases of self-deception are not.

Certain cases of monothematic delusion display the unstable character of self-deception we have identified. A very typical form of anosognosia involves denial of hemiplegia (paralysis or weakness) in the left side. There are various possibilities for how we might describe the anomaly in experience that gives rise to the denial. It may be that the denial is partly based upon the *lack* of the unusual experience of a failure of motor movement or a loss of sensation in the limbs on the left side. Perhaps this is coupled with an experience of intending to move the left arm or leg that makes a subject think that they are moving it. Maybe a hallucination of the left arm moving. We won't try to resolve the matter here although we suspect that the denial that one is paralyzed is partly because of experiences or lack of experiences of this kind. The important point concerns another aspect of these cases: the extent to which they display the distinctive instability identified earlier.

In his discussion of a patient with anosognosia, V. S. Ramachandran writes the following:

> At this point, I wondered what would happen if I kept pushing the patient further. I did so with some hesitation, for fear of precipitating what Kurt Goldstein has called a "catastrophic reaction" which is simply medical jargon for "The patient becomes depressed and starts crying because her defences crumble." (Ramachandran 1996: 348)

The pushing described is trying to get the patient to acknowledge their left hemiplegia by providing further evidence of it. Patients with this kind of anosognosia can be brought to acknowledge their left hemiplegia and some display the reaction that Ramachandran fears.

This is prima facie evidence that there is the kind of instability that we argued is distinctive of self-deception. There is an alternative explanation though. The patients don't believe that they have left hemiplegia, or that the evidence indicates that they have, but when they are pressed they form this belief and it is the belief that causes the catastrophic reaction. For this reason, it is helpful to consider another observation concerning such patients, the strange phenomenon of ice-cold water irrigation of the left ear canal. On doing this, a patient who had denied left hemiplegia acknowledged it. Ramachandran reproduces this sample of the conversation:

VSR: Do you feel okay?
BM: My ear is very cold but other than that I am fine.
VSR: Can you use your hands?
BM: I can use my right arm but not my left arm. I want to move it but it doesn't move.
VSR: Mrs M, how long has your arm been paralyzed? Did it start now or earlier?
BM: It has been paralyzed continuously for several days now . . . (Ramachandran 1996: 355)

The working hypothesis is that ice-cold water irrigation in the left ear canal stimulates the right hemisphere which is responsible for detection of anomalies between what you consciously believe, or claim to be the case, and what you otherwise believe is the case. If stimulation of the right hemisphere had led to an acknowledgment of left hemiplegia but no acknowledgment that the arm had been paralyzed for several days, it is conceivable that the acknowledgment could result from the evidence that the patient just obtained (e.g., trying to move their arm). However, since they also acknowledged that the arm had been paralyzed for several days, this suggests that they had a belief about the paralysis of their arm earlier but the belief that their arm was not paralyzed hadn't been checked against this other belief earlier. Put these two pieces of evidence together and it seems the patient had a prior belief that they were paralyzed that is a basis for the instability of the belief that they are not paralyzed distinctive of self-deception.

This conclusion doesn't depend upon endorsing all of Ramachandran's proposals concerning self-deception in this case. His idea is that the left hemisphere seeks to maintain a consistent model of the self that is the basis of stable behavior. We might take this to be supported by the motivational or agential structure of self-deception already identified. When the right hemisphere is damaged—as it tends to be in cases of anosognosia relating to left hemiplegia—the standard checking of this motivational structure to ensure that the model reflects the way things are with oneself no longer takes place so effectively. Self-deception, in other words, comes about because of the inhibition of an inhibitor.

Standard cases of self-deception, without damage we may presume, wouldn't involve Ramachandran's idea of the inhibition of an inhibitor. We might take this as evidence that standard cases of self-deception involve an even stronger motivational element which overwhelms the inhibition of motivationally supported but evidentially unsupported beliefs. Just in case you think that this is implausible because becoming paralyzed might be very bad, and thus this would surely be a candidate for particularly strong self-deception, it is worth noting that cases of anosognosia due to right hemiplegia are rare which rather suggests that subjects generally don't deceive themselves about whether or not they are paralyzed. So even when there are cases of monothematic delusion that involve strong self-deception, the kind of self-deception involved doesn't involve nonrational motivational elements to the same degree. While there might be a type of brain damage that introduces with it a particular form of self-deception (inhibition of the inhibitor), the kind of irrationality that holds as a consequence is still, in an important sense, milder than the everyday irrationality that results in self-deception.

5.5 Concluding Remarks

Everyday irrationality is instructive for research into monothematic delusion in two respects. As we saw in the first three sections of the chapter, paranormal and other irrational beliefs result from strange experiences plus a normal range of cognitive styles not constitutive of clinical irrationality. No appeal is made to a clinically significant factor like a deficit resulting from brain damage or a distinctive form of bias. This throws into question the claim that delusion involves some more substantial form of irrationality than everyday irrationality. Second, monothematic delusions can display components of everyday motivated irrationalities like wishful thinking/weak self-deception and strong self-deception. However, these components constitute the ways in which more profound irrationality is involved and, often, the irrationality that occurs is less severe than everyday cases of motivated irrationality. In general, there is no need to take delusion to involve a distinctive further irrationality that goes beyond the everyday and, indeed, many monothematic delusions involve less substantial irrationalities than many everyday ones in either cold or hot forms.

Acknowledgments

With thanks to the Arts and Humanities Research Council for funding the research of which this chapter is a part (*Deluded by Experience,* grant no. AH/T013486/1). We are grateful for comments on an earlier version of the chapter received from the audience at the Delusion Formation Workshop.

Notes

1 We assume doxasticism about delusion (and indeed self-deception) in this chapter, that is, the view that the delusional attitude is a *belief*. Although far from settled in either case, it is an assumption shared by the various literatures, philosophers, and psychologists we engage with here. For defenses of doxasticism see Bortolotti (2009) and Bayne and Pacherie (2005) (delusion), and Van Leeuwen (2007) (self-deception).
2 This definition is wider than that used in earlier work on paranormal belief, the presence of which was assessed by "sheep-goat scales" devised to select participants who believed in ESP in particular (see Irwin 1993 for discussion). The studies we discuss here were generally broader, with measures of paranormal belief being based on the Paranormal Belief Scale (Tobacyk 1988, later revised in 2004) or the Belief in the Paranormal Scale (Jones, Russel, and Nickel 1977).

3   See Sullivan-Bissett (2020) for an argument that those interested in delusion formation have much to learn from the case of alien abduction belief.
4   We interpret the empirical work on paranormal experience and belief in empiricist terms, that is, as the cited experiences preceding the belief. However, a non-experiential cognitive single factor may well be more plausible in the paranormal case than the delusion case, given the cultural grounding of paranormal beliefs and the testimony of others that give these beliefs currency. We don't want to rule out that in many cases, experiences are interpreted as paranormal in character because of an existing belief in the possibility of such goings on. This is the *cultural source* hypothesis according to which "paranormal belief creates or shapes experience and cultural traditions influence interpretation of bizarre experiences" (Dagnall et al. 2020, see Hufford 1982 and McClenon 1994 for representative views). Lindeman and Aarnio found that "the general tendency to believe in paranormal phenomena was the strongest predictor of all specific paranormal beliefs" (2006: 598), and Dagnall and colleagues note that positive societal depictions might make more plausible paranormal explanations of puzzling experiences (10–11). We note then that the bizarreness and relative rarity of delusions might be in part explained not by a corresponding rarity in particular cognitive contributions but rather by the absence of positive societal depictions of their contents.
5   There has also been substantial research into other contributory factors such as sex, socioeconomic status, ethnicity, level of education, and IQ (see Irwin 1993 for an overview).
6   Pennycook and colleagues (2012) also found this, although they did not control for cognitive ability. Their view is that belief formation is Spinozan and that supernatural thinking is the default state, with analytical reasoning undermining the beliefs arising from the default state.
7   This may seem too modest; it might seem as though Capgras subjects straightforwardly *do not* start from a place of high subjective probability in the possibility of imposters, and furthermore, that the Capgras belief *contradicts* the backgrounds beliefs such a subject began with (McLaughlin 2009: 143). We have argued elsewhere that this is overstated (see §5.1 of Noordhof and Sullivan-Bissett 2021).
8   Although they are likely not as clear-cut as we present them here, and so an objection of this kind may well be relying on exaggerated differences. As noted, testimonial transmission may occur in cases of folie á deux. With respect to relevant background beliefs, we see some potential in the idea that these can be explanatory in cases of delusion. However, this idea has been relatively underexplored since the research focus in investigations of delusion formation is not one of identifying how everyday irrationalities (including relevant background beliefs) might go into the explanatory mix, but has rather been one of seeking clinical abnormality. Irwin and colleagues (2012) have argued that paranormal beliefs and delusions share a common etiology, but our claim is significantly more modest.
9   We are grateful to Fiona Macpherson for raising this concern.

References

Alexander, M. P., D. T. Struss, and D. F. Benson (1979), "Capgras Syndrome: A Reduplicative Phenomenon," *Neurobiology*, 29: 334–9.

American Psychiatric Association (2000), *Diagnostic Statistical Manual of Mental Disorders*, 4th ed., Text Revision (DSM-IV-TR). Arlington, VA.
American Psychiatric Association (2013), *Diagnostic Statistical Manual of Mental Disorders*, 4th edn, Text Revision (DSM-V-TR). Arlington, VA.
Ames, David (1984), "Self-Shooting of a Phantom Head," *British Journal of Psychiatry*, 145 (2): 193–4.
Barnes, Annette (1997), *Seeing Through Self-Deception*, Cambridge: Cambridge University Press.
Bayne, Tim and Elisabeth Pacherie (2005), "In Defence of the Doxastic Conception of Delusions," *Mind & Language*, 20 (2): 164–88.
Beyerstein, Barry L. (2007), "The Neurology of the Weird: Brain States and Anomalous Experience," in Sergio Della Sala (ed.), *Tall Tales About the Mind and Brain: Separating Fact from Fiction*, 314–35, New York: Oxford University Press.
Blackmore, Susan (1984), "A Postal Survey of OBEs and Other Experience," *Journal of the Society for Psychical Research*, 52: 225–44.
Blackmore, Susan (1997), "Probability Misjudgement and Belief in the Paranormal," *British Journal of Psychology*, 88 (4): 683–9.
Blackmore, Susan and Rachel Moore (1994), "Seeing Things: Visual Recognition and Belief in the Paranormal," *European Journal of Parapsychology*, 10: 91–103.
Blackmore, Susan and Tom Trościanko (1985), "Belief in the Paranormal: Probability Judgements, Illusory Control, and the 'Chance Baselines Shift,'" *British Journal of Psychology*, 76 (4): 459–68.
Bortolotti, Lisa (2009), *Delusions and Other Irrational Beliefs*, New York: Oxford University Press.
Brugger, P., M. Regard, T. Landis, N. Cook, D. Krebs, and J. Niderberger (1993), "'Meaningful' Patterns in Visual Noise: Effects of Lateral Stimulation and the Observer's Belief in ESP," *Psychopathology*, 26 (5–6): 261–5.
Chapman, L. K. and J. P. Chapman (1988), "The Genesis of Delusions," in T. Oltmanns and B. Maher (eds.), *Delusional Beliefs*, 167–83, John Wiley and Sons.
Clarke, Dave (1990), "Experience and Other Reasons Given for Belief and Disbelief in Paranormal and Religious Phenomena," *Journal of the Society for Psychical Research*, 60: 371–84.
Coltheart, Max (2005), "Conscious Experience and Delusional Belief," *Philosophy, Psychiatry & Psychology*, 12: 153–7.
Coltheart, M. (2015), "From the Internal Lexicon to Delusional Belief," *AVANT*, 3: 19–29.
Coltheart, Max, Robyn Langdon, and Ryan McKay (2007), "Schizophrenia and Monothematic Delusions," *Schizophrenia Bulletin*, 33 (3): 642–47.
Corlett, Philip R. (2019), "Factor One, Familiarity and Frontal Cortex, a Challenge to the Two Factor Theory of Delusions," *Cognitive Neuropsychiatry*, 24 (3): 165–77.
Dagnall, Neil, Kevin Drinkwater, Andrew Parker, and Peter Cloug (2020), "Paranormal Experience, Belief in the Paranormal and Anomalous Beliefs," *Parantropology*, 7 (1): 4–14.
Davies, M. and M. Coltheart (2000), "Introduction: Pathologies of Belief," *Mind & Language*, 15 (1): 1–46.
Davies, Martin, Max Coltheart, Robyn Langdon, and Nora Breen (2001), "Monothematic Delusions: Towards a Two-Factor Account," *Philosophy, Psychiatry, & Psychology*, 8 (2): 133–58.

Davies, M., A. Davies, and M. Coltheart (2005), "Anosognosia and the Two-Factor Theory of Delusion," *Mind and Language*, 20 (2): 209–36.

Dudley, Robert, Peter Taylor, Sophie Wickham, and Paul Hutton (2015), "Psychosis, Delusions and the 'Jumping to Conclusions' Reasoning Bias: A Systematic Review and Meta-analysis," *Schizophrenia Bulletin*, 42 (3): 652–65.

Ellis, Haydn D. and Andrew W. Young (1990), "Accounting for Delusional Misidentification," *British Journal of Psychiatry*, 157 (2): 239–48.

Ellis, Haydn D., Andrew W. Young, Angela H. Quayle, and Karel W. De Pauw (1997), "Reduced Autonomic Responses to Faces in Capgras Delusion," *Proceedings of the Royal Society of London, Series B*, 264 (1384): 1085–92.

Enoch, David and William Threthowan (1991), *Uncommon Psychiatric Syndromes*, Oxford: Butterworth-Heinemann.

Fleminger, Simon and Alistair Burns (1993), "The Delusional Misidentification Syndromes in Patients with and Without Evidence of Organic Cerebral Disorder: A Structured Review of Case Reports," *Biological Psychiatry*, 33 (1): 22–32.

French, Christopher C. and Krissy Wilson (2007), "Cognitive Factors Underlying Paranormal Beliefs and Experiences," in Sergio Della Sala (ed.), *Tall Tales About the Mind and Brain: Separating Fact from Fiction*, 3–22, New York: Oxford University Press.

Garety, Philippa A. and Daniel Freeman (1999), "Cognitive Approaches to Delusions: A Critical Review of Theories and Evidence," *British Journal of Clinical Psychology*, 38 (2): 113–54.

Garety, Phillipa A., D. R. Hemsley, and S. Wessely (1991), "Reasoning in Deluded Schizophrenic and Paranoid Patients Biases in Performance on a Probabilistic Inference Task," *Journal of Nervous and Mental Disease*, 179 (4): 194–201.

Gerrans, Philip (2001), "Delusions as Performance Failures," *Cognitive Neuropsychiatry*, 6 (3): 161–73.

Glicksohn, J. (1990), "Belief in the Paranormal and Subjective Paranormal Experience," *Personality and Individual Differences*, 11 (7): 675–83.

Hirstein, William (2006), *Brain Fiction*, Cambridge, MA: The MIT Press.

Hufford, D. J. (1982), *The Terror that Comes in the Night: An Experience-Centered Study of Supernatural Assault Traditions*, Philadelphia, PA: University of Pennsylvania Press.

Huq, S. F., P. A. Garety, and D. R. Hemsley (1988), "Probabilistic Judgments in Deluded and Nondeluded Subjects," *Quarterly Journal of Experimental Psychology Section A*, 40A: 801–12.

Irwin, Harvey J. (1990), "Fantasy Proneness and Paranormal Beliefs," *Psychological Reports*, 6 (2): 655–8.

Irwin, Harvey J. (1991), "A Study of Paranormal Belief, Psychological Adjustment, and Fantasy Proneness," *Journal of the American Society for Psychical Research*, 85: 317–31.

Irwin, Harvey J. (1993), "Belief in the Paranormal: A Review of the Empirical Literature," *Journal of the American Society for Psychical Research*, 87 (1): 1–39.

Irwin, Harvey J., Neil Dagnall, and Kenneth Drinkwater (2012), "Paranormal Beliefs and Cognitive Processes Underlying the Formation of Delusions," *Australian Journal of Parapsychology*, 12 (2): 107–26.

Johnston, Mark (1988), "Self-Deception and the Nature of the Mind," in B. McLaughlin and Amelie Oksenberg Rorty (eds.), *Perspectives on Self-Deception*, 63–91, Berkeley, CA: University of California Press.

Jones, W. H., D. W. Russel, and T. W. Nickel (1977), "Belief in the Paranormal Scale: An Objective Instrument to Measure Belief in Magical Phenomena and Causes," *JSAS Catalog of Selected Documents in Psychology*, 7 (100): 1577.

Lamont, Peter (2007), "Critically Thinking About Paranormal Belief," in Sergio Della Sala (ed.), *Tall Tales About the Mind and Brain: Separating Fact from Fiction*, 23–35, New York: Oxford University Press.

Lindeman, Marjaana (2017), "Paranormal Beliefs," in V. Zeigler-Hill and T. K. Shackelford (ed.), *Encyclopedia of Personality and Individual Differences*, 1–4, Cham: Springer International Publishing.

Lindeman, Marjaana and Kia Aarnio (2006), "Paranormal Beliefs: Their Dimensionality and Correlates," *European Journal of Personality*, 20 (7): 585–602.

Maher, Brendan (1988), "Anomalous Experience and Delusional Thinking: The Logic of Explanations," in Thomas Oltmanns and Brendan Maher (eds.), *Delusional Beliefs*, 15–33, John Wiley and Sons.

McKay, R., R. Langdon, and M. Coltheart (2009), "'Sleights of Mind': Delusions and Self-deception," in T. Bayne and J. Fernandez (eds.), *Delusion and Self-Deception*, 165–85, New York and London: Taylor and Francis.

McLaughlin, B. P. (2009), "Monothematic Delusions and Existential Feelings," in T. Bayne and J. Fernández (eds.), *Delusion and Self-Deception: Affective and Motivational Influences on Belief Formation*, 139–64, Psychology Press.

McClenon, J. (1994), *Wondrous Events: Foundations of Religious Beliefs*, Philadelphia, PA: University of Pennsylvania Press.

McNally, Robert and Susan A. Clancy (2005), "Sleep Paralysis, Sexual Abuse, and Space Alien Abduction," *Transcultural Psychiatry*, 42 (1): 113–22.

Mele, Alfred (2001), *Self-Deception Unmasked*, Princeton, NJ: Princeton University Press.

Mele, Alfred (2009), "Self-Deception and Delusions," in Tim Bayne and Jordi Fernandez (eds.), *Delusion and Self-Deception*, 55–69, New York, NY and London: Taylor and Francis.

Musch, J. and K. Ehrenberg (2002), "Probability Misjudgment, Cognitive Ability, and Belief in the Paranormal," *British Journal of Psychology*, 93 (2): 169–78.

Noordhof, Paul (2003), "Self-Deception, Interpretation and Consciousness," *Philosophy and Phenomenological Research*, 67 (1): 75–100.

Noordhof, Paul (2008), "Expressive Perception as Projective Imagining," *Mind and Language*, 23 (3): 329–58.

Noordhof, Paul (2009), "The Essential Instability of Self-Deception," *Social Theory and Practice*, 35 (1): 45–71.

Noordhof, Paul and Ema Sullivan-Bissett (2021), "The Clinical Significance of Anomalous Experience in the Explanation of Delusion Formation," *Synthese*. https://doi.org/10.1007/s11229-021-03245-x.

Pennycook, Gordon, James Allan Cheyne, Paul Seli, Derek J. Koehler, and Jonathan A. Fugelsang (2012), "Analytic Cognitive Style Predicts Religious and Paranormal Belief," *Cognition*, 123 (3): 335–46.

Ramachandran, V. S. (1996), "The Evolutionary Biology of Self-Deception, Laughter, Dreaming and Depression: Some Clues from Anosognosia," *Medical Hypotheses*, 47 (5): 347–62.

Ratter, S. L. and K. Burski (2001), "Investigating the Personality Correlates of Paranormal Belief and Precognitive Experience," *Personality and Individual Differences*, 31: 433–44.

Ross, Robert, Ryan McKay, Max Coltheart, and Robyn Langdon (2015), "Jumping to Conclusions About the Beads Task? A Meta-Analysis of Delusional Ideation and Data-Gathering," *Schizophrenia Bulletin*, 41 (5): 1183–91.

Stone, Tony and Andrew Young (1997), "Delusions and Brain Injury: The Philosophy and Psychology of Belief," *Mind and Language*, 12 (3&4): 327–64.

Sullivan-Bissett, Ema (2020), "Unimpaired Abduction to Alien Abduction: Lessons on Delusion Formation," *Philosophical Psychology,* 33 (5): 679–704.

Tobacyk, Jerome J. (1988), *A Revised Paranormal Belief Scale*, Ruston, LA: Louisiana Tech University.

Tobacyk, Jerome J. (2004), "A Revised Paranormal Belief Scale," *International Journal of Transpersonal Studies,* 23 (1): 94–8.

Todd, J. (1957), "The Syndrome of Capgras," *Psychiatric Quarterly*, 31 (2): 250–65.

Tranel, Daniel, Hanna Damasio, and Antonio R. Damasio (1995), "Double Dissociation Between Overt and Covert Face Recognition," *Journal of Cognitive Neuroscience*, 7 (4): 425–32.

Van Leeuwen, Neil (2007), "The Product of Self-Deception," *Erkenntnis*, 67 (3): 419–37.

Vogel, Frank (1974), "The Capgras Syndrome and Its Psychopathology," *American Journal of Psychiatry*, 131 (8): 922–4.

Wierzbicki, Michael (1985), "Reasoning Errors and Belief in the Paranormal," *Journal of Social Psychology*, 125 (4): 489–94.

Wilkinson, Sam (2015), "Delusions, Dreams and the Nature of Identification," *Philosophical Psychology*, 28 (2): 203–26.

Wilson, Sheryl C. and Theodore X. Barber (1983), "The Fantasy-Prone Personality: Implications for Understanding Imagery, Hypnosis, and Parapsychological Phenomena," in A. A. Sheikh (ed.), *Imagery: Current Theory, Research, and Application*, 340–87, New York, NY: Wiley.

Winters, Ken C. and John M. Neale (1983), "Delusions and Delusional Thinking in Psychotics: A Review of the Literature," *Clinical Psychology Review*, 3 (2): 227–353.

Young, A. and K. W. de Pauw (2002), "One Stafe is not Enough," *Philosophy, Psychiatry, and Psychology*, 9 (1): 55–9.

Young, A. W., I. H. Robertson, D. J. Hellawell, K. W. de Pauw, and B. Pentland (1992), "Cotard Delusion After Brain Injury," *Psychological Medicine*, 22 (3): 799–804.

6

Truth, Perspective, and Norms of Assertion

New Findings and Theoretical Advances

John Turri

6.1 Introduction

Communication is essential to any social species. In addition to our onboard equipment of perception, memory, and inference, communication is an indispensable means of learning things about the world. Much of what we know arrives this way, by trusting others. But trust isn't an unalloyed good. It has a dark side too: it leaves us vulnerable to manipulation and betrayal. Somehow a balance must be struck to achieve some benefits without being swamped by costs.

How do we establish and maintain the bonds of trust essential to effective communication? This is not a uniquely human question. A challenge facing any communication system is that the interests of sender (speaker) and receiver (audience) often diverge, which can lead to dishonesty and deception, such as false predator alarm calls in bird and monkey species. If this happens too often, the communication channel will be ignored and rendered worthless. This is why stable and enduring communication systems include mechanisms that promote honest signaling.

Life scientists have found that animals establish and maintain trust by instinctively following certain behavioral rules (Bradbury and Vehrencamp 2011). One rule is to attend preferentially to "information-constrained" signals, or signals that only individuals with particular knowledge would produce. For instance, a sparrow needs to distinguish other sparrows ("conspecifics") who are invading its territory from those who innocently occupy neighboring territory. A sparrow does this by paying attention to whether the conspecific imitates the song the sparrow just sang ("song matching"), or sings a different song that the sparrow sang previously ("repertoire matching"). A neighbor has had time to memorize other songs that the sparrow sang, but an invader has not. This makes repertoire matching an information-constrained signal of neighborhood, which sparrows instinctively rely on when deciding how to respond to nearby conspecifics (Beecher et al. 2000).

In humans, assertion is a principal means of communication. What prevents us from dishonestly asserting enough to destabilize the practice? According to the *knowledge-rule hypothesis*, our practice of assertion is at least partially sustained by an unwritten, socially policed rule that *assertions should express knowledge*.

This is an empirical hypothesis about a biological, social phenomenon. It attempts to shed light on assertion by placing it in a broader context of scientific understanding of animal communication. In particular, on this approach, our practice of assertion is partly sustained by mechanisms similar to those that sustain nonhuman communication systems: information-constrained signaling and social policing. This provides the view with a deep and principled theoretical motivation.

In these respects, my proposal must be distinguished from superficially similar but fundamentally different views from the theoretical philosophy literature. Deliberately, it is not a logical definition or conceptual analysis in terms of necessary or sufficient conditions, just as it is purposely framed in terms of "should" rather than "must," "permissible," or other terminology importing questionable, speculative assumptions from philosophical writings on assertion. Neither does my proposal close off obviously legitimate questions. For example, it is not "pointless to ask" why assertion has the rules it does, as some philosophers claim (Williamson 2000: 267). To the contrary, available evidence supports a specific and informative answer: our practice includes the rule *assertions should express knowledge* because *the point* of assertion is to transmit knowledge (Turri 2016c). By following the rule, speakers do their part in achieving the practice's point. This connects with another theme in the broader study of animal communication, where, in an evolutionary context, biologists propose that sharing information for use in decision-making is a signal's function (Bradbury and Vehrencamp 2011: 4, 17).

Philosophical writings often assume, among other things, that there is a single, exceptionless rule pertaining to what speakers "must" do (for details, see Turri 2014a, Turri 2016b: ch. 4). The only evidence philosophers offer for these and other strong assumptions is that their truth would be "theoretically satisfying" (Williamson 2000: 242). Others follow along, often without even acknowledging, much less questioning, the extraordinary amount of unargued baggage being carried into the arena of dialectic (e.g., Marsili 2018).

Obviously, scholars are free to make as many pleasing yet unsupported assumptions as they wish. But, equally obviously, their satisfaction places no genuine constraints on research in this area, or any other, for that matter.

A legitimate alternative—one that some of us find theoretically satisfying—is to start with fewer strong assumptions and fill in the details based on evidence as it accumulates. In other words, we could view many of these issues as open questions to be answered in the course of inquiry, perhaps to our dismay, rather than stipulated from the armchair in advance to our satisfaction.

The knowledge-rule hypothesis makes testable predictions. In particular, it predicts a central tendency to link judgments about what is *true* and *known* to judgments about what *should be asserted* in the behavior of competent language users, who are the practice's practitioners. Its central prediction has been verified and replicated many times across a range of contexts and by multiple research groups, including defenders of opposing views (e.g., Kneer 2018; Reuter and Brössel 2018; Marsili and Wiegmann 2020). This is in addition to the precedential evidence from biology about animal communication systems, observational data in naturalistic contexts, and convergent evidence from human development, cross-cultural studies, and historical linguistics (for discussion, reviews, and findings, see Turri 2014a, 2016b, 2017c; Turri and Park 2018).

The hypothesis also receives appreciable, albeit more indirect, support from its deep coherence with accounts of the norms of pedagogy, the norms of other speech acts (questioning, guaranteeing, explanation, assurance), epistemic value, rule-breaking, and lying (Turri 2016b: ch. 2, 2015c). Every major objection raised against the view has been addressed (Turri 2016b: ch. 3). No competing account of assertoric norms can explain even a small fraction of existing evidence, much less explain it all equally well. Nor is any competing account similarly grounded in the broader scientific context of animal communication studies, social cognition, and norm psychology.

Overall, the amount and variety of evidence supporting the knowledge-rule hypothesis is formidable and, as far as I am aware, unsurpassed in philosophy's recent history. We are far past the point where it is reasonable to doubt that knowledge is a central norm of our social practice of assertion. Nevertheless, in good scientific spirit, it shouldn't be and has not been spared critical scrutiny. This is a good thing because there is much left to learn, at least if its leading proponents are to be believed (for a partial accounting, see Turri 2016b: ch. 4).

Unfortunately, the view has yet to attract criticism worthy of its strengths. Critics tend to ignore the vast majority of evidence, argument, and theory supporting the hypothesis (e.g., Marsili 2018; Marsili and Wiegmann 2020). Instead, they focus narrowly on data points in isolation or aspects of individual studies, argue that these suffer from various defects, and then rashly conclude that the knowledge-rule hypothesis is false (e.g., Reuter and Brössel 2018). For instance, despite ignoring almost all of the evidence supporting the knowledge-rule hypothesis—including previous studies that stated, tested, and ruled out their primary concern—some critics declare that with one study they have "shown" that "truth and hence knowledge are not an integral part of the norm of assertion" (Reuter and Brössel 2018: 18).

The present research addresses three weaknesses in the evidence supporting the knowledge-rule hypothesis. First, one might question whether judgments favoring true assertions are due to subtle aspects of stimulus selection. This is relevant to the knowledge-rule hypothesis because *assertions expressing knowledge* are a subset of *assertions expressing truth*. The knowledge-rule is a *factive* (or *truth-sensitive*) rule. An opposing group of hypotheses claims that assertion has only *non-factive* (or *truth-insensitive*) rules, which welcome false assertions if they are, for instance, sincere (i.e., the speaker actually believes the false proposition) or supported by the evidence (i.e., the speaker is "justified" in believing the false proposition).

Not all ways of lodging this objection hit their mark. For example, theorists have objected to testing people's judgments about cases featuring imperfect or fallible evidence (Reuter and Brössel 2018). However, a preregistered experiment directly tested the objection and conclusively ruled it out: truth had just as large an effect on assertability judgments regardless of whether fallibility was mentioned (Turri 2020a: experiment 1).

Regardless of the shortcomings of previous criticisms along these lines, important work remains to be done. Although a range of key findings have been observed using different stimuli (e.g., Turri 2015a; Turri, Friedman, and Keefner 2017), using various questioning procedures (e.g., Turri 2013, 2017b), by different research groups (e.g., Kneer 2018; Reuter and Brössel 2018; Marsili and Wiegmann 2020), and cross-culturally and -linguistically (Turri and Park 2018), no previous research has accounted for the variability due to stimulus selection and used that information when estimating the effect of truth-value on assertability judgments. Thus the possibility remains that previously observed effects of truth-value are stimuli-specific and might not broadly generalize.

This possibility seems unlikely given the variety of replications on record and the convergent evidence from biology, naturalistic observation, cross-cultural studies, historical linguistics, and human development, but it is still worth investigating directly. To make progress on this front, I studied a range of different scenarios involving what is widely taken to be *the strongest challenge* to factive accounts. More specifically, I focused on scenarios involving the assertion of "unlucky falsehoods," or propositions which turn out to be false despite the agent's evidence and outside of his awareness.

Second, researchers have cautioned against assuming that there is a unique norm of assertion or focusing exclusively on one normative term (e.g., Turri 2013: 281, 2014a, 2016b, 2017c). Even though most research has focused on the standard associated with what *should* be asserted, some findings pertain to *criticism* or *blame*, or whether an assertion is *incorrect*. This research provides evidence that people distinguish assertions that should not be made from blameworthy assertions (e.g., Turri 2013), just as people reliably distinguish between someone failing a moral obligation and being blameworthy for failing it (Buckwalter and Turri 2015; Turri 2017d; Henne et al. 2016), and between someone forming a belief that they shouldn't form and being blameworthy for forming it (Turri 2015b).

Recently researchers have tested other vocabulary, including what is "appropriate," "permissible," or "justified" (Kneer 2018; Reuter and Brössel 2018). But even though *blame* was already known to differ from *should*, this research didn't collect judgments about blame for comparison. So it can't tell us whether the judgments studied express a standard different from *blame*. Also, some of this research fails to replicate. For example, researchers claimed to find that assertion has a truth-insensitive standard of *justification* determined by the speaker's evidence, rather than objective facts (Reuter and Brössel 2018). But a preregistered experiment directly tested this claim and falsified it: participants judged that a false assertion is not justified, while they judged that the (otherwise objectively similar) true assertion is justified (Turri 2020a: experiment 2).

Third, as is often the case in human social cognition, perspective-taking can play an important role in how people evaluate assertions. Perspective-taking is the act of considering or describing a situation from another's perspective, which might differ from one's own and be objectively mistaken.

Different probes can promote or inhibit perspective-taking. For example, research on knowledge attributions has found that people are more likely to attribute knowledge when the answer options are "does know"/"doesn't know" (*plain options*) than when the options are "actually knows"/"only thinks he knows" (*contrast options*)

(Cullen 2010; Buckwalter 2014; Turri 2014b). Indeed, when plain options are used, people are surprisingly willing to attribute *false knowledge*—that is to agents who have false beliefs—whereas the contrast options inhibit the attribution of false knowledge. Contrast options don't force participants to choose between responding accurately and acknowledging the agent's perspective. Instead they enable participants to distinguish appearance from reality while minimizing the risk of appearing oblivious or insensitive. Relatedly, recent work on lie attributions found that when an agent makes a deceptively motivated statement that, despite his evidence, turns out to be true, people classify it as a lie when the options are "he lied"/"he didn't lie," but they deny that it is a lie when the options are "he actually lied"/"he only thinks he lied" (Turri and Turri 2015, 2018).

Similarly, work on assertion has found that when people evaluate an assertion supported by misleading evidence, they are more likely to respond affirmatively if the options are "should assert"/"shouldn't assert" than if they are "actually should assert"/"only thinks he should assert" (Turri 2016a, 2018). However, in a surprising oversight, with the exception of *justification*, no research has investigated whether other evaluations of assertion, especially *blame*, are similarly affected by the difference between plain and contrast options. Thus existing evidence does not rule out the possibility that there is only a single standard associated with assertion and the apparent difference between *should* and *blame* was due to perspective-taking. In my view, this is the most serious limitation of earlier research on the topic, and I am disappointed that it took me so long to correct it.

The present research significantly advances our understanding by addressing all three of the weaknesses identified earlier. First, I gathered assertability evaluations across a range of scenarios and treated scenario as a random factor in a linear mixed effects analysis of the data. This allows us to statistically account for the variability in participant response due to stimulus selection when estimating the effects of other independent variables, including truth-value and perspective-taking. Second, I studied a much wider range of normative vocabulary than previous research on norms of assertion, including not only when an assertion should be made or is blameworthy, but also when it would be good, justified, appropriate, permissible, acceptable, reasonable, and right. Third, I varied whether participants recorded judgments using plain or contrast response options for a wide range of evaluations.

6.2 General Methods

All manipulations, measures, and exclusion criteria are reported. All participants were adult residents of the United States. I recruited and tested people using an online platform of Amazon Mechanical Turk (https://www.mturk.com), TurkPrime (Litman, Robinson, and Abberbock 2017), and Qualtrics (https://www.qualtrics.com). Participants completed a brief demographic questionnaire after testing. I used R 3.5.2 for all analyses (R Core Team 2018). All stimuli and data are available through an Open Science Foundation project (https://osf.io/btqz3/?view_only=65db0d6de3cc476 68669241d6ae26752). All studies were preregistered.

6.3 Experiment 1

6.3.1 Method

Following previous research on this topic (Turri 2018), I decided in advance to recruit 50 participants per condition, plus some extra as a precaution against attrition (see preregistration).

6.3.1.1 *Participants*

Out of 1,025 participants recruited, 43 (4%) failed a comprehension question and were excluded from further analysis (preregistered exclusion), yielding a final sample of 982. Their mean age was 38.34 years (range = 18–77, sd = 12.45), 50 percent (495 of 982) were female, and 94 percent reported native competence in English.

6.3.1.2 *Materials and Procedure*

Participants were randomly assigned to one of twenty conditions in a 2 (Truth-value: false, true) × 2 (Option: plain, contrast) × 5 (Scenario: various) experimental design. Participants first read a brief scenario (one example is described as follows) about an agent who is asked a question. Then they responded to a comprehension question and three test statements (within-subjects): whether an assertion should be made, is justified, and is appropriate. The truth-value factor manipulated whether the relevant proposition was false or true. The option factor manipulated the answer options for the test items. The scenario factor was not of independent theoretical interest and was included to support generalization of the results beyond the specific stimuli studied here (Clark 1973; Baayen, Davidson, and Bates 2008; Judd, Westfall, and Kenny 2012). The order of the three test statements was randomized; the comprehension check always appeared first; the order of all response options was randomized.

All stimuli used in this study are available through an Open Science Foundation project (linked earlier). To give readers a sense of the materials, I include one scenario (adapted from Kneer 2018) and the dependent measures. The truth-value manipulation is included in brackets in the text. Both pairs of response options are also included. The plain option appears first, followed by the contrast option. Participants in plain conditions saw the plain options for each test item, whereas participants in contrast conditions saw the contrast options for each test item. (In other words, the type of response option, plain or contrast, was not manipulated within-subjects.)

> June is at the train station talking to her friend Joe on the phone. At some stage, Joe asks her what time it is, because he wants to go for a run before it gets dark. June looks at the platform clock, which says that it's 5:30. So she concludes that it's 5:30. June is unaware that a janitor recently [broke / cleaned] the clock. The actual time is [4:18 / 5:30].
>
> What time is it where June is at? [4:18 / 5:30] (comprehension)

June _____ tell Joe that it is 5:30. (should)
- should not / should
- only thinks she should / actually should

June _____ in telling Joe that it is 5:30. (justified)
- is not justified / is justified
- only thinks she is justified / actually is justified

It _____ for June to tell Joe that it is 5:30. (appropriate)
- is not appropriate / is appropriate
- only seems appropriate / actually is appropriate

6.3.1.3 Coding

I interpreted the options appearing on the right side of all the pairs listed earlier as *attributions* (coded as 1), whereas I interpreted the options appearing on the left side as *denials* (coded as 0). Accordingly, a response of "should," "actually should," "is justified," "actually is justified," "is appropriate," or "actually is appropriate" was counted as an attribution, whereas all other responses were counted as a denial.

6.3.1.4 Data Analysis

The principal research questions are whether people will distinguish between different normative statuses when evaluating assertions and whether truth-value and answer options affect those evaluations. To answer these questions, I analyzed participant responses using a generalized linear mixed effects model with fixed effects of truth-value (false, true), option (plain, contrast), judgment (within-subjects: justified, should, appropriate), and participant age and sex, and random intercepts for scenario and participant nested within scenario. I followed this up with proportion tests on attribution rates in the relevant conditions.

6.4 Results

There were main effects of truth-value, option, and judgment, and an interaction of truth-value and option (see Figure 6.1 and the appendix of tables, accessible from the Open Science Foundation project for this research). The attribution rate was higher in true conditions (92.6%) than in false conditions (51.1%). It was higher in plain conditions (83.2%) than in contrast conditions (61.6%). And it was higher for "justified" (76.3%) than for "should" (69.5%). When switching from plain to contrast options, the drop in attribution was larger in false conditions (a 50.95% relative reduction from 68.3% to 33.5%) than in true conditions (a 10.05% relative reduction from 97.5% to 87.7%). There was an unpredicted interaction between truth-value and judgment, which occurred because the switch from false to true boosted attribution for "should" more than "justified." There was also an unpredicted three way interaction between truth-value, option, and judgment, which occurred because the interaction between truth-value and option was smaller for "appropriate" than for "justified." In

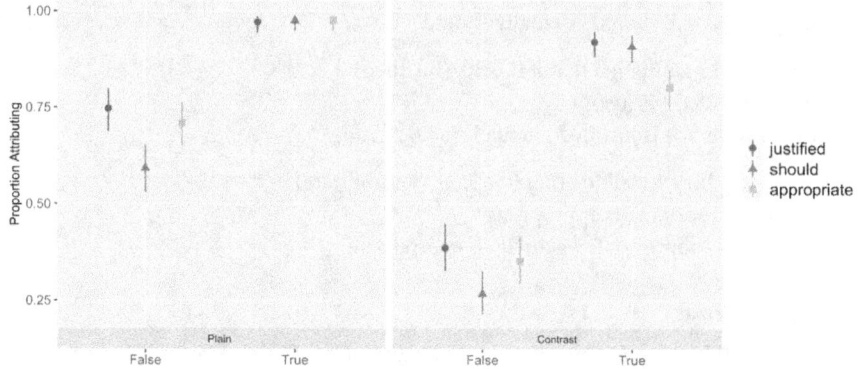

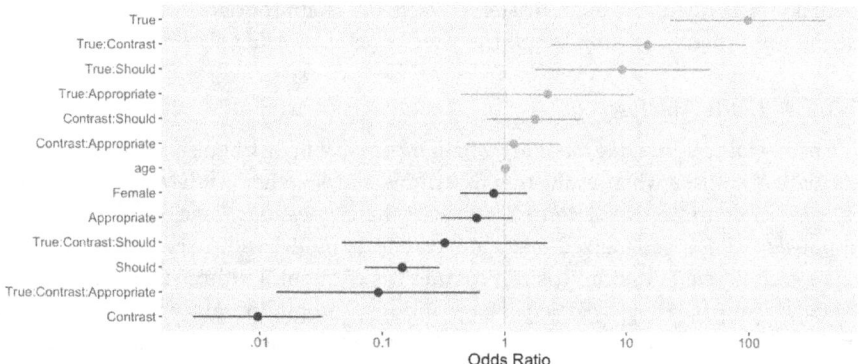

Figure 6.1 Experiment 1. (a) Rates of attribution for three judgments (within-subjects: justified, should, appropriate) across four conditions (between-subjects): truth-value (false, true) x option (plain, contrast). (b) Visualization of generalized linear mixed model predicting attribution, showing odds ratios. Error bars show 95 percent confidence intervals. © John Turri.

particular, when switching from plain to contrast options, the switch from false to true boosted attribution for "appropriate" slightly less (see Figure 6.1).

Follow-up McNemar's tests revealed that attribution did not differ between "should" and "appropriate" (71.6%), χ^2 (1) = 3.05, p = .081. Although the difference between "appropriate" and "justified" did not reach significance in the full model, the attribution rate for "appropriate" was significantly lower in a direct comparison, $\chi^2(1)$ = 15.82, $p < .001$, h = −0.11. For each judgment in all four conditions created by crossing truth-value and option, the attribution rate differed significantly from chance, $ps < .005$, test proportion = .5. In each case, all three judgments differed from chance in the same direction. That is, either they were all above chance, or they were all below chance.

6.5 Discussion

This experiment studied the relationship among different normative vocabulary for evaluating assertion, the truth-value of an assertion, and the type of response options used to probe for evaluations. Participants distinguished between what an agent is *justified* in asserting, on the one hand, and whether the assertion *should* be made or is *appropriate*, on the other hand. The objective truth-value of an assertion affected all three evaluations, with true assertions much more likely to be positively evaluated. Nevertheless, "should" evaluations were more strongly affected by truth-value than "justification" evaluations. The answer options also affected all three evaluations, with options that distinguished appearance from reality ("contrast" options) making a positive evaluation less likely compared to options that did not ("plain" options). There was also an interaction whereby the effect of response options depended on the assertion's truth-value. When an assertion was false, the difference between plain and contrast options was large, reversing the central tendency for all three evaluations from attribution of positive status (for plain options) to denial (for contrast options). By contrast, when the proposition was true, the difference between plain and contrast options was much smaller, with the central tendency being attribution for both options for all three evaluations.

This experiment is limited in at least two ways. First, the fact that participants made several evaluations on the same screen could have influenced responses. Participants might have felt pressure to answer them all similarly. For instance, after judging that the agent should not make an assertion, participants might have been less likely to answer that the assertion is justified. Or participants might have felt pressure to answer them differently. For instance, when asked both whether an assertion should be made and whether it is justified, participants might infer that they are expected to distinguish between the two statuses, even if they would not naturally do this when making such judgments. Second, the comprehension question about truth-value appeared on the same page as the evaluations, which might have caused participants to give truth greater weight than they otherwise would have.

The next experiment avoids both of those limitations by having participants record only a single evaluation on the first screen, followed by a comprehension question on a second screen. The next experiment also examines a wider range of normative vocabulary for evaluating assertions. However, in order to keep the experiment of manageable size, it only studies a single scenario, which is a limitation not shared by Experiment 1.

6.6 Experiment 2

6.6.1 Method

6.6.1.1 Participants

Out of 1,622 participants recruited, 96 (6%) failed a comprehension question and were excluded from further analysis (preregistered exclusion), yielding a final sample of

1,526. Their mean age was 38.11 years (range = 6–82, sd = 12.17), 56 percent (848 of 1,526) were female, and 95 percent reported native competence in English.

6.6.1.2 Materials and Procedure

Participants were randomly assigned to one of thirty-two conditions in a 2 (Truth-value: false, true) × 2 (Option: plain, contrast) × 8 (Judgment: should, good, justified, permissible, right, acceptable, reasonable, blameless) between-subjects design. Participants first read a brief scenario about an agent who is asked a question, then responded to a test statement on the same screen, then went to a new screen and answered a comprehension question from memory.

The truth-value and option factors were the same as in Experiment 1: the truth-value factor manipulated whether the relevant proposition was false or true, and the option factor manipulated the answer options for the test items. The judgment factor manipulated which evaluation of the assertion participants made.

In order to keep the experiment of manageable size, I tested only a single scenario, the clock scenario from Experiment 1, rather than crossing the other factors with a scenario manipulation. (A fully crossed design of that sort would have one hundred sixty conditions.) Following are the eight different evaluations, followed first by the pair of plain options, then by the pair of contrast options. Options were always rotated randomly. The comprehension question was the same as in Experiment 1.

June _____ tell Joe that it is 5:30. (should)
- should not / should
- only thinks she should / actually should

It _____ for June to tell Joe that it is 5:30. (good)
- is not good / is good
- only seems good / actually is good

June _____ in telling Joe that it is 5:30. (justified)
- is not justified / is justified
- only thinks she is justified / actually is justified

It _____ for June to tell Joe that it is 5:30. (permissible)
- is not permissible / is permissible
- only seems permissible / actually is permissible

June _____ to tell Joe that it is 5:30. (right)
- does not have a right / does have a right
- only thinks she has a right / actually does have a right

It _____ for June to tell Joe that it is 5:30. (acceptable)
- is not acceptable / is acceptable
- only seems acceptable / actually is acceptable

It _____ for June to tell Joe that it is 5:30. (reasonable)
- is not reasonable / is reasonable
- only seems reasonable / actually is reasonable

June _____ for telling Joe that it is 5:30. (blameless)
- is not blameless / is blameless
- only seems blameless / actually is blameless

6.6.1.3 Coding

Just as in Experiment 1, I interpreted the options appearing on the right side of all the pairs listed earlier as *attributions* (coded as 1), whereas I interpreted the options appearing on the left side as *denials* (coded as 0).

6.6.1.4 Data Analysis

The principal research questions are whether people will distinguish between different normative statuses when evaluating assertions and whether truth-value and answer options affect those evaluations. To answer these questions, I analyzed participant responses using a generalized linear model with truth-value, option, judgment, and participant age and sex as predictors. I followed this up with simpler generalized linear models for each judgment separately with truth-value and option as predictors.

6.7 Results

In one of the conditions (true-plain-appropriate), 100 percent of participants attributed the status, resulting in complete separation when fitting the model. To address this, I fit the model using a penalized likelihood method (Firth 1993; Heinze 2006). The model revealed main effects of truth-value, option, and judgment, and several interactions (see the appendix of tables, accessible from the Open Science Foundation project for this research).

Replicating findings from Experiment 1, attribution was higher when the proposition was true and when using plain options. Unlike in Experiment 1, the interaction between truth-value and option was not significant, although the interpretation of this is complicated by the fact that truth-value and option entered into interactions with specific judgments. In particular, when compared to "should," the switch from false to true mattered less for "permissible" and "blameless." The switch from plain to contrast options depressed attribution for "blameless" significantly less than for "should." When compared to "should," overall attribution was significantly higher for all judgments except for "good," which did not differ significantly. Participant age had a small, unpredicted effect whereby older participants were more likely to attribute positive status. Each year increased the odds of a positive attribution by a factor of 1.01.

In order to better understand the effect of truth-value and option on the eight judgments, I followed up with a generalized linear model for each judgment separately with truth-value and option as predictors (see Figure 6.2). For all judgments, the switch from false to true numerically increased the odds of an attribution, although this increase reached statistical significance only for "should," "good," "right," and "acceptable." For all judgments except "blameless," the switch from plain to contrast options decreased

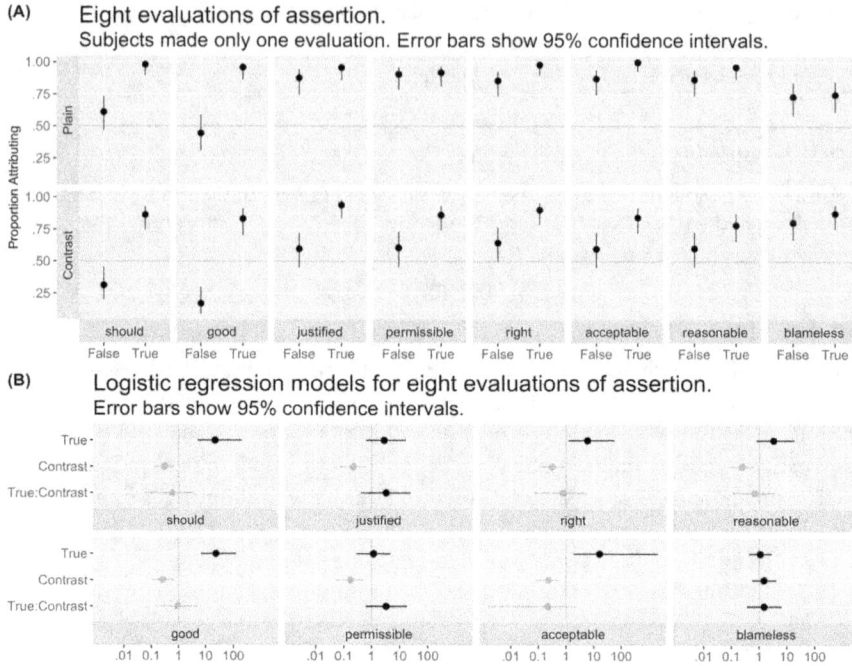

Figure 6.2 Experiment 2. (a) Rates of attribution for eight evaluations of assertion across four conditions: truth-value (false, true) x option (plain, contrast). (b) Visualization of generalized linear models predicting each of the evaluations, showing odds ratios. Error bars show 95 percent confidence intervals. © John Turri.

the odds of an attribution, and this decrease reached statistical significance in each case. Blamelessness was the only judgment that was not significantly affected by truth-value, option, or both. Attributions of blamelessness remained high in all four conditions.

6.8 Discussion

This experiment studied the effect of truth-value and response options on eight evaluations of assertion that involved different normative vocabulary: "should," "good," "justified," "permissible," "right," "acceptable," "reasonable," and "blameless." Replicating findings from Experiment 1, overall, attributions were higher when the assertion was true rather than false, and attributions were lower when response options provided an appearance/reality distinction. There were also a number of interactions between truth-value, response options, and type of judgment. Three interesting observations emerge from the findings. First, "should" and "good" appear very similar, both in their attribution rates and their sensitivity to truth-value and response options. Second, "justified," "right," "reasonable," "acceptable," and "permissible" resemble one another in their attribution rates and sensitivity to the independent variables. Third, blamelessness was unique in remaining uniformly high in all four conditions and being unaffected by either independent variable.

Although blamelessness was consistently high in all four conditions, some might be surprised that it wasn't even higher. Approximately 75 percent to 85 percent of participants in all conditions judged that the speaker was blameless. But why would 15 percent to 25 percent of people think that she was to blame? This can seem especially puzzling in the case where she provides a relevant, true answer to a question directly posed to her.

One possibility is that some people interpreted the question comparatively and causally, rather than normatively, along the following lines. (A causal reading of "blame" can be natural, as when one blames a patch of ice for a fall.) *Someone* is responsible for providing the information, and *who else* could it possibly be? So yes, she's to blame in the sense of clearly being the responsible party. This explanation has the virtue of applying equally to all four conditions, thereby potentially explaining not only why some people would have answered this way, but also why they would do so at roughly equal rates in all conditions.

6.9 Analysis of Comprehension Questions

While reviewing the data from Experiment 2, a couple hypotheses occurred to me. On the one hand, scrolling through the sorted datafile, it seemed like more participants were failing the comprehension question in false conditions. On the other hand, I reasoned that participants might have been more likely to fail the comprehension question in Experiment 2 than in Experiment 1 because of procedural differences. In Experiment 1, the comprehension question was answered on the same screen as the other judgments and with the scenario visible on the screen. In Experiment 2, by contrast, the comprehension question was answered from memory, by itself, on a separate screen.

To begin assessing these hypotheses, I conducted some exploratory analyses. I first constructed a generalized linear model for each experiment separately to predict comprehension (i.e., correctly answering the comprehension question). In each case, the model included truth-value, option, and participant age and sex as predictors. The model for Experiment 2 also included judgment type as a predictor. In each case, the only significant predictor was truth-value. So I combined the data from the two experiments and constructed a generalized linear model to predict comprehension. The model included truth-value (true, false) and experiment (1, 2) as predictors. This model cohered with both hypotheses that motivated it. There was an effect of experiment whereby participants were more likely to fail the comprehension question in Experiment 2. This was qualified by an interaction whereby being assigned to a true condition boosted the odds of comprehension more in Experiment 2.

In Experiment 1, 93.5 percent of participants passed in false conditions and 98.1 percent passed in true conditions. In Experiment 2, 89.4 percent of participants passed in false conditions and 98.8 percent passed in true conditions.

These analyses must be treated as exploratory because they occurred after inspecting the data. Bearing that in mind, they suggest that comprehension failure could be additional evidence that perspective-taking affects how participants evaluate false assertions based on misleading evidence. For example, in the debriefing portion of a prior study that examined people's judgments about whether an assertion counted as a lie, one participant told researchers, "Well, I could have answered some of those stories the other way. I wasn't sure whether to answer in terms of what really happened, or what Chris [the character in the story] believed" (Strichartz and Burton 1990; see also Turri and Turri 2018). In the present studies, when the speaker presumably blamelessly formed a false opinion about the subject matter at hand, that might have encouraged some participants to answer in terms of what the speaker believed, rather than what really happened. Yet this tendency might have been reduced when a comprehension question (about what really happened) appeared on the same page. Nevertheless, given how infrequent, in absolute terms, comprehension failure was, it's possible that appreciable evidence of such dynamics will be detected only by a very highly powered study, such as the ones reported here.

6.10 Reanalysis of Clustered Judgments

In the Discussion of Experiment 2, I noted that the judgments seemed to fall into three clusters. For convenience, I will give the clusters the following labels (whose rationale is discussed in the General Discussion):

1. Blame: "blameless"
2. Mixed: "justified," "right," "reasonable," "acceptable," and "permissible"
3. Conformity: "should" and "good"

To explore this clustering hypothesis, I conducted some exploratory analyses. I first constructed a generalized linear model predicting assertability evaluations from the data in the mixed and conformity clusters, respectively. Each model contained as predictors truth-value, option, judgment, participant sex, and participant age. Neither model found an effect of judgment or any interaction involving judgment. I then constructed a generalized linear model predicting assertability judgments using the entire dataset. The model was specified in the exact same way, except that in place of judgment (an eight-level independent variable) I substituted the clustering variable (a three-level calculated variable) with blame as the reference cluster. The purpose of this analysis was to explore whether blame attributions differed from the other clusters and whether there were any interactions with truth-value and option (Figure 6.3).

Attribution was lower in the conformity cluster than for blame. This was qualified by two interactions: the switch from false to true boosted attribution in the conformity cluster more than for blame, and the switch from plain to contrast options depressed attribution more in the conformity cluster than for blame. Attribution was higher in the mixed cluster than for blame. This also was qualified by two interactions: the switch

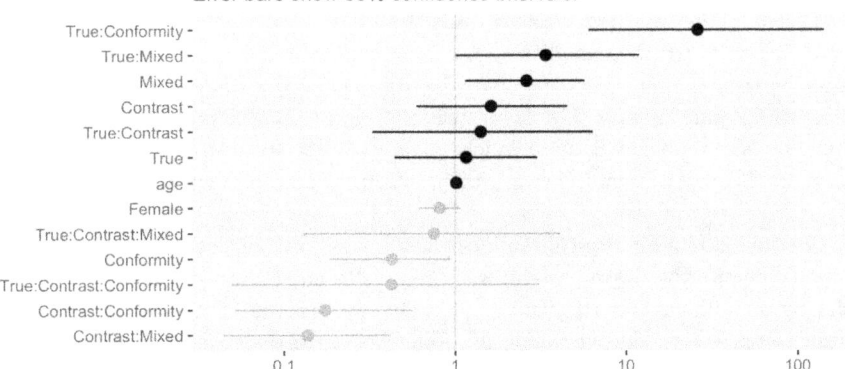

Figure 6.3 Experiment 2. Visualization of a generalized linear model predicting evaluations of assertion when clustering judgments into three groups (blame, mixed, and conformity). Error bars show 95 percent confidence intervals. © John Turri.

from false to true boosted attribution in the mixed cluster more than for blame, and the switch from plain to contrast options depressed attribution more in the mixed cluster than for blame. This pattern of results coheres with the impression gleaned from inspecting the visualization of attribution rates and odds ratios for Experiment 2. I will return to the clustering hypothesis in the General Discussion.

6.11 General Discussion

Results from two large experiments advanced our understanding of the social practice of assertion. Each study found that evaluations of assertion are affected by truth-value, with positive evaluations significantly more likely for true assertions. Each study also found that evaluations of assertion are affected by the answer options, with positive evaluations significantly less likely for options that inhibit perspective-taking by encoding an appearance/reality distinction. And these two factors can interact to affect evaluations of assertion, with the effect of truth-value being significantly larger when the answer options inhibit perspective-taking.

People distinguish between different normative vocabulary when evaluating assertions, and the two factors mentioned earlier—truth-value and answer options—do not affect all evaluations similarly. This replicates previous findings from less ambitious studies that provided evidence that what *should* be asserted differs from what is *blamelessly* asserted (e.g., Turri 2013), but the present studies go much further. For example, judgments about whether an assertion *should* be made or is *good* can differ from judgments about whether an assertion is *justified, permissible, acceptable, reasonable*, or within a speaker's *rights*. Judgments involving *should* and *good* appear to be more sensitive to truth-value than the other judgments. And *blamelessness* differed from all the other judgments tested: it was the only one insensitive to truth-value and unaffected by the appearance/reality distinction.

The effect of truth-value observed in these studies was very large, recording odds ratios between 20 and 100, but one might suspect that this *underestimates* the actual effect truth-value tends to have on evaluations. Here I focused on scenarios involving "unlucky falsehoods," which are widely taken to be the strongest challenge to factive accounts. If there is anything to critics' intuitions, then this is where truth-value will make its poorest showing.

The point about focusing on "unlucky falsehoods" has a flip side: the large observed effect of perspective-taking might *overestimate* its actual effect on these evaluations. Making an unlucky assertion is like accidentally breaking a rule. You're trying to measure up to the relevant standards. Your heart is in the right place. You aren't to blame. It's a blameless transgression.

Blameless transgressions can trigger *excuse validation* (Turri 2013, 2019; Turri and Blouw 2015). When participants know that an agent reasonably but falsely believes she is following the rules, roughly half of people sacrifice accuracy in their answers in order to avoid unfairness. For instance, even when everyone agrees that Shawn is driving 60 miles per hour and that the speed limit is 55 miles per hour, roughly half of people might still deny that Shawn is breaking the speed limit, if he is trusting a faulty speedometer in a car that was just serviced. The effect is so powerful that it can even lead people to conspicuously contradict themselves: many judge *both* that Shawn is not breaking the speed limit *and* that he is unintentionally breaking the speed limit!

Excuse validation has been observed only when people are given specific exculpatory information about how things seem from the agent's perspective—in particular, that the agent's evidence makes it seem like she is following the rules. Excuse validation wasn't observed to occur merely because the agent believes, sincerely believes, or even is tricked into believing that she is following the rules (Turri and Blouw 2015: experiment 3). This raises the following suspicion about the present studies on assertability judgments: if we sampled an even wider range of cases—instead of restricting our sample to unlucky falsehoods apt to trigger excuse validation—then the effect of perspective-taking would diminish.

Inspecting the visualizations of attribution rates and odds ratios from the two experiments, one interpretation is that the judgments studied here cluster into three groups (called "the clustering hypothesis" earlier). First, "should" and "good" appear very similar, both in their attribution rates and their sensitivity to truth-value and response options (Experiment 2). "Appropriate" could also fall into this group (Experiment 1). Second, "justified," "right," "reasonable," "acceptable," and "permissible" resemble one another in their attribution rates and sensitivity to the independent variables (Experiment 2). Third, blamelessness is unique in remaining uniformly high and unaffected by manipulations of truth-value or response options (Experiment 2).

Based on those observations, I propose the following theory of evaluations of assertability. The theory has two parts.

First, there are two basic norms of assertion. On the one hand, an assertion can objectively conform to the rules of our social information-sharing practice. These rules enjoin, prescribe, or recommend assertions to express (known) truths. False assertions don't meet this standard. (Note: the precise quality and strength of the factive norm are open questions to be settled by further investigation; see Turri 2014a, 2016b, and 2017c for discussion of these and other theoretical parameters.) On the other hand, an assertion can be blameless. Just like actions of other types, assertions can be blameless even when they should not occur. This implies that some false assertions will be counted as blameless.

Second, evaluations of assertion can be more or less focused on conformity or blamelessness. This could happen for multiple reasons. On the one hand, answer options enabling participants to comfortably distinguish appearance from reality will facilitate judgments about conformance to the rules. By contrast, answer options preventing participants from comfortably doing so can inhibit judgments about conformity, especially when an agent blamelessly fails to conform. On the other hand, different normative vocabulary is more or less likely to focus attention on conformity or blame. "Blame," its cognates, and nearby terms such as "criticism" are obviously most apt for evaluations of blame. "Should," "good," and perhaps also "appropriate" are more apt for evaluations of conformity. The other terminology—"justified," "acceptable," "permissible," "reasonable," and "rights"—falls somewhere in between, capable of being associated with either status but with greater variability and a tendency to align more with blamelessness.

Put simply, according to this theory, (i) there is *what should be asserted* and *what is blamelessly asserted*, and (ii) different normative vocabulary is more or less apt for expressing those two different norms.

In the Introduction, I discussed previous evidence that assertion has a factive rule for what should be asserted (*assertions should express knowledge*); the present findings add to that already-conclusive case. And I reviewed the explanation for why assertion has that rule: the point of assertion is to transmit knowledge.

Why would evaluations of assertion be concerned with blame? I propose that this reflects a general concern for fairness in human affairs. Human prosociality is constituted by a suite of psychological traits, including a tendency to respect order and authority, follow rules, and police norms by punishing rule-breakers (Tomasello and Vaish 2013; Fehr and Fischbacher 2004; McAuliffe, Jordan, and Warneken 2015; Cushman 2015). It is also constituted by our ability and willingness to consider other people's perspectives, take extenuating circumstances into account, and excuse transgressions when appropriate (Tomasello 2008; Martin and Cushman 2016; Tetlock, Self, and Singh 2010; Schroeder and Linder 1976; Turri and Blouw 2015).

As a matter of justice, we feel that it is important to hold people responsible for breaking rules. But as a matter of fairness, we feel that not all rule-breaking is created equal. Mitigating circumstances and the agent's capabilities and state of mind can prompt forgiveness (e.g., Cushman 2008; Buckwalter and Turri 2015; for a review, see Malle, Guglielmo, and Monroe 2014). Reflecting these intuitions, the legal system also gives these factors weight when determining guilt and punishment (Barnett, Brodsky, and Davis 2004; Shen et al. 2011; MacLeod 2016), and someone who habitually ignored them could be viewed as insensitive or even cruel. On this approach, the salience of blamelessness in evaluating assertions is a specific example of the human tendency to be sensitive to exculpatory information in social evaluations (Turri 2017a).

Overall, then, the present discussion offers an explanation for why the human practice of assertion has a factive rule, why evaluations of assertion are sensitive to truth-value and answer options conveying an appearance/reality distinction, and why blamelessness is a salient concern when making such evaluations.

Additionally, it offers an explanation for the present findings regarding the effect of different normative vocabulary. Judgments featuring "should" and "good" seem more apt for expressing judgments of conformity. Trivially, judgments about "blame" are especially apt for expressing evaluations pertaining to blame. The remainder of the vocabulary—"justified," "permissible," "right," "reasonable," and "acceptable"—falls somewhere in between, exhibiting some of the sensitivities of "should" and "good," but also resembling blamelessness in some respects. To the extent that it is not entirely clear what status is under consideration, people must make a decision about whether the evaluation pertains to conformity or blame. It seems reasonable that people would tend to err on the side of caution and treat it as an evaluation of blame, especially when they are asked to evaluate a blameless transgression. This tendency would produce a pattern that looked more like explicit judgments about "blame" than about "should," despite bearing some similarities to both.

Interestingly, the first experimental paper on norms of assertion found a similar pattern (Turri 2013). It found strong evidence of a factive norm for what should be asserted, with the vast majority judging that a false assertion should not be made; it found strong evidence of a non-factive norm for blamelessness, with the vast majority judging that the same false assertion doesn't merit criticism; and it found that about half of participants agreed that the false assertion was "incorrect."

If this is all on the right track, then existing evidence cannot be explained by a theory proposing a single norm of assertion. But it can be explained by the hypothesis that our social practice of assertion has two norms. And no third norm is needed to explain any finding up to this point.

I want to explicitly note that this dual-norm hypothesis pertains to what is expected of *speakers*. Other norms might encapsulate expectations for *questioners* and *auditors*. This is fertile ground for future research.

Of course, even if no third (or fourth, etc.) norm is strictly necessary to explain the findings up to this point, such explanations can still be offered and, in the long run, might even be preferable. Future research could profitably explore this possibility.

Even if the dual-norm hypothesis turns out to be incorrect in some respects, the present findings support several conclusions. First, assertion has at least two norms, one concerned with truth and the other with blame. In order to make the case that a third status is involved, future research must show that it is distinct from both of them. This should be accompanied by placing the findings in a broader context of scientific understanding of communication systems, social cognition, and norm psychology. Indeed, that context could be essential in making the case for a third status because, as explained earlier, a "mixed" pattern of sensitivities might just reflect a mix of the other two judgments. It is not automatically evidence of a third status, especially when excuse validation is potentially playing a role. But by casting a wider net in our theorizing about assertion, we might catch hold of a reason why some particular "mixed" pattern is best interpreted as evidence of a third status.

Second, the effect of truth-value on evaluations of assertion is large and robust across stimuli, terminology, and questioning procedures. We now have conclusive evidence that it is not an artifact of testing a specific scenario, probing with a specific normative term (e.g., "should"), or questioning procedures. Nevertheless, this does not imply that the effect, or our ability to detect it, is *unlimited*. To undermine the interpretation of prior findings as evidence of a factive norm, future research must do more than obtain different results conditional on some combination of changes to stimuli, terminology, and procedures. Instead, it will also come to terms with the entire range of evidence from multiple disciplines, social observation, and dozens of experimental studies conducted using diverse protocols. And it will do so in relation to plausible theories of factive norms informed by current evidence, not implausible or outdated theories from decades past.

Third, the motivation to perspective-take or excuse blameless failure can interfere with evaluations of assertability. If forced to choose between these motivations and responding accurately on a categorization task, many participants choose the former. Of all the evaluations studied here, only blame was unaffected by this phenomenon. Accordingly, future research cannot responsibly ignore the importance of response options that inhibit task-substitution. At a minimum, future research should show that a finding of interest replicates with response options distinguishing appearance from reality.

Finally, if there is to be any hope for sustained, cumulative, shared progress in this area, future research should not reimport false, counterproductive, or entirely speculative assumptions from armchair philosophical writings on assertion.

One question that deserves further attention is whether the practice of assertion has not only multiple *norms*, but also multiple *points* or *purposes*. Up until now, I have claimed that "the point" of assertion is to transmit knowledge. But that is surely too ambitious in light of existing evidence. Instead, I should say that transmitting knowledge is *a principal point* of the practice, allowing for multiple aims, just as there are multiple norms.

In closing, I urge critics aiming to make a contribution to ***stop taking shortcuts***. Ignoring evidence, attacking strawmen, peddling sloppy experiments, and angling for a return to dialectical stalemates of old—that way lies the intellectual graveyard of fabulists and petty pretenders. It just wastes people's time and distorts the research record. Yes, there is a lot of evidence to sort through. It would be so much more convenient if it could all be boiled down to a data point or two. Yes, the leading theory in this area is formidable in its multidisciplinary grounding, refinement, evidential support, and explanatory power. It would be so much easier to confront a slick slogan. And yes, it is unusual nowadays for a philosophical research program to so quickly and decisively cut through the tangles of disputation and speculation that, to our detriment, we are conditioned to expect. It would be so much simpler to just trade intuitions and distinctions and congratulate ourselves on making "progress" in better understanding one another's assumptions. A meeting of the minds is hardly anything to write home about.

There is a lot of work left to do and, other things being equal, the more the merrier. But if you take shortcuts and get called out, remember: you were given notice.

Acknowledgments

For helpful feedback and discussion, I thank Wesley Buckwalter, Ori Friedman, Paul Henne, Markus Kneer, Samuel Murray, Angelo Turri, and Sarah Turri. This research was supported by the Canada Research Chairs program and the Social Sciences and Humanities Research Council of Canada.

References

Baayen, R. H., D. J. Davidson, and D. M. Bates (2008), "Mixed-Effects Modeling with Crossed Random Effects for Subjects and Items," *Journal of Memory and Language*, 59 (4): 390–412.

Barnett, Michelle E., Stanley L. Brodsky, and Cali Manning Davis (2004), "When Mitigation Evidence Makes a Difference: Effects of Psychological Mitigating Evidence on Sentencing Decisions in Capital Trials," *Behavioral Sciences & the Law*, 22 (6): 751–70.

Beecher, M. D., S. E. Campbell, J. M. Burt, C. E. Hill, and J. C. Nordby (2000), "Song-Type Matching between Neighbouring Song Sparrows," *Animal Behaviour*, 59 (1): 21–7. https://doi.org/10.1006/anbe.1999.1276.

Bradbury, Jack W. and Sandra L. Vehrencamp (2011), *Principles of Animal Communication*, 2nd edn, Sunderland, MA: Sinauer Associates.

Buckwalter, Wesley (2014), "Factive Verbs and Protagonist Projection," *Episteme*, 11 (4): 391–409.

Buckwalter, Wesley and John Turri (2015), "Inability and Obligation in Moral Judgment," *PLOS ONE*, 10 (8): e0136589.

Clark, Herbert H. (1973), "The Language-as-Fixed-Effect Fallacy: A Critique of Language Statistics in Psychological Research," *Journal of Verbal Learning and Verbal Behavior*, 12 (4): 335–59.

Cullen, Simon (2010), "Survey-Driven Romanticism," *Review of Philosophy and Psychology*, 1 (2): 275–96.

Cushman, Fiery (2008), "Crime and Punishment: Distinguishing the Roles of Causal and Intentional Analyses in Moral Judgment," *Cognition*, 108 (2): 353–80.

Cushman, Fiery (2015), "Punishment in Humans: From Intuitions to Institutions," *Philosophy Compass*, 10 (2): 117–33.

Fehr, E. and U. Fischbacher (2004), "Social Norms and Human Cooperation," *Trends in Cognitive Sciences*, 8 (4): 185–90.

Firth, David (1993), "Bias Reduction of Maximum Likelihood Estimates," *Biometrika*, 80 (1): 27–38.

Heinze, Georg (2006), "A Comparative Investigation of Methods for Logistic Regression with Separated or Nearly Separated Data," *Statistics in Medicine*, 25 (24): 4216–26.

Henne, Paul, Vladimir Chituc, Felipe De Brigard, and Walter Sinnott-Armstrong (2016), "An Empirical Refutation of 'Ought' Implies 'Can,'" *Analysis*, 76 (3): 283–90.

Judd, Charles M., Jacob Westfall, and David A. Kenny (2012), "Treating Stimuli as a Random Factor in Social Psychology: A New and Comprehensive Solution to a Pervasive but Largely Ignored Problem," *Journal of Personality and Social Psychology*, 103 (1): 54–69.

Kneer, Markus (2018), "The Norm of Assertion: Empirical Data," *Cognition*, 177: 165–71.

Litman, Leib, Jonathan Robinson, and Tzvi Abberbock (2017). "TurkPrime.com: A Versatile Crowdsourcing Data Acquisition Platform for the Behavioral Sciences," *Behavioral Research Methods*, 49 (2): 1–10.

MacLeod, James A. (2016), "Belief States in Criminal Law," *Oklahoma Law Review*, 68 (3): 497–554.

Malle, Bertram F., Steve Guglielmo, and Andrew E. Monroe (2014), "A Theory of Blame," *Psychological Inquiry*, 25 (2): 147–86.

Marsili, Neri (2018), "Truth and Assertion: Rules Versus Aims," *Analysis*, 78 (4): 638–48. https://doi.org/10.1093/analys/any008.

Marsili, Neri and Alex Wiegmann (2020), "Should I Say That? An Experimental Investigation of the Norm of Assertion." https://doi.org/10.31234/osf.io/cs45j.

Martin, Justin W. and Fiery Cushman (2016), "Why We Forgive What Can't Be Controlled," *Cognition*, 147 (C): 133–43.

McAuliffe, Katherine, Jillian J. Jordan, and Felix Warneken (2015), "Costly Third-Party Punishment in Young Children," *Cognition*, 134 (C): 1–10.

R Core Team (2018), *R: A Language and Environment for Statistical Computing*, Vienna, Austria: R Foundation for Statistical Computing.

Reuter, Kevin and Peter Brössel (2018), "No Knowledge Required," *Episteme*, 134: 1–19. https://doi.org/10.1017/epi.2018.10.

Schroeder, David A. and Darwyn E. Linder (1976), "Effects of Actor's Causal Role, Outcome Severity, and Knowledge of Prior Accidents upon Attributions of Responsibility," *Journal of Experimental Social Psychology*, 12 (4): 340–56.

Shen, Francix X., Morris B. Hoffman, Owen D. Jones, and Joshua D. Greene (2011), "Sorting Guilty Minds," *New York University Law Review*, 86: 1306–60.

Strichartz, Abigail F. and Roger V. Burton (1990), "Lies and Truth: A Study of the Development of the Concept," *Child Development*, 61 (1): 211–20.

Tetlock, Philip E., William T. Self, and Ramadhar Singh (2010), "The Punitiveness Paradox: When is External Pressure Exculpatory – And When a Signal Just to Spread Blame?," *Journal of Experimental Social Psychology*, 46 (2): 388–95.

Tomasello, Michael (2008), *Origins of Human Communication*, Cambridge, MA: MIT Press.

Tomasello, Michael and Amrisha Vaish (2013), "Origins of Human Cooperation and Morality," *Annual Review of Psychology*, 64 (1): 231–55.

Turri, Angelo and John Turri (2015), "The Truth About Lying," *Cognition*, 138 (C): 161–68.

Turri, Angelo and John Turri (2018), "Lying, Fast and Slow," *Synthese*, 198: 1–19. https://doi.org/10.1007/s11229-018-02062-z.

Turri, John (2013), "The Test of Truth: An Experimental Investigation of the Norm of Assertion," *Cognition*, 129 (2): 279–91.

Turri, John (2014a), "Knowledge and Suberogatory Assertion," *Philosophical Studies*, 167 (3): 557–67. https://doi.org/10.1007/s11098-013-0112-z.

Turri, John (2014b), "The Problem of ESEE Knowledge," *Ergo*, 1 (4): 101–27.

Turri, John (2015a), "Knowledge and the Norm of Assertion: A Simple Test," *Synthese*, 192 (2): 385–92.

Turri, John (2015b), "The Radicalism of Truth-Insensitive Epistemology: Truth's Profound Effect on the Evaluation of Belief," *Philosophy and Phenomenological Research*, 93 (2): 348–67.

Turri, John (2015c), "Assertion and Assurance: Some Empirical Evidence," *Philosophy and Phenomenological Research*, 90 (1): 214–22. https://doi.org/10.1111/phpr.12160.

Turri, John (2016a), "Knowledge and Assertion in 'Gettier' Cases," *Philosophical Psychology*, 29 (5): 759–75.

Turri, John (2016b), *Knowledge and the Norm of Assertion: An Essay in Philosophical Science*, Cambridge: Open Book Publishers.

Turri, John (2016c), "The Point of Assertion is to Transmit Knowledge," *Analysis*, 76 (2): 130–36.

Turri, John (2017a), "Sustaining Rules: A Model and Application," in J. Adam Carter, Emma C. Gordon, and Benjamin Jarvis (eds.), *Knowledge First*, 259–77, New York: Oxford University Press.

Turri, John (2017b), "The Distinctive 'Should' of Assertability," *Philosophical Psychology*, 30 (4): 481–89.

Turri, John (2017c), "Experimental Work on the Norms of Assertion," *Philosophy Compass*, 12 (7): e12425.

Turri, John (2017d), "How 'Ought' Exceeds but Implies 'Can': Description and Encouragement in Moral Judgment," *Cognition*, 168 (November): 267–75.

Turri, John (2018), "Revisiting Norms of Assertion," *Cognition*, 177 (March): 8–11.

Turri, John (2019), "Excuse Validation: A Cross-Cultural Study," *Cognitive Science*, 43 (8): 1–14. https://doi.org/10.1007/s11098-014-0322-z.

Turri, John (2020), "Truth, Fallibility, and Justification: New Studies in the Norms of Assertion," *Synthese*, 1–12. https://doi.org/10.1007/s11229-020-02558-7.

Turri, John and Peter Blouw (2015), "Excuse Validation: A Study in Rule-Breaking," *Philosophical Studies*, 172 (3): 615–34.

Turri, John, Ori Friedman, and Ashley Keefner (2017), "Knowledge Central: A Central Role for Knowledge Attributions in Social Evaluations," *Quarterly Journal of Experimental Psychology*, 70 (3): 504–15.

Turri, John and YeounJun David Park (2018), "Knowledge and Assertion in Korean," *Cognitive Science*, 42 (6): 2060–80.

Williamson, Timothy (2000), *Knowledge and Its Limits*, New York: Oxford University Press.

7

The Distinct Functions of Belief and Desire in Intentional Action Explanation

Joanna Korman[1]

7.1 Rationality in Action: Teleological versus Intentional Stances

Infants and adults alike understand intentional actions by inferring the *goals* of those actions. They infer these goals by appeal to what researchers have dubbed the "teleological stance" or the "principle of rational action": an interpretive stance that relates the action to the goal object or location and constraints of the physical environment (Gergely and Csibra 2003; Gergely et al. 1995). For example, when observing an agent traveling through an open environment without encountering barriers on the path toward a goal, both infants (after goal habituation) and adults expect the agent to take the most efficient path to the goal. In fact, when presented with an action that moves inefficiently through the environment with respect to one physical goal, adults may infer that the goal has more likely changed to a different location—one for which that path is more efficient (Baker, Saxe, and Tennenbaum 2009).

These same researchers (Gergely et al. 1995; Baker, Saxe, and Tenenbaum 2009) have also argued that this teleological stance, and its accompanying principle of rational action, is analogous to another stance held by adults: an *intentional* stance informed by a *rationality assumption* (e.g., Dennett 1987; Davidson 1963). Under this assumption, actions are performed to satisfy the agent's desires in light of the beliefs she holds. Like the teleological stance, the intentional stance relates three components to one another: actions, goals, and constraints on the fulfillment of those goals.

However, there are at least two key distinctions between the two stances. The first distinction concerns a difference in the key inferences made by observers of action in each stance. According to the teleological principle of rational action, the observer of an action infers a goal that itself (even though it is reached after the action) serves as the Aristotelian "final cause" of the action; that is, the observer infers that the agent pursues a particular action along a particular path *so that* she can achieve a particular goal (Lombrozo and Carey 2006). Thus, in a teleological explanation of action, the most important inference is a goal inference (see measures used in Gergely and Csibra 1995; Baker, Saxe, and Tenenbaum 2009; Schachner and Carey 2013). By contrast, an observer who takes a fully intentional stance toward an agent's action also adopts a fully mentalistic "rationality assumption." Beyond the inference of a goal, this assumption relies on the unique informativeness of two distinct mental state representations for explanation: beliefs and desires. The observer of an agent's action infers that the agent chooses to perform a particular action because she has a *desire* for a particular outcome and a *belief* that her action will serve to bring about that outcome. Distinct from the "final cause" status of goals in the teleological stance, the observer of action infers that the two mental states must be (or have been) on the agent's mind as *prior* causes of the action. And, in addition to serving as causes of the action, the observer takes these mental states to rationalize the action in the mind of that agent, serving not only as causes of the action from the observer's perspective, but also as subjective *grounds* for the action. In this mentalistic rationality assumption, the focus of inference shifts from the features of the observable action and its physical goal to how the action resulted from the mutually reinforcing mental states–the beliefs and desires—of the agent who carried it out.

The information captured by beliefs and desires is also distinct from the goal and means information found in the teleological stance. Fully mentalistic desires refer not only to goals that can be easily "read" off of common actions in the physical world (e.g., closing the window shade), but also to abstract, higher-order goals that must be inferred from those actions (e.g., to avoid being woken up by the sun, or to experience deep, restorative sleep). Indeed, for purposes of achieving the most complete comprehension of an action, higher-level descriptions of the desires fulfilled by an action are often preferred (Vallacher and Wegner 1987). In addition, when taking the intentional stance observers consider not only the physical constraints the agent's environment places on her action, but also how an agent's subjective representations—her beliefs—inform her choice of actions. Regardless of how an action may appear on the surface, a wide diversity of distinct beliefs may underlie it—including false or highly abstract ones.

A long tradition of research on theory of mind has investigated the use of these mental state concepts in a variety of contexts. For example, research on the belief concept highlights the capacity for beliefs to represent false contents or contents that differ from an agent's own current knowledge state (e.g., Wellman, Cross, and Watson 2001; Hogrefe, Wimmer, and Perner 1986; Wimmer and Perner 1983). In contrast, desires are described primarily in terms of their functions in representing different goals for different individuals, even with respect to the same object or situation (e.g., Wellman and Wooley 1990, Repacholi and Gopnik 1997). Beliefs and desires are also distinct in their developmental trajectories (with desire emerging before belief in development) and in the degree to which they are grasped by primates (who come to grasp desire but never belief, Premack 2010; Premack and Woodruff 1978, though see Krupenye et al. 2016 and Buttelmann et al. 2017 for evidence that primates have a rudimentary understanding of the basis of action in belief even if they routinely fail explicit false belief tasks). However, many of these investigations have focused on functions served by these mental states other than those specific to the context of action explanation, such as straightforward communication of one's own or another person's epistemic state or object of desire (Bartsch and Wellman 1995). There is evidence for a distinction in how people use these two mental states in social interactions; for example, people use beliefs and desires differently for purposes of impression formation, explaining their actions with more beliefs if they seek to appear rational to others (Malle et al. 2000), or providing more desires if they seek to excuse a negative behavior (Korman et al. 2014). However, if beliefs and desires serve distinct cognitive functions in the explanation of intentional action in mature adult observers, these have yet to be demonstrated.

7.2 Probing the Distinct Cognitive Functions of Belief and Desire: A Proposal

While there is no direct prior treatment of the issue, contemporary work on people's rational understanding of action does suggest one possible account of the distinct cognitive functions of belief and desire. In work on the teleological stance, researchers argue that if the social perceiver can identify that any two of the three main components of action, goal, and environmental constraints are present, then the third should be inferable from these two (Gergely and Csibra 2003; Baker, Saxe, and Tenenbaum 2009). If beliefs and desires can be thought of as analogous to constraints and goals, respectively, then we might expect that a similar inferential rule would hold for belief, desire, and action. However, a previous study found no evidence for this hypothesis (Korman and Malle 2016). When we provided participants with intentional actions paired with either a belief or a desire, people offered the same number of beliefs and desires in their explanations regardless of which mental state was paired with the action in the stimulus.

One interpretation of this result is that beliefs and desires do not serve fundamentally different cognitive functions in explanations of human action. Indeed, previous work shows that people tend to give about one reason (belief or desire) explanation for every behavior they explain (Korman and Malle 2016). This finding supports the notion that perhaps *both* mental states are not required, as a single mental state—*either* a belief or a desire—will often suffice to make the action intelligible to the explainer. This idea is especially plausible when we consider the fact that, in some cases, belief and desire may deliver the same types of contents in only very slightly different forms (Ross 1977; Malle et al. 2000). This point can be demonstrated by considering the following action explanation pairs:

(a) He gave chicken soup to his sick grandmother because he **wanted** her to feel better.
(b) He gave chicken soup to his sick grandmother because he **knew** it would make her feel better.

Such a simple action (giving chicken soup to one's grandmother) relies on widely accepted knowledge structures (social scripts) that already clearly make the action comprehensible. Because the existing action description already delivers full comprehension (see Figure 7.1a), stating a belief or desire reason does not introduce any novel explanatory information. It therefore seems that if beliefs and desires serve

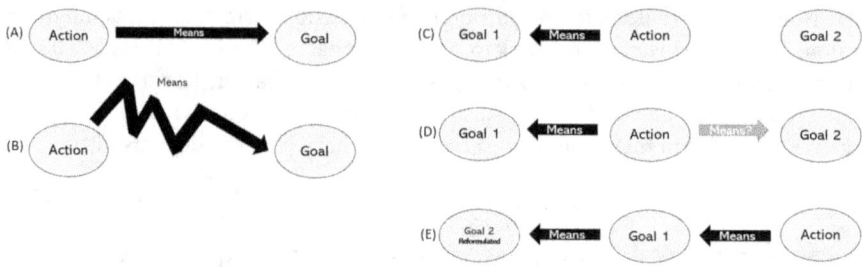

Figure 7.1 (a) When an action and a belief or desire explanation with which it is paired already conform to a common knowledge structure, knowledge about the action's goal comes with knowledge of the means, and vice versa. To the social perceiver, the goal is clear, and the choice of means is appropriate. The action is thus comprehensible without the addition of the missing "third element" (belief or desire). (b) When the agent pursues her goal by a puzzling means as in the arrow in (b), the social perceiver understands what the goal is, but not why the actor would choose this apparently inefficient means to reach the goal (e.g., taking cross-country skis to the grocery store). Although an alternative approach to the puzzle would be to posit one or more subgoals (additional desires) en route to the final goal (e.g., she wanted to create visible ski tracks on every street corner along her path to the store), this approach is neither parsimonious nor illuminating: it still does not explain why the agent would have chosen a convoluted, multi-goal route to the original goal in the first place. Only a belief (e.g., the agent knows the roads are impassable to cars due to a recent snowstorm) provides a clear solution: it explains how the agent's choice of means *is* an intelligible way to reach the agent's goal, *given the constraints she is aware of*. The addition of the belief thus makes the action once again appear as a rational means to the goal as in (a). (c) Schematic of a Goal-Blocking puzzle. Goal-blocking puzzles present an action that implies the fulfillment of one goal (Goal 1), but the agent also wants that action to fulfill a second, incompatible goal (Goal 2). (d) Belief "solution" to a Goal-Blocking puzzle. A belief may posit (rather uninformatively) that the agent falsely believes that the action serves as a means to the fulfillment of Goal 2, but such a belief is unlikely to enhance the intelligibility of the action. It is still unclear how the *same* action that strongly implies Goal 1 could also achieve a seemingly incompatible goal. (e) Desire solution to a Goal-Blocking puzzle. A common way to resolve this puzzle would be to reformulate Goal 2 (without negating it) so that the fulfillment of Goal 1 can also serve as a means to the fulfillment of Goal 2. If the status of Goal 1 as a means to the fulfillment of the reformulated version of Goal 2 (the new desire explanation provided by the explainer/observer) is not obvious, an additional belief can be provided, but providing the reformulation of Goal 2 (the new desire) is primary to resolving the puzzle. © Joanna Korman.

distinct cognitive functions, these functions will not be easily revealed in explanations for such simple actions.

The present chapter proposes and tests a theory asserting that belief and desire do indeed serve distinct cognitive functions in action explanation. The theory relates three key elements of the rationality assumption of the intentional stance: people explain an intentional action by attributing mental states (beliefs and desires) that connect the *action* to the end *goal*, and specify how the action serves as a *means to that goal*. Following Dretske (1988), I argue that beliefs and desires draw on these elements differently. First, desires provide the crucial "destination" of the action—the end goal toward which the action is ultimately aimed (Dretske 1988: 132). Most fundamentally, a desire represents the goal that the agent has on her mind before acting, and that motivates her decision to act. Consistent with findings on the teleological stance in young infants, which focus on the identification of goals as primary in action understanding, desires also appear to be primary in adults' understanding of intentional action, and are inferred before beliefs, when adult social perceivers observe such actions (Malle and Holbrook 2012; Haigh and Bonnefon 2015).

In the presence of a clear goal, inferring the agent's belief provides the social perceiver with a subjective understanding of how the agent sees the action as a *means* to that goal, shedding light on an agent's decision to achieve her goal by performing that particular action. In other words, beliefs provide the social perceiver with the "map by means of which an [agent] [has] steer[ed]" her action toward that goal (Dretske 1988: 79). For example, one participant provided this belief explanation to show how a man's action of *purchasing an expensive oriental rug* would serve as a means to the goal of *improving his vision*: "He thought that staring on the patterns on the rug would improve his vision" (Korman and Malle 2016: Study 4).

7.3 Two Types of Puzzles

If the earlier proposal is true—desires serve to provide destinations, or end goals, and beliefs serve to provide "maps" that specify how particular actions lead toward those destinations—how should this proposal be tested?

As already noted in (a) and (b), drawing on action explanation pairs that are already easily comprehensible will not be a good approach. Widely accepted knowledge structures already contain within them links to particular end goals ("destinations") with particular actions-as-means ("maps") toward those goals. The belief that connects the action to the goal (knowing that chicken soup will make Grandma feel better) already implies the destination (to make her feel better), and vice versa, so there is no way to disentangle which of these functions might be uniquely fulfilled by belief or desire in a less obvious case.

These distinctions may be more likely to reveal themselves when puzzling incongruities between agent's observed action, presumed goal, and choice of means are presented. Specifically, the present study investigates how beliefs and desires may be distinguished in being each uniquely suited to respond to a particular type of explanatory puzzle (Bromberger 1970; Hilton 1990). These puzzles and the function of each explanation type in providing solutions are outlined in what follows.

7.3.1 Eliciting Belief Explanations: Means-End Puzzles

If beliefs are map-like indicators of Means-End relationships, they should be especially apt answers to explanatory puzzles that arise when an action is difficult to understand as a **means** to its goal. In such cases, the goal is either explicitly stated or strongly (and uncontroversially) implied, and it is action's proposed *path to fulfillment* of the goal that is puzzling—not the goal itself. Notably, beyond its representation as a *physical* path to achievement that is perceived as either "efficient" or "inefficient" in reaching objects in space, the efficiency with which an action achieves its goal is determined by more general knowledge about the means people commonly choose for the achievement of (physical or nonphysical) goals. These *Means-End* puzzles thus violate the typical means for the given goal (see Figure 7.1b).

For example, an agent who straps on her cross-country skis with the goal of making it to the supermarket on time is fulfilling this goal in an atypical fashion. We predict that in response to such puzzles participants will provide *belief* explanations, which will clarify how, in the agent's mind, the action actually serves as a means to the given goal. In response to this example, the social perceiver might respond that the agent *knew that the roads were blocked with snow* and *she realized that the only way to get around was on cross-country skis*. This prediction is also consistent with findings in the action identification literature (Vallacher and Wegner 1987), which suggest that people tend to focus on the details of an action (descriptions of the low-level actions that serve as a means to the achievement of a more abstract goal) when they achieve that goal by complex, difficult, or unfamiliar means. For example, Wegner and Vallacher (1987) describe an earlier study (Wegner, Connally, Shearer, and Vallacher 1983) in which all subjects were instructed to eat Cheetos. Some of the participants were instructed to eat Cheetos with their hands (the typical way), and others were asked to use a pair of chopsticks. In comparison to the participants who ate Cheetos in the typical way, when asked what they had done, those who used chopsticks tended to describe the action in lower-level terms such as " 'chewing,' 'swallowing,' and 'moving my hands,'" while those who ate with their hands described the action in higher level, more abstract terms, such as "getting nutrition" and "reducing hunger" (Wegner et al. 1983, as cited in Vallacher and Wegner 1987: 5–6).

7.3.2 Eliciting Desire Explanations: Goal-Blocking Puzzles

As discussed earlier, desires are the agent's mental representations of her goal. In many cases, the desire behind a person's action can be easily generated just by observing or hearing about that action; for example, people typically go to the pool because they want *to swim* and to the theater because they want to *see a show*. However, if an action lacks a clear, single end goal (e.g., "He plucked a single blade of grass"), people may need to provide desire explanations in order to clarify the action's final destination. Our *Goal-blocking* puzzles sought to create such ambiguity by presenting actions that contained multiple, inconsistent goals.

Many actions can be described as having multiple goals. However, in order for these goals to all be goals of that *same* action, they must be arranged in a hierarchical, consistent structure such that there is only one end goal that is specified by a desire motivating the action. This desire provides a structure under which each goal of the action is consistent with the other goals also achieved by that action. Consider the following: *Jane went to the department store. Her goal was to get her mother a present. She did that in order to make her mother feel happy on her birthday.* Jane's action fulfills a series of hierarchically related goals: getting the present is both a fulfilled goal and an action that fulfills further goals with one *end* goal: to make her mother feel happy on her birthday. When an action is performed in service of multiple, *inconsistent* goals—when the pursuit of one goal actually runs *counter* to the achievement of another goal, thus effectively blocking its achievement in that same action—an explanatory gap opens up (see Figure 7.1c–e). For example, consider the following statement: "He hung up on his sister because he wanted her to know how much he loved her." Generally, one person hangs up on another person to show displeasure, and showing displeasure tends to be mutually exclusive with the demonstration of love for another person; that is, they cannot normally be executed in the very same action.

In response to Goal-Blocking puzzles like the one just presented, it is of course possible that people would provide false belief explanations; for example, they could explain the earlier example by saying, "The man falsely thought that hanging up on his sister would effectively communicate his love." However, I argue that such puzzles will primarily elicit desire explanations for two reasons. First, in the context of Goal-Blocking puzzles, many belief explanations—including false beliefs—will amount to uninformative confabulations about hypothetical means-end relationships (e.g., about how the man believes that his action will, in some unspecified way, fulfill his desire to express love for his sister) with no inferential grounding in the stimulus itself.[2] Because prior knowledge dictates that the goal achieved by the stated action largely contradicts the stated desire, an ad hoc statement that the agent believes otherwise is unlikely to contribute to genuine understanding (see Figure 7.1d).

Second, and more fundamentally, I argue that when there is an absence of any clear end goal, or final "destination" at all, as is the case in Goal-Blocking puzzles, participants' understanding will be enhanced most significantly by providing such an end goal. They will do this by providing one or more desires that subsume the existing goals under a single, hierarchical structure. For example, by responding that "the man wanted to show 'tough love' to his sister," a person provides a new desire explanation (a reformulation of the original "Goal 2" as labeled in Figure 7.1e, the content of which is *to show his love for his sister*) that subsumes the goal of *showing displeasure* (or Goal 1 in Figure 7.1e) under the goal of showing love.

One complication does arise, however. As Figure 7.1e shows, introducing a new or reformulated desire in a hierarchical structure also means introducing a new means-end relationship: this time, showing how the old goal (e.g., expressing displeasure, Goal 1 in Figure 7.1e, which itself is a kind of action description) serves as a means to the achievement of the new desire (labeled "Goal 2, reformulated" in Figure 7.1e). If the new desire is a good "fit" with the existing goals in prior knowledge, this means-end relationship will be implied (e.g., it is fairly obvious that communicating displeasure can be a way to show "tough love"). However, if participants' newly provided desire explanation ("Goal 2, reformulated") is not a perfect fit, an additional belief explanation may be required to show just precisely how the goals are hierarchically related. Crucially, however, even if a connecting belief is required, I predict that it cannot be an effective solution to a Goal-Blocking puzzle unless it is accompanied by a desire explanation (otherwise there is no new goal for the new belief to tie to the original goal). Furthermore, if a desire can resolve the puzzle by itself without additional support from a belief, this is the most parsimonious solution to the puzzle (see Harman 1965 and Keil 2006 for a discussion of the role of parsimony in explanations).

7.4 Methods

Puzzling stimulus sentences were created by pairing actions with puzzling belief or desire explanations for those actions, for example, "The lawyer placed a call to one of his clients [action] because he wanted to see what the weather was like [desire reason]." Use of these action-reason pairs allowed for the creation of two different puzzle types. While Goal-Blocking puzzles presented two inconsistent goals (one implied in the action, one stated or implied in the reason, e.g., "The chef baked peanuts into the bride's dessert because he knew she had a serious peanut allergy"), Means-End puzzles presented a goal (stated or implied in the reason) that was achieved via an atypical means (the action), for example, "He picked up his frying pan because it was time to put together the Ikea furniture." While desires explicitly stated a goal (e.g., "because he wanted to . . . "), beliefs only implied this goal (e.g., "because she knew the supermarket was about to close.") In the final set of items, stimulus reason type (belief or desire) was fully crossed with puzzle type.

Pretesting. A total of twenty-one stimulus sentences containing actions paired with ill-fitting reasons were pretested on two main dimensions, *goal compatibility* (to select Goal-Blocking items) and *action commonality* (a test of the commonness with which a particular action is used as a means to achieve a particular goal, to select means-end items). Eight of these items, four in each group and two of each reason type (belief or desire) per group, were ultimately selected for use in the study.

The format of pretest questions varied as a function of the type of explicit reason with which the stimulus was paired (belief or desire). These differences are noted for each dimension. Because of slight differences in the instructions across these item types, items containing belief and desire reasons were pretested between subjects.

Goal Compatibility. Consider a belief-containing sentence: "She strapped on her cross-country skis because [she believed][3] the supermarket was about to close." Pretest participants initially read the first part of the sentence, "She strapped on her cross-country skis," and then answered the question "What was her goal?" (e.g., "to enjoy herself in the snow."). Then they read the entire sentence ("Actually what happened was the following . . . [full sentence]") and were asked, "Now that you've seen the whole sentence, what do you think her goal was?" (e.g., "to get to the supermarket on time"). Then, for goal compatibility, participants rated how *compatible* the initial goal that they had provided was with the final goal on a scale of 0 (Totally incompatible) to 8 (Perfectly compatible). For a desire-containing sentence, for example, "The woman sent her friend a check for $1,000 because she wanted to pay her back for lunch," the first goal question was the same as for the belief version. The second goal question was omitted, however, because the second half of the sentence (e.g., "she wanted to pay her back for lunch") itself provided the overarching goal of the behavior. This goal content was used as the second goal in the goal-compatibility question.

Action commonality. For belief-containing items, participants rated how common it was for a person to perform the initial action (e.g., "strapping on her cross-country skis") when trying to achieve the final goal inferred by the participant (e.g., "getting to the supermarket on time") on a scale of 0 (Not at all common) to 8 (Very common). For desire-containing items, participants rated how common it was for a person to perform the initial action (e.g., "A woman sending a $1,000 check") when trying to achieve the final goal specified in the desire contained in the stimulus sentence ("paying the friend back for lunch").

General puzzlingness. In addition to the individual puzzle types, we also pretested for the general puzzlingness of each stimulus sentence in a third set of subjects. This question was worded as an "understanding" question: "Given this explanation, how well do you *understand* this action?" and "puzzlingness" ratings were created using the formula $P = 8 - U$.

Stimulus selection. Four items were selected for inclusion in the means-end category, and four in the Goal-Blocking category. For each dimension, items were eligible for selection if they were below their respective scale midpoints (4). Goal-blocking items had a mean of $M = 2.02$ ($SD = 0.45$) on the goal-compatibility question, and means-end items had a mean of $M = 2.72$ ($SD = 0.98$) on the action commonality question.[4] In addition, while item selection was based on a single-question criterion, participants responded to both questions for each item. Thus, a single composite score for each item could also be calculated by subtracting that item's action commonality score from its goal-compatibility score; on this composite score, a more positive score indicated higher goal compatibility than goal commonality, while a negative score indicated the reverse.

Task and design. The task was identical to that presented in Studies 1, 2, and 4 of Korman and Malle (2016). Participants read the stimulus sentences one by one and were invited to "add whatever information you think is needed for the sentence above to make better sense." The eight items were presented to participants in two forms, consisting of one pseudorandom order and its reverse.

Participants. Seventy-nine participants (thirty-nine female) completed the task on Amazon Mechanical Turk in exchange for monetary compensation. Their average age was thirty-four years, and 51 percent had a four-year college degree or higher level of education.

Data Treatment. Two coders (one blind to condition) were involved in the classification of 632 explanations using the F.Ex coding scheme (Malle 1998/2004), which classifies mental state explanations into belief and desire reasons, as well as distinguishing between mental state and non-mental state (causal history of reason) explanations (see Malle 1999, for more details and evidence on this distinction). For reliability purposes, the two coders each classified responses into 128 items. Coders reached 100 percent agreement on whether a statement was codable as an explanation ($K = .68$), and 96 percent on mental state reasons versus causal history explanations ($K = .69$), and 99 percent agreement on belief versus desire reasons ($K = .86$). Both coders independently classified a second group of 437 responses; disagreements were resolved in discussion. A final sixty-four responses were then classified by a single coder.

7.5 Results and Discussion

Aggregate analysis. First, the number of explanations provided by each participant was aggregated over category such that each participant received a mean score for beliefs and desires for Means-End puzzles and Goal-Blocking puzzles (a total of four scores). A 2 (Goal-blocking vs. Means-end puzzle type) X 2 (Belief vs. Desire reason) repeated measures ANOVA revealed a significant interaction, $F(1, 70) = 31.02, p < .001$, partial $\eta^2 = .31$. Bonferoni-adjusted simple-effects comparisons revealed that participants provided more beliefs in response to Means-End puzzles ($M = 0.86, SD = 0.37$) than in response to Goal-Blocking puzzles ($M = 0.59, SD = 0.47, p < .001$, 95 percent CI for the difference = .14 to .37), while they provided more desires in response to Goal-Blocking puzzles ($M = .71, SD = .44$) than in response to Means-End puzzles ($M = 0.39, SD = .32, p < .001$, 95 percent CI of the difference = .22 to .44).

There was also a main effect of explanation type, with participants providing more belief ($M = .74, SD = .34$) than desire explanations overall ($M = .54, SD = .31$), $F(1, 70) = 5.29, p = .02$, partial $\eta^2 = .07$.

Disaggregated analysis: Multilevel Poisson regression. To examine the effects of individual items' pretested Goal-Blocking and means-end ratings on specific rates of explanations given, a multilevel Poisson regression was performed for the number of each type of explanation (Belief vs. Desire) given by each participant in response to each of the eight items (for a total of sixteen data points per participant). The Poisson distribution was chosen as a commonly used distribution for (disaggregated) count data, as ordinary least squares regression is generally a poor choice for such data (O'Hara and Kotze 2010).[5] An analysis of random effects revealed that 0 percent of the variance in the number of explanations provided was explained by including a unique intercept for each subject. In addition, the inclusion of random slope for number of explanations in each category (belief or desire) by subject also did not improve the performance of the model, $\chi^2(3) = 1.94$, *ns*. With no significant contributions from random effects, the analysis proceeded with the consideration of fixed effects only.

In addition to the type of explanation (Belief vs. Desire) given for each item, each item's pretested rating for action commonality, goal compatibility, and general puzzlingness was entered into the model as a continuous predictor. Interactions between explanation type with goal compatibility, action commonality, and puzzlingness were also included in the full model.

Action commonality alone did not significantly predict the number of explanations participants provided, nor did the interaction between action commonality and explanation type. The final model included goal compatibility, puzzlingness, explanation type, and interaction terms for each of the continuous measures with explanation type. There was a significant interaction between goal compatibility and explanation type; for every increase of one unit in goal compatibility, participants gave 22 percent more belief explanations ($p < .01$, 95 percent CI, 7 percent to 39 percent) and 36 percent fewer desire explanations ($p < .001$, 95 percent CI, a 21 percent to 48 percent decrease). In addition, there was a significant interaction between ratings of the puzzlingness of an item and explanation type. Participants increased the number of belief explanations they provided by 23 percent ($p = .01$, 95 percent CI, 5 percent to 37 percent) and decreased the number of desire explanations by 25 percent ($p = .04$, 95 percent CI 2 percent to 54 percent) for every unit of increase in the item's puzzlingness.

Why might puzzlingness ratings have superseded action commonality in the prediction of participants' providing beliefs? One notable point is that action commonality ratings were actually quite similar across means-end and Goal-Blocking items ($M = 2.72$, $M = 2.25$, respectively) so the two groups of items were much better distinguished by the goal-compatibility dimension than the action commonality dimension. Because in the present pretests, action commonality and puzzlingness ratings were collected in separate groups of subjects, we could not compare the covariances between these two dimensions directly. However, an earlier set of pretests drawing on the same theoretical framework (DiGiovanni, Korman, and Malle 2016) elicited both action commonality and puzzlingness ratings for each item. Similar to the present study, these earlier pretests also showed no initial difference between Means-end and Goal-blocking items on action commonality ratings, but when puzzlingness ratings were entered as a covariate, the two groups of items differed significantly on action commonality. This effect occurred because means-end items were overall less puzzling than Goal-Blocking items and, once this difference was accounted for, the items differed on action commonality. While not definitive, this finding suggests that the failure of action commonality to directly predict participants' belief usage may have been a consequence of means-end items being less puzzling than goal-compatibility items.

7.6 General Discussion and Future Directions

What are the primary determinants of the choice between beliefs and desires in action explanation? The present results suggest that the more incompatible the initial goal implied by the action was with another goal the agent had in performing that same action, the more likely participants were to provide desires, and the less likely they were to provide beliefs. This finding confirms the prediction that, when an action lacks a clear goal, people will search, first and foremost, for the "final destination" of that action, providing desire explanations.

However, in response to Goal-Blocking puzzles, participants did not cease to give belief explanations entirely. In fact, although they provided fewer beliefs for Goal-blocking puzzles than for Means-End puzzles, participants still provided more beliefs for Goal-Blocking puzzles than they did desires for Means-End puzzles, $t(70) = 2.76$, $p < .01$). This result suggests that, in keeping with the predictions outlined in Figure 7.1c–e, beliefs may also be an important, if secondary, component when responding to Goal-Blocking puzzles. In contrast, and in keeping with the prediction that desires are a largely uninformative and inefficient way to resolve Means-End puzzles, participants gave very few desires in this case (less than half as many desires as beliefs).

Two limitations of the present study should be noted. First, the use of only eight unique items in total limited the variability of items along the two main pretest dimensions. Future studies with a larger number of items and a more variable range of scores over the two dimensions should replicate the present finding. Secondly, while the use of actions paired with puzzling reasons as stimuli did supply sufficient variation to differentially elicit beliefs and desires as a function of puzzle type, these stimuli in particular, both in the present study and in a previous study (Korman and Malle 2016: Study 3), elicit a greater number of belief than desire explanations overall. This prevalence of belief stands in contrast to much of the literature on action understanding, which suggests that desires are the much more frequent inference. Thus, if the current findings are to be generalized to settings of more naturalistic human action understanding, they should be replicated with more naturalistic behaviors.

In spite of these limitations, the present study makes a distinct contribution to the study of the roles of belief and desire in action understanding. Previous work examining the role of both mental states within a single study is limited (especially in adults), and generally queries the distinct roles of belief and desire into structured questions posed to the social perceiver in response to an action that is primarily physical in nature (e.g., Baker, Tenenbaum, and Schulz 2014; Richardson et al. 2012). For example, Richardson et al. (2012) probed participants' abilities to make joint inferences of belief and desire by depicting an agent (bunny) navigating toward one of three fruits in a 3D animated environment. In that study, for example, if the bunny passes the first piece of fruit in plain view in favor of walking around a wall toward a hidden fruit, participants should infer that the bunny does not prefer (desire) the first fruit, since he clearly knows it is there (belief) yet does not pick it up. The current study was distinct from this earlier work in two important respects. First, similar to explanations for actions in the real world, the contents of mental representations were limited only by participants' prior knowledge—not by the tight constraints of an agent moving in a physical environment. In order to resolve the puzzles, participants had to construct rich representations of the agent's beliefs, and, distinct from prior work, often also her subjective, nonphysically realized desires. Second, in contrast to the previous use of forced-choice and probability-based measures, participants' open-ended, self-generated representations of agents' mental states were elicited. This methodology reveals that the apparent differences in structure between belief and desire in action explanation—suggested by only a small number of earlier studies in adults—are not the mere consequence of a constrained response medium.

Acknowledgments

Thanks to Corey Cusimano, Baxter DiFabrizio, Maddy DiGiovanni, Bertram Malle, and Stuti Thapa.

Notes

1 The views expressed in this chapter are the author's alone and do not represent those of any other entity.

2 If, for example, the stimulus offered some compelling background to motivate why the agent might have this particular false belief in this case, the structure of the puzzle would fundamentally change.
3 Even without use of mental state markers such as "he believed," such formulations are still considered by explainers to be beliefs of the agent (Malle et al. 2000). There are, of course, pragmatic distinctions between the choice to use or omit a mental state marker.
4 Despite several rounds of pretesting, it was not possible to distinguish the categories along both dimensions. In a test that included six out of the eight selected items, the two categories differed on the goal-compatibility dimension, $t(69) = 3.4$, $p <.01$, but not on the action commonality dimension, $t(69) =.58$, ns. The consequences of this asymmetric differentiation are detailed in the analysis section.
5 The data were somewhat underdispersed ($M = 0.66$, $SD = 0.43$, Deviance/$df = .78$) compared to the Poisson distribution, which assumes the mean and variance are equal. An alternative model was thus considered as well. Since the modal values in the count data were "0" (no explanations of a given type) and "1" (one explanation of a given type), transforming the response variable (number of explanations of each type) into a binary (either providing an explanation of that type, "1," or not providing any explanations of that type, "0") provided an alternative approach. This did lead to some loss of information, but it enabled a multilevel logistic regression, which requires less stringent distributional assumptions. This model was distinguished from the Poisson model primarily by a significant improvement in model fit when a random slope for number of belief vs. desire explanations by participant ID was also included ($\chi^2(3) = 32.52$, $p < .001$). While this model led to somewhat different values for regression coefficients, the overall interpretation of fixed effects in the model did not differ from the Poisson model, nor did it differ from a version of the logistic model run without random effects parameters.

References

Baker, C. L., R. Saxe, and J. B. Tenenbaum (2009), "Action Understanding as Inverse Planning," *Cognition*, 113 (3): 329–49.

Baker, C. L., J. B. Tenenbaum, and L. E. Schulz (2014), "Joint Inferences of Belief and Desire from Facial Expressions," in N. Miyake, D. Peebles, and R. P. Cooper (eds.), Proceedings of the Thirty-Fourth Annual Conference of the Cognitive Science Society, 923–8. Austin, TX: Cognitive Science Society.

Bartsch, K. and H. M. Wellman (1995), *Children Talk About the Mind*, New York: Oxford University Press.

Bromberger, S. (1970), "Why-Questions," in B. Brody (ed.), *Readings in the Philosophy of Science*, Englewood Cliffs, NJ: Prentice-Hall.

Buttelmann, D., F. Buttelmann, M. Carpenter, J. Call, and M. Tomasello (2017), "Great Apes Distinguish True from False Beliefs in an Interactive Helping Task," *PLOS ONE*, 12 (4): e0173793.

Davidson, D. (1963), "Actions, Reasons, and Causes," *The Journal of Philosophy*, 60 (23): 685–700.

Dennett, D. C. (1987), *The Intentional Stance*, Cambridge, MA: MIT Press.

DiGiovanni, M., J. Korman, and B. F. Malle (2016, August), "How We Explain Puzzling Behavior: The Differential Use of Beliefs and Desires," Poster presented to the *Brown Summer Research Symposium*, Providence, RI.

Dretske, F. (1988/1992), *Explaining Behavior: Reasons in a World of Causes*, Cambridge, MA: MIT Press.
Gergely, G. and G. Csibra (2003), "Teleological Reasoning in Infancy: The Naıve Theory of Rational Action," *Trends in Cognitive Sciences*, 7 (7): 287–92.
Gergely, G., Z. Nádasdy, G. Csibra, and S. Bíró (1995), "Taking the Intentional Stance at 12 Months of Age," *Cognition*, 56 (2): 165–93.
Haigh, M. and J.-F. Bonnefon (2015), "Eye Movements Reveal How Readers Infer Intentions from the Beliefs and Desires of Others," *Experimental Psychology*, 62 (3): 206–13.
Harman, G. H. (1965), "The Inference to the Best Explanation," *The Philosophical Review*, 74 (1): 88–95.
Hilton, D. J. (1990), "Conversational Processes and Causal Explanation," *Psychological Bulletin*. Available online: http://psycnet.apa.org/journals/bul/107/1/65/.
Juergen Hogrefe, G., H. Wimmer, and J. Perner (1986), "Ignorance Versus False Belief: A Developmental Lag in Attribution of Epistemic States," *Child Development*, 57 (3): 567–82.
Keil, F. C. (2006), "Explanation and Understanding," *Annual Review of Psychology*, 57: 227–54.
Korman, J., C. Cusimano, A. Monroe, J. Smith, and B. F. Malle (2014, July), Not so Bad After All? The Role of Explanation Features in Blame Mitigation. Poster presented at the *Annual Meeting of the Cognitive Science Society*, Quebec City, Canada.
Korman, J. and B. F. Malle (2016), "Grasping for Traits or Reasons? How People Grapple with Puzzling Social Behaviors," *Personality and Social Psychology Bulletin*, 42 (11): 1451–65.
Krupenye, C., F. Kano, S. Hirata, J. Call, and M. Tomasello (2016), "Great Apes Anticipate Agents' Actions Based on Their False Beliefs," *Science*, 354 (6308): 110–14.
Lombrozo, T. and S. Carey (2006), "Functional Explanation and the Function of Explanation," *Cognition*, 99 (2): 167–204.
Malle, B. F. (1998/2004), F.Ex: Coding Scheme for People's Folk Explanations of Behavior. Available online: http://research.clps.brown.edu/SocCogSci/CodingSchemes.html (Accessed July 2015).
Malle, B. F. (1999), "How People Explain Behavior: A New Theoretical Framework," *Personality and Social Psychology Review*, 3 (1): 23–48.
Malle, B. F. and J. Holbrook (2012), "Is There a Hierarchy of Social Inferences? The Likelihood and Speed of Inferring Intentionality, Mind, and Personality," *Journal of Personality and Social Psychology*, 102 (4): 661–84.
Malle, B. F., K. Joshua, M. J. O'Laughlin, G. E. Pearce, and S. E. Nelson (2000), "Conceptual Structure and Social Functions of Behavior Explanations: Beyond Person-Situation Attributions," *Journal of Personality and Social Psychology*, 79 (3): 309–26.
O'hara, R. B. and D. J. Kotze (2010), "Do Not Log-Transform Count Data," *Methods in Ecology and Evolution, British Ecological Society*. Available online: http://onlinelibrary.wiley.com/doi/10.1111/j.2041-210X.2010.00021.x/full.
Premack, D. (2010), "Why Humans Are Unique: Three Theories," *Perspectives on Psychological Science: A Journal of the Association for Psychological Science*, 5 (1): 22–32.
Premack, D. and G. Woodruff (1978), "Does the Chimpanzee Have a Theory of Mind?," *The Behavioral and Brain Sciences*, 1 (04): 515–26.
Repacholi, B. M. and A. Gopnik (1997), "Early Reasoning About Desires: Evidence from 14- and 18-Month-Olds," *Developmental Psychology*, 33 (1): 12–21.

Richardson, H. L., C. L. Baker, J. B. Tenenbaum, and R. R. Saxe (2012), "The Development of Joint Belief-Desire Inferences," in N. Miyake, D. Peebles, and R. P. Cooper (eds.), Proceedings of the Thirty-Fourth Annual Conference of the Cognitive Science Society, 923–8. Austin, TX: Cognitive Science Society.

Ross, L. (1977), "The Intuitive Psychologist and His Shortcomings: Distortions in the Attribution Process," in L. Berkowitz (ed.), *Advances in Experimental Social Psychology*, vol. 10, New York, NY: Academic Press.

Schachner, A. and S. Carey (2013), "Reasoning About 'Irrational' Actions: When Intentional Movements Cannot Be Explained, the Movements Themselves Are Seen as the Goal," *Cognition*, 129 (2): 309–27.

Vallacher, R. R. and D. M. Wegner (1987), "What Do People Think They're Doing? Action Identification and Human Behavior," *Psychological Review*, 94 (1): 3.

Wegner, D. M., D. Connally, D. Shearer, and R. R. Vallacher (1983), "[Disruptions and Identifications in the Act of Eating.]" Unpublished research data.

Wellman, H. M., D. Cross, and J. Watson (2001), "Meta-analysis of Theory of Mind Development: The Truth About False Belief," *Child Development*, 72 (3): 655–84.

Wellman, H. M. and J. D. Woolley (1990), "From Simple Desires to Ordinary Beliefs: The Early Development of Everyday Psychology," *Cognition*, 35 (3): 245–75.

Wimmer, H. and J. Perner (1983), "Beliefs About Beliefs: Representation and Constraining Function of Wrong Beliefs in Young Children's Understanding of Deception," *Cognition*, 13 (1): 103–28.

8

Free Enough

Human Cognition (And Cultural Interests) Warrant Responsibility

Cory J. Clark, Heather M. Maranges, Brian B. Boutwell, and Roy F. Baumeister

Ongoing debates about the existence of free will (e.g., Baumeister, Clark, and Luguri 2015; Dennett 2004; Pereboom 2006) have compelled debates about definitions of free will (e.g., Frankfurt 1969; van Inwagen 1983; Wolf 1990) and how everyday people conceptualize free will (Feltz, Cokely, and Nadelhoffer 2009; Knobe et al. 2012; Nahmias et al. 2006; Nichols and Knobe 2007). We doubt very much that all of that will be settled anytime soon, in part because such debates are often normative rather than empirical (e.g., the level of freedom needed to warrant moral responsibility) and in part because everyday people likely lack a coherent, stable conception of free will and perhaps even the ability to comprehend relevant components of free will debates (such as determinism; Clark, Winegard, and Baumeister 2019; Murray, Dykhuis, and Nadelhoffer 2022). However, these debates and corresponding research make clear that people *care* about the existence of free will, that ordinary people *believe* in free will (Dennett 2015; Nahmias et al. 2005; Sarkissian et al. 2010), and that scholars and ordinary people alike have intuitions that the existence of free will *matters* (Kane 1998; Shariff et al. 2014).

Although there is no universally agreed-upon definition of free will, one commonality among varying definitions is that exercising free will requires choosing among more than one possible outcome, whether the possible outcomes are real or imagined. For example, many compatibilists define free will in a way that presumes the ability to act on the basis of rational deliberation over *epistemically* possible actions in the absence of coercion (Kapitan 1986; Pereboom 2008); many incompatibilists define free will in a way that presumes the ability to act on the basis of rational deliberation over *metaphysically* possible actions in the absence of coercion and deterministic constraints, entailing the genuine possibility of acting in different possible ways even given identical causal histories (Haggard et al. 2015; Taylor 1963; Van Inwagen 1983); and when everyday people are asked to generate definitions of free will, they mention the ability to make decisions or choices (Monroe and Malle 2010).

Deliberations about multiple possible futures (regardless of whether those multiple possible futures truly exist) *cause* human behavior at least as part of a string of other causes (Baumeister et al. 2018; Baumeister, Maranges, and Sjastad 2018). Unlike a Labrador Retriever with an impulse to eat all available food as quickly as possible with minimal capacity for reflecting on possible negative consequences of doing so, humans can often imagine the intensity and duration of pleasure they would enjoy from indulging in a high-calorie treat, anticipate possible negative consequences of indulging (e.g., physical discomfort, putting on weight), and use that tradeoff calculation as an input into the decision of whether to indulge. Thus, humans are able to simulate mentally various possible choices and anticipate the likely consequences of those choices (e.g., De Brigard, Henne, and Stanley 2021).

This capacity may be *unique* to humans—at least in its level of sophistication—and may justify conceiving humans as uniquely responsible for their behavior. This capacity may be evolutionarily advantageous for individual humans by promoting decisions with better long-term outcomes. For instance, people can observe others' use or failure to use this capacity to make better choices (e.g., exercising self-control in personal and professional domains) and choose to affiliate with and reward those who exhibit high self-control and avoid and punish those who exhibit low self-control. This tendency can incentivize better behavior within individuals because risks of punishment and reputational costs cause people to behave more cooperatively (Gächter and Fehr 1999; Engelmann and Fischbacher 2009; Van Vugt and Hardy 2010). Thus, the capacity to simulate possible futures and associated beliefs in free will and moral responsibility may promote more desirable behavior within human societies broadly as well as contribute to more socially advantageous decision-making for individuals.

In the present chapter, we discuss recent research in experimental philosophy and related disciplines that support the significance of perceptions of choice, control, multiple possibilities, and free will for understanding human behavior, promoting better individual decision-making, and fostering large-scale cooperation within human societies. We first discuss the significance of counterfactual reasoning and prospection about the future for facilitating better decision-making, self-control, and more prosocial behavior. We argue that such human capacities may be sufficient to warrant conceiving of humans as *responsible* for their behavior. Last, we argue that conceptions of responsibility may help facilitate more prosocial behavior and cooperation in human social groups. When an individual creates costs for the social group (e.g., by behaving selfishly or impulsively), blaming and attributing responsibility to that individual creates costs for the individual thus disincentivizing behavior that is socially costly. This creates benefits for society (because people behave more prosocially) and for the individual (because prosocial behavior is rewarded with social benefits). So although we do not claim to settle any definitional or metaphysical disputes about free will, we argue that conceptions of free will and responsibility serve crucial social and cultural functions. These reflections may help explain why people care so much about what free will is and whether it exists.

8.1 Causal Calculations and Counterfactual Reasoning

The mathematician and computer scientist Stan Franklin once asserted that a mind's chief function is to answer the question of "what do I do now" (Franklin, 1995: 233).

What we might refer to as "Franklin's question," and the mind's strategies for solving it, remain poorly understood. It is clear, however, that these strategies involve a flood of informational processing carried out by the brain, including many tasks that are essential to life but outside the arena of conscious awareness (e.g., Baumeister et al. 2017). Maintaining homeostasis by regulating respiration, modulating hormone levels, along with a host of other duties are all varieties of "what do I do now" that come in a "never-conscious" form and are handled well outside of our volitional reach (Baars 1983; Baars and Franklin 2009).

More pertinent to this discussion are decisions made in the wake of what others have referred to as a conscious broadcast (Baars 1983; Baars and Franklin 2003). When Baars and Franklin (2009: 170) define the concept, they did so in an intuitive fashion, simply noting that: "This broadcast is hypothesized to correspond to phenomenal consciousness" (see also Baars 1983; Baars and Franklin 2009). The conscious thought experienced during a broadcast, then, is considered to be a necessity for many of the most sophisticated human behaviors, such as communication and group decision-making (Baumeister et al. 2018), that are responsible for facilitating complex human culture (Baumeister 2005). Conscious contemplations often involve morally tinged choices (Baars and Franklin 2009; Franklin 2003) and the creation of imaginary worlds (Pearl 2009; Pearl and MacKenzie 2018).

These alternative worlds encapsulate paths that we *might* travel, with a variety of consequences that *might* play out creating a menu of mental options. Among other things, it seems that consciousness enables humans (and possibly nonhumans) to engage in mental simulations in order to make predictions about the future, to evaluate the likelihood that certain effects will result from possible causal events, and to mentally undo certain events to predict what *could have* happened in alternate realities (e.g., Kahneman and Tversky 1982). This type of deliberative contemplation implies a need to "simulate" a variety of different scenarios which could unfold in unique ways depending on what choices are made. This type of psychological world-building and imagination allows individual actors to mentally experiment with different actions, without actually undertaking them in the real world.

Considered as more formal concepts, these psychological simulations of what *might happen* in the future or what *could have happened* in the past bleed seamlessly into the philosophical and scientific conception of a counterfactual (Byrne 2016; De Brigard et al. 2019; Pearl 2009). Or, the notion that B will only happen if I do A, so failing at A means missing out on B. Counterfactuals are thoughts about what could have happened in a given situation (as opposed to what did happen). Such thoughts form a basis for evaluating one's satisfaction with reality because one can compare reality to imagined alternative possibilities (both positive and negative) (see De Brigard et al. 2019). Consequently, counterfactual thinking can lead to negative affect, a temporarily displeasing state, which can motivate persistence, planning, and better decision-making in the future (Boninger, Gleicher, and Strathman 1994; Markman et al. 1993; Markman, McMullen, and Elizaga 2008). Anticipation of negative counterfactuals, for instance, reduced intentions to engage in future unethical behavior (Celuch and Saxby 2013). Counterfactual thinking is believed to help people prepare for the future and learn from past mistakes (Alquist et al. 2015; Byrne 2016; Smallman 2013).

It is possible that other strategies (besides counterfactual forms of thinking) are employed in causal reasoning. Put another way, it is not a foregone conclusion that counterfactual thinking is always required for humans to make judgments about causality, and indeed others have proposed alternative models (see Kelley 1973; Wolff 2006). Something akin to raw correlational analysis, for example, could be the mind's primary way to record, catalogue, and track data about the world. Not unlike a formal correlational analysis, a mental correlation analysis would function to link events in the world that co-occur at high frequencies (Gerstenberg et al. 2017). Observing that some trees produce more fruit following a rainy stretch, for example, may lead to the assessment that fruit *usually* follows rain, without an explicit counterfactual assessment. Indeed, associational data alone can be used to build a prediction model and may serve individuals quite well in terms of anticipating what outcomes are likely given certain circumstances (see Gerstenberg et al. 2017).

But likely both processes inform our causal judgments, with counterfactual logic used alongside correlational insight. Gerstenberg and colleagues (2017) endeavored to better understand which cognitive approach might be deployed and when. In setting the stage for their study, the authors described an area of human cultural life where counterfactually based cognitive processing seems essential: sports. Adopting their example, (American) football limits the extent to which defensive players can attempt to prevent an offensive player from catching a pass. Overly aggressive obstruction is penalized; a key caveat, however, is that the pass intended for the receiver must be "catchable." This provision implies that a pass far over the receiver's head would render the interference moot. Counterfactual thinking requires *imagining* what might happen were the quarterback to throw a variety of different passes—some of which might be catchable and others not. From these imagined alternative worlds, one can impose a causal assessment as to whether defensive interference did indeed *cause* the receiver to miss the catch. Pondering the role of counterfactual thinking in areas beyond sports, Gerstenberg and colleagues (2017: 1731) observed:

> Of course, counterfactuals arise not only in sports. We use them to make sense of history (Ferguson, 2000), to determine causation in the law (Hart & Honoré, 1959/1985), and to understand our own and other people's actions and emotions (Alicke, Mandel, Hilton, Gerstenberg, & Lagnado, 2015; Kahneman & Miller, 1986; Roese, 1997). We ponder over near misses (Kahneman & Varey, 1990) and regret decisions that could have turned out better. (Loomes & Sugden, 1982; Zeelenberg et al. 1998)

Participants in the study were fitted with eye-tracking equipment, watched various scenarios in which billiard balls collided with one another, and they were asked to make judgments about possible outcomes of colliding balls if certain things were to change, such as if one billiard ball was removed from the table. Participants' eye movements revealed that participants were cognitively simulating probable locations of the target ball in these counterfactual scenarios, suggesting that people rely on counterfactual thinking when making causal judgments. A single study is far from dispositive, but outside of the laboratory, counterfactual logic has long been foundational in areas of high societal consequence, especially in criminal justice and assessing the culpability of offenders (Gerstenberg et al. 2017; Niemi et al. 2016). Had some person *not* acted violently, we reason that their victim would be unharmed. Had someone not acted recklessly, some innocent person would have avoided injury (Gerstenberg et al. 2021). There is an assumption that different responses to the same situation were *possible* (Byrne 1997), that these differences would have caused different outcomes (some causing harm and some not), and that moral culpability depends on those differences. Beyond these lofty legal principles, of course, reside our daily appraisals of significant life choices (De Brigard et al. 2019). Whether we chose the right college major, took the right job, or married the right partner are all of great import, and each choice is bound up in counterfactual thinking about where we would be now had we made different choices then.

Such considerations enable humans to do something that perhaps no other animal can: use fictional realities about possible futures as inputs into one's own decision-making (Pearl and MacKenzie 2018; Phillips, Morris, and Cushman 2019). Whereas other animals may have the capacity to learn from events of the past (e.g., by forming associations) and alter future behaviors accordingly, humans can learn in a proactive manner by imagining possible futures and using those to-date unrealized possibilities to better their decision-making. Moreover, basing one's decisions today on expectations about long-term outcomes facilitates human culture by encouraging short-term costly investments that turn into much larger long-term rewards (e.g., investments in agriculture, education, infrastructure, governments, and criminal justice systems).

Deliberating about possible actions by imagining different outcomes seems to be a fundamental psychological ability for humans, one enriched by using counterfactual logic, directed toward the goal of figuring out what the appropriate next action should be. None of this suggests that humans always or even frequently make well-informed, well-reasoned decisions. Any particular bit of reasoning, counterfactually underpinned or not, may be warped and bent by our current level of self-control, to mention just one example. Overall though, counterfactual reasoning appears capable of facilitating better decision-making at the individual level, which can then promote group coordination on a societal level by helping people learn from the past and prepare for the future (Byrne 2016). And by benefiting society, individuals receive the social benefits of acceptance and affiliation in a prosperous society.

8.2 Prospection, Self-control, and Decision-Making

Humans likely evolved the ability to prospect, to mentally simulate the future in order to consciously deliberate over multiple, alternative possibilities, because it conferred advantages to individual and group decision-making. Prospection allows analysis of one's possible decisions and actions and the possible results of those decisions and actions, enabling better *right now* choices that will lead to better *later* outcomes. For example, if a person has an 8:00 a.m. meeting tomorrow, they can anticipate that binge-watching Netflix until 3:00 a.m. will likely cause a rather painful morning, decide they would like to avoid that outcome, and go to bed earlier.

A key function of consciousness may be to allow people to conceptualize the future as a *matrix of maybe* (Baumeister, Maranges, and Vohs 2018)—that is, as containing multiple alternative possibilities—and thus as highly changeable and dependent on one's own choices and behavior. When people consciously consider the future, they believe that they can change it by their own volitional will (Helzer and Gilovich 2012). That belief likely motivates conscious prospection and planning and thinking through "If, then" scenarios to behave in ways likely to bring about desired future outcomes. Indeed, most prospective thinking *is* planning, to narrow the field of possible undesirable futures or to grow the field of desirable futures. The vast majority (75%) of peoples' thoughts about the future entail considering what might be *and* actively devising strategies to reach their goals via future actions, choices, and performances (Baumeister et al. 2020).

The ability to represent the future also facilitates an essential function of the human self—*information agency* (Baumeister, Maranges, and Vohs 2018). Information agency is the process by which individuals in a group contribute to building the group's shared knowledge. Living as a member of a cultural group confers many advantages to survival and reproduction, including shared knowledge and resources, division of labor and specialization, and protection in numbers. Cultural groups (and individuals) are stronger to the extent that they can function on a shared store of knowledge and beliefs (Fernbach and Light 2020) and form joint intentions (Engelmann and Tomasello 2018), such that interactions from basic exchanges with strangers to large-scale cooperation are made easier. To maintain collectively held beliefs and knowledge—what we follow the sociologist Bourdieu (1977) in calling the "doxa"—individuals within the group act as information agents: each person seeks out information, communicates one's knowledge to others, passes along knowledge received from others, and criticizes and refines information (Baumeister, Maranges, and Vohs 2018). Given that power comes with widely shared beliefs, they also maintain shared reality (often by prioritizing consensus over truth [Clark and Winegard 2020]), disseminate false information, and strategically withhold information. For example, people might choose to withhold information from others because they believe that information has potential to cause harm (e.g., Clark, Graso, et al. 2022; Davison 1983; Gunther and Mundy 1993; Rojas, Shah, and Faber 1996). Deciding which information and beliefs are important for the cultural group, cooperation, and one's own interest thus requires that people consider possible futures—what effects are desired, what effects are undesired, and what ideas will increase the likelihood of the desired ones and decrease the likelihood of the undesired ones. Imagining the potential impact of information enables maintenance of shared reality and avoidance of pernicious narratives.

Also conferring advantages to the cultural group is *self-control*, individuals' ability to regulate their thoughts, feelings, and behaviors, to act volitionally according to their will, goals, or important norms, and to suppress short-term desires to attain longer-term goals (Baumeister 2018). Self-control varies across people and predicts normative decision-making across many contexts (e.g., health, academics, relationships, criminal behavior, career outcomes; Tangney, Baumeister, and Boone 2004). After intelligence, self-control might be the second most important individual difference variable for predicting positive life outcomes across numerous otherwise unrelated domains (Baumeister 2018; although the two are also positively correlated [Meldrum et al. 2017]).

Self-control may have evolved to mediate between one's own desires, interests, and goals and the well-being of the group. Self-control may enable people to overcome impulses with short-term benefits (e.g., laziness and crime) to obtain longer-term benefits by contributing to the social group (e.g., working hard to obtain prestige and status) (Gottfredson and Hirschi 1990). Indeed, people higher in self-control less often lie, cheat, and steal to benefit themselves at the cost of others, and this is explained by stronger internalization and automatization of the morally right inclination and reduced moral temptations (Maranges et al. 2022a). People higher in self-control also engage in more other-focused complex moral decision-making that balances the well-being of the individual and the group on moral dilemmas (Maranges et al. 2022b). Moral dilemmas are cases in which doing some harm, often to one individual, may maximize outcomes for many people, or increase overall well-being. Consider a dilemma in which a doctor must decide whether to give community members a vaccine. For most people, the vaccine will have no side effects and will keep them safe from a deadly disease, but for some people, the vaccine will cause severe side effects. Researchers can measure both the tendency to avoid harm (i.e., refusing to give the vaccine; consistent with deontological ethics) and the tendency to maximize outcomes (e.g., giving the vaccine; consistent with utilitarian ethics) (Conway and Gawronski 2013). People higher, versus lower, in self-control demonstrate both tendencies to a greater extent (minimizing harm *and* maximizing outcomes), largely because they integrate empathetic feelings and deliberate reasoning (Maranges et al. 2022b). Volitional control, then, facilitates normative decision-making that benefits both individuals *and* the cultural group. And because people give status and awards to beneficial group members, this then feeds back to give more benefits to the individual (e.g., Buss et al. 2020; Clark, Keighley, and Vsiljevic 2022; Durkee, Lukaszewski, and Buss 2020).

These abilities to prospect, plan, socially coordinate, and consciously forego short-term benefits for long-term ones are not *free will* necessarily, a human capacity many regard as a prerequisite for *responsibility* (Frankfurt 1971; Shariff et al. 2014; Van Inwagen 1983; Wolf 1990). However, these abilities are unique to humans in their level of sophistication, which may justify conceiving humans as uniquely responsible for their behavior. Moreover, holding humans responsible likely encourages better behavior in others, and so regardless of whether it is truly *justified* (which is more of a normative than an empirical question anyway), holding humans responsible may be necessary for a thriving society.

8.3 Facilitating Responsibility

Because humans evolved to detect, blame, and punish costly members of the social group (Axelrod and Hamilton 1981; Fehr, Fischbacher, and Gächter 2002; Kurzban and Leary 2001; Nowak and Sigmund 1998; Trivers 1971) humans also evolved to manage their reputations as prosocial and valuable members of their social groups in order to avoid punishment and ostracization (Clark, Keighley, and Vasiljevic, 2022; Fehr 2004; Sperber and Baumard 2012; Tennie, Frith, and Frith 2010; Vonasch et al. 2018). When people know their reputations are imperiled (e.g., because their behavior is publicly visible), they behave better (Wu, Balliet, and Van Lange 2016a, 2016b).

Consequently, making reputational judgments about other people effectively punishes and discourages certain behaviors in other people, and judging that other people are *responsible* for their bad behavior likely is a key ingredient in making these reputational judgments (Clark 2022).

One could imagine an alternative reality where transgressions were generally treated with sympathy and understanding (e.g., "Well, I am not happy that you stole my car, but it's not your fault—your genes made you do it. Tough break for both of us."). Possibly in some cases (especially those in which the offender was already unlikely to reoffend), this might be a suitable reaction. But adopted at large, it seems it would be less effective at deterring future transgressions (in both the perpetrator and third-party observers of the transgression response) than more reputationally damaging reactions (e.g., labeling the perpetrator a criminal and publishing the transgression in the public record). People likely evolved to make reputational judgments and assign morally disparaging labels to harmdoers (such as liar, cheater, thief, crook, scoundrel, scalawag, lowlife, knave, fink, jerk, miscreant, hoodlum, rapscallion, ne'er-do-well, buttface, meanie, asshat) in part because they were and are effective deterrents for antisocial behavior, which creates a more prosperous environment for humans on whole. This fact may explain why humans are less inclined to make moral reputational judgments toward harmdoers who have little concern for preserving their moral reputations (e.g., we have never heard anyone describe a baby's or animal's misbehavior as *morally wrong*), because moral judgments would not be particularly effective in such cases (Clark 2022). Although assigning responsibility to an individual actor may communicate many things (e.g., regarding the actor's presumed intentions and obligations; Murray and Vargas 2020), responsibility-laden reputational judgments may ultimately function as a means of deterring undesirable behavior in both the transgressor and third-party observers of the transgression response.

Consistent with this possibility, judgments about how much freedom and control people have over their behavior appear *motivated* by desires to hold others morally responsible for their bad behavior. *Motivated* reasoning refers to the tendency for people's reasoning, and consequently, judgments and beliefs, to be influenced by their desires. Rather than dispassionately and objectively observing the world and drawing the most rational and accurate conclusions, it often seems that reasoning is motivated to pursue certain goals (e.g., to justify preferred beliefs and conclusions, to conform to local beliefs; e.g., Baumeister and Newman 1994; Ditto et al. 2019a, 2019b; Ditto and Lopez 1992; Haidt 2001, 2012; Kunda 1990; Mercier and Sperber 2011).[1] A useful metaphor often invoked is that sometimes people seem to reason more like lawyers—starting with a desired conclusion and then organizing the evidence to support that conclusion—than like (ideal) scientists—evenhandedly piecing the evidence together to come to the most accurate conclusion.

In the context of attributions of responsibility, people attribute more intentionality, freedom, free will, choice, and causal control to others for behaviors with harmful outcomes than for very similar or identical behaviors with helpful or neutral outcomes (e.g., Alicke 1992; 2000; Clark, Chen, and Ditto 2015; Clark et al. 2017; 2018; Cushman 2008; Nadelhoffer et al. 2020; Knobe 2003, 2006; Knobe and Fraser 2008; Reeder and Spores 1983; Walster 1966). For example, people attributed greater causal control to a speeding driver who caused a car accident when he was said to be speeding home to hide a vial of cocaine than when he was said to be speeding home to hide an anniversary present (Alicke 1992). These and many similar findings (e.g., Clark et al. 2014; Everett et al. 2020) suggest that desires to blame and punish harmdoers *motivate* perceptions that harmdoers are morally responsible for their bad behavior.

Similarly, when faced with others' harmful behaviors, people also report stronger beliefs in free will *in general*, are more likely to reject science that challenges free will, and seek to uphold human moral responsibility broadly (Clark, Graso et al. 2014; 2022; Clark, Winegard, and Baumeister 2019). For example, in one study, students in a psychology course were randomly assigned to receive different emails from their professor shortly after a midterm exam. One set of emails informed the students that one of their classmates had cheated on the exam, whereas the control email simply informed the students that there would be an activity in the next class. All emails contained a link directing the students to a survey which included a measure of free will belief and a brief questionnaire about how severely students should be punished for cheating on exams. Students who believed one of their classmates had cheated thought cheaters deserved harsher punishments and believed more in free will than students who believed they were completing the measures as part of class activity (Clark et al. 2014). Such findings suggest that upholding free will and moral responsibility is particularly crucial when dealing with the harmful norm-violating behaviors of others.

The Don Corleone Principle (Clark 2022) describes a tendency for people to have such pro-blame biases (to view others are more responsible for bringing about harmful outcomes than neutral or positive outcomes) because under-blaming is evolutionarily costly. *Not* holding people morally responsible for their bad behavior can signal to others that one is easily exploitable, and that selfish behavior may be tolerated. Not only can under-blaming incentive perpetrators to reoffend, but it can also demonstrate to third-party observers that the rewards of selfish behavior outweigh their costs. On a large scale, diminishing responsibility for harmful outcomes could normalize selfish, antisocial behavior.

Although free will and other responsibility judgments might be *motivated* by desires to blame others for their harmful behavior, these are likely minor adjustments on top of otherwise more *rational* processes. In many cases, people assess how much freedom and control people have, and update judgments of blame and punishment rationally and systematically on the basis of receiving new evidence (e.g., Guglielmo, Monroe, and Malle 2009; Malle, Guglielmo, and Monroe 2014; Monroe and Malle 2019). Moral judgments vary with attributions of free will, and attributions of free will vary with the history of the agent being evaluated. For example, across studies in which Mary, a perpetrator of harm (i.e., killing her neighbor), had desires, values, and beliefs that made her want to commit that harm, people judged her as having free will and being morally responsible and blameworthy (Taylor and Maranges 2019). However, when those same desires, values, and beliefs emerged because scientists had implanted them or a tumor was causing them in Mary's brain, people viewed Mary as less morally responsible and blameworthy. These judgments were accounted for by perceptions of attenuated free will, both in terms of freedom to act and freedom to develop (two lay conceptions of free will, Gill and Cerce 2017). Similarly, people judge harmdoers less harshly and attribute less free will when agents cause harm after becoming addicted to some substance and while seeking out that substance (Taylor et al. 2021). Responsibility and blame judgments are even further diminished when the harmdoer did not consent or was forced to consume the addictive substance in the past, and this is partially explained by perceptions that the actor had little free will (Taylor et al. 2021).

In general, perceptions of intentions and desires to cause harm increase blame (e.g., Cushman 2008; Monroe and Malle 2017; Monroe and Ysidron 2020; Schein and Gray 2018), and those who are believed to have a choice and causal control over their behavior and outcomes are blamed more harshly. Indeed, perceptions of choice and causal control are correlated with moral wrongness and blameworthiness judgments for homosexuality (Haider-Markel and Joslyn 2008), obesity and schizophrenia (Chandrashekar 2020), pedophilia, drug addiction, psychopathy, having a fetish, being racist, being transgender, and depression (Mercier, Clark, and Shariff 2019). When people perceive such behaviors, conditions, and life outcomes as controllable, the expression of them may be viewed as a marker of self-control (or a lack thereof), and people may use these markers to judge the morality and cooperative partner value of others. People judge others stereotyped as having lower self-control (e.g., people with obesity) as less moral and less trustworthy and are less interested in working with such people than those with more moderate body weight when given the choice of cooperative partner (Maranges, Ainsworth, and March 2022). People may use superficial cues of self-control as personality indicators to affiliate with disciplined others who are likely to benefit the self. And although these cues are not perfect indicators of underlying traits (and people may occasionally cause overestimations of how much control people have over their expression), they may not be completely useless either insofar as self-control really is correlated with various undesirable behaviors and outcomes. Consistent with this line of reasoning, Righetti and Finkenauer (2011) found that people have higher trust in others who exhibit better self-control.

In turn, awareness that one is being judged for expressions of self-control (or expressions of failed self-control) likely contributes to some degree of behavioral regulation by encouraging people to make better choices without the need for interventions from authorities. For example, the stigmatization of cigarette smoking appears to have contributed to the decline in tobacco use (Bayer 2008). Social judgment—although often viewed as an inherent bad—can promote more desirable decisions among individuals, which generally also contributes to the public good, without paternalistic top-down impingement on peoples' freedom (e.g., by outlawing smoking).

At the same time, people may seek ways of dodging responsibility for their own harmful behavior by downplaying their own abilities to regulate their behavior and outcomes. This may explain why people report having less free will and personal responsibility when they have caused harmful outcomes themselves—they may want others to interpret their harmful behaviors as caused by external factors rather than their own lack of self-discipline. For example, in one study, participants wrote about a time their addictive behavior led to harmful consequences or more neutral consequences and then reported how much free will they had themselves. Those who wrote about the harmful consequences of their addictive behavior downplayed their free will more than those who wrote about neutral consequences (Vonasch et al. 2018). People who engage in harmful behaviors might prefer to explain their own harmful behavior as the result of external forces to dissociate it from their personal characteristics and minimize blame and reputational judgments. This same set of studies also found evidence for a self-fulfilling prophecy: reducing beliefs in one's own free will increased perceptions of how addictive various substances and activities were and lowered perceptions of one's own self-control. Thus, minimizing perceptions of one's own free will could lead to feelings of defeat over short-term impulses and reduced self-control in ways that are harmful to the person seeking to avoid responsibility.

On concrete constructs *related* to free will, it appears that reduced feelings of personal responsibility are associated with undesirable outcomes, or conversely, that high feelings of personal responsibility are associated with desirable ones. For example, perceived regulatory self-efficacy was associated with scholastic achievement, prosocial behavior, and reduced vulnerability to feelings of futility and depression (Bandura et al. 1996), higher job satisfaction and performance (Saragih 2015), and perseverance (Gist 1987). Taking responsibility for wronging others was associated with more prosocial responses to the wrongdoing (Fisher and Exline 2006), and feelings of personal responsibility can promote well-being (Langer and Rodin 1976). In the experimental psychology and philosophy literatures, however, it remains unclear whether and how much decreasing free will *beliefs* influence prosocial behavior on average (Baumeister, Masicampo, and DeWall 2009; Genschow et al. 2021; Nadelhoffer et al. 2020; Vohs and Schooler 2008). Not only have there been failures to replicate the impact of reduced free will beliefs on prosocial behavior (Nadelhoffer et al. 2020), current methodological attempts to reduce free will beliefs may be largely ineffective (Genschow et al. 2021). Reducing free will beliefs may not be possible, especially if they are held with the conviction of other kinds of moral and religious beliefs. But attempting to identify ways to reduce free will beliefs (at least temporarily) may be useful to better explore whether scholars' intuitions about the potential consequences of reduced free will beliefs are borne out.

More research is needed to understand the full range of possible consequences of minimizing feelings of personal responsibility, but these findings do raise an interesting dilemma. Often, arguments against free will treat perpetrators as victims—victims of their personal life circumstances, of their genes, of the luck-based lottery of life (e.g., Caruso 2016). And there is some merit to this perspective. After all, human behavior is caused by a combination of genes and environments, and people have little control over either (Clark 2020). It can thus seem harsh and unjust to hold people responsible for their behaviors and life outcomes—they did not choose the genes and environments that ultimately caused them to commit their transgressions. From a practical perspective, however, it is worth considering whether responsibility judgments, on whole, improve the lives and well-being of most people (perpetrators, victims, and broader society). People likely evolved pro-blame biases—attributing more free will, responsibility, and causal control to those who cause harm than to similarly situated actors who cause neutral or helpful consequences—because it effectively deters others from causing harm. Just as a person might avoid speeding while driving next to a police officer who might issue a pricey ticket, people might avoid committing selfish or harmful behaviors in front of others who might judge them and smear their reputations. Indeed, criminal justice systems are one cultural solution to promoting group cooperation and cohesion, but they are costly, complicated, and limited. Tendencies to blame and morally judge harmdoers are one of perhaps many psychological adaptations that similarly promote socially advantageous behavior *without* the need for complex and expensive institutions.

At the same time, people likely evolved to consider how much freedom and control harmdoers had when deciding how much blame is warranted because the harm caused under conditions of greater freedom and control are more malleable (i.e., capable of being deterred) and more diagnostic of harmdoers' underlying characteristics and cooperative partner value. The risk of being evaluated negatively likely incentivizes the use of self-control to make decisions more beneficial to the social group (which in turn benefits the self).

Insofar as responsibility judgments (and corresponding punishments) incentivize prosocial behavior, deter antisocial behavior, and motivate people to avoid risky short-term benefits (such as criminal behavior and unhealthy lifestyle behaviors) to obtain long-term benefits, upholding human responsibility may help most people come closer to the best versions of themselves. And minor improvements in each individual can have large and widespread benefits for society as a whole. In other words, social environments that emphasize personal responsibility may create more individual-level and group-level prospering. Perhaps ironically, if humans lack free will because their behaviors are fully caused by their genes and environments, we should treat people as though they have free will because such an environment may facilitate more socially productive decision-making (Clark and Winegard 2019; Smilansky 2000). The belief in free will is an environmental feature that positively influences human behavior.

8.4 Conclusion

Although scholars may never agree upon a single definition of free will or whether the causes of human behavior warrant the label "free will," human cognition has numerous unique capabilities that may warrant conceiving humans as uniquely responsible for their behaviors. By consciously imagining alternative past outcomes and simulating likely future outcomes of various behaviors, people can use such calculations to make better decisions. Whereas other animals may make decisions by relying on intuitions and learned associations from the past, humans can use their imaginations of past and future possibilities to forego short-term benefits to obtain longer-term rewards. Insofar as humans are often *aware* of likely future outcomes of their behaviors before engaging in them (e.g., if I shoplift, I may get arrested, which creates costs for taxpayers, and I will almost certainly contribute to higher priced goods for non-shoplifters), it may not be unreasonable to consider humans as responsible for the outcomes caused by their behaviors (at least in some cases).

Moreover, treating people *as though* they have free will and are responsible for their behavior may incentivize more socially desirable behavior, which in turn benefits the individual through earned social status and affiliations (and disincentivizes socially undesirable behavior, which protects against status and affiliation losses). When those who generate costs to the social group (e.g., by harming others or consuming resources without pulling their weight) are viewed as responsible for those costs and subsequently viewed negatively by others, this creates costs to the individual, which incentivizes a purely self-interested person to behave in ways that benefit the group. Thus, responsibility narratives may be the solution to a critical problem: how to make individuals who evolved to behave in ways that selfishly promote their own thriving to behave in ways that cooperatively promote the thriving of the social group.

Note

1 Although see also Pennycook and Rand, 2019; Monroe and Ysidron, 2020.

References

Alicke, M. D. (1992), "Culpable Causation," *Journal of Personality and Social Psychology*, 63 (3): 368–78.
Alicke, M. D. (2000), "Culpable Control and the Psychology of Blame," *Psychological Bulletin*, 126 (4): 556–74.
Alquist, J. L., S. E. Ainsworth, R. F. Baumeister, M. Daly, and T. F. Stillman (2015), "The Making of Might-Have-Beens: Effects of Free Will Belief on Counterfactual Thinking," *Personality and Social Psychology Bulletin*, 41 (2): 268–83.
Axelrod, R. and W. D. Hamilton (1981), "The Evolution of Cooperation," *Science*, 211 (4489): 1390–6.
Baars, B. J. (1983), "Conscious Contents Provide the Nervous System with Coherent, Global Information," in *Consciousness and Self-regulation*, 41–79, Boston, MA: Springer.
Baars, B. J. and S. Franklin (2009), "Consciousness is Computational: The LIDA Model of Global Workspace Theory," *International Journal of Machine Consciousness*, 1 (01): 23–32.
Bandura, A., C. Barbaranelli, G. V. Caprara, and C. Pastorelli (1996), "Multifaceted Impact of Self-Efficacy Beliefs on Academic Functioning," *Child Development*, 67 (3): 1206–22.
Baumeister, R. (2018), *Self-Regulation and Self-Control: Selected Works of Roy F. Baumeister*, London: Routledge.
Baumeister, R. F. (2005), *The Cultural Animal: Human Nature, Meaning, and Social Life*, New York: Oxford University Press.
Baumeister, R. F., C. J. Clark, J. Kim, and S. Lau (2017), "Consumers (and Consumer Researchers) Need Conscious Thinking in Addition to Unconscious Processes: A Call for Integrative Models, a Commentary on Williams and Poehlman," *Journal of Consumer Research*, 44 (2): 252–7.
Baumeister, R. F., C. J. Clark, and J. Luguri (2015), "Free Will: Belief and Reality," in A. Mele (ed.), *Surrounding Free Will*, 49–71, New York: Oxford University Press.
Baumeister, R. F., W. Hofmann, A. Summerville, P. T. Reiss, and K. D. Vohs (2020), "Everyday Thoughts in Time: Experience Sampling Studies of Mental Time Travel," *Personality and Social Psychology Bulletin*, 46 (12): 1631–48.

Baumeister, R. F., S. Lau, H. M. Maranges, and C. J. Clark (2018), "On the Necessity of Consciousness for Sophisticated Human Action," *Frontiers in Psychology*, 9: 1925.

Baumeister, R. F., H. M. Maranges, and H. Sjastad (2018), "Consciousness of the Future as a Matrix of Maybe: Pragmatic Prospection and the Simulation of Alternative Possibilities," *Psychology of Consciousness: Theory, Research, and Practice*, 5 (3): 223–38. https://doi.org/10.1037/cns0000154.

Baumeister, R. F., H. M. Maranges, and K. D. Vohs (2018), "Human Self as Information Agent: Functioning in a Social Environment Based on Shared Meanings," *Review of General Psychology*, 22 (1): 36–47. https://doi.org/10.1037/gpr0000114.

Baumeister, R. F., E. J. Masicampo, and C. N. DeWall (2009), "Prosocial Benefits of Feeling Free: Disbelief in Free Will Increases Aggression and Reduces Helpfulness," *Personality and Social Psychology Bulletin*, 35 (2): 260–8.

Baumeister, R. F. and L. S. Newman (1994), "Self-Regulation of Cognitive Inference and Decision Processes," *Personality and Social Psychology Bulletin*, 20 (1): 3–19.

Bayer, R. (2008), "Stigma and the Ethics of Public Health: Not Can We but Should We," *Social Science & Medicine*, 67 (3): 463–72.

Boninger, D. S., F. Gleicher, and A. Strathman (1994), "Counterfactual Thinking: From What Might Have Been to What May Be," *Journal of Personality and Social Psychology*, 67 (2): 297–307.

Buss, D. M., P. K. Durkee, T. K. Shackelford, B. F. Bowdle, D. P. Schmitt, G. L. Brase, J. C. Choe, and I. Trofimova (2020), "Human Status Criteria: Sex Differences and Similarities Across 14 Nations," *Journal of Personality and Social Psychology*, 119 (5): 979–98.

Byrne, R. M. (2016), "Counterfactual Thought," *Annual Review of Psychology*, 67: 135–57.

Byrne, R. M. J. (1997), "Cognitive Processes in Counterfactual Thinking About What Might Have Been," in D. L. Medin (ed.), *Psychology of Learning and Motivation: Advances in Research and Theory*, vol. 37, 105–54, San Diego, CA: Academic Press.

Caruso, G. D. (2016), "Free Will Skepticism and Criminal Behavior: A Public Health-Quarantine Model," *Southwest Philosophy Review*, 32 (1): 25–48.

Celuch, K. and C. Saxby (2013), "Counterfactual Thinking and Ethical Decision Making: A New Approach to an Old Problem for Marketing Education," *Journal of Marketing Education*, 35 (2): 155–67.

Chandrashekar, S. P. (2020), "It's in Your Control: Free Will Beliefs and Attribution of Blame to Obese People and People with Mental Illness," *Collabra: Psychology*, 6 (1): 29.

Clark, C. J. (2020), "The Social Sciences Have No Use for Undetermined Free Will," *Philosopher*, 108: 61–80.

Clark, C. J. (2022), "The Blame Efficiency Hypothesis: An Evolutionary Framework to Resolve Rationalist and Intuitionist Theories of Moral Condemnation," in T. Nadelhoffer and A. Monroe (eds.), *Advances in Experimental Philosophy of Free Will and Responsibility*, 27–44, London: Bloomsbury Publishing.

Clark, C. J., C. W. Bauman, S. V. Kamble, and E. D. Knowles (2017), "Intentional Sin and Accidental Virtue? Cultural Differences in Moral Systems Influence Perceived Intentionality," *Social Psychological and Personality Science*, 8 (1): 74–82.

Clark, C. J., E. E. Chen, and P. H. Ditto (2015), "Moral Coherence Processes: Constructing Culpability and Consequences," *Current Opinion in Psychology*, 6: 123–8.

Clark, C. J., M. Graso, I. Redstone, and P. E. Tetlock (2022), "Harm Hypervigilance in Public Reactions to Scientific Evidence." Manuscript under review, in press.

Clark, C. J., N. Honeycutt, and L. Jussim (2022), "Replicability and the Psychology of Science," in S. Lilienfeld, A. Masuda, and W. O'Donohue (eds.), *Questionable Research Practices in Psychology*, 45–71, New York: Springer.

Clark, C. J., D. Keighley, and M. Vasiljevic (2022), "Being Bad to Look Good: Competence Reputational Stakes Can Increase Unethical Behavior," *Evolutionary Behavioral Sciences*. Online first.

Clark, C. J., J. B. Luguri, P. H. Ditto, J. Knobe, A. F. Shariff, and R. F. Baumeister (2014), "Free to Punish: A Motivated Account of Free Will Belief," *Journal of Personality and Social Psychology*, 106 (4): 501–13.

Clark, C. J., A. Shniderman, J. B. Luguri, R. F. Baumeister, and P. H. Ditto (2018), "Are Morally Good Actions Ever Free?," *Consciousness and Cognition*, 63: 161–82.

Clark, C. J. and B. M. Winegard (2019), "An Evolutionary Perspective on Free Will Belief," Science Trends. Available online: https://sciencetrends.com/an-evolutionary-perspective-on-free-will.

Clark, C. J. and B. M. Winegard (2020), "Tribalism in War and Peace: The Nature and Evolution of Ideological Epistemology and Its Significance for Modern Social Science," *Psychological Inquiry*, 31 (1): 1–22.

Clark, C. J., B. M. Winegard, and R. F. Baumeister (2019), "Forget the Folk: Moral Responsibility Preservation Motives and Other Conditions for Compatibilism," *Frontiers in Psychology*, 10: 215.

Clark, C. J., B. M. Winegard, and A. F. Shariff (2021), "Motivated Free Will Beliefs: The Theory, New (Preregistered) Studies, and Three Meta-analyses," *Journal of Experimental Psychology: General*, 150 (7): e22.

Conway, P. and B. Gawronski (2013), "Deontological and Utilitarian Inclinations in Moral Decision Making: A Process Dissociation Approach," *Journal of Personality and Social Psychology*, 104 (2): 216–35. https://doi.org/10.1037/a0031021.

Cushman, F. (2008), "Crime and Punishment: Distinguishing the Roles of Causal and Intentional Analyses in Moral Judgment," *Cognition*, 108 (2): 353–80.

Davison, W. P. (1983), "The Third-Person Effect in Communication," *Public Opinion Quarterly*, 47 (1): 1–15.

De Brigard, F., E. Hanna, P. L. St. Jacques, and D. L. Schacter (2019), "How Thinking About What Could Have Been Affects How We Feel About What Was," *Cognition and Emotion*, 33 (4): 646–59.

De Brigard, F., P. Henne, and M. L. Stanley (2021), "Perceived Similarity of Imagined Possible Worlds Affects Judgments of Counterfactual Plausibility," *Cognition*, 209: 104574.

Dennett, D. C. (2004), *Freedom Evolves*, New York: Penguin.

Dennett, D. C. (2015), *Elbow Room: The Varieties of Free Will Worth Wanting*, Cambridge, MA: MIT Press.

Ditto, P. H., C. J. Clark, B. S. Liu, S. P. Wojcik, E. E. Chen, R. H. Grady, J. B. Celniker, and J. F. Zinger (2019b), "Partisan Bias and Its Discontents," *Perspectives on Psychological Science*, 14 (2): 304–16.

Ditto, P. H., B. S. Liu, C. J. Clark, S. P. Wojcik, E. E. Chen, R. H. Grady, J. B. Celniker, and J. F. Zinger (2019a), "At Least Bias is Bipartisan: A Meta-analytic Comparison of Partisan Bias in Liberals and Conservatives," *Perspectives on Psychological Science*, 14 (2): 273–91.

Ditto, P. H. and D. F. Lopez (1992), "Motivated Skepticism: Use of Differential Decision Criteria for Preferred and Nonpreferred Conclusions," *Journal of Personality and Social Psychology*, 63 (4): 568–84.

Durkee, P. K., A. W. Lukaszewski, and D. M. Buss (2020), "Psychological Foundations of Human Status Allocation," *Proceedings of the National Academy of Sciences*, 117 (35): 21235–41.
Engelmann, D. and U. Fischbacher (2009), "Indirect Reciprocity and Strategic Reputation Building in an Experimental Helping Game," *Games and Economic Behavior*, 67 (2): 399–407.
Engelmann, J. M. and M. Tomasello (2018), "The Middle Step: Joint Intentionality as a Human-Unique Form of Second-Personal Engagement," in M. Jankovic and K. Ludwig (eds.), *The Routledge Handbook of Collective Intentionality*, 433–46, London: Routledge/Taylor & Francis Group.
Fehr, E. (2004), "Don't Lose Your Reputation," *Nature*, 432 (7016): 449–50.
Fehr, E., U. Fischbacher, and S. Gächter (2002), "Strong Reciprocity, Human Cooperation, and the Enforcement of Social Norms," *Human Nature*, 13 (1): 1–25.
Feltz, A., E. T. Cokely, and T. Nadelhoffer (2009), "Natural Compatibilism Versus Natural Incompatibilism: Back to the Drawing Board," *Mind & Language*, 24 (1): 1–23.
Fernbach, P. M. and N. Light (2020), "Knowledge is Shared," *Psychological Inquiry*, 31 (1): 26–8.
Fisher, M. L. and J. J. Exline (2006), "Self-Forgiveness Versus Excusing: The Roles of Remorse, Effort, and Acceptance of Responsibility," *Self and Identity*, 5 (02): 127–46.
Frankfurt, H. G. (1969), "Alternate Possibilities and Moral Responsibility," *Journal of Philosophy*, 66 (23): 829–39.
Frankfurt, H. G. (1971), "Freedom of the Will and the Concept of a Person," *Journal of Philosophy*, 68 (1): 5–20.
Franklin, S. (1995), *Artificial Minds*, Cambridge, MA: MIT Press.
Franklin, S. (2003), "A Conscious Artifact?," *Journal of Consciousness Studies*, 10: 47–66.
Gächter, S. and E. Fehr (1999), "Collective Action as a Social Exchange," *Journal of Economic Behavior & Organization*, 39 (4): 341–69.
Genschow, O., E. Cracco, J. Schneider, J. Protzko, D. Wisniewski, M. Brass, and J. Schooler (2021), "Meta-analysis on Belief in Free Will Manipulations." https://doi.org/10.31234/osf.io/quwgr.
Gerstenberg, T., N. D. Goodman, D. A. Lagnado, and J. B. Tenenbaum (2021), "A Counterfactual Simulation Model of Causal Judgments for Physical Events," *Psychological Review* [Advance online publication]. https://doi.org/10.1037/rev0000281.
Gerstenberg, T., M. F. Peterson, N. D. Goodman, D. A. Lagnado, and J. B. Tenenbaum (2017), "Eye-Tracking Causality," *Psychological Science*, 28 (12): 1731–44.
Gill, M. J. and S. C. Cerce (2017), "He Never Willed to have the Will he has: Historicist Narratives, "civilized" Blame, and the Need to Distinguish Two Notions of Free Will," *Journal of Personality and Social Psychology*, 112 (3): 361–82.
Gist, M. E. (1987), "Self-Efficacy: Implications for Organizational Behavior and Human Resource Management," *Academy of Management Review*, 12 (3): 472–85.
Gottfredson, M. R. and T. Hirschi (1990), *A General Theory of Crime*, Palo Alto, CA: Stanford University Press.
Guglielmo, S., A. E. Monroe, and B. F. Malle (2009), "At the Heart of Morality Lies Folk Psychology," *Inquiry*, 52 (5): 449–66.
Gunther, A. C. and P. Mundy (1993), "Biased Optimism and the Third-Person Effect," *Journalism Quarterly*, 70 (1): 58–67.

Haggard, P., A. Mele, T. O'Connor, and K. Vohs (2015), "Free Will Lexicon," in A. R. Mele (ed.), *Surrounding Free Will*, 319–26, New York: Oxford University Press.

Haider-Markel, D. P. and M. R. Joslyn (2008), "Beliefs About the Origins of Homosexuality and Support for Gay Rights: An Empirical Test of Attribution Theory," *Public Opinion Quarterly*, 72 (2): 291–310.

Haidt, J. (2001), "The Emotional Dog and Its Rational Tail: A Social Intuitionist Approach to Moral Judgment," *Psychological Review*, 108 (4): 814–34.

Haidt, J. (2012), *The Righteous Mind*, New York: Penguin Books.

Helzer, E. G. and T. Gilovich (2012), "Whatever is Willed Will Be: A Temporal Asymmetry in Attributions to Will," *Personality and Social Psychology Bulletin*, 38 (10): 1235–46.

Kahneman, D. and A. Tversky (1982), "Availability and the Simulation Heuristic," in D. Kahneman, P. Slovic, and A. Tversky (eds.), *Judgment Under Uncertainty: Heuristics and Biases*, 201–8, New York: Oxford University Press.

Kane, R. (1998), *The Significance of Free Will*, New York: Oxford University Press.

Kapitan, T. (1986), "Deliberation and the Presumption of Open Alternatives," *The Philosophical Quarterly*, 36 (143): 230–51.

Kelley, H. H. (1973), "The Processes of Causal Attribution," *American Psychologist*, 28 (2): 107–28.

Knobe, J. (2003), "Intentional Action and Side Effects in Ordinary Language," *Analysis*, 63 (3): 190–4.

Knobe, J. (2006), "The Concept of Intentional Action: A Case Study in the Uses of Folk Psychology," *Philosophical Studies*, 130 (2): 203–31.

Knobe, J., W. Buckwalter, S. Nichols, P. Robbins, H. Sarkissian, and T. Sommers (2012), "Experimental Philosophy," *Annual Review of Psychology*, 63: 81–99.

Knobe, J. and B. Fraser (2008), "Causal Judgment and Moral Judgment: Two Experiments," *Moral Psychology*, 2: 441–8.

Kunda, Z. (1990), "The Case for Motivated Reasoning," *Psychological Bulletin*, 108 (3): 480–98.

Kurzban, R. and M. R. Leary (2001), "Evolutionary Origins of Stigmatization: The Functions of Social Exclusion," *Psychological Bulletin*, 127 (2): 187–208.

Langer, E. J. and J. Rodin (1976), "The Effects of Choice and Enhanced Personal Responsibility for the Aged: A Field Experiment in an Institutional Setting," *Journal of Personality and Social Psychology*, 34 (2): 191.

Malle, B. F., S. Guglielmo, and A. E. Monroe (2014), "A Theory of Blame," *Psychological Inquiry*, 25 (2): 147–86.

Maranges, H. M., S. E. Ainsworth, and D. S. March (2022), "Concerns about Self-Control Underlie Moralized Prejudice Against People with Obesity." *Manuscript submitted for publication*.

Maranges, H. M., M. A. Dieciuc, A. J. Vonasch, M. Taylor, and D. S. March (2022a), "Trait Self-Control Predicts Moral Decision Making Through Reduced Automatic Temptation." *Manuscript submitted for publication*.

Maranges, H. M., T. A. Reynolds, D. S. March, R. F. Baumeister, and P. J. Conway (2022b), "Self-Control as the Moral Dilemma Muscle: Trait Self-Control Predicts Both Deontological and Utilitarian Moral Judgments." *Manuscript submitted for publication*.

Markman, K. D., I. Gavanski, S. J. Sherman, and M. N. McMullen (1993), "The Mental Simulation of Better and Worse Possible Worlds," *Journal of Experimental Social Psychology*, 29 (1): 87–109.

Markman, K. D., M. N. McMullen, and R. A. Elizaga (2008), "Counterfactual Thinking, Persistence, and Performance: A Test of the Reflection and Evaluation Model," *Journal of Experimental Social Psychology*, 44 (2): 421–8.

Meldrum, R. C., M. A. Petkovsek, B. B. Boutwell, and J. T. Young (2017), "Reassessing the Relationship Between General Intelligence and Self-Control in Childhood," *Intelligence*, 60: 1–9.

Mercier, B., C. J. Clark, and A. F. Shariff (2019), *Correlates of Perceived Mental Illness* [Unpublished manuscript], Irvine, CA: Department of Psychological Science, University of California, Irvine.

Mercier, H. and D. Sperber (2011), "Why Do Humans Reason? Arguments for an Argumentative Theory," *Behavioral and Brain Sciences*, 34 (2): 57–74.

Monroe, A. E. and B. F. Malle (2010), "From Uncaused Will to Conscious Choice: The Need to Study, Not Speculate About People's Folk Concept of Free Will," *Review of Philosophy and Psychology*, 1 (2): 211–24.

Monroe, A. E. and B. F. Malle (2017), "Two Paths to Blame: Intentionality Directs Moral Information Processing Along Two Distinct Tracks," *Journal of Experimental Psychology: General*, 146 (1): 123–33.

Monroe, A. E. and B. F. Malle (2019), "People Systematically Update Moral Judgments of Blame," *Journal of Personality and Social Psychology*, 116 (2): 215–36.

Monroe, A. E. and D. W. Ysidron (2020), "Not so Motivated After All? Three Replication Attempts and a Theoretical Challenge to a Morally Motivated Belief in Free Will," *Journal of Experimental Psychology: General*, 150 (1): e1–ee12.

Murray, S., E. Dykhuis, and T. Nadelhoffer (2022), "Do People Understand Determinism? The Tracking Problem for Measuring Free Will Beliefs." *Manuscript submitted for publication.*

Murray, S. and M. Vargas (2020), "Vigilance and Control," *Philosophical Studies*, 177 (3): 825–43.

Nadelhoffer, T., Shepard, J., Crone, D. L., Everett, J. A., Earp, B. D., and Levy, N. (2020), "Does Encouraging a Belief in Determinism Increase Cheating? Reconsidering the Value of Believing in Free Will," *Cognition*, 203: 104342.

Nahmias, E., S. G. Morris, T. Nadelhoffer, and J. Turner (2006), "Is Incompatibilism Intuitive?," *Philosophy and Phenomenological Research*, 73 (1): 28–53.

Nahmias, E., S. Morris, T. Nadelhoffer, and J. Turner (2005), "Surveying Freedom: Folk Intuitions About Free Will and Moral Responsibility," *Philosophical Psychology*, 18 (5): 561–84.

Nichols, S. and J. Knobe (2007), "Moral Responsibility and Determinism: The Cognitive Science of Folk Intuitions," *Nous*, 41 (4): 663–85.

Niemi, L., J. Hartshorne, T. Gerstenberg, and L. Young (2016), "Implicit Measurement of Motivated Causal Attribution," in A. Papafragou, D. Grodner, D. Mirman, and J. C. Trueswell (eds.), Proceedings of the 38th Annual Conference of the Cognitive Science Society, 1745–50, Austin, TX: Cognitive Science Society.

Nowak, M. A. and K. Sigmund (1998), "Evolution of Indirect Reciprocity by Image Scoring," *Nature*, 393 (6685): 573–7.

Pearl, J. (2009), *Causality*, New York,: Cambridge University Press.

Pearl, J. and D. Mackenzie (2018), *The Book of Why: The New Science of Cause and Effect*, New York: Basic Books.

Pennycook, G. and D. G. Rand (2019), "Lazy, Not Biased: Susceptibility to Partisan Fake News is Better Explained by Lack of Reasoning than by Motivated Reasoning," *Cognition*, 188: 39–50.

Pereboom, D. (2006), *Living Without Free Will*, New York: Cambridge University Press.
Pereboom, D. (2008), "A Compatibilist Account of the Epistemic Conditions on Rational Deliberation," *The Journal of Ethics*, 12 (3–4): 287–306.
Phillips, J., A. Morris, and F. Cushman (2019), "How We Know What not to Think," *Trends in Cognitive Sciences*, 23 (12): 1026–40.
Reeder, G. D. and J. M. Spores (1983), "The Attribution of Morality," *Journal of Personality and Social Psychology*, 44 (4): 736–45.
Righetti, F. and C. Finkenauer (2011), "If You Are Able to Control Yourself, I Will Trust You: The Role of Perceived Self-Control in Interpersonal Trust," *Journal of Personality and Social Psychology*, 100 (5): 874–86.
Rojas, H., D. V. Shah, and R. J. Faber (1996), "For the Good of Others: Censorship and the Third-Person Effect," *International Journal of Public Opinion Research*, 8 (2): 163–86.
Saragih, S. (2015), "The Effects of Job Autonomy on Work Outcomes: Self Efficacy as an Intervening Variable," *International Research Journal of Business Studies*, 4 (3): 203–15.
Sarkissian, H., A. Chatterjee, F. De Brigard, J. Knobe, S. Nichols, and S. Sirker (2010), "Is Belief in Free Will a Cultural Universal?," *Mind & Language*, 25 (3): 346–58.
Schein, C. and K. Gray (2018), "The Theory of Dyadic Morality: Reinventing Moral Judgment by Redefining Harm," *Personality and Social Psychology Review*, 22 (1): 32–70.
Shariff, A. F., J. D. Greene, J. C. Karremans, J. B. Luguri, C. J. Clark, J. W. Schooler, R. F. Baumeister, and K. D. Vohs (2014), "Free Will and Punishment: A Mechanistic View of Human Nature Reduces Retribution," *Psychological Science*, 25 (8): 1563–70.
Smallman, R. (2013), "It's What's Inside that Counts: The Role of Counterfactual Content in Intention Formation," *Journal of Experimental Social Psychology*, 49 (5): 842–51.
Smilansky, S. (2000), *Free Will and Illusion*, New York: Oxford University Press.
Sperber, D. and N. Baumard (2012), "Moral Reputation: An Evolutionary and Cognitive Perspective," *Mind & Language*, 27 (5): 495–518.
Tangney, J. P., R. F. Baumeister, and A. L. Boone (2004), "High Self-control Predicts Good Adjustment, Less Pathology, Better Grades, and Interpersonal Success," *Journal of Personality*, 72: 271–324. doi:10.1111/j.0022-3506.2004.00263.x.
Taylor, M. C. and H. M. Maranges (2019), "Are the Folk Historicists About Moral Responsibility?," *Philosophical Psychology*, 33: 1–22. https://doi.org/10.1080/09515089.2019.1695045.
Taylor, M. C., H. M. Maranges, S. K. Chen, and A. J. Vonasch (2021), "Direct and Indirect Freedom in Addiction: Folk Free Will and Blame Judgments Are Sensitive to the Choice History of Drug Users." *Consciousness and Cognition*, 94: 103170.
Taylor, R. (1963), *Metaphysics*, Englewood Cliffs, NJ: Prentice-Hall.
Tennie, C., U. Frith, and C. D. Frith (2010), "Reputation Management in the Age of the World-Wide Web," *Trends in Cognitive Sciences*, 14 (11): 482–8.
Trivers, R. L. (1971), "The Evolution of Reciprocal Altruism," *The Quarterly Review of Biology*, 46 (1): 35–57.
Van Inwagen, P. (1983), *An Essay on Free Will*, New York: Oxford University Press.
Van Vugt, M. and C. L. Hardy (2010), "Cooperation for Reputation: Wasteful Contributions as Costly Signals in Public Goods," *Group Processes & Intergroup Relations*, 13 (1): 101–11.
Vohs, K. D. and J. W. Schooler (2008), "The Value of Believing in Free Will: Encouraging a Belief in Determinism Increases Cheating," *Psychological Science*, 19 (1): 49–54.

Vonasch, A. J., T. Reynolds, B. M. Winegard, and R. F. Baumeister (2018), "Death Before Dishonor: Incurring Costs to Protect Moral Reputation," *Social Psychological and Personality Science*, 9 (5): 604–13.

Walster, E. (1966), "Assignment of Responsibility for an Accident," *Journal of Personality and Social Psychology*, 3 (1): 73–9.

Wolf, S. (1990), *Freedom Within Reason*, New York: Oxford University Press.

Wolff, P. (2006), "Dynamics and the Perception of Causal Events," in T. Shipley and J. Zacks (eds.), *Understanding Events: How Humans See, Represent, and Act on Events*, 555–86, New York: Oxford University Press.

Wu, J., D. Balliet, and P. A. Van Lange (2016a), "Reputation Management: Why and How Gossip Enhances Generosity," *Evolution and Human Behavior*, 37 (3): 193–201.

Wu, J., D. Balliet, and P. A. Van Lange (2016b), "Reputation, Gossip, and Human Cooperation," *Social and Personality Psychology Compass*, 10 (6): 350–64.

9

Beyond the Courtroom

Agency and the Perception of Free Will

Edouard Machery, Markus Kneer, Pascale Willemsen,
and Albert Newen

9.1 Introduction

Philosophers, psychologists, and neuroscientists have proposed two different families of models of mindreading, that is, how we ascribe mental states, such as beliefs, desires, action plans, or intentions: the Theory Theory (e.g., Gopnik and Wellman 1992; Nichols and Stich 2003) and Simulation Theory (e.g., Goldman 1992, 2006). Theory Theory Models claim that we ascribe mental states on the basis of a folk psychological theory, while Simulation Theory models hold that mental state attribution results from the ascriber simulating what kind of mental states they would have, were they in the ascribee's situation. Despite their disagreements, both the Theory Theory and Simulation Theory, at least in their original variants (but see Gallese and Goldman 1998), are committed to the view that mindreading belongs to higher cognition. According to the Theory Theory, mindreading results from some form of theoretical reasoning, and, according to Simulation Theory, it requires understanding how one's situation is similar to, and differs from, the assignee's situation.

However, in the last two decades, cognitive-scientific research has revealed that philosophers, psychologists, and neuroscientists had often overlooked at least one important additional access to understanding others, namely a low-level response to a variety of perceptual, particularly visual, cues. This shift in perspective is illustrated by the research on *implicit* false belief understanding[1] (Baillargeon, Scott, and He 2010), which is measured by the observation of gaze direction and duration as well as anticipatory looking. Furthermore, in philosophy, it led to arguments for the direct perception of some mental phenomena (Carruthers 2015; Gallagher 2008; Newen, Welpinghus, and Juckel 2015) and, in psychology, to the investigation of the perception of goals in adults, children, and babies (e.g., Csibra et al. 1999; Reid 2007). Perceptual access to mental states appears not to require reasoning; rather, perceptual cues lead to the experience and judgment that the perceived object is an agent with some specific goals.

In this chapter, we argue that a similar shift in perspective is necessary for understanding the attribution of free will. Judgments based on visual cues have not only been overlooked for understanding the attribution of beliefs, desires, intentions, and so on (what we will call "mindedness"), but also for understanding the attribution of free will. Experimental philosophers working on free will seem to assume that determining whether an agent has free will or performed an action freely is a higher cognitive endeavor. For them, it would seem, we *reason* about free will and control. There has been much theoretical and empirical debate, for instance, about whether or not laypeople consider determinism consistent with free will (e.g., Hannikainen et al. 2019; Murray and Nahmias 2014; Nahmias et al. 2005; Nichols 2004; Nichols and Knobe 2007; Sarkissian et al. 2010). Because people are asked whether some unexpected or unusual conditions would defeat their usual expectation that people are in control of their actions, they are primed to engage in some form of conscious or unconscious reasoning, even if their judgments are influenced by emotions, as some have claimed (Nichols and Knobe 2007; but see Feltz and Cova 2014). We will call this way of studying the psychology of free will attribution *the courtroom approach* because it treats the attribution of free will as similar to what a judge does when she decides whether an agent had the capacity to control her behavior (Hollander-Blumoff 2012). We believe it is no accident that experimental-philosophical debates have taken place against a background of concerns about responsibility and punishment in the law and morality.

While the attribution of free will can sometimes involve reasoning, real-life judgments about whether an agent acts freely are often elicited more directly by the perception of the assignee's behavior. In everyday life, we do not merely reason to free will, we *see* it. The first contribution of this chapter is thus to invite experimental philosophers and psychologists to go beyond the courtroom approach and pay greater attention to the *perception* of free will and control in our everyday interactions. Thus, we develop a new paradigm to study free will judgments: *the perceptual approach*.

What makes us see free will? The second contribution of our chapter is to argue that free will is often attributed on the basis of the very cues that lead to the perception of agency. When someone is perceived as an agent, we also tend to perceive them as acting freely. Thus, on our view, in many everyday interactive situations, the attribution of free will is primarily a perception-based judgment that is anchored in the perception of agency. We call this model *"the agency model of free will attribution."*

Here is how we will proceed. In Section 9.2, we contrast the perceptual approach with previous studies of free will in psychology and experimental philosophy, and we propose our new model of free will attribution. In Section 9.3, we describe the new experimental materials that were developed to bring about the perceptual approach. Section 9.4 reports our results. Section 9.5 discusses their significance both for the agency model of free will attribution and for the existing debates about free will judgment in psychology and experimental philosophy, and it also highlights the limitations of our work.

9.2 The Agency Model of Free Will Attribution

In 1944, Heider and Simmel presented subjects with a short, black-and-white, animated video in which three geometrical figures (a circle and two triangles of different sizes) move across a surface (Heider and Simmel 1944). In addition, the video showed a fixed, large, rectangular object that could be opened and closed. Although the three geometrical figures looked nothing like actual agents (people or animals), the vast majority of participants in this famous study readily perceived them as agents, and they described the scene in agentic terms, attributing intentions, desires, and beliefs. The only agency cues participants saw were the movements of the geometrical figures, which seemed purposeful, with the figures changing direction, accelerating, and decelerating, often in response to the other figures' movements. Perception of agency on the basis of this kind of cues is robust across individuals, including children, and cultures (e.g., Barrett et al. 2005; Bowler and Thommen 2000; Gao, McCarthy, and Scholl 2010), while being highly sensitive to small variations in the stimuli (Gao, McCarthy, and Scholl 2010). The perception of agentic behavior appears to depend largely on three features—directionality, discontinuity, and responsiveness (Santos et al. 2008)—which we will call "agency cues." The object must not follow a physically determined trajectory. Instead of moving in a straight line, the object changes course without any contact with other physical objects. It should display a discontinuous movement pattern. For instance, it can stop and accelerate. Finally, the object should respond and react to other objects in its environment.

We propose that when we see an entity as an agent, we tend to see it as having a host of other properties. Previous research suggests that once an entity is perceived as an agent, we are disposed not only to attribute to it mental states such as intentions, desires, and beliefs but also to see it as conscious (Arico et al. 2011). The agency model of free will attribution hypothesizes that perceptual cues of agency lead to viewing the entity as not only minded and conscious, but also as free and in control of its own behavior. When we see the geometrical figures in Heidel and Simmel's experiment as agentive, we also tend to view them as being in control of their behavior, thus as being free to move one way or another. We thus predict that if an entity as simple as a geometrical figure moves in a directional, discontinuous, and responsive manner, it will be perceived as free.

Noticeably, the agency model of free will attribution is third-personal. It grounds free will judgment in the third-personal perception of others' agency. In this respect, it differs from approaches that highlight the first-personal experience of one's own actions. Wegner (2002 2003), for instance, has related the belief in free will to the conscious experience of one's own will as the source of one's intentional actions.

We acknowledge that the agency model of free will attribution is underspecified in important respects. For one, the relation between the perceptions of agency, mindedness, and free will is not specified. Perceptual cues could, for instance, lead us to perceive an object as an agent, and this perception could dispose us to view it as minded and free (Figure 9.1, left panel). Alternatively, agency, mindedness, and free will (as well, perhaps, as consciousness) could be part of a single package, which we tend to perceive in response to some low-level perceptual cues (Figure 9.1, right panel).

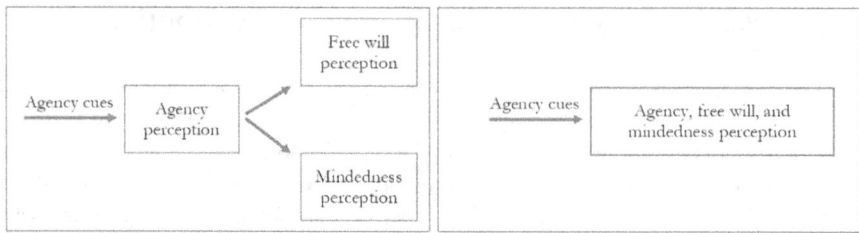

Figure 9.1 Two versions of the Agency Model. © Edouard Machery, Markus Kneer, Pascale Willemsen, and Albert Newen.

In addition, we remain noncommittal about the exact nature of the experience of free will (for related debates on the perception of agency, see Scholl and Gao 2013): Is it genuinely perceptual? If so, in what sense? Is it affected by beliefs, desires, and expectations? We believe that we are not yet in a position to address these gaps. Our goal is more modest. We want to loosen the grip of the courtroom approach on the study of free will attribution in experimental philosophy and psychology, developing experimental tools to examine the perception of free will, and we want to show that there is a plausible connection between the perception of agency and free will.

We would also like to emphasize that the agency model does not deny the relevance of reasoning for the attribution of free will. We do sometimes reason to decide whether someone was in control of her actions. The experimental philosophy studies treating free will judgments as the output of some form of reasoning might thus be onto something. That said, we aim to demonstrate that there is more to the psychology of free will attribution than reasoning.

9.3 Designing New Materials for the Perceptual Approach

As noted in the introduction, one of the goals of this chapter is to develop an alternative to the courtroom approach to free will attribution, which acknowledges that many of our judgments about control and free will result from the perceptual experience of free will. Studying the perception of free will requires developing new experimental stimuli. Experimental philosophy stimuli about free will are typically verbal (e.g., Hannikainen et al. 2019; Murray and Nahmias 2014; Nahmias et al. 2005), describing the behavior of an agent in various situations (e.g., in a deterministic world or in a situation where the agent could not have done otherwise). Shortcomings of the vignettes often used to study free will judgment in experimental philosophy have already been discussed (Clark, Winegard, and Baumeister 2019; Nadelhoffer et al. 2020; Rose, Buckwalter, and Nichols 2017), but our concern here is different: While such stimuli might make sense to study reasoning-based free will judgments, they are inadequate to study the perception of free will since they do not involve any perceptual cues.

To develop new experimental materials, we were inspired by Heider and Simmel's experimental paradigm, which examined the perception of agency and mindedness by presenting participants with simple visual cues embodied by geometrical figures. Similarly, we developed short animated videos displaying the movement of a marble and its interactions with its environment (for a related approach to the study of moral judgment, see Sosa et al. 2021).[2] Agency cues are manipulated across animated videos to determine whether, as predicted by the agency model, participants treat a simple geometrical figure (a marble) as free when it embodies agency cues. In half of the experimental conditions, a simple marble follows a path clearly determined by the layout of the room and its original motion. In the other half, the marble embodies the agency cues: Its movement is clearly not determined by the layout of the room, it is discontinuous, and the marble interacts with its environment (Figure 9.2).

We also manipulated the moral valence of the interactions of the marble. Experimental philosophy studies have shown that moral valence influences judgments of various kinds, including causal judgment (Hitchcock and Knobe 2009; Willemsen and Kirfel 2019, and Sytsma 2020), judgment about the true self (Newman, Bloom, and Knobe 2014), attribution of intentionality (e.g., Knobe 2003), conative states (Tannenbaum, Ditto, and Pizarro 2007), and doxastic states (e.g., Beebe and Buckwalter 2010; Kneer 2018 2021; Kneer et al. 2021). What's more, using verbal stimuli, psychologists have found that people ascribe more free will for morally bad actions than morally good actions (e.g., Clark et al. 2014; Monroe and Ysidron 2021).

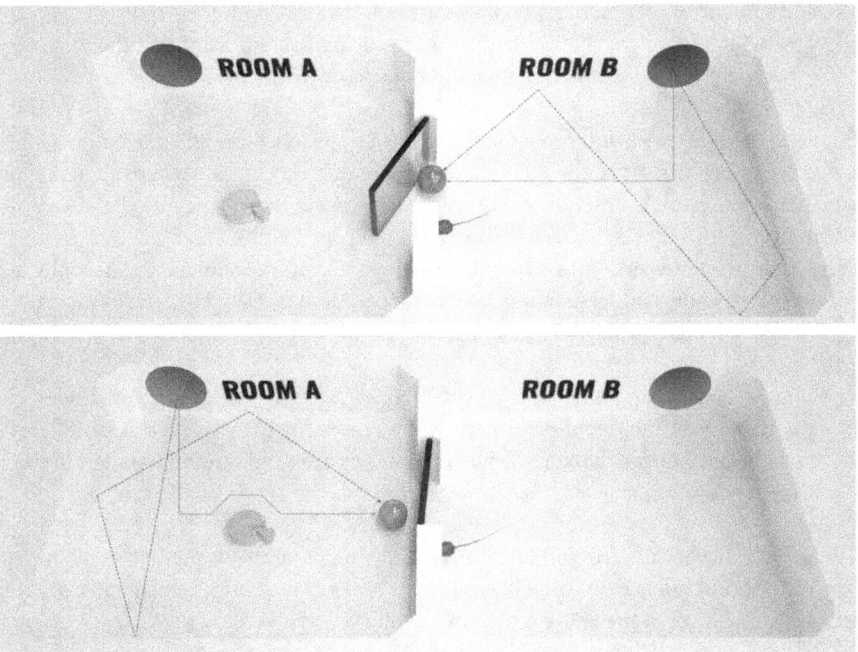

Figure 9.2 Top panel depicts Help condition (Continuous Path Indicates Agency and Dotted Path No Agency). Bottom panel depicts Hinder Condition (Continuous Path Indicates Agency and Dotted Path No Agency). © Edouard Machery, Markus Kneer, Pascale Willemsen, and Albert Newen.

On the other hand, Danks, Rose, and Machery (2014) have provided evidence that at least for causal judgments, the influence of moral valence might be limited to verbal stimuli and be absent when the stimuli are visual (but see Gerstenberg and Icard 2020 and Henne et al. 2021). In half of the experimental conditions, the marble enters the scene and allows a character (a mouse) to bring about its goal; in the other half, the marble prevents the mouse from bringing about its goal. The marble fosters or hinders the mouse's goal by following either a purely physical path or an animate movement pattern.

Thus, in a fully factorial 2 × 2 design (Agency: Agent vs. Object; Valence: Help vs. Hinder), participants were randomly presented with one of four animated videos. In the four videos, a mouse is trying to open a door to enter into the neighboring room, which contains cheese. In the two Help conditions, the marble opens the door; in the two Hinder conditions, it prevents the mouse from opening the door. In the two Object conditions, the marble follows a simple physical trajectory that obeys the mechanical laws of motion. In the two Agent conditions, the marble's movement is self-propelled and discontinuous, and the marble interacts with the mouse.

Given these stimuli, the agency model of free will attribution makes the following predictions:

(i) Participants in the Agent condition will be more likely to treat the marble as free and in control of its actions than those in the Object condition.
(ii) Free will judgments will not depend on participants' judgment that the movement of the marble is determined.

Prediction (ii) follows from the fact that the agency model of free will attribution singles out simple visual cues (viz. the agency cues). Since the relevant visual cues are not about whether every event is determined by antecedent causes, the agency model of free will attribution does not take determinism to be relevant for the experience of free will. Prediction (ii) stands in contrast with the usual practice in experimental philosophy that connects lay people's understanding of free will with issues related to determinism.

We also predicted that we would observe an effect of the Agency variable on the attribution of mindedness:

(iii) Participants in the Agent conditions will be more likely to assign doxastic states (beliefs and knowledge) and conative states (desires and intentions) than in the Object condition.

The agency model of free will attribution does not make any prediction about the impact of moral valence on free will judgments and existing work is inconclusive about it as well. This part of the study is thus exploratory.

(iv) The existing literature on the impact of moral valence on judgment suggests that participants will be more likely to treat the agent as having doxastic states (Beebe and Buckwalter 2010), conative states (Knobe 2003), and possibly free will (Clark et al. 2014) in the Hinder condition than in the Help condition. On the other hand, moral valence will not impact judgment when the stimuli are visual rather than verbal if morality influences judgment only for verbal stimuli (Danks, Rose, and Machery 2014).

9.4 Experiment

9.4.1 Participants

We recruited 813 participants on Prolific. In line with the preregistered criteria, thirty-one participants who were not native English speakers or failed an attention check ("how many rooms are there in the video?" on a 7-point scale from 1 to 7) were excluded, leaving a sample of 782 participants (female: 64 percent; age M=39 years, SD=13 years, range: 18–83 years).[3]

9.4.2 Methods and Materials

The experiment followed a 2 (Agency: Agent vs. Object) × 2 (Valence: Help vs. Hinder) between-subjects fully crossed factorial design, and participants were randomly assigned to one of the four conditions. In all conditions, participants saw a 12-second movie. The four movies showed the marble entering one of the rooms, A or B, via the holes (Figure 9.2). Depending on the Agency condition, it followed a path corresponding to the law of physics (blue, dotted path indicating the Object condition) or a path clearly violating the law of physics (red, continuous path indicating the Agent condition).

Having watched one of the four animated videos, participants read the following ten questions in a list. They then had to watch the video again before answering the same questions in random order. All responses were collected on 7-point Likert scales, anchored at 1 with "definitely not" and at 7 with "definitely yes" (unless otherwise indicated).[4]

Free will
Did the marble seem to [open/block] the door of its own free will?
Did the marble seem to have control over its movements?
Doxastic states
Did the marble seem to believe that the mouse wanted to open the door?
Did the marble seem to know that the mouse was interested in the cheese?
Conative states
Did the marble seem to intentionally allow the mouse to enter [prevent the mouse from entering] the other room?
Did the marble seem to want to [open/block] the door?
Moral judgments
Did it seem the case that the marble should be punished or rewarded for [opening/blocking] the door? (1 = definitely punished and 7 = definitely rewarded)
Did the marble seem blameworthy or praiseworthy for [opening/blocking] the door? (1 = definitely blameworthy and 7 = definitely praiseworthy)

Determinism
Did the movement of the marble seem to obey the laws of physical movement?
Did the path of the marble seem to be determined by the way it entered the room and the shape of the room?

9.4.3 Results

The alpha coefficients for all pairs of dependent variables were larger than .7 (Table 9.1).

As preregistered, we created five dependent variables (free will, doxastic states, conative states, moral judgment, and determinism) by taking the means of the responses to the relevant pair of dependent variables. As was also preregistered, we analyzed the data by means of ANOVAs (with the significance level set at .005 following Benjamin et al. 2018) and conducted mediation analyses (with the significance level at .05). We report the results in what follows.

9.4.3.1 Between-Subjects ANOVAs and Pairwise Comparisons

A series of between-subjects ANOVAs (see Appendix B for details[5]) determined that aggregating across the Help and Hinder conditions participants were more inclined to ascribe free will ($F(1,778) = 550.88$, $p < .001$, $\eta p2 = .41[.37,.46]$, a large effect), doxastic states ($F(1,778) = 563.72$, $p < .001$, $\eta p2 = .42[.37,.46]$, a large effect), and conative states ($F(1,778) = 682.23$, $p < .001$, $\eta p2 = .47[.42,.51]$, a large effect) to the marble in the Agent condition compared to the Object condition. Focusing on the Help condition, participants further judged the marble morally better ($F(1,778) = 68.29$, $p < .001$, $\eta p2 = .08[.05,.12]$, a medium effect) and to be less determined ($F(1,778) = 328.39$, $p < .001$, $\eta p2 = .30[.25,.35]$, a large effect) in the Agent condition compared to the Object condition (Figure 9.3 for pairwise effects).

Moreover, participants were more inclined to ascribe free will ($F(1,778) = 8.43$, $p = .004$, $\eta p2 = .01[.00,.03]$, a small effect) to the marble and judged the marble morally better ($F(1,778) = 41.16$, $p < .001$, $\eta p2 = .05[.02,.08]$, a small effect), and to be more determined ($F(1,778) = 6.50$, $p = .011$, $\eta p2 = .01[.00,.03]$, a large effect) in the Help condition than in the Hinder condition, although this last effect is only suggestive and calls for caution (Figure 9.4[6] for pairwise effects).

Table 9.1 Alpha Coefficients for the Five Pairs of Dependent Variables © Edouard Machery, Markus Kneer, Pascale Willemsen, and Albert Newen

DV	Raw Alpha	Std Alpha
Free Will	0.81	0.81
Doxastic States	0.92	0.92
Conative States	0.93	0.93
Determinism	0.83	0.83
Moral Judgments	0.77	0.77

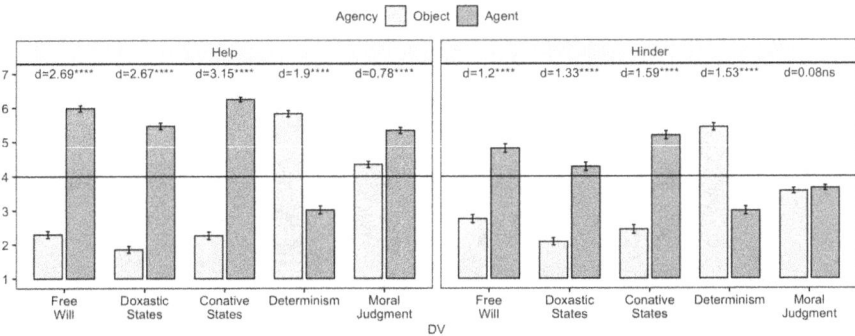

Figure 9.3 Mean ratings for all aggregated DVs across Agency (Agent vs. Object) and Valence (Help vs. Hinder). Error bars denote standard errors. Cohen's d for the pairwise effects of Agency (Agent vs. Object). © Edouard Machery, Markus Kneer, Pascale Willemsen, and Albert Newen.

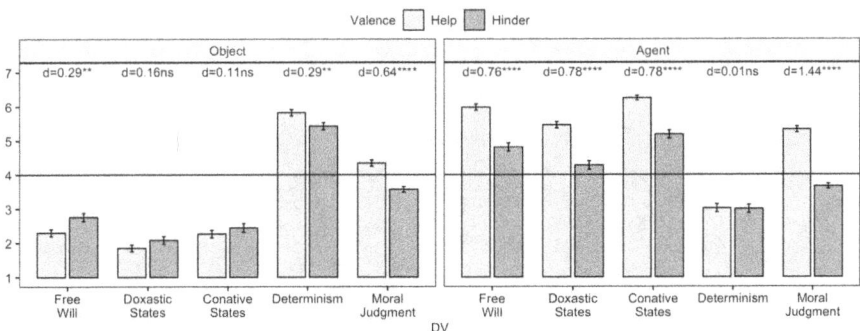

Figure 9.4 Mean ratings for all aggregated DVs across Agency (Agent vs. Object) and Valence (Help vs. Hinder). Error bars denote standard errors. Cohen's d for the pairwise effects of Valence (Help vs. Hinder). © Edouard Machery, Markus Kneer, Pascale Willemsen, and Albert Newen.

The results further revealed significant interactions for the attribution of free will ($F(1,778) = 53.82, p < .001, \eta p2 = .06[.04,.10]$, a medium effect), doxastic mental states ($F(1,778) = 43.75, p < .001, \eta p2 = .05[.03,.09]$, a small effect), and conative mental states ($F(1,778) = 33.24, p < .001, \eta p2 = .04[.02,.07]$, a small effect) as well as on moral judgment ($F(1,778) = 28.23, p < .001, \eta p2 = .04[.01,.06]$, a small effect).

9.4.3.2 Mediation Analyses

To examine further the impact of agency on free will, multiple mediation analysis revealed doxastic states and conative states to be significant mediators at the .05 level (all $ps < .009$), whereas determinism and moral judgment proved nonsignificant ($ps > .070$) (Figure 9.5).[7] The impact of agency on free will is largely mediated by the two significant factors, though a small, yet significant direct effect remained ($p = .005$).

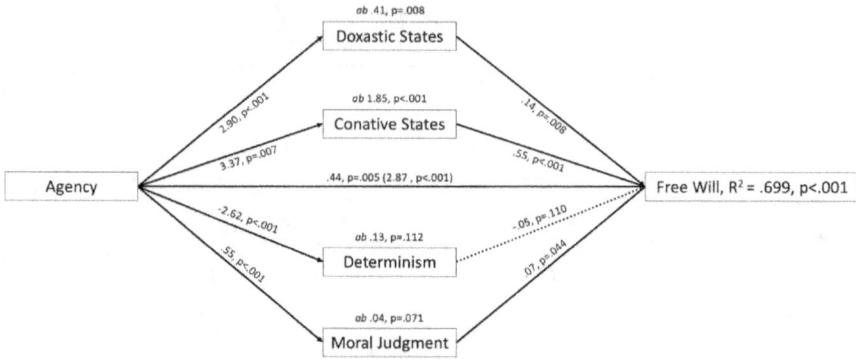

Figure 9.5 Mediation analysis for the impact of agency on free will with doxastic states, conative states, determinism, and moral judgment as mediators. © Edouard Machery, Markus Kneer, Pascale Willemsen, and Albert Newen.

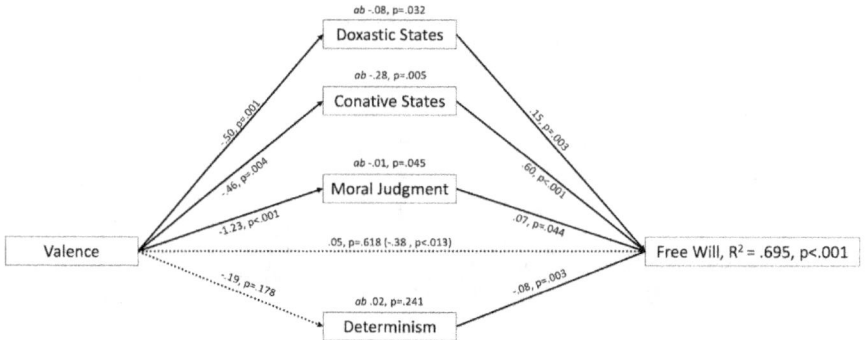

Figure 9.6 Mediation analysis for the impact of valence on free will with doxastic states, conative states, determinism, and moral judgment as mediators. © Edouard Machery, Markus Kneer, Pascale Willemsen, and Albert Newen.

As concerns the impact of valence on free will, a multiple mediation analysis revealed a different pattern: All potential mediators proved significant ($ps < .046$) except for determinism ($p = .241$) (Figure 9.6). Jointly, the three mediators render the impact of valence on free will nonsignificant ($p = .618$), suggesting that there is no direct effect of valence on free will.

Appendix F[8] reports the exploratory analyses specified in the preregistration (factor analysis and demographic analysis).

9.4.4 Discussion

In line with the agency model of free will attribution (prediction i), a simple geometrical figure, such as a marble, is viewed as minded and free when it embodies the agency cues that researchers in the Heider and Simmel tradition have identified. Agency cues lead people to see objects as minded agents that are in control of their behavior. In line with the agency model (prediction ii), the presence of agency cues did not influence free will judgment by influencing judgments about whether the motion of the marble was physically and mechanistically determined. When it comes to the perception of free will, determinism does not seem to matter.

The valence of the marble's interaction with the mouse matters too, as revealed by the interaction between valence and agency for the attribution of free will, conative states, and doxastic states. Whether a mere object helps or hinders another agent in pursuing their goal makes no difference for the attribution of conative and doxastic states. By contrast, when an object behaves like an agent, people are more willing to assign free will, conative states, and doxastic states when it does something good, such as fostering someone's goals, than something bad, such as hindering someone's goals. This finding seems at odds with the large literature on the impact of moral valence on the attribution of conative and doxastic states as well as the application of other concepts, which has repeatedly found that people are more willing to assign doxastic and conative states when the agent does something bad. The results are also at odds with the smaller literature failing to find any effect of valence when the stimuli are visual instead of verbal (Danks, Rose, and Machery 2014). We come back to this matter in the next section.

Finally, also noteworthy is the finding that when the marble prevents the mouse to satisfy its desire, the marble's behavior was judged to be morally similar whether it is an agent or an object. We also come back to this matter in the next section.

9.5 Perceiving Free Will on the Basis of Agency

9.5.1 Agency and Free Will

Our results provide support for the agency model of free will attribution. Adding agency cues, such as nonmechanical motion that is discontinuous and responsive, to a geometrical figure as simple as a marble is sufficient to prompt people to not only see it as minded, that is, as having conative and doxastic states, but also as free. Not only do we reason to free will judgment, we also experience free will in our everyday life in relation to agency. This experimental finding is consistent with our own experiences of stimuli similar to Heider and Simmel's: We view their geometrical figures as being in control of their behavior.

These results illustrate the importance of going beyond the courtroom approach and of embracing the perceptual approach. While we undoubtedly reason about free will and control in some situations and while the features that determine whether we treat someone as free in such situations matter, in much of our everyday life free will attribution is a low-level process. We treat agents around us as free and in control either because agency, mindedness, free will, and perhaps even consciousness are attributed together in response to agency cues or because agency primes us to view agents as free.

What is more, the manipulation of agency cues did not influence free will judgments through judgments of determinism. Agency cues lead to free will judgment independently of reasoning about issues related to determinism. Much of the discussion of free will attribution in experimental philosophy has focused on whether determinism undermines free will attribution, and if so, why. Our results show that this focus is myopic since we did not find any evidence that determinism influence the experience of free will.

9.5.2 The Psychology of Free Will

How do our results bear on the psychology of free will? Experimental philosophers have mostly been concerned with making explicit lay people's implicit theory of free will and, relatedly, responsibility (e.g., Hannikainen et al. 2019; Murray and Nahmias 2014; Nahmias et al. 2005; Nichols 2004; Nichols and Knobe 2007; Sarkissian et al. 2010): Is this theory compatibilist? Why or why not? Is it committed to the principle of alternate possibilities? On this view, people's understanding of free will has, just like contemporary philosophers', something to do with issues related to determinism, although it is not settled whether laypeople are compatibilists, whether they are committed to the principle of alternate possibilities, whether the folk theory is universal or varies across cultures, etc. Experimental philosophers' approach to the lay concept of free will is echoed by others, for example, Bloom (2012), who writes the following:

> [c]ommon sense tells us that we exist outside of the material world—we are connected to our bodies and our brains, but we are not ourselves material beings, and so we can act in ways that are exempt from physical law. (1)

Like most experimental philosophers, Bloom connects the folk understanding of free will with the question of determinism (see also Wegner 2002, 2003).

Clark, Baumeister, and colleagues reject this approach (e.g., Clark et al. 2014; Clark, Baumeister, and Ditto 2017; Clark, Winegard, and Baumeister 2019). On their view, lay people are committed to holding others responsible for their actions (in order to blame or, to a lesser extent, praise them) and as a result to treating them as free (for critical discussion, see Monroe and Ysidron 2021). This view is inspired by Nietzsche, who wrote (1889/1954):

> Today we no longer have any pity for the concept of "free will": we know only too well what it really is—the foulest of all theologians' artifices, aimed at making mankind "responsible" in their sense.... Wherever responsibilities are sought, it is usually the instinct of wanting to judge and punish which is at work. (499)

Lay people embrace any view of free will that allows them to keep holding others free and responsible, even if it means embracing incompatible positions from one occasion to the next. As Clark and colleagues put it (2019), "people do not have one intuition about whether free will is compatible with determinism. Instead, people report that free will is compatible with determinism when desiring to uphold moral responsibility." That is, on this view, lay people do not really have a theory of free will, and experimental philosophers have mistakenly assumed they do.

Monroe and Malle (2010) have also rejected the experimental-philosophical approach to free will, which ties the folk conception of free will to issues related to determinism, but they hold, in contrast to Clark and colleagues, that there is a stable lay concept of free will that turns around the notion of choice and unconstrained action (see also; Feldman, Baumeister, and Wong 2014; Monroe, Dillon, and Malle 2014, 2017; Stillman, Baumeister, and Mele 2011). Monroe and Malle (2010: 211) write that "the core of people's concept of free will is a choice that fulfills one's desires and is free from internal or external constraints. No evidence was found for metaphysical assumptions about dualism or indeterminism."

How do our results bear on these main psychological theories of free will judgment? First and foremost, none of them embraces the perceptual approach that we have been touting in this chapter: They do not examine how perceptual cues can lead people to make free will judgments. Second, they have little to say about the relation between agency and free will judgment. Third, the experimental-philosophical research and Clark and colleagues' theory both exaggerate the connection between the lay understanding of free will with decisions about how blame and praise should be apportioned. Similarly, as noted, the focus on the relation between determinism and free will attribution has misled many (though not all) researchers: Perceptual judgments about free will have nothing to do with determinism.

Our findings also seem to challenge Clark et al.'s (2014) asymmetry between praise and blame: On their view, free will attribution is particularly important to justify blame and punishment. What we found however is that more free will was assigned when the marble was viewed as an agent and helped compared to when it hindered someone's goal.

What could explain the surprising effect of praise and blame in our study, that is, the finding that, when something behaves like an agent, people are more willing to assign free will, conative states, and doxastic states when it does something good than something bad? Stuart and Kneer (2021) have found that people assign more knowledge and blame to an autonomously acting robot when it doesn't commit any harm compared to when it commits harm. This "inverse outcome effect" mirrors the results found in our study. Stuart and Kneer propose that people are willing to assign mental states to robots and other entities that are not full-fledged moral agents when there is little at stake in doing so; when the stakes are higher, for instance, when these entities would have to be blamed or punished, people are more reluctant to do so, treating them as the kind of things that can't be blamed or punished because they do not have mental states. This proposal can be easily combined with the agency model of free will attribution: People are primed to assign conative and doxastic states as well as free will in response to agency cues, but they can override or modulate this tendency when the stakes are higher (e.g., when blame is at stake). We speculate that stakes being higher is just one way of triggering reasoning-based judgments, which go beyond the more basic perception-based judgments that are the default in everyday life. Thus, people override the disposition to assign mental states and free will in the Hinder condition to avoid blaming a marble, but not in the Helping condition.

While we believe the challenge to Clark et al.'s theory is genuine and while we take the explanation just provided to be plausible, we should mention another possible explanation of why participants gave higher ratings to the free will, conative states, and doxastic states dependent variables in the Help compared to the Hinder condition. Despite our best efforts, the epistemic situation of the marble when it embodies agency cues is not the same in the Hinder and Help conditions. In the Help conditions the marble can see, so to speak, the mouse's efforts to open the door and it is pretty clear that the mouse wants to open the door. Someone watching the animated video can thus be fairly confident about what the marble knows and believes about the mouse as well as fairly confident about what it wants do to. In the Hinder condition, however, the marble doesn't have visual access to the mouse's efforts, and someone watching the animated video is probably less likely to be confident about the marble's conative and doxastic states. This epistemic asymmetry could explain the differences between the Help and Hinder conditions just discussed. Further research should balance the epistemic status of the marble better across conditions to find out whether this potential confound can explain away our findings.

9.5.3 Limitations

Our study is limited in some respects. We have already discussed a possible confound, but a second one should be mentioned too. On average participants gave similar answers to the moral judgment dependent variable in the Agent and Object conditions when the marble hinders the mouse's goal. Why is that? A possible explanation is that it isn't clear whether preventing a mouse from eating cheese is blameworthy and deserves punishment. If it isn't clear, people should give an average answer near the midpoint, which they should also do for the Object condition. This hypothesis could explain why we failed to find any difference in moral judgment between the Agency and Object conditions when the marble hinders' the mouse's goal. In addition, the study didn't examine how the agency cues trigger a free will attribution nor did it examine in what sense people perceive or experience free will. We call for more research about these issues. Finally, we do not deny that reasoning plays a role in free will judgment. Reasoning and low-level cues might interact in a complex manner even in the kind of situations used in this study. Future work should investigate this interaction.

9.6 Conclusion

This chapter has made a plea for a new approach to free will attribution: the perceptual approach. We not only reason to free will—the topic of most of the experimental philosophy of free will—but we also see free will. We have proposed that the cues that lead people to see agency also lead them to see free will. Visual stimuli were developed to study the attribution of free will that is grounded in perception, and our results show that agency cues matter for free will attribution. Finally, these results reveal that concerns with determinism and with moral judgment that have been central to much of the psychology of free will judgment are not central to our everyday experience of free will.

Acknowledgments

The video stimuli were produced by Uber Eck (www.ubereck.com). Particular thanks go to Niklaus Hofer for his great work.

Pascale Willemsen's research was supported by the Swiss National Science Foundation, Grant Number: PCEFP1_181082 and PZ00P1_201737.

Markus Kneer's research was supported by the Swiss National Science Foundation, Grant Number: PZ00P1_179912.

Albert Newen's research was supported by Deutsche Forschungsgemeinschaft (DFG)—Projekt number GRK-2185/1 (DFG-Graduiertenkolleg Situated Cognition) and by the DFG-project (NE 576/14-1) "The structure and development of understanding actions and reasons."

Notes

1. We note, however, serious concerns with the replicability of implicit belief understanding studies (see, e.g., Kulke and Rakoczy 2018; Poulin-Dubois et al. 2018; Kampis et al. 2021).
2. All supplementary material, including data files, statistical analyses, and the video stimuli can be found here: https://osf.io/8vdgz/?view_only=98e6b67573b94d3094d1cfc5f2b7ffa3.
3. See as predicted.org/rf37v.pdf. Because of technical issues (the timing wasn't set to begin at the right point in the chapter), we were not able to implement one of the three exclusion criteria (duration).
4. The midpoint was not labeled.
5. https://mfr.de-1.osf.io/render?url=https://osf.io/vn7kz/?direct%26mode=render%26action=download%26mode=render
6. Figure 9.4 merely displays the data in another way, but we find this alternative presentation more suited to visualize the pairwise comparisons.
7. We had preregistered a simple mediation analysis with determinism as a mediator. However, during data analysis we concluded that any effect observed in this analysis could be misleading if the other variables were not taken into account. In a mediation analysis with determinism as the single potential mediator, the latter also proved nonsignificant as regards the relation between valence and free will. It was significant for the relation between agency and free will, although the indirect effect was rather small (see Appendix C: https://mfr.de-1.osf.io/render?url=https://osf.io/su5h9/?direct%26mode=render%26action=download%26mode=render). Further, the multiple mediation analysis suggests that determinism is not a mediator.
8. https://mfr.de-1.osf.io/render?url=https://osf.io/u4dvr/?direct%26mode=render%26action=download%26mode=render

References

Arico, A., B. Fiala, R. F. Goldberg, and S. Nichols (2011), "The Folk Psychology of Consciousness," *Mind & Language*, 26 (3): 327–52. https://doi.org/10.1111/j.1468-0017.2011.01420.x.

Baillargeon, R., R. M. Scott, and Z. He (2010), "False-Belief Understanding in Infants," *Trends in Cognitive Sciences*, 14 (3): 110–18. https://doi.org/10.1016/j.tics.2009.12.006.

Barrett, C., P. M. Todd, G. F. Miller, and P. W. Blythe (2005), "Accurate Judgments of Intention from Motion Cues Alone: A Cross-Cultural Study," *Evolution and Human Behavior*, 26 (4): 313–31. https://doi.org/10.1016/j.evolhumbehav.2004.08.015.

Beebe, J. and W. Buckwalter (2010), "The Epistemic Side-Effect Effect," *Mind & Language*, 25 (4): 474–98. https://doi.org/10.1111/j.1468-0017.2010.01398.x.

Benjamin, D. J., J. O. Berger, M. Johannesson, B. A. Nosek, E. J. Wagenmakers, R. Berk, et al. (2018), "Redefine Statistical Significance," *Nature Human Behaviour*, 2 (1): 6–10.

Bloom, P. (2012, March 18), "Free Will Does Not Exist. So What?," The Chronicle of Higher Education. Available online: https://www.chronicle.com/article/free-will-does-not-exist-so-what.

Bowler, D. and E. Thommen (2000), "Attribution of Mechanical and Social Causality to Animated Displays by Children with Autism," *Autism*, 4 (2): 147–71. https://doi.org/10.1177/1362361300004002004.

Carruthers, P. (2015), "Perceiving Mental States," *Consciousness and Cognition: An International Journal*, 36: 498–507. https://doi.org/10.1016/j.concog.2015.04.009.

Clark, C. J., R. F. Baumeister, and P. H. Ditto (2017), "Making Punishment Palatable: Belief in Free Will Alleviates Punitive Distress," *Consciousness and Cognition: An International Journal*, 51: 193–211. https://doi.org/10.1016/j.concog.2017.03.010.

Clark, C. J., J. B. Luguri, P. H. Ditto, J. Knobe, A. F. Shariff, and R. F. Baumeister (2014), "Free to Punish: A Motivated Account of Free Will Belief," *Journal of Personality and Social Psychology*, 106 (4): 501–13. https://doi.org/10.1037/a0035880.

Clark, C. J., B. M. Winegard, and R. F. Baumeister (2019), "Forget the Folk: Moral Responsibility Preservation Motives and Other Conditions for Compatibilism," *Frontiers in Psychology*, 10: Article 215. https://doi.org/10.3389/fpsyg.2019.00215.

Csibra, G., G. Gergely, S. Bíró, O. Koos, and M. Brockbank (1999), "Goal Attribution Without Agency Cues: The Perception of 'Pure Reason' in Infancy," *Cognition*, 72 (3): 237–67. https://doi.org/10.1016/S0010-0277(99)00039-6.

Danks, D., D. Rose, and E. Machery (2014), "Demoralizing Causation," *Philosophical Studies*, 171 (2): 251–77. https://doi.org/10.1007/s11098-013-0266-8.

Feldman, G., R. F. Baumeister, and K. F. E. Wong (2014), "Free Will is About Choosing: The Link Between Choice and the Belief in Free Will," *Journal of Experimental Social Psychology*, 55: 239–45. https://doi.org/10.1016/j.jesp.2014.07.012.

Feltz, A. and F. Cova (2014), "Moral Responsibility and Free Will: A Meta-analysis," *Consciousness and Cognition: An International Journal*, 30: 234–46. https://doi.org/10.1016/j.concog.2014.08.012.

Gallagher, S. (2008), "Direct Perception in the Intersubjective Context," *Consciousness and Cognition: An International Journal*, 17 (2): 535–43. https://doi.org/10.1016/j.concog.2008.03.003.

Gallese, V. and A. I. Goldman (1998), "Mirror Neurons and the Simulation Theory of Mind-Reading," *Trends in Cognitive Sciences*, 2 (12): 493–501. https://doi.org/10.1016/S1364-6613(98)01262-5.

Gao, T., G. McCarthy, and B. J. Scholl (2010), "The Wolfpack Effect: Perception of Animacy Irresistibly Influences Interactive Behavior," *Psychological Science*, 21 (12): 1845–53. https://doi.org/10.1177/0956797610388814.

Gerstenberg, T. and T. Icard (2020), "Expectations Affect Physical Causation Judgments," *Journal of Experimental Psychology: General*, 149 (3): 599–607. https://doi.org/10.1037/xge0000670.

Goldman, A. I. (1992), "In Defense of the Simulation Theory," *Mind & Language*, 7 (1–2): 104–19. https://doi.org/10.1111/j.1468-0017.1992.tb00200.x.

Goldman, A. I. (2006), *Simulating Minds. The Philosophy, Psychology, and Neuroscience of Mindreading*. New York: Oxford University Press. https://doi.org/10.1093/0195138929.001.0001.

Gopnik, A. and H. M. Wellman (1992), "Why the Child's Theory of Mind Really is a Theory," *Mind & Language*, 7 (1–2): 145–71. https://doi.org/10.1111/j.1468-0017.1992.tb00202.x.

Hannikainen, I. R., E. Machery, D. Rose, S. Stich, C. Y. Olivola, P. Sousa, et al. (2019), "For Whom Does Determinism Undermine Moral Responsibility? Surveying the Conditions for Free Will Across Cultures," *Frontiers in Psychology*, 10: 2428. https://doi.org/10.3389/fpsyg.2019.02428.

Heider, F. and M. Simmel (1944), "An Experimental Study of Apparent Behavior," *American Journal of Psychology*, 57 (2): 243–59.

Henne, P., K. O'Neill, P. Bello, S. Khemlani, and F. De Brigard (2021), "Norms Affect Prospective Causal Judgments," *Cognitive Science*, 45 (1): e12931.

Hitchcock, C. and J. Knobe (2009), "Cause and Norm," *The Journal of Philosophy*, 106 (11): 587–612. https://doi.org/10.5840/jphil20091061128.

Hollander-Blumoff, R. E. (2012), "Crime, Punishment, and the Psychology of Self-Control," *Emory Law Journal*, 61 (3): 501–52.

Kampis, D., P. Karman, G. Csibra, V. Southgate, and M. Hernik (2021), "A Two-Lab Direct Replication Attempt of Southgate, Senju and Csibra (2007)," *Royal Society Open Science*, 8 (8): 210190.

Kneer, M. (2018), "Perspective and Epistemic State Ascriptions," *Review of Philosophy and Psychology*, 9 (2): 313–41. https://doi.org/10.1007/s13164-017-0361-4.

Kneer, M. (2021), "Reasonableness on the Clapham Omnibus: Exploring the Folk Concept of Reasonable," in P. Bystranowski, B. Janik, and M. Prochnicki (eds.), *Judicial Decision-Making: Integrating Empirical and Theoretical Perspectives*, 25–48, Cham: Springer Nature.

Kneer, M., D. Colaço, J. Alexander, and E. Machery (2021), "On Second Thought: Reflection on the Reflection Defense," in T. Lombrozo, J. Knobe, and S. Nichols (eds.), *Oxford Studies in Experimental Philosophy*, vol. 4, 257–96, New York: Oxford University Press.

Knobe, J. (2003), "Intentional Action and Side Effects in Ordinary Language," *Analysis*, 63 (3): 190–4. https://doi.org/10.1111/1467-8284.00419.

Kulke, L. and H. Rakoczy (2018), "Implicit Theory of Mind–An Overview of Current Replications and Non-replications," *Data in Brief*, 16: 101–4.

Monroe, A. E., G. L. Brady, and B. F. Malle (2017), "This Isn't the Free Will Worth Looking For: General Free Will Beliefs Do Not Influence Moral Judgments, Agent-Specific Choice Ascriptions Do," *Social Psychological and Personality Science*, 8 (2): 191–9. https://doi.org/10.1177/1948550616667616.

Monroe, A. E., K. D. Dillon, and B. F. Malle (2014), "Bringing Free Will Down to Earth: People's Psychological Concept of Free Will and Its Role in Moral Judgment," *Consciousness and Cognition: An International Journal*, 27: 100–8. https://doi.org/10.1016/j.concog.2014.04.011.

Monroe, A. E. and B. F. Malle (2010), "From Uncaused Will to Conscious Choice: The Need to Study, Not Speculate About People's Folk Concept of Free Will," *Review of Philosophy and Psychology*, 1 (2): 211–24. https://doi.org/10.1007/s13164-009-0010-7.

Monroe, A. E. and D. W. Ysidron (2021), "Not so Motivated After All? Three Replication Attempts and a Theoretical Challenge to a Morally Motivated Belief in Free Will,"

Journal of Experimental Psychology: General, 150 (1): e1–ee12. https://doi.org/10.1037/xge0000788.

Murray, D. and E. Nahmias (2014), "Explaining Away Incompatibilist Intuitions," Philosophy and Phenomenological Research, 88 (2): 434–67. https://doi.org/10.1111/j.1933-1592.2012.00609.x.

Nadelhoffer, T., D. Rose, W. Buckwalter, and S. Nichols (2020), "Natural Compatibilism, Indeterminism, and Intrusive Metaphysics," Cognitive Science, 44 (8): Article e12873. https://doi.org/10.1111/cogs.12873.

Nahmias, E., S. Morris, T. Nadelhoffer, and J. Turner (2005), "Surveying Freedom: Folk Intuitions About Free Will and Moral Responsibility," Philosophical Psychology, 18 (5): 561–84. https://doi.org/10.1080/09515080500264180.

Newen, A., A. Welpinghus, and G. Juckel (2015), "Emotion Recognition as Pattern Recognition: The Relevance of Perception," Mind & Language, 30 (2): 187–208. https://doi.org/10.1111/mila.12077.

Newman, G. E., P. Bloom, and J. Knobe (2014), "Value Judgments and the True Self," Personality and Social Psychology Bulletin, 40 (2): 203–16. https://doi.org/10.1177/0146167213508791.

Nichols, S. (2004), "The Folk Psychology of Free Will: Fits and Starts," Mind & Language, 19 (5): 473–502. https://doi.org/10.1111/j.0268-1064.2004.00269.x.

Nichols, S. and J. Knobe (2007), "Moral Responsibility and Determinism: The Cognitive Science of Folk Intuitions," Noûs, 41 (4): 663–85. https://doi.org/10.1111/j.1468-0068.2007.00666.x.

Nichols, S. and S. Stich (2003), Mindreading: An Integrated Account of Pretence, Self-Awareness, and Understanding Other Minds. New York: Oxford University Press. https://doi.org/10.1093/0198236107.001.0001

Nietzsche, F. (1954), Twilight of the Idols Trans. W. Kaufmann, New York: Penguin Books. (Original work published 1889).

Poulin-Dubois, D., H. Rakoczy, K. Burnside, C. Crivello, S. Dörrenberg, K. Edwards, et al. (2018), "Do Infants Understand False Beliefs? We Don't Know yet–A Commentary on Baillargeon, Buttelmann and Southgate's Commentary," Cognitive Development, 48: 302–15.

Reid, V. M., G. Csibra, J. Belsky, and M. H. Johnson (2007), "Neural Correlates of the Perception of Goal-Directed Action in Infants," Acta Psychologica, 124 (1): 129–38. https://doi.org/10.1016/j.actpsy.2006.09.010.

Rose, D., W. Buckwalter, and S. Nichols (2017), "Neuroscientific Prediction and the Intrusion of Intuitive Metaphysics," Cognitive Science, 41 (2): 482–502. https://doi.org/10.1111/cogs.12310.

Santos, N. S., N. David, G. Bente, and K. Vogeley (2008), "Parametric Induction of Animacy Experience," Consciousness and Cognition: An International Journal, 17 (2): 425–37. https://doi.org/10.1016/j.concog.2008.03.012.

Sarkissian, H., A. Chatterjee, F. De Brigard, J. Knobe, S. Nichols, and S. Sirker (2010), "Is Belief in Free Will a Cultural Universal?," Mind & Language, 25 (3): 346–58. https://doi.org/10.1111/j.1468-0017.2010.01393.x.

Scholl, B. J. and T. Gao (2013), "Perceiving Animacy and Intentionality: Visual Processing or Higher-Level Judgment?," in M. D. Rutherford and V. A. Kuhlmeier (eds.), Social Perception: Detection and Interpretation of Animacy, Agency, and Intention, 197–230. MIT Press. https://doi.org/10.7551/mitpress/9780262019279.001.0001.

Sosa, F. A., T. Ullman, J. B. Tenenbaum, S. J. Gershman, and T. Gerstenberg (2021), "Moral Dynamics: Grounding Moral Judgment in Intuitive Physics and Intuitive Psychology," Cognition, 217: 104890.

Stillman, T. F., R. F. Baumeister, and A. R. Mele (2011), "Free Will in Everyday Life: Autobiographical Accounts of Free and Unfree Actions," *Philosophical Psychology*, 24 (3): 381–94. https://doi.org/10.1080/09515089.2011.556607.

Stuart, M. T. and M. Kneer (2021), "Guilty Artificial Minds: Folk Attributions of Mens Rea and Culpability to Artificially Intelligent Agents," *Proceedings of the ACM on Human-Computer Interaction*, 5: Article 363. https://doi.org/10.1145/3479507.

Sytsma, J. (2020), "Causation, Responsibility, and Typicality," *Review of Philosophy and Psychology*, 1–21. https://doi.org/10.1007/s13164-020-00498-2.

Tannenbaum, D., P. H. Ditto, and D. A. Pizarro (2007), *Different Moral Values Produce Different Judgments of Intentional Action* [Unpublished manuscript], University of California-Irvine. Available online: https://citeseerx.ist.psu.edu/viewdoc/download?doi =10.1.1.306.9800&rep=rep1&type=pdf.

Wegner, D. M. (2002), *The Illusion of Conscious Will*, Cambridge, MA: MIT Press.

Wegner, D. M. (2003), "The Mind's Best Trick: How We Experience Conscious Will," *Trends in Cognitive Sciences*, 7 (2): 65–9. https://doi.org/10.1016/S1364 -6613(03)00002-0.

Willemsen, P. and L. Kirfel (2019), "Recent Empirical Work on the Relationship Between Causal Judgements and Norms," *Philosophy Compass*, 14 (1): Article e12562. https://doi .org/10.1111/phc3.12562.

10

Do Rape Cases Sit in a Moral Blindspot? The Dual-Process Theory of Moral Judgment and Rape

Katrina L. Sifferd

Common sense seems to indicate that people are only responsible for things that are under their control. This is called the "control principle" by philosophers, and it seems to be a feature of our folk psychology: as Oliver Wendell Holmes noted, even a dog knows the difference between being kicked and being stumbled over. However, there are also cases where we seem to violate the control principle when making moral judgments. Imagine that Jorge has the desire to kill Lucinda. He buys a gun for this purpose and lies in wait behind a tree to shoot Lucinda as she leaves her office building. When Lucinda appears, Jorge pulls the trigger, but at that moment a very fat Canadian goose flies right in the path of the bullet and is killed instead. Jorge will be charged with attempted murder due to the lucky (or unlucky, depending on perspective) circumstance of the goose dying instead of Lucinda. It is likely that a judge or jury will apply somewhat lesser penalties to Jorge for attempt than would be applied if he had committed a first-degree murder. This is the case even though Jorge clearly pulled the trigger with the aim of Lucinda's death.[1]

This criminal case is a slightly altered version of the classic moral luck thought experiment in philosophy, which highlights what some philosophers call the "difference intuition," a principle that runs counter to the control principle (Nagel 1993). The difference intuition holds that there is a moral difference between two duplicate cases where the same mental states and related actions yield different consequences and that this difference justifies a difference in punishment (Kneer and Machery 2019). Legal practice reflects this intuition by stipulating a difference between attempted murder and successful murder. While treating these two types of cases differently seems correct, there does not seem to be any morally relevant behavioral or psychological differences between agents on which such an intuition might rest: two cases can be identical regarding their actions and intentions but produce very different results. Even so, it seems our folk psychology—the process of attributing mental states to others in order to understand and predict their behavior (Sifferd 2006)—is not always committed to the control principle or to only holding persons responsible for what is attributable to persons as agents.

This is the puzzle of moral luck. In the earlier case, resultant luck—luck based on the results produced by an action—seems to impact the moral assessment of action. Data from experimental philosophy indicate that results matter specifically to how much punishment is deemed to be appropriate, although it may not affect assessments of wrongdoing or permissibility (Cushman 2008, 2015; Kneer and Machery 2019). In this chapter I will discuss one proposed solution to the problem of moral luck, which offers a normative justification for treating cases differently based on results (Kumar 2019). This solution focuses on consequentialist aims that may be served when moral judgments track publicly available results. However, crimes that do not involve publicly available results, including rape, pose a problem for this solution. In such cases, moral judgments and attributions of punishment may rely instead upon biased inferential processes to establish a private outcome (often, the mental states of a victim), and consequentialist aims may not be met. Before delving into the specific case of rape, however, I will provide a quick, general account of the dual-process theory of moral judgment and the way in which it gives rise to the claim that punishment judgments track outcomes of action. I will then review attempts to further characterize and solve the moral luck puzzle generated by dual-process theory, focusing on Victor Kumar's 2019 paper.

10.1 The Dual-Process Theory of Moral Judgment and the Puzzle of Moral Luck

In a series of landmark papers, Fiery Cushman asked subjects to engage in a variety of moral judgments.[2] Cushman's studies found that moral judgment is not a unitary process, but instead, is accomplished by parallel, dissociable processes (Cushman 2008). Cushman concluded that there are two processes of moral judgment; one which begins with harmful consequences and then seeks a causally responsible agent to produce a judgment related to punishment, and another that begins with an action and analyzes the mental states responsible for that action to produce a judgment related to wrongdoing.

Cushman hypothesizes that the problem of moral luck may arise when judgments generated by the two processes conflict (Cushman 2008). Responsibility attributions where an agent committed a failed attempt, but the harm still occurred by some independent means, seem to provide evidence for this hypothesis. An example would be if Jorge had fired at Lucinda and hit the goose, but Lucinda had been killed anyway because a tree fell on her. In such cases, causal responsibility is assigned to the other causal factor (the tree, in my example), and assessment of the culpable mental state of the agent seems to be competitively blocked, leading to a decreased assessment of responsibility (Cushman 2008: 376). So, tracking the harm to the tree that fell on Lucinda ends up blocking an assessment of Jorge's mental states, despite the fact that Jorge intended to shoot (and tried to shoot) Lucinda. However, in cases of attempt where no harm at all occurs—where Lucinda emerges unscathed—causal responsibility is not assigned, and then assessment of mental culpability dominates. That is, in this case, persons look to Jorge's mental states with regard to his attempt, which leads to judgments of punishment and blame based upon these mental states (Cushman 2008: 376). Cushman's studies found subjects could be made to rely more heavily on one process or the other, and the processes appeared to operate in parallel and generate cognitive conflict (Cushman 2008: 378).[3]

Recent work has focused on the way in which Cushman's dual-process theory generates the problem of moral luck. In a 2019 paper, Kneer and Machery claimed the problem may affect a narrower set of cases than previously thought. They found that in within-participants experiments favorable to reflective deliberation, people tended to judge a lucky and unlucky agents equally blameworthy and their actions as equally wrong and permissible. However, Kneer and Machery replicated Cushman's findings that punishment judgments were significantly more outcome-dependent than wrongness, blame, and permissibility judgments. They found that a sizable portion of subjects judged morally lucky and unlucky agents should be punished differently in both comparative contexts and when reporting their abstract principles (Kneer and Machery 2019: 16).

Kneer and Machery explained the sensitivity of subjects to resultant luck by appealing to the mediating role of negligence (failure to take reasonable care). They noted that subjects seemed to infer from the fact that harm did occur that it had a higher probability of occurring, and thus they were more likely to assume the actor was negligent in acting (Kneer and Machery 2019). In a recent paper, Machery calls this "hindsight bias" (Machery and Scoczen, in progress). So, for example, if Tonya fails to take her car to the mechanic when a check engine light goes on, in the case where the car breaks down she may be deemed more negligent than when the car continues to run, even though her mental states and action (of failing to take the car to the shop) are exactly the same in both cases. However, Kneer and Machery found the influence of outcomes on punishment judgments was only partly due to varying ascriptions of negligence (Kneer and Machery 2019: 16). Even once the mediator of negligence was removed, the outcome seemed to have a direct effect on a substantial number of punishment judgments. Kneer and Machery conclude that the "puzzle of moral luck exists after all," though its scope is restricted (Kneer and Machery 2019). They note, however, that the tendency to punish unlucky agents more harshly may not be all that philosophically puzzling if there are good normative reasons to make punishment partly dependent on the consequences of actions. In a more recent paper, however, Machery and Szcocen claim that if factors unrelated to moral assessment, but relevant to punishment, account for the effect of outcome on punishment judgments, the problem of moral luck doesn't exist (Machery and Szcocsen, in progress: 24–5).

Kumar (2019) offers a normative justification of the sort that might indeed solve—or dissolve—the problem of moral luck. He argues that the folk's tendency to apply greater punishments to unlucky versus lucky outcomes may be justified by instrumental aims (Kumar 2019). Like Kneer and Machery, Kumar embraces a dual-process model of moral judgment, and claims the total amount of blame and punishment assigned depends on the contribution of both processes. This means resultant luck can impact punishment in most cases (Kumar 2019: 991).

Kumar argues that the folk's focus on results serves the instrumental end of increasing certainty and uniformity in punishment (Kumar 2019). Punishments are outcome sensitive because outcomes are more reliable and publicly available than intentions (Kumar 2019). Kumar notes that studies show subjects reliably hold people responsible based on outcomes, even where intentions are fixed (Kumar 2019: 997). Again, this is because publicly available outcomes drive judgments regarding appropriate levels of punishment.

To summarize: Experimental philosophy supports a dual process of moral judgment, and indicates this model gives rise to the puzzle of moral luck, although the puzzle may apply to a fairly narrow set of cases. One way to resolve the problem of moral luck is to offer a normative justification for treating cases differently based on results. Kumar provides such a justification by claiming that consequentialist aims may be met when we punish based on publicly available results. As we will see in the next section, Kumar specifically argues that his analysis can justify the criminal law's focus on results by pointing to instrumental effects.

10.2 The Dual-Process Model and Criminal Responsibility and Punishment

The rest of this chapter will explore how the dual-process theory of moral judgment, and Kumar's response to the problem of moral luck, may be related to arrests, prosecutions, and punishments in the criminal law for crimes that may lack publicly available results. Specifically, I will argue that the crime of rape poses special challenges for Kumar's solution to moral luck because it is a crime that often lacks publicly available outcomes. Either the results-oriented process of moral judgment is not tracking public results in such rape cases, or it is not used. In this case one might assume moral judgments about rape rest upon the process focused on actions and intentions. However, because attributing mental states or intentions to determine responsibility in rape cases is often difficult and subject to biases related to gender and credibility, sex, and trauma, such judgments are problematic.

In the criminal law, verdicts and punishments are largely dependent on both a defendant's mental states (*mens rea*) and the type and degree of harm caused (a death, a fire, a stolen car). Criminal guilt also requires that the criminal harm be related to a voluntary act by the defendant (*actus reus*). Voluntary acts are typically defined by exclusion: they are not bodily movements that are best understood as a seizure or a fall, for example. Together, these factors—mental states, voluntariness, and level of harm—determine the type of crime one may be charged with and found guilty of, where the level of charge carries with it a certain level of criminal punishment, usually stipulated in a range by statute.[4]

Resultant luck can affect either the crime with which one is charged—like in the drunk driving case—or the punishment assigned within a given statutory range. Jorge's voluntary act was pulling the trigger of a gun aimed at Lucinda. The mental states relevant to Jorge's criminal culpability are that he committed this act for the purpose of killing Lucinda.⁵ This mental state qualifies Jorge for first-degree murder in a case where his act caused Lucinda's death and for attempted first-degree murder where the goose dies instead.⁶ Even in jurisdictions where both charges carry the same range of possible punishments, the judge or jury may be more likely to apply punishment at the severe end in the former case and apply a lesser punishment in the latter case. This highlights the fact that criminal court procedures can reflect the dual-process model of moral judgment and, accordingly, are subject to the same problem of moral luck arising from it.

10.2.1 Levels of Justification for the Criminal Law

Kumar notes that legal scholar HLA Hart argued for a two-level theory of justification of the criminal law, where different justifications might apply to the different levels (Kumar 2019: 1000). Institutions and norms associated with the criminal law must be justified on what I will call the *institutional* level. At this level the very existence of institutions and public policies that operate to infringe on persons' liberty by forbidding certain behaviors and imposing censure or hardships in the form of punishment needs justification. On another level, which I term the *agential* level, applications of moral and legal norms as a response to particular acts by particular persons must be justified. The state must be able to justify finding any one person guilty of a crime, as well as justifying punishment that follows. An unjustifiable criminal justice *system*—say, one that criminalized race or religion—may still apply a just punishment to a particular *individual* (e.g., for murder), and a just system of criminal law and punishment can still impose punishment in an unjust way (e.g., punish Black offenders more harshly than White offenders who commit the same crime).⁷

The US Model code endorses a mixed theory of the justification of punishment that appeals to both retributive and instrumental aims (Model Penal Code Sentencing Provisions 2017). The dual-process model of responsibility, argues Kumar, describes the psychology of holding persons responsible in a way that supports this sort of mixed justification of criminal law and punishment with different justifications at each level (Kumar 2019). At the agential level, intentions and outcomes determine what a person deserves or merits in a retributive sense. But at the institutional level, these norms of desert or merit have a consequentialist rationale (Kumar 2019: 1000). That is, at the agential level we attribute culpable mental states to justify a particular criminal verdict that this person is a wrongdoer who deserves punishment for a particular act, but at the institutional level we may offer forward-looking aims like deterrence to justify criminalization and particular categories or levels of punishment in response to certain harmful results. Kumar tells an evolutionary story to support this latter consequentialist rationale, indicating that our practices of blame and punishment became sensitive to outcomes *because* this sensitivity yields positive consequences (Kumar 2019: 1001). Punishment encourages people to be prosocial by introducing disincentives for harmful behavior that we can track and respond to, says Kumar (Kumar 2019: 1002).

Sensitivity to outcomes supports prosocial behavior because outcomes are "typically much easier to identify than intentions. It is usually obvious whether or not harm occurred" (Kumar 2019: 998). Blaming and punishing people "strictly for their intentions would be unreliable," whereas punishing based on publicly available outcomes is more reliable. Again, Kumar indicates that linking punishments to publicly available results has reliable forward-looking effects because it sends a clear message to the public regarding what sort of outcomes must be avoided. This allows persons to regulate behavior more effectively, resulting in lower levels of crime (Kumar 2019: 998). Thus, only rigid, outcome-based punishment provides a learning environment that truly favors prosociality (Kumar 2019: 1003).

10.2.2 Different Justifications within Levels

While I agree that a mental state-driven process of moral judgment may ground assessment of guilt at the agential level in the criminal law, I think results-driven moral judgments are also involved at the agential level—not just the institutional one—in the generation of criminal verdicts and sentences.[8] I have watched prosecuting attorneys attempt to trigger strong feelings of blame and punishment by highlighting harmful results. For the prosecution, often the most riveting and convincing way to provoke moral judgment in a homicide is to ask the factfinder to imagine the lifeless body of a victim in detail (or even more effective, to look at pictures or a video). After establishing the presence of serious harm, the prosecutor will then ask the court to trace backward in time from the body to the defendant's actions that purportedly caused the death, which may have been performed purposely, recklessly, or negligently.

Other criminal results are also easily identified to trigger blame and punishment judgments in court. In battery cases the prosecution can display evidence of bruising and broken bones; and in the case of arson the burned rubble of a former home. Even where the result is a thing gone missing a prosecutor can tell a story depicting publicly available harm: for example, they may ask the court to consider what it was like for the victim to hurry outside to go to work only to discover an empty driveway where his car should have been. We might imagine that in some cases the defense will counter with an attempt to trigger a responsibility judgment focused primarily on the defendant's mental states and their relationship to his action—to see the crime from the defendant's perspective as an actor. This could serve the defendant's purposes if they were seriously mentally ill, very emotional, or suffered from a cognitive impairment.

Moving back to the institutional level, the results-oriented process of moral judgment may be reflected in the codification of certain harmful results as criminal. Statues also stipulate ranges of punishment for different harms.[9] Remember, Kumar claims outcome-based punishment provides a learning environment that favors prosocial behavior. This means statutes ought to make clear the outcomes that are forbidden by criminalizing results or outcomes that the public can easily identify. Statutes that refer to publicly available outcomes will serve the forward-looking justification of enhancing moral agency by making forbidden harms salient, thereby reducing crime and increasing social order.

It certainly seems right that it would be less effective and successful for the law to criminalize thoughts or intentions rather than publicly available acts, at least as measured by the forward-looking aims just described. First, it seems way beyond the power of the State to expect people to manage or censor their thoughts or be subject to criminal prosecution. Second, trying to forbid harmful thoughts via criminal liability may be futile for several reasons, including: (1) the occurrence of such thoughts is not subject to the same level of control as actions—we very often cannot control what we think; and (2) thoughts are private such that proof of them in a legal setting (often months or years after an arrest) is extremely difficult. It seems easier, although still difficult, to criminalize results and move backward to a causal agent and an assessment of a particular set of mental states regarding that result. In general, when assessing criminal guilt the court is not looking to describe the specific mental states held by the defendant at the time of the crime. Instead, the court seeks to classify those mental states within a categorical level of intention required under the law; for example, the categories given in the Model Penal Code (MPC). Under the MPC, a crime can be committed purposely, knowingly, recklessly, or negligently.

Even if one agrees with Kumar's claim that results-oriented punishment leads to prosociality and provides stronger deterrence than a process that focuses on mental states, there is a question on how to determine what counts as a result. This matters because for some crimes, like trespass, there is no obvious result separate from the criminal act. Can the act of trespass itself count as a result? Under the dual-process theory of moral judgment, it would seem not, because this would collapse the main difference between the two processes where one is triggered by results and moves to a causal actor, and the other focuses on an act and simultaneous mental states. However, in the next section I will further explore this issue further by examining the crime of rape. Like trespass, in the paradigm case of rape, the act itself, and not harm caused by the act, is forbidden by the criminal law.

10.3 Moral Judgment and Sexual Assault

In this section I will focus primarily on "simple" rape, with the idea of narrowing a more complicated larger category of sexual assault that includes, among other crimes, sexual assault by extortion (MPC 213.4) and deception (MPC 213.5) and sex trafficking (MPC 213.9). In the United States and elsewhere, the present legal definition of rape is sexual intercourse without consent (Temkin 2002: 90), and I will focus on the baseline crime of sexual assault in the absence of consent (MPC 213.6) with the idea that this essential crime can be made more serious where other elements are present, including aggravated physical force or restraint (MPC 213.1). The newly redesigned MPC offense of sexual assault in the absence of consent, which I will also call rape, requires proof beyond a reasonable doubt of: (1) an act of sexual penetration or oral sex, (2) the absence of the complainant's consent, and (3) the defendant's recklessness as to each of these elements (Tentative Draft No. 4, pg. 226, lines 20–3).[10]

As already noted, rape is an interesting test case for Kumar's theory of criminal punishments because it is difficult to posit a publicly available harmful result—the forbidden criminal harm is a particular act performed in the context of the defendant and victim's mental states, and not any result that might flow from that act. Although "rape kits" can collect evidence that sex occurred, and in some cases that sex caused physical harm or damage, there are cases where the only difference between legal sex and rape is lack of consent. Physical harm is not required by the MPC rape statute, and for good reason: nonconsensual sex is rape even if it does not cause physical damage, and consensual sex that does cause physical damage is not rape. Obviously, consent is a private state-of-affairs as it concerns the victim's state of mind, although there must have been enough of an outward expression of nonconsent that the offender can be deemed reckless regarding the victim's state of mind. However, the disjunctive ways in which nonconsent can be expressed are too numerous and varied to be the target of statutory language; hence, sex without consent is itself criminalized.

I do not think that the act of nonconsensual sex itself can be conceived of as the harmful result of rape. In addition to the worry that this collapses the two processes of moral judgment, another worry is that the victim's mental state of nonconsent is crucial to a rape charge, so analysis of the defendant's mental state and act alone is not sufficient to make a moral judgment about a rape. From the perspective of the difference principle, in a rape case both lucky and unlucky actors have sex, but in one case it's rape due to nonconsent and in the other it's consensual sex. The difference between these cases is not a public result, but the presence or absence of a particular state of mind on the part of the victim. Further, the defendant's private mental states are necessarily relevant to moral judgments about such cases, as what he knew about the victim's nonconsent is crucial to his culpability. So, trying to understand the results of rape takes us directly back to an act and the mental states associated with it, where these mental states include those that can be attributed to both the defendant and the victim. Because of this, the assessment of culpability and punishment in cases of rape would seem to be driven not by the results-based process of judgment, but by the mental-states-based process.

We may be further convinced that the act/intention process of moral judgment is likely to be used in rape cases when we consider how a prosecutor might attempt to trigger the results-oriented process of moral judgment about a rape in court. What result could a prosecutor gesture toward (in physical images or in the courts' mind's eye) in cases of rape, especially those cases where the victim did not suffer serious physical harm? I have seen prosecutors attempt to describe the victim's traumatized behavior after the attack as an outcome of the crime; however, normal emotional reactions to rape can be withdrawal and numbness, which can then fail to signal the trauma a survivor experienced.[11] Although it is often assumed that in the immediate aftermath of a rape "the victim will be hysterical and tearful," one study found that many victims "have a controlled response in which they mask their feelings and appear calm and composed" (Temkin 2002). Very often, there are no pictures of serious physical injuries to introduce, no pictures of intimate physical violence the victim wants the court to see or imagine, and no stories of a sobbing, inconsolable victim in a public setting. There may be no public result for the prosecutor to linger upon, and any proof of public harm is offered primarily to influence the court's mental state attributions.

All of this indicates that while Kumar may be right that result-oriented moral judgments can justify criminalization of acts at the institutional level—and I might be right the result-oriented process is also used at the agential level—the nature of rape is such that the results-driven process may either not be triggered such that the act/intention process must be activated, or may be tuned to things that are not, in fact, publicly available results. If Kumar is correct that punishing based on public outcomes is more effective and reliable than punishment focused on mental states, then this could have important consequences for criminal law. I posit that if the results-oriented process of moral judgment is unavailable or ineffective in rape cases we might expect three things: first, the lack of public results may mean that laws that criminalize and punish rape are generated by intuitions about wrongdoing by the act/intention system which tracks mental states. Attribution of mental states in rape cases, however, is often based upon biased and unreliable inferential processes which are not reliably linked to judgments about deserved punishment. As a result, at the institutional level, we might expect less agreement and a wider variety in statutes criminalizing rape, and a wider range of applicable punishments. Second, because the process of discerning mental states in rape cases is difficult and subject to gendered expectations and bias which tends to discount victims' testimony; and because the act/intention process of moral judgment will often depend upon testimony from defendants and victims regarding their mental states ("he said, she said"), we might expect to see fewer investigations and prosecutions for rape crimes given the number of rapes that seem to occur. Third, due to the lack of publicly available results in rape cases and thus the lessened deterrent effect of rape statutes and norms, we might see higher levels of recidivism among sexual assault offenders.

In the next three sections, I will argue that all three of these things are the case, taking the United States as an example.

10.3.1 Rape Law

A recent American Law Institute commission has been tasked with updating the MPC's sexual assault provisions. They said the following regarding existing sexual assault statutes in the United States:

> [E]xisting law defies ready characterization. As a general matter, state laws exhibit a patchwork of penal philosophies. With specific regard to sexual offenses, there is no clear consensus about the amount of punishment that should apply to particular offenses, and a breadth of punishments are authorized for similar conduct across the states. Consider an offense such as engaging in sexual intercourse with an adult who is unconscious. One jurisdiction punishes the offense with a maximum of five years' incarceration; another with life without parole. (Institute August 18, 2020) (1–2)

As this quote makes clear, US sexual assault statutes vary wildly, and the sentences offenders serve are haphazard. Jurisdictions cannot even agree whether sexual assault in the absence of consent (without other aggravating factors) is rape and should be criminalized: only 68 percent of US jurisdictions punish sexual penetration solely on the basis of absence of consent (Institute August 18, 2020: 239). (The proposed changes to the MPC lament this, and, as already noted, claim nonconsensual sex should be a crime where the defendant shows recklessness regarding consent.) The exact same sexual offense may generate a fairly short or extremely long sentence of incarceration. For example, the jurisdictions that do criminalize nonconsensual sex vary wildly in their gradation and punishment of the offense. For example, among the twelve jurisdictions that treat absence of consent as sufficient but do not define consent, three authorize a maximum penalty of twenty years, one authorizes up to five years, one up to two years, and seven impose misdemeanor penalties of up to a year. For the twenty-four jurisdictions that define consent as either affirmative consent or to be determined given the context of the circumstances, some impose felony sanctions with maximum sentences of twenty years to life, some with a maximum of ten to fifteen years, some with a maximum of five to seven years, and two with a maximum of eighteen months and two years (American Law Institute 2020)(247–8). Truly, the sentencing of offenders who commit rape is variable to the point of being chaotic and unjust.[12]

The variations between jurisdictions regarding both the basic elements of rape and the gradations or seriousness of sexual offenses may be seen as supporting Kumar's claims that punishing based on results is more effective in accomplishing forward-looking aims and reliable than punishment based upon private mental states. Moral judgments related to punishment in rape cases based upon attributions of these mental states—on dual-process theory, generated primarily using the act/intention or mental state process—seem to be less stable and more variable, and rape statutes reflect this process. The private nature of the harm in many rape cases, and the difficulty and bias inherent in attributing mental states in such cases, discussed in detail as follows, may be one reason legislatures and courts have handled such cases—through statute and case law—in a highly inconsistent (and often ineffective) way.

10.3.2 Lower Levels of Report, Investigation, Arrest, and Conviction for Rape

We might also expect the lack of publicly available results in many rape cases to lead to lower levels of report, investigation, arrest, and conviction of such cases when compared to other violent crimes, especially if I am right that the results-oriented process often supports criminal verdicts at the agential level. If the act/intention process of moral judgment is heavily relied upon in rape cases, we ought not to think this would *necessarily* lead to weaker moral judgments, possibly even about punishment: the system focused on permissibility and wrongdoing might generate strongly consistent judgments of wrongdoing and blameworthiness, which could then result in related retributive judgments regarding proportional punishments. For example, if a person commits an act that is clearly impermissible (e.g., hitting someone) and the mental states associated with the act are fairly easy to surmise (e.g., the hitter yells "You'll be sorry!" while throwing the punch), then moral judgments regarding the act should be somewhat consistent. There is still a question regarding whether judgments about proportional punishment will also be consistent—punishment judgments show anchoring effects, for example (Enough and Mussweiler 2006). But we can imagine that it is at least possible that a criminal verdict and sentence or a criminal statute resting primarily on the act/intentions system of moral judgment could be fair and justifiable, even if such a judgment had poorer forward-looking effects than judgments based upon results.

However, as already indicated, in many rape cases the defendant's mental states may be difficult to discern, and a judgment in such cases is also dependent on an assessment of the victim's mental states, which is equally difficult. Proofs of both typically rest on testimonial evidence. Understanding the nature of a victim's nonconsent and how it interacted with her behavior is very often complicated—for example, both saying "no" and freezing up, and saying nothing can be related to the mental state of nonconsent. To make matters worse, law enforcement and factfinders' attempts to use their folk psychology to attribute mental states in rape cases are subject to social norms and biases regarding male and female sexual behavior and testimonial credibility, as well as gendered expectations related to violence and trauma. As legal theorist Kimberly Ferzan puts it: "Rape law has typically conceptualized rape as a 'she said/he said.' . . . And, because the existence of semen is fully consistent with consent in cases of acquaintances, trials can easily come down to credibility contests" (Ferzan 2022: 28).

Generally, when we ascribe mental states to others, we utilize cues we take to indicate a person's prior behavior, character, appearance, demeanor, and the larger circumstances within which they are acting (Sifferd 2006). In the recent past these types of facts were often crucial to proving—or not proving—a rape case. And for women, reliance on such facts proved to be a disaster because they were interpreted against the backdrop of gendered and biased norms of sexual behavior. For example, courts assumed that if a person had had sex with a partner before they must have consented this time; that if a female victim dressed a certain way or was drunk at the time of the rape, these factors indicated consent; or that it was reasonable the defendant thought they consented (Temkin 2002). But these factors are not relevant to whether a rape occurred. One might consent to sex in one circumstance and not consent to sex with the same person in another circumstance; one might flirt or leave a party with someone never planning to consent to sex; and a person who drinks too much should not be seen as consenting to sex just due to their alcohol intake. Just the existence of a public awareness campaign that "no means no" indicates that there was massive societal misunderstanding regarding the nature of sexual consent.[13]

Today, rape shield laws have removed the court's ability to infer a lack of credibility and consent from a victim's sexual history (Temkin 2002: 30). But rape cases still very often rest on credibility, and patriarchal and even misogynist views and values can influence our folk psychology when we are making moral judgments regarding rape (Manne 2017). These views can specifically taint a person's assessment of a victim's credibility and responsibility. Of course, some subsets of the population may be more biased against victims than others. In a study by Niemi and Young, subjects who more strongly held the values of loyalty, obedience to authority, and purity—called "binding values" by the authors—were more likely to consider victims of sexual and nonsexual crimes as contaminated; they were also more likely to blame victims and hold them responsible (Niemi and Young 2016). Women subjects overall, however, considered sexual crime victims less contaminated and more injured; but of course, police officers, prosecutors, and judges are very often men. Subjects who held binding values were also more likely to have increased perceptions of victims' (versus perpetrators') behaviors as contributing to the outcome or harm, and decreased focus on perpetrators (Niemi and Young 2016). Interestingly, these patterns persisted even when the authors controlled for subject's political views.

Because mental state attributions in rape cases are likely to be made in ways that depend crucially on testimony, attributing mental states in rape cases is also impacted by all the ways in which men's testimony may be privileged over women's testimony (Fricker 2007; Manne 2017). Legal scholar Deborah Turkheimer has noted that juries in rape cases seem to default to distrust regarding accounts from women that they were raped (Turkheimer 2017). Kimberly Ferzan notes that a major obstacle to justice in rape cases is law enforcement's search for a "righteous victim," and prosecutors' unwillingness to pursue cases where they don't think the victim will be seen as likable and sympathetic (Ferzan 2022). Victim testimony alone is very often not enough for a rape conviction: in 2009, the Chicago Alliance against Sexual Exploitation wrote to the Cook County State's attorney alleging that there was strong evidence the office did not bring rape cases unless there was bodily injury, a third-party witness, or an offender confession (Turkheimer 2017: 34).

If the results-driven process of moral judgment is not available, and the act/intention or mental state process is severely compromised due to bias, especially from the perspective of victims, we ought not to be surprised that rape is underreported, underinvestigated, and underprosecuted. While large-scale victimization studies indicate that between 15 and 20 percent of adult American women are raped at some time in their lives, the vast majority of these are not reported or investigated (Tjaden and Thoennes 2000).[14] Overall, it is likely fewer than 1–3 percent of rapes result in an arrest and conviction.[15] Even when reported, arrest and conviction rates are shockingly low. One study found that for every 100 rapes reported to police—and again, one must assume many rapes are not reported—only eighteen led to arrest, and even fewer resulted in a conviction (Morabito, Williams, and Pattavina 2019). Overall, fewer than seven percent of the rapes reported ended up in conviction (Morabito, Williams, and Pattavina 2019). In Chicago, one of the largest criminal justice jurisdictions in the United States, 80 to 90 percent of sexual harm reports to the Chicago Police Department over the past ten years did not result in an arrest.[16] In sum, rape, when compared to other violent crimes, has lower rates of reporting, investigation, arrest, and conviction (Kyckelhahn and Cohen 2004).[17]

There is an additional confounding possibility related to the low arrest and conviction rate in rape cases. Earlier, I indicated that it is unlikely that the results-driven process of moral judgment is engaged with regard to rape due to the lack of publicly available results. As I noted, another possibility is that the rape itself is seen as a result, and when making moral judgments people focus on this result and attempt to trace from the rape to a causal actor. One might assume this causal actor identified in a rape would be the defendant, but instead, it might be that both the defendant and the victim—or even, just the victim—are seen as the actor causally related to the rape. Ferzan reports findings that "most observers agree that decisions in acquaintance rape cases are strongly affected by the purported victim's *contributory negligence*, and by her perceived immorality" (Ferzan 2022: 31, quoting Bryden and Lengnick 1997: 1232). Relatedly, subjects in Neimi and Young's study that held binding values were also more likely to have increased perceptions of victims' (versus perpetrators') behaviors as contributing to the outcome or harm, and decreased focus on perpetrators (Niemi and Young 2016).

Remember that hindsight bias and attribution of contributory negligence are the factors identified by Kneer and Machery (2019) and Kneer and Scoczen (in progress) as explaining and mediating responsibility assessments that were results-oriented. They note that subjects seemed to infer from the fact that harm did occur that it had a higher probability of occurring, thus the actor was negligent in acting. In rape cases, where the only result to be identified is the act of rape, this may work against victims if they are seen as the relevant causal actor: that the rape occurred seems to make it more likely that the victim is seen as negligent in creating circumstances where the rape happens, instead of making it seem more likely the defendant was negligent in not garnering consent.[18] The two processes of moral judgment operate in competition with one another. If the results-oriented process is triggered, and a moral judgment about rape traces back to the victim as a negligent causal actor, then a responsibility judgment focused on the defendant may be effectively blocked, especially where it is not easy to attribute to him an intent to rape or recklessness regarding consent.

All told, our processes of moral judgment seem to be ill-equipped to handle rape cases, especially in cases where physical violence and serious bodily harm are difficult to discern. If dual-process theory is correct, it seems that cases of rape may sit within a moral blind spot, as neither process is well-suited to generate reliable judgments of wrongdoing or appropriate punishment.[19] If this is true, we ought not to be surprised that the enforcement and application of the criminal law regarding rape cases would be similarly compromised.

10.3.3 Higher Levels of Recidivism for Sexual Assault

Earlier, I have shown that categories and gradations of sexual assault crimes and their related punishments are highly inconsistent across jurisdictions, and that rape reports, arrests, and convictions are low in comparison to other crimes. If Kumar's theory regarding the instrumental justification of results-oriented moral judgments is correct, we might also expect that rape law would have a lessened deterrent effect on the general population and on offenders.

Criminal law and punishment are thought to have a general deterrent effect on the population such that fewer people commit crimes than would have if criminal law did not exist. Of course, we cannot compare current rates of rape with those that might occur if the harm in rape cases and norms related to rape were more consistent, reliable, and salient, and we cannot compare current rates with what rates would be if rape were not criminalized at all.

However, it is worth noting that rates of recidivism among sexual offenders are higher than for other types of offenders, even violent offenders—but only with regard to sex crimes.[20] That is, sex offenders are *less likely* than other offenders to commit another crime, but four times *more likely* to commit another sex crime. There is evidence that over 40 percent of heterosexual adult sexual offenders commit another sexual offense (Przybylski 2015). In one study, sex offenders had a lower overall rearrest rate than non-sex offenders (43 percent compared to 68 percent), but their sex crime rearrest rate was four times higher than the rate for non-sex offenders (Langan and Levin 2002). Similar patterns are consistently found in other studies that compare sex offender and non-sex offender recidivism (see, e.g., Sample and Bray 2003; Hanson, Scott, and Steffy 1995). In another study, sex offenders in Illinois did not appear to commit future offenses, in general, at a higher rate than do other offenders. However, they had higher levels of recidivism regarding the sex crime category for which they were arrested (Przybylski 2015). Like sex offenders overall, rapists had a lower overall recidivism rate than non-sex offenders in the study (46 percent compared to 68 percent), but a higher sexual recidivism rate (5 percent compared to 1.3 percent) (Przybylski 2015). About half of the rapists with more than one prior arrest were rearrested within three years of their release, a rearrest rate nearly double (49.6 percent compared to 28.3 percent) that of rapists with just one prior arrest (Przybylski 2015).

It is important to remember that these studies indicated a high rate of re-offense is among defendants who are convicted of a sexual offense, not persons who have committed a sexual offense but who have not been convicted. However, when the Cleveland Police Department embarked upon a massive rape kit testing initiative, they identified 207 suspected serial rapists responsible for almost 600 attacks across the greater Cleveland area. Many of these men had never been arrested for a sex crime, and several were linked to over five instances of rape each.[21] Researchers have noted that "the historic under-prosecution of sexual assault means that recidivism studies likely underestimate the scope of serial sexual perpetration" (Campbell et al. 2019).

Overall, there seems to be evidence that rape law may have a weaker effect on encouraging prosocial behavior and discouraging offending than laws about other violent offenses. This is something we might expect if Kumar is correct that we may be more sensitive and responsive to moral and criminal norms that identify publicly available results, as these public results are lacking in the crime of "simple" rape.

10.4 Conclusions

Work in experimental philosophy indicates that humans use at least two separate cognitive processes to make moral judgments: one that focuses on an act and intentions or mental states and one that focuses on outcomes or results and then looks for a causal actor. Conflict between these two processes can give rise to puzzle of moral luck, which arises when persons who commit the same acts with the same associated mental states are punished differently when these acts have different results. Kumar (2019) has argued that one resolution to the puzzle of moral luck as it arises in the criminal law is to claim instrumental aims like deterrence and social order are achieved by the law treating cases differently based on results.

However, rape is a crime that, by definition, may be lacking a publicly available outcome. This means moral judgments about rape may not engage the results-oriented system; or may engage it less often and less effectively. Criminal statutes, police investigations, arrests, prosecutions, verdicts, and punishment for rape are more likely to be related to moral judgments that assess acts and intentions. I have argued that the act/intention process of moral judgment is also poorly equipped with regard to rape cases. In the end, the variability in statutes criminalizing and punishing rape; the low number of reports, arrests, and convictions for rape; and the higher rates of recidivism for rapists all support the claim that instances of rape may not produce high-quality judgments from either the results-oriented or the act/mental state systems of moral judgment. If this is true, rape—and other crimes that lack a publicly available result—may sit in a moral judgment blind spot.

Acknowledgments

The author would like to thank the two editors of this volume, Sam Murray and Paul Henne, for extensive and insightful comments on an earlier draft that resulted in this much-improved chapter. The remaining confusions are not their fault.

Notes

1. Although both attempted murder and murder are considered very serious felonies (both are Class X felonies in jurisdictions such as Illinois), *in practice* attempted murder tends to carry a lower punishment than murder. For example, Jorge might earn a sentence at the lower end of the Class X range, twenty years, for attempted murder, and a sentence at the higher end, sixty years, for murder.
2. For Cushman's work on related topics, see Martin and Cushman (2015) and Martin and Cushman (2016).
3. Interestingly, Cushman's experiments indicated that judgments of wrongfulness and permissibility are more heavily determined by belief than desire (Cushman 2008). So, where mental states mattered, belief that one will cause harm mattered more than the desire to cause harm. This is interesting from a legal perspective because the Model Penal Code separates the mental states of "purposely" and "knowingly," and crimes committed purposely are considered more serious.
4. Whether a defendant has an excuse for his action, or a justification for his action, will also affect whether and to what extent he can be criminally charged for that action and its related harm.
5. According to the US Model Penal Code, Jorge killed "purposely" Model Penal Code section 2.02.
6. Note that a certain level of mental capacity is also necessary for Jorge to be legally culpable. If he is deemed incapable of forming the requisite *mens rea* due to a serious mental illness or juvenile status (i.e., if Jorge were deemed legally insane or if he were eleven years old), then he would not qualify for punishment despite his mental states and voluntary act.

7 Thank you to Sam Murray for noting that this distinction is reminiscent of Rawls' (1955) two-tiered view of utilitarianism, and for making this point clear via an analogy: in chess, particular moves are justified in virtue of the aims of the players as constrained by the rules of the game. But, when we ask about why the rules are justified, we can appeal to prospective or broadly consequentialist considerations.
8 This makes sense given Cushman's claim that the two processes often work in parallel and to some extent competitively to produce moral judgments.
9 There are also retributive, or legal moralist, reasons why certain harmful results are criminalized. So, to my mind we might see both retributive and consequentialist justifications of the criminal law at the institutional and the agential level. (What the "best" mixed justification for the criminal law looks like is another matter.)
10 Rape is not a term used in the MPC. Recklessness is sufficient to be found guilty under MPC 213.6.
11 Common responses to rape and other trauma are the "shut down" and dissociation often associated with PTSD. "When a parasympathetically dominated 'shut-down' was the prominent peri-traumatic response during the traumatic incident, comparable dissociative responses may dominate responding to subsequently experienced threat and may also reappear when the traumatic memory is reactivated" (Shauer and Elbert 2015).
12 Depending on attendant circumstances, especially where serious physical force was used or where there is a certain relationship between the offender and the victim (e.g., teacher and student), long terms of incarceration for rape are not uncommon. Only murderers serve longer sentences overall (Temkin 2002). But there are also examples of high-profile rape cases where the sentences seem too lenient to be proportional. For example, Kate Manne (2017) discusses the case of Stanford University student and swimmer Brock Turner at length in her book *Down Girl*. Mr. Turner only served three months after being found guilty of sexually penetrating an intoxicated person. The judge in the case lamented the possibility of giving Turner a harsh sentence, indicating that Turner did not deserve to have his life ruined over one mistake. This mistake was having sex with an unconscious victim.
13 For a review of the "no means no" campaign against rape, and its insufficiency, see this Atlantic article: https://www.theatlantic.com/entertainment/archive/2018/08/the-dangerous-insufficiency-of-no-means-no/566465/
14 The number reported by the Office of Justice Programs in 2000 was 17.9 percent. See Full Report of the Prevalence, Incidence, and Consequences of Violence Against Women: https://www.ojp.gov/pdffiles1/nij/183781.pdf.
15 https://www.washingtonpost.com/business/2018/10/06/less-than-percent-rapes-lead-felony-convictions-least-percent-victims-face-emotional-physical-consequences/
16 https://www.caase.org/cpd-response-sex-crimes/
17 Studies have found that defendants are charged with rape at roughly the same rate as they are charged with murder, which is striking given the vast difference in estimated numbers of rapes versus murders. For example, an estimated 57,497 felony cases were filed in the US state courts in the seventy-five largest counties during May 2004. About a quarter of defendants were charged with a violent offense, usually robbery or assault (figure 2). Less than 1 percent of defendants were charged with murder (0.6 percent) or rape (0.9 percent). https://bjs.ojp.gov/content/pub/pdf/fdluc04.pdf.
18 In a new paper, Kneer and Scoczen (in progress) performed studies focused on ways to counter the hindsight bias. They found that, "Although the hindsight bias is

robust, pervasive and its consequences can be daunting ... there are measures that can be taken. Whereas the practical import of probability anchoring is small ... both probability stabilizing and prompting people to entertain alternative outcomes hold a lot of promise. They block the hindsight bias, the distorted ascription of risk-related types of mens rea (negligence and recklessness) and decrease the outcome bias on blame substantially or cancel it out." This may mean there are ways to counter biased attributions of negligence to rape victims.
19 I'd like to thank Tyler Fagan for this turn of phrase.
20 Unfortunately, here I must shift to discussing sex offenders more generally, instead of rapists. This is because this is the way much of the data about recidivism is coded.
21 https://www.cleveland.com/rape-kits/2015/03/authorities_believe_serial_rap.html

References

Bryden, D. and S. Lengnick (1997), "Rape in the Criminal Justice System," *Journal of Criminal Law and Criminology*, 87 (4): 1194–384.
Campbell, R., Steven J. Pierce, Dhruv Sharma, Hannah Feeney, Rachael Goodman-Williams, and Wenjuan Ma. (2019), "Serial Sexual Assaults: A Longitudinal Examination of Offending Patterns Using DNA Evidence," Report for the Office of Justice Programs. Available online: https://www.ojp.gov/pdffiles1/nij/grants/252707.pdf.
Cushman, F. (2008), "Crime and Punishment: Distinguishing the Roles of Causal and Intentional Analyses in Moral Judgment," *Cognition*, 108 (2): 353–80.
Cushman, F. (2015), "Punishment in Humans: From Intuitions to Institutions," *Philosophy Compass*, 10 (2): 117–33.
Enough, B. and T. Mussweiler (2006), "Sentencing Under Uncertainty: Anchoring Effects in the Courtroom," *Journal of Applied Social Psychology*, 31 (7): 1535–51.
Ferzan, K. (2022), "#WeToo," *Florida State Law Review*, 49 (3): 693–753.
Fricker, M. (2007), *Epistemic Injustice: Power and the Ethics of Knowing*, New York: Oxford University Press.
Hanson, R., H. Karl, and R. A. Steffy (1995), "A Comparison of Child Molesters and Nonsexual Criminals: Risk Predictors and Long-Term Recidivism," *Journal of Research in Crime and Delinquency*, 32 (3): 325–37.
Kneer, M. and E. Machery (2019), "No Luck for Moral Luck," *Cognition*, 182: 331–48.
Kneer, M. and I. Skoczeń (in progress), "Outcome Effects, Moral Luck and Hindsight Bias," [Preprint]. Available online: https://psyarxiv.com/k6fpa/. https://papers.ssrn.com/sol3/papers.cfm?abstract_id=3810220
Kumar, V. (2019), "Empirical Vindication of Moral Luck," *Nous*, 53 (4): 987–1007.
Kyckelhahn, T. and J. Cohen (2004), "Felony Defendants in Large Urban Counties," Report for the Bureau of Justice Statistics. Available online: https://bjs.ojp.gov/content/pub/pdf/fdluc04.pdf.
Langan, P. and D. Levin (2002), "Recidivism of Prisoners Released in 1994." *Report for the Bureau of Justice Statistics*.
Manne, K. (2017), *Down Girl: The Logic of Misogyny*, New York: Oxford University Press.
Martin, J. and F. Cushman (2015), "To Punish or to Leave: Distinct Cognitive Processes Underlie Partner Control and Partner Choice Behaviors," *PLOS ONE*, 10 (4): 1–14.

Martin, J. and F. Cushman (2016), "The Adaptive Logic of Moral Luck," in J. Sytsma and W. Buckwalter (eds.), *Blackwell Companion to Experimental Philosophy*, 190–202, West Sussex: Wiley.

Morabito, M., Linda M. Williams, and April Pattavina. (2019), "Decision Making in Sexual Assault Cases: Replication Research on Sexual Violence: Case Attrition in the U.S.," *Report Through the NCJRS*. Available online: https://www.ojp.gov/pdffiles1/nij/grants/252689.pdf.

Nagel, T. (1993), "Moral Luck," in D. Statman (ed.), *Moral Luck*, 141–66, Albany, NY: New York Press.

Niemi, L. and L. Young (2016), "When and Why We See Victims as Responsible: The Impact of Ideology on Attitudes Toward Victims," *Personality and Social Psychology Bulletin*, 42 (9): 1227–42.

Przybylski, R. (2015), "Recidivism of Adult Sexual Offenders," Report for the Office of Justice Programs. Available online: https://smart.ojp.gov/sites/g/files/xyckuh231/files/media/document/recidivismofadultsexualoffenders.pdf.

Rawls, J. (1955), "Two Concepts of Rules," *The Philosophical Review*, 64 (1): 3–32. Available online: https://doi.org/10.2307/2182230.

Sample, Lisa L. and Timothy M. Bray (2003), "Are Sex Offenders Dangerous?," *Criminology and Public Policy*, 3 (1): 59–62.

Shauer, M., and T. Elbert (2015), "Dissociation Following Traumatic Stress," *Zeitschrift für Psychologie / Journal of Psychology*, 218 (2): 109–27.

Sifferd, K. L. (2006), "In Defense of the Use of Commonsense Psychology in the Criminal Law," *Law and Philosophy*, 25 (6): 571–612.

Temkin, J. (2002), *Rape and the Legal Process*, New York: Oxford University Press.

The American Law Institute (2017), *Model Penal Code Sentencing Provisions*, section 102 (2).

The American Law Institute (2020, August 18), *Model Penal Code: Sexual Assault and Related Offenses*, tentative draft no. 4.

Tjaden, P., and N. Thoennes (2000), "Full Report of the Prevalence, Incidence, and Consequences of Violence Against Women," *Report for the Office of Justice Programs*, National Institute of Justice. Available online: https://www.ojp.gov/pdffiles1/nij/183781.pdf.

Turkheimer, D. (2017), "Incredible Women: Sexual Violence and the Credibility Discount," *University of Pennsylvania Law Review*, 166 (1): 1–58.

11

How People Think about Moral Excellence

The Role of Counterfactual Thoughts in Reasoning about Morally Good Actions

Shane Timmons and Ruth M. J. Byrne

11.1 Moral Goodness

Our aim in this chapter is to consider how people think about morally good actions. In daily life, we often hear about the morally bad things that people have done, in reports of criminal acts of assault or murder, burglary or mugging, in discussions of racism, misogyny, and homophobia, and everyday acts of discrimination, intolerance, and cruelty. Less often, we hear about the best of humanity, the morally good things that people have done, feats of heroism and self-sacrifice, exceptional acts of kindness and generosity, and extraordinary benevolence and charity. Similarly, although research on moral cognition has received extensive attention in the past decade, most of it has focused on judgments about moral violations. Consideration of moral responsibility has often concentrated on judgments of blame, fault, accountability, and punishment (e.g., Greene et al. 2001; Haidt 2001; Lagnado, Gerstenberg, and Zoltan 2013; Schein and Gray 2018; Young and Koenigs 2007). By comparison there has been very little research on how people reason about acts of moral excellence, and few studies have considered moral responsibility for good outcomes, and judgments of moral credit, praise, virtue, or merit (e.g., Algoe and Haidt 2009; Anderson, Crockett, and Pizarro 2020; Clark et al. 2018; Goodwin 2015; Knobe 2010). Our aim is to contribute to redressing this imbalance, and to advance the nascent field of judgments of moral goodness.

Most of the existing research on morally good actions has focused on emotional responses. For example, when people observe an act of moral goodness they experience an emotional uplift or "moral elevation" (e.g., Algoe and Haidt 2009; Aquino, McFerran, and Laven 2011; Diessner et al. 2013; Schnall and Roper 2012). They often wish to emulate such witnessed prosocial behavior, to do something good themselves that will help others (e.g., Cox 2010; Freeman, Aquino, and McFerran 2009; Schnall, Roper, and Fessler 2010). Little is known about the cognitive processes that underlie judgments about morally good actions. Our recent work has focused on the development of a theory of how people reason about moral goodness. To do so, we have considered fundamental questions such as whether cognitive processes about nonmoral matters are recruited to reason about moral matters, and whether there are asymmetries in how people think about morally good actions compared to morally bad ones.

Our starting point has been to explore the idea that the experience of moral elevation may lead to the formation of intentions to emulate in part because people think about how things could turn out differently if the morally good action had not been taken. People may spontaneously create alternatives to reality that envisage how things could have been different when they witness morally excellent events. The suggestion originates from the observation that actions that inspire moral elevation often seem exceptional, and it is well established that exceptional events prompt people to spontaneously create counterfactual alternatives to reality (e.g., Byrne 2005; Kahneman and Tversky 1982; Roese and Epstude 2017). Moreover, people tend to think about how things could have turned out differently not only after bad outcomes but also after unexpected and unusually good ones (e.g., Dixon and Byrne 2011; Kahneman and Tversky 1982; McEleney and Byrne 2006; Sanna and Turley 1996). Hence, we considered that creating an imagined alternative to reality may be one of the cognitive ingredients in the formation of an intention to emulate moral goodness. A core function of counterfactual thoughts appears to be to help people to form intentions (e.g., Roese and Epstude 2017). For example, in one study, people imagined an everyday event with a bad outcome, such as that they had got bad sunburn the day before, and then read either a counterfactual assertion about how it could have turned out differently, such as that they could have worn sun-cream, or a factual assertion, such as that they wore sun-cream in the past. They subsequently responded faster (pressing yes or no) after they read the counterfactual assertion, compared to the factual assertion, to a description of an intention that would prevent the event from recurring in the future, such as that they would now wear sun-cream (Smallman and Roese 2009; see also Smallman and McCulloch 2012). Counterfactual thoughts may help people to prepare for the future, especially when counterfactuals focus on how something someone did could have turned out better (e.g., Ferante, Girotto, and Walsh 2013; McCloy and Byrne 2000; Walsh and Byrne 2007; see also Fazelpour 2020). Our theoretical proposal is that counterfactual thoughts about how things could have turned out differently about a morally elevating event drive the formation of pro-social intentions to emulate moral excellence. In several series of experiments, we have examined how people think about moral goodness to test these theoretical ideas.

We consider three questions in this chapter. Our first question is, do people rely on different sorts of cognitive processes to reason about moral excellence compared to reasoning about moral violations? Our focus is on exemplary actions rather than exemplary character (e.g., Goodwin 2015). We consider how people reflect on their episodic memories of events they have witnessed in which someone demonstrated humanity's higher or better nature, that is, observations of someone doing something good, honorable, or charitable for someone else. We discuss the implications of evidence that shows that people tend to construct very different sorts of imagined alternatives to morally good acts compared to bad ones (Timmons et al. 2021). Our second question is, how do people reason about whether a morally good action should be taken? For example, what sorts of cognitive processes underlie a self-sacrificial decision to run into traffic in front of a truck to save a child who has fallen there? We consider the phenomenon of *moral hindsight,* the tendency for people to judge that a good action should have been taken when the outcome turned out well—for example, the child rescued from the oncoming truck sustained just minor bruises, compared to when the outcome did not turn out well—for example, the child sustained life-threatening injuries (Byrne and Timmons 2018). We also discuss the implications of evidence that judgments about whether the morally good action should have been carried out are affected by imagined counterfactual alternatives. Our third question is, what sorts of causal mental models do people construct of a morally good action and its outcome? We consider evidence that when people have carried out a demanding cognitive task, they tend to judge that a self-sacrificial action, such as jumping onto railway tracks to save a person who has fallen there, need not be taken, compared to individuals who are not tired (Timmons and Byrne 2019). We discuss the cognitive resources required to construct a causal model that explicitly links an action to its outcome, compared to a simplified model of an action. We also consider the observation that the effects of cognitive fatigue occur when people focus solely on the sacrifice, jumping on the tracks, but not when they focus on its good outcome, saving the life of the person who has fallen. We consider the implications of the results for the role of cognitive processes for reasoning about nonmoral matters, such as the construction of models, in reasoning about moral matters. In the following sections we consider each of these questions in turn, and in the final section of the chapter we discuss their implications for alternative theories of the cognitive processes underlying reasoning about moral matters, and for potential future directions of research on moral goodness.

11.2 What Sorts of Cognitive Processes Underlie Reasoning about Moral Excellence?

The cognitive processes that people rely on to reason about moral goodness may share many elements in common with reasoning about moral violations, and with reasoning about nonmoral matters (e.g., Bucciarelli, Khemlani, and Johnson-Laird 2008; see also Cushman and Young 2011; Landy and Royzman 2018; Phillips, Leguri, and Knobe 2015). People tend to reason about most events by simulating them, imagining the potential consequences of different actions, and hypothesizing about the possible antecedents to various actions (e.g., Byrne and Johnson-Laird 2020; Johnson-Laird and Byrne 2002). They construct a model of an event, and modify some aspects of it to consider counterfactual alternatives to reality (e.g., Byrne 2016; Kahneman and Tversky 1982; Roese and Epstude 2017). We have explored the idea that people form intentions to emulate morally good acts when they experience moral elevation in part because people imagine how things could have been different when they reflect on a morally good event.

What kinds of alternatives to reality do people imagine when they recall someone carrying out an act of moral excellence? In a series of experiments, we explored how people reflect on episodic memories from their past about events they witnessed that epitomize moral goodness, such as a memory of a neighbor taking in an elderly person who had become confused until their relative could be located (Timmons et al. 2021). We asked people to write about a time they witnessed someone doing something good for someone else. We then asked them to think about how things could have turned out differently. We coded the counterfactuals they generated according to whether they described the event as turning out *better*—an upward comparison to a better situation, or *worse*—a downward comparison to a worse situation (e.g., Roese 1997; Roese and Epstude 2017). We also coded them according to whether the participant *added* something that had not happened or *subtracted* something that had happened (e.g., Kahneman and Tversky 1982; Roese and Epstude 2017). For example, one participant recalled witnessing a woman offer help to a homeless man. The participant imagined how things could have been *better* by *adding* something that had not happened: they imagined the man could have been helped more if they themselves had stopped to help him too. It is just as plausible to imagine instead how things could have been *worse* by *subtracting* something that happened: they could have imagined the man would have received no assistance if the woman had not offered to help him. We wished to test whether there were systematic patterns in the types of counterfactuals that people imagined for memories of morally good actions compared to morally bad ones. Accordingly, we asked some of the participants to write about a time they witnessed someone doing something good for someone else, and others to write about a time they witnessed someone doing something bad to someone else.

We were also interested in the intentions people form after they recall memories of morally good actions compared to morally bad ones. When people witness or hear about acts of moral excellence, they often intend to act in morally good ways themselves in the future (e.g., Pohling and Diessner 2016). People can form intentions that are general aspirations—for example, "I will be more caring,"—or ones that are specific plans—for example, "If I see a homeless person looking for food, I will give them money." However, general aspirations are less likely to be acted upon than specific plans (e.g., Gollwitzer and Sheeran 2006). Hence, after participants recalled a morally good action (or a bad one), and imagined how it could have turned out differently, we also asked them about their intentions for the future. We coded their intentions as general aspirations or specific intentions.

In two experiments, we invited over 230 members of the general public who visited a science exhibition to write about a memory they had of someone acting in a morally good way, when they witnessed someone "demonstrating humanity's higher or better nature . . . someone did something good, honorable, or charitable for someone else" (adapted from Algoe and Haidt 2009). Participants were assigned at random to two groups, one group was asked to recall a memory of a morally good action, the other group was asked to recall a memory of a morally bad action, "humanity's lower or worse nature . . . something bad, dishonorable, or uncharitable." People appear readily able to recall such memories, and they remembered various different sorts of morally good actions such as a brother as a child returning cash he found to an elderly man, or an acquaintance donating a kidney to a relative. They also recalled various sorts of morally bad actions, such as girls in school bullying a classmate, or a wealthy person sneering at a homeless man. They were then prompted to write about how things could have turned out differently. They were also asked whether they thought about changing their own behavior and, if so, to describe their intentions. Both experiments showed that, for morally good acts, people *subtracted* something from reality and imagined how things could have been *worse*, whereas for morally bad acts they *added* something to reality and imagined how things could have been *better*. This pattern is similar to the sorts of counterfactuals that people create for good and bad nonmoral events (e.g., Epstude and Roese 2017). It suggests a shared set of cognitive processes underlies thinking about moral and nonmoral matters. The results support the idea that, as with reasoning about moral violations, reasoning about moral excellence relies at least in part on domain-general processes (e.g., Bucciarelli, Khemlani, and Johnson-Laird 2008; Gubbins and Byrne 2014), rather than a domain-specific moral faculty (e.g., Mikhail 2007). The results also showed that after recalling a morally good action, participants who intended to behave differently in the future were more likely to report *general aspirations*, whereas those who recalled a morally bad action were more likely to report *specific intentions* (see also Janoff-Bulman, Sheikh, and Hepp 2009). The finding is also consistent with research on counterfactuals and intentions for nonmoral events (e.g., Smallman 2013). Importantly, counterfactuals that add something to reality to make it better tend to provide blueprints for future behavior (Epstude and Roese 2008). However, participants rarely imagined counterfactuals that add something to reality when they thought about an act of moral goodness. This discovery provides a clue about why the desire to emulate the morally good actions of others rarely translates into sustained future behavior change.

We sought to determine whether the outcome of morally good actions matters. In another two experiments our comparison was between, not morally good actions and morally bad ones, but morally good actions with a successful good outcome, and morally good actions with a bad outcome. Over 130 university students were asked to recall an act of moral excellence that had a good outcome, "a situation that resulted in a good outcome—a situation where the person's actions were successful in helping another person." Participants were assigned at random to two groups, one group was asked to recall a memory of a morally good action with a good outcome, the other group was asked to recall a memory of a morally good action with a bad outcome, "a situation that did not result in a good outcome—a situation where the person's actions were not successful in helping another person." People were readily able to recall morally good actions with bad outcomes, for example, one participant remembered witnessing a woman trying to give money to a man begging on the street who was shouted at by the man. They were then prompted to imagine how things could have turned out differently and they were asked to write about any intentions they had for the future. Each participant was tested individually in the lab, and when they had completed the tasks, the experimenter "accidentally" knocked a cup of pens off the table. We recorded whether the participant helped to pick them up. The action is an indirect test of moral prosocial behavior (van Baaren et al. 2004). The experimenter (the first author) was unaware of which experimental condition the participant had been assigned to by the computer program. We explained the mild deception to participants in their individual debriefing, none of the participants were distressed by it, and only one indicated he had thought it might be part of the experiment.

The results of these two experiments show striking similarities in how people think about actions that are morally bad, examined in our two earlier experiments, and actions that are morally good but have bad outcomes. Participants who recalled good actions that led to good outcomes tended to generate *subtractive* counterfactuals about how things could have been *worse*, just as they did in the first two experiments for morally good actions. But when the morally good action had a bad outcome, participants created *additive* counterfactuals about things that could have been *better*, just as they did in the first two experiments for morally *bad* actions. Similarly, participants formed *general aspirations* to change when they recalled good actions that had good outcomes, just as they did for morally good actions in the earlier experiments, but they formed *specific intentions* when the good actions had bad outcomes, just as they did for morally *bad* actions in the earlier experiments. Even though the action itself was morally good, its failed outcome led participants to create counterfactuals and intentions similar to those generated for morally bad actions. Strikingly, participants tended to spontaneously help to pick up the pens more often when they recalled a morally good act with a good outcome than when they recalled a morally good act with a bad outcome. The finding demonstrates for the first time that the outcomes of morally good actions matter for the desire to emulate moral goodness. Previous experiments have compared the positive emotion of moral elevation to other positive emotions, but the results of our experiments identify an important boundary condition for morally good actions to encourage emulation (e.g., Pohling and Diessner 2016).

We replicated the results in a subsequent experiment with over 100 participants recruited online that included a control group who were not instructed to imagine how things could have been different but instead just to reflect on the facts. The results showed that the difference in general aspirations versus specific plans after people had thought about morally good actions with good or bad outcomes occurred only when people imagined how things could have turned out differently, and not when they focused just on the facts. The results also showed that participants who recalled good actions with bad outcomes were less likely to donate some of their participant payment to charity than those who recalled good actions with good outcomes, replicating the finding that a good outcome appears necessary if a morally good act is to create the desire to be emulated (see also Yao and Enright 2018).

This series of experiments shows that when people think about how an act of moral excellence that successfully helped someone could have turned out differently, they imagine how it could have turned out *worse* by *subtracting* something that happened, as Figure 11.1a illustrates. But when they think about a morally bad act, or an act of moral excellence that failed to help someone, they imagine how it could have turned out *better* by *adding* something. When people think about an act of moral excellence that successfully helped someone, they form intentions to emulate that tend to be *general* aspirations rather than *specific* intentions, compared to when they think about a morally bad action, or a morally good action that failed to help someone, as Figure 11.1b shows. The difference in the types of intentions that people form depends on their imagination of an alternative to reality; it is not observed when they reflect only

How People Think about Moral Excellence 215

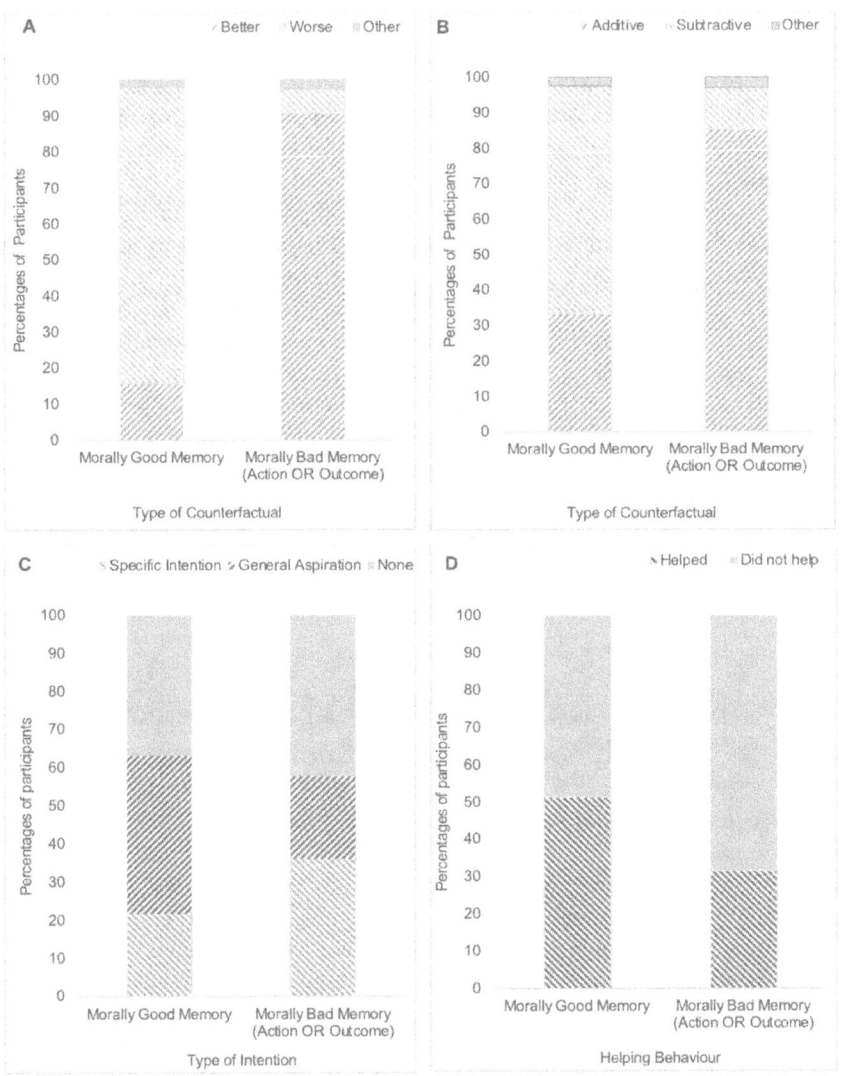

Figure 11.1 Types of counterfactuals that participants created: better or worse (a), and additive or subtractive (b); types of intentions that participants created (c), and their spontaneous helping behavior (d), after they recalled a morally good action with a good outcome, versus a morally bad action, or a morally good action with a bad outcome. Adapted from Timmons et al. 2021, with pooled data from five experiments (participants who were asked to reflect only on the facts are not included). Helping behavior was measured in three experiments only.

on the facts of the event. Intriguingly, the creation of counterfactuals about how an action could have turned out *worse* that *subtract* something that happened, and the formation of *general* aspiration intentions, is observed only when a morally good action has a good outcome. When people recall good acts that have bad outcomes, they create counterfactuals and intentions that are similar to those they form when they recall morally bad actions, they imagine how the events could have turned out *better* by *adding* something, and they form a *specific* intention for the future. Moreover, the likelihood that good actions are emulated in prosocial helping behavior immediately after they are recalled depends on whether their outcome was good or bad. Specific intentions may be more conducive than general aspirations to bringing about prosocial change in the long-term, but in the immediate aftermath of recalling a good action with a good outcome, helping behavior increases.

The cognitive processes that underlie reasoning about moral excellence are similar to those that underlie reasoning about moral violations, with regard to the creation of counterfactual alternatives. Nonetheless people create very different counterfactuals and intentions for morally good actions with good outcomes, compared to those with bad outcomes, and compared to morally bad actions. The differences may reflect the nature of the causal links made between actions and their outcomes, to which we now turn.

11.3 How Do People Reason about Whether a Morally Good Action Should Be Taken?

When people reason about nonmoral matters, they tend to show a "hindsight bias," that is, when they are given information about an outcome, they believe they would have predicted it all along (e.g., Fischhoff 1975; Roese and Vohs 2012). Judgments about morally bad actions too are influenced by outcome knowledge (e.g., Baron and Hershey 1988; Fleischhut, Meder, and Gigerenzer 2017; Oeberst and Goeckenjan 2016; see also Rozin and Royzman 2001). For example, when people read about a boy who threw a brick from an overpass bridge that hit a car passing underneath and injured a driver, they judge that he should be punished, far more so than when they read about a boy whose brick fell without causing injury. Both boys carried out the same action with the same beliefs and same intentions and it is a matter of luck whether the outcome was bad or not for each one (e.g., Lench et al. 2015; Martin and Cushman 2016a; see also Cushman 2008; Young, Nichols, and Saxe 2010; Kneer and Machery 2019). Yet people's judgments of punishment are influenced by whether the intended outcome occurred or not. Do similar effects occur for morally good outcomes? We examined whether judgments that a morally good action should have been taken are affected by outcome knowledge about whether it succeeded or failed (Byrne and Timmons 2018). In a series of experiments, we gave participants stories to read, for example, about Ann who ran into traffic to save Jill who had fallen in front of an oncoming truck. We examined how people thought about whether Ann should have carried out the morally good action, when they believed that her heroic action succeeded—Jill was saved with just minor bruises, or when they believed her action failed—Jill sustained life-threatening injuries.

We also examined the effects of imagined alternatives to the outcome. An imagined alternative to an outcome affects moral judgments for stories about bad actions. For example, for the boy who threw a brick that did not hurt anyone, when people read a counterfactual about how things would have turned out worse, e.g., if he had thrown the brick from another section of the bridge he would have hit a car, their judgments that he should be punished increased (e.g., Parkinson and Byrne 2017; see also Lench et al. 2015). Counterfactuals amplify moral judgments about many sorts of bad outcomes (e.g., Branscombe et al. 1996; see also Alicke et al. 2008; Malle, Guglielmo, and Monroe 2014; Markman, Mizoguchi, and McMullen 2008). Do similar effects occur for morally good outcomes? We examined whether judgments that a morally good action should have been taken are affected by the sorts of alternatives that people imagine. We compared judgments when people heard a counterfactual about how the outcome would have been worse if the action had not been taken, "if Ann had not rushed to help, Jill's injuries would have been worse," compared to judgments when they heard a "semi-factual" about how the outcome would have been the same even if the action had not been taken, "even if Ann had not rushed to help, Jill's injuries would have been the same." People make different inferences from counterfactual "if only" subjunctive conditionals compared to semi-factual "even if" subjunctive conditionals (e.g., Moreno-Rios, Garcia-Madruga, and Byrne 2008; see also Santamaria, Espino, and Byrne 2005). And when they reason about nonmoral matters, the nature of an imagined alternative to an outcome influences their causal judgments. For example, people judged that a painkiller caused a runner to lose a race due to the side effects of fatigue. Their causal judgments were amplified when they heard about a counterfactual alternative—another painkiller with no side effects—and so they could imagine that if the runner had taken the other painkiller she would not have lost the race. Their causal judgments were diminished when they heard about a semi-factual alternative—another painkiller with the same side effects—and so they could imagine that even if the runner had taken the other painkiller she still would have lost the race (e.g., McCloy and Byrne 2002).

In one of our experiments, we gave over 150 volunteers from the general public the following story:

> Ann is waiting for a bus with her son. Nearby a young child, Jill trips over an uneven pavement stone and stumbles into the road and falls down near the traffic lights at the busy intersection. Just then, a very large truck drives through the intersection. Ann rushes to help, she can see that the truck driver cannot see Jill struggling on the ground and will not be able to stop in time. She decides that the only way to help is to run into the road and hold Jill down so they both lie still as the truck passes over them. She knows that there is a terrible risk that the truck could crush them both.

We also told them the outcome:

> Ann ran into the road and held Jill down. When the truck drove on and passersby got to them, Jill had sustained only minor bumps and bruises from the truck.

One group of participants in the experiment read a counterfactual ending:

> The police examined the videos of the incident later and observed that if Ann had not rushed to help, Jill's injuries would have been worse.

A second group read a semi-factual ending:

> The police examined the videos of the incident later and observed that even if Ann had not rushed to help, Jill's injuries would have been the same.

The third group read a factual ending:

> The police examined the videos of the incident later and observed Ann rushing to help and Jill sustaining injuries from the truck.

Participants completed two judgments, one just before they read the outcome:

> Ann should run into the road to help Jill.

And one after they had read the whole story:

> Knowing what I know now, I believe Ann should have run into the road to help Jill.

They indicated whether they agreed or disagreed with the sentences (on a 1–7 scale with 1 labeled "agree" and 7 labeled "disagree"). In a second experiment, a different set of over 140 volunteers from the general public read a version of the story but this time about a failed attempt to help, in which the outcome was that the child, Jill, had sustained serious life-threatening injuries.

The experiments reveal two discoveries which are illustrated in Figure 11.2a. The first finding is that people tended to judge that the action should have been taken after they heard the good outcome and the facts, more so than they judged it should be taken *before* they heard the good outcome. The result demonstrates for the first time a moral hindsight effect for morally good actions with good outcomes. There was no such hindsight effect for bad outcomes. Across the two experiments, participants judged that the action should have been taken more often for good outcomes than bad ones when they knew the outcome.

The results support the proposal that people make moral judgments by attempting to construct a causal mental model to connect an action to its intended, expected outcome (e.g., Cushman 2013; Timmons and Byrne 2019). When they identify a causal link between the action and the outcome, they believe the actor could have known what the outcome would be (e.g., Baron and Hershey 1988; Martin and Cushman 2016b). On this proposal, they judge a morally good action should have been taken more often when they know it succeeded, compared to when they do not know the outcome, because the good outcome provides confirmation of its causal link to the action, for example, Ann could have known that her action would save Jill. However, they judge

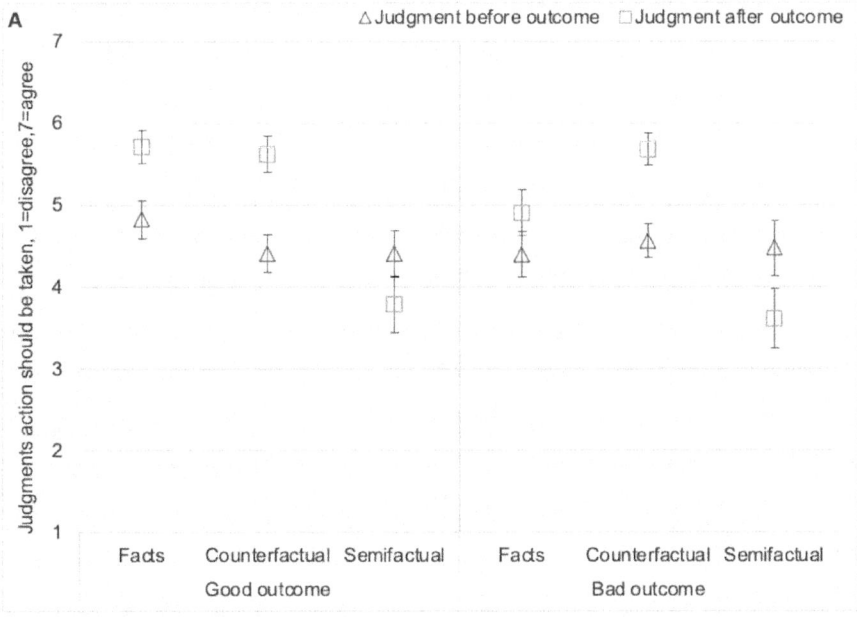
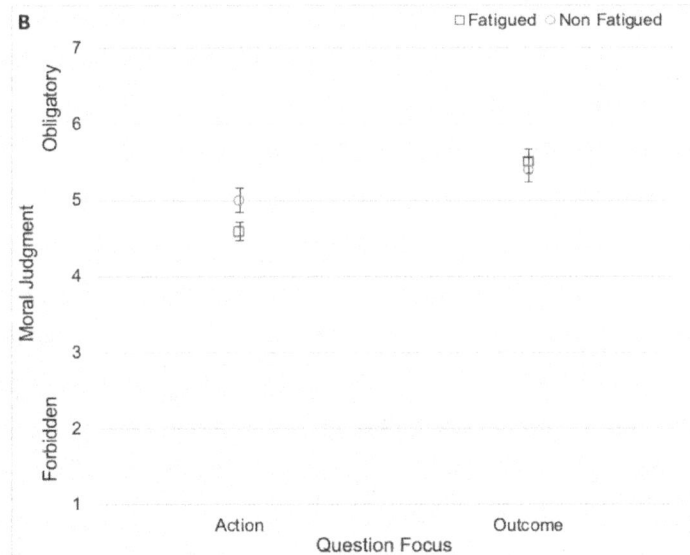

Figure 11.2 (a) Judgments that an action should have been taken, before and after information about the outcome and an assertion of the facts, counterfactual, or semifactual for a good outcome and a bad outcome (adapted from Byrne and Timmons 2018: Experiments 1 and 2). Responses are reverse scored. (b) Judgments that a good action was morally obliged, made by fatigued and non-fatigued participants in response to action-focused and outcome-focused questions (adapted from Timmons and Byrne 2019). Error bars are standard error of the mean.

a good action should have been taken just as often when they know it failed compared to when they do not know the outcome, because the bad outcome is not interpreted as disconfirming the causal link between the good action and the expected good outcome, as they recognize that other factors could have prevented the intended outcome (see also Kominsky et al. 2015; Sarin, Lagnado, and Burgess 2017). Our subsequent experiments in this series replicated the results and showed the hindsight effect occurs for judgments about morally good actions in a range of different sorts of domains, such as sports.

The second discovery is that judgments that the action should have been taken were amplified when people heard a counterfactual that the outcome would have been worse if the action hadn't been taken, and diminished when they heard a semi-factual that the outcome would have been the same if the action hadn't been taken. The effect of these imagined alternatives occurred for both the good outcome version and the bad outcome version of the story, as Figure 11.2a also shows. The result provides further evidence for the proposal that the counterfactual makes a comparison that emphasizes the causal link between the action and its outcome, whereas the semi-factual makes a comparison to a world in which the outcome is the same, and denies a causal link between the action and its outcome (e.g., Branscombe et al. 1996; McCloy and Byrne 2002).

The results provide insights into the cognitive processes that underlie how people reason about whether an act of moral excellence should be taken. The effects of moral hindsight indicate that people construct causal mental models that make explicit the links between an action and its outcome. A counterfactual further emphasizes the causal link between the action and its outcome. The asymmetric hindsight effects indicate that judgments about the necessity to engage in moral excellence are particularly sensitive to the efficacy of actions in leading to successful outcomes.

11.4 What Sorts of Models Do People Construct of a Morally Good Action?

Causal mental models that link actions to outcomes are important for judgments about morally bad actions (e.g., Crockett 2013; Cushman 2013; see also Cushman and Young 2011; Siegel, Crockett, and Dolan 2017). Is the construction of a model that links actions to outcomes important for judgments about morally good actions too? In the third series of experiments we examined how people's judgments about whether to engage in morally good actions are affected by whether they focus on the self-sacrificial action or its beneficial outcome (Timmons and Byrne 2019). In one of the experiments, we presented over 180 participants with real news stories that described acts of moral heroism, such as a story about Mr. Autrey who jumped onto the New York subway train tracks in front of an oncoming train to save Mr. Hollopeter who had fallen there. We asked them to judge how obligatory the morally good act was, and they chose their answer on a 1–7 scale:

In your opinion, Mr. Autrey jumping in front of the train in this case was morally

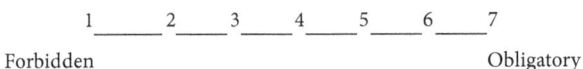

We expected that participants would judge that the action with its successful outcome was morally obligatory.

We hypothesized that participants would consider that the person was obliged to carry out the morally exemplary action with its excellent outcome provided that they have constructed a model that makes explicit the causal link between the action and its outcome. They must mentally represent the action, for example, Mr. Autrey jumping onto the tracks, and the outcome, for example, Mr. Hollopeter being saved from the oncoming train. But they must also simulate the causal relationship between the action and the outcome in their representation of the events (e.g., Byrne and Johnson-Laird 2020; Johnson-Laird and Khemlani 2017). If they construct only a simple initial model that represents the events but does not explicitly simulate the causal relationship between them, then they will be less inclined to judge that the person was obliged to carry out the action.

People tend to construct an initial set of models rather than a fully explicit set of models, given the limitations of working memory (Byrne and Johnson-Laird 2020; Johnson-Laird and Byrne 2002). They must have sufficient cognitive resources to construct a model that makes explicit the causal connections between the action and its outcome. As a result, we expected that if participants did not have sufficient cognitive resources, they would not construct the explicit causal mental model, and so they would not tend to judge the action to be obligatory, to the same extent as participants who had the cognitive resources to construct the more complex, fully explicit model. To test this idea, we gave one group of participants a cognitively demanding task, known to reduce cognitive resources (e.g., Inzlicht and Schmeichel 2012; Schmeichel, Vohs, and Baumesiter 2003). We compared their judgments to those of a second group of participants who were not cognitively fatigued in this manner.

We also compared two ways of asking whether the action was obligatory. We asked half of the participants a question designed to focus only on the self-sacrificial action, for example, "In your opinion, Mr. Autrey jumping in front of the train in this case was morally . . . " (and they choose their answer on the 1–7 scale from "forbidden" to "obligatory"). We asked the other half of the participants a question designed to focus also on the beneficial outcome, for example, "In your opinion, doing this to save Mr. Hollopeter was morally . . . ."

We expected to observe an interaction between fatigue and question focus: the outcome-focused question can help cognitively fatigued participants to overcome the limitation of tiredness and construct the more complex model that incorporates the outcome and makes explicit the causal links between it and the action. The action-focused question does not help in this way. Hence, we predicted that cognitively fatigued participants who answered action-focused questions would judge the morally good action to be less obligatory compared to participants who answered the outcome-focused questions and compared to participants who were not fatigued.

The results showed that participants tended to judge the actions to be somewhat obligatory, as Figure 11.2b illustrates, with overall mean judgments of 5 on the 1–7 scale (in which 7 is obligatory), significantly above the midpoint. Non-fatigued participants tended to judge that the action was obligatory regardless of the framing of the question, whereas fatigued participants tended to judge the action was obligatory more often when they answered the question that focused on the beneficial outcome, than when they answered the one that focused on the sacrificial action. Participants who completed a cognitively demanding task and then read an action-focused question judged the morally good action to be significantly less obligatory than participants in the other conditions, as Figure 11.2b shows. Participants who completed the cognitively demanding task and then read an outcome-focused question were helped by its framing to create an explicit model of the causal links between the action and the outcome, and so they responded similarly to non-fatigued participants.

When creating a complex mental model is difficult, for example when people are cognitively fatigued, they construct a simpler model of the action and outcome that does not make fully explicit the nature of their causal relationship. If these actions are potentially self-sacrificial, as is the case for some acts of moral excellence, people are not inclined to decide that the morally good act is obligatory. These findings suggest that people evaluate good actions based on the causal link between them and their outcomes. They do not evaluate the morally good action on its own merits in a vacuum.

11.5 Conclusions

When people reason about a morally good action, they construct a causal mental model of the action and its outcome, and imagine alternative possibilities in which the action was not carried out, and the outcome turned out worse. Our first question was whether people rely on different sorts of cognitive processes to reason about moral excellence compared to reasoning about moral violations. The evidence from people's episodic memories of events that they have witnessed in which someone demonstrated humanity's better nature shows that they tend to construct very different sorts of imagined alternatives about morally good acts compared to bad ones (Timmons et al. 2021). For episodic memories of a morally good act, they tend to imagine how things could have been *worse*, by mentally *subtracting* something that happened, for example, a confused elderly person could have got lost if their neighbor had not taken them in; whereas for memories of a morally bad act, they imagine how things could have been *better*, by mentally *adding* something new. The pattern occurs for memories of a good act that succeeded and so had a good outcome, but not for good acts that failed and so had a bad outcome. These different sorts of counterfactual thoughts lead to the formulation of different sorts of intentions, either *general* aspirations or *specific* plans. Moreover, spontaneous helping is greater immediately after people recall morally good actions with good outcomes compared to those with bad outcomes. However, our results suggest that emulation intentions about future prosocial behavior are affected by the nature of the counterfactual alternatives that people create. The nature of the cognitive processes that intervene between elevation and emulation is not always conducive to sustained behavioral change because intentions to emulate are more likely to take the form of general aspirations rather than specific plans, after recalling morally good actions with good outcomes. A potential question for future research is whether the tendency to help others could be encouraged further by ensuring that they imagine counterfactuals about how things could be better that add something new to the situation, or transform their general aspirations into specific plans.

Our second question was how people reason about whether a morally good action should have been taken. People exhibit pronounced moral hindsight, and judge that a good action should have been taken when the outcome turned out well, for example, a child rescued from an oncoming truck sustained just minor bruises, compared to when the outcome does not turn out well, for example, the child sustained life-threatening injuries (Byrne and Timmons 2018). Their judgments about whether the morally good action should have been carried out are affected by the alternatives they imagine. For example, their judgments that the action should have been taken increase when they imagine counterfactual alternatives such as that if the good action had not been taken, the outcome would have been worse. In contrast, their judgments that the action should have been taken *decrease* when they imagine semi-factual alternatives such as that even if the good action had not been taken, the outcome would have been just the same anyway. The counterfactual amplifies the causal link between the action and its outcome—people can infer that Ann running into traffic in front of the truck caused Jill to escape with minor injuries, since they can imagine that if Ann had not rushed to help, Jill's injuries would have been worse. The semi-factual diminishes the causal link between the action and its outcome—people can infer that Ann running into traffic in front of the truck did not cause Jill to escape with minor injuries, since they can imagine that even if Ann had not rushed to help, Jill's injuries would have been the same. A potential question for future research is whether moral hindsight is also influenced by inferences about the likelihood of success, for example, inferences about whether a person running into traffic is probably going to succeed or not in the effort to save a fallen child.

Our third question was how people construct causal mental models that link a morally good action to its outcome. When people have carried out a demanding cognitive task, they tend to judge that a self-sacrificial action, such as jumping onto railway tracks to save a person who has fallen there, need not be taken, compared to individuals who are not tired (Timmons and Byrne 2019). The effect occurs when they focus solely on the sacrifice, jumping on the tracks, but not when they focus on its good outcome, saving the life of the person who has fallen. The process of constructing a causal mental model that links the morally good action to its outcome requires cognitive resources, and when they are not available, people construct a simpler, initial mental model that does not make explicit the causal links between the action and its outcome. A potential question for future research is whether other means to ensure the construction of an explicit causal mental model, such as making causal inferences, affect judgments about whether a morally good action should be taken.

Together, our empirical discoveries imply that people do not think about morally good actions on their own merit, without also thinking about their consequences. When people recall a good action that lead to a bad outcome, the counterfactual alternatives to reality that they imagine mirror those they create when they recall a moral violation, they imagine a world in which something *better* happened by *adding* some new action. However, when they recall a good action that lead to a good outcome, their counterfactuals are strikingly different. They imagine a world in which something *worse* happened by *subtracting* some action. The desire to emulate a morally good action is also influenced by its consequences. A good outcome appears to be essential for a morally elevating action to be subsequently emulated, for example, spontaneous helping is less likely when people recall a morally good action that did not turn out well compared to when they recall one that did turn out well. Moreover, judgments that good actions should be taken are amplified when people discover the outcome was good, a striking instance of moral hindsight. Such judgments are also amplified when people imagine that the outcome would have been different had the action not been taken, and not when they imagine the same outcome would have occurred had the action not been taken. Accordingly, people judge acts of heroism to be morally obligatory when they have constructed a causal mental model linking the action to its outcome, more so than when they have focused solely on the action. These discoveries demonstrate for the first time that the outcomes of morally good actions play an important role in how people reason about acts of moral excellence, just as they do when people reason about moral violations, and when they reason about nonmoral matters.

Acknowledgments

We thank our collaborators Eoin Gubbins and Tiago Almeida for discussions of these topics. The research on which this chapter was based was funded by a postgraduate scholarship from Trinity College Dublin awarded to Shane Timmons, and a grant from the John Templeton Foundation, grant number 48054 awarded to Ruth Byrne.

References

Algoe, S. B. and J. Haidt (2009), "Witnessing Excellence in Action," *Journal of Positive Psychology*, 4 (2): 105–27.

Alicke, M. D., J. Buckingham, E. Zell, and T. Davis (2008), "Culpable Control and Counterfactual Reasoning in the Psychology of Blame," *Personality and Social Psychology Bulletin*, 34 (10): 1371–81.

Anderson, R. A., M. J. Crockett, and D. A. Pizarro (2020), "A Theory of Moral Praise," *Trends in Cognitive Sciences*, 24 (9): 694–703.

Aquino, K., B. McFerran, and M. Laven (2011), "Moral Identity and the Experience of Moral Elevation in Response to Acts of Uncommon Goodness," *Journal of Personality and Social Psychology*, 100 (4): 703.

Baron, J. and J. Hershey (1988), "Outcome Bias in Decision Evaluation," *Journal of Personality and Social Psychology*, 54 (4): 569–79.

Branscombe, N. R., S. Owen, T. A. Garstka, and J. Coleman (1996), "Rape and Accident Counterfactuals," *Journal of Applied Social Psychology*, 26 (12): 1042–67.

Bucciarelli, M., S. Khemlani, and P. N. Johnson-Laird (2008), "The Psychology of Moral Reasoning," *Judgment and Decision Making*, 3 (2): 121.

Byrne, R. M. J. (2005), *The Rational Imagination: How People Create Alternatives to Reality*, Cambridge, MA: MIT Press.
Byrne, R. M. J. (2016), "Counterfactual Thought," *Annual Review of Psychology*, 67: 153–7.
Byrne, R. M. J. (2017), "Counterfactual Thinking: From Logic to Morality," *Current Directions in Psychological Science*, 26 (4): 314–22.
Byrne, R. M. and P. N. Johnson-Laird (2020), "If and Or: Real and Counterfactual Possibilities in Their Truth and Probability," *Journal of Experimental Psychology: Learning, Memory, and Cognition*, 46 (4): 760.
Byrne, R. M. and S. Timmons (2018), "Moral Hindsight for Good Actions and the Effects of Imagined Alternatives to Reality," *Cognition*, 178: 82–91.
Clark, C. J., A. Shniderman, J. B. Luguri, R. F. Baumeister, and P. H. Ditto (2018), "Are Morally Good Actions Ever Free?," *Consciousness and Cognition*, 63: 161–82. https://doi.org/10.1016/j.concog.2018.05.006.
Cox, K. S. (2010), "Elevation Predicts Domain-Specific Volunteerism 3 Months Later," *Journal of Positive Psychology*, 5 (5): 333–41.
Crockett, M. J. (2013), "Models of Morality," *Trends in Cognitive Sciences*, 17 (8): 363–6.
Cushman, F. (2008), "Crime and Punishment," *Cognition*, 108 (2): 353–80.
Cushman, F. (2013), "Action, Outcome, and Value," *Personality and Social Psychology Review*, 17 (3): 273–92.
Cushman, F. and L. Young (2011), "Patterns of Moral Judgment Derive from Nonmoral Psychological Representations," *Cognitive Science*, 35 (6): 1052–75.
Diessner, R., R. Iyer, M. M. Smith, and J. Haidt (2013), "Who Engages with Moral Beauty?," *Journal of Moral Education*, 42 (2): 139–63.
Dixon, J. E. and R. M. Byrne (2011), "'If Only' Counterfactual Thoughts About Exceptional Actions," *Memory & Cognition*, 39 (7): 1317–31.
Epstude, K. and N. J. Roese (2008), "The Functional Theory of Counterfactual Thinking," *Personality and Social Psychology Review*, 12 (2): 168–92.
Fazelpour, S. (2020), "Norms in Counterfactual Selection," *Philosophy and Phenomenological Research*. https://doi.org/10.1111/phpr.12691.
Ferrante, D., V. Girotto, M. Stragà, and C. Walsh (2013), "Improving the Past and the Future: A Temporal Asymmetry in Hypothetical Thinking," *Journal of Experimental Psychology: General*, 142 (1): 23.
Fischhoff, B. (1975), "Hindsight Does Not Equal Foresight," *Journal of Experimental Psychology: Human Perception and Performance*, 1: 288–99.
Fleischhut, N., B. Meder, and G. Gigerenzer (2017), "Moral Hindsight," *Experimental Psychology*, 64 (2): 110–23.
Freeman, D., K. Aquino, and B. McFerran (2009), "Overcoming Beneficiary Race as an Impediment to Charitable Donations," *Personality and Social Psychology Bulletin*, 35 (1): 72–84.
Gollwitzer, P. M. and P. Sheeran (2006), "Implementation Intentions and Goal Achievement: A Meta-analysis of Effects and Processes," *Advances in Experimental Social Psychology*, 38: 69–119.
Goodwin, G. P. (2015), "Moral Character in Person Perception," *Current Directions in Psychological Science*, 24 (1): 38–44.
Greene, J. D., R. B. Sommerville, L. E. Nystrom, J. M. Darley, and J. D. Cohen (2001), "An fMRI Investigation of Emotional Engagement in Moral Judgment," *Science*, 293 (5537): 2105–8.
Gubbins, E. and R. M. Byrne (2014), "Dual Processes of Emotion and Reason in Judgments About Moral Dilemmas," *Thinking & Reasoning*, 20 (2): 245–68.

Haidt, J. (2001), "The Emotional Dog and Its Rational Tail: A Social Intuitionist Approach to Moral Judgment," *Psychological Review*, 108 (4): 814–34.
Inzlicht, M. and B. J. Schmeichel (2012), "What is Ego Depletion? Toward a Mechanistic Revision of the Resource Model of Self-Control," *Perspectives on Psychological Science*, 7 (5): 450–63.
Janoff-Bulman, R., S. Sheikh, and S. Hepp (2009), "Proscriptive Versus Prescriptive Morality: Two Faces of Moral Regulation," *Journal of Personality and Social Psychology*, 96 (3): 521–37.
Johnson-Laird, P. N. and R. M. Byrne (2002), "Conditionals: A Theory of Meaning, Pragmatics, and Inference," *Psychological Review*, 109 (4): 646–78.
Johnson-Laird, P. N. and S. Khemlani (2017), "Mental Models and Causation," in M. Waldman (ed.), *Oxford Handbook of Causal Reasoning*, 169–88, New York: Oxford University Press.
Kahneman, D. and A. Tversky (1982), "The Simulation Heuristic," in D. Kahneman, P. Slovic, and A. Tversky (eds.), *Judgment Under Uncertainty: Heuristics and Biases*, Cambridge: Cambridge University Press.
Kneer, M. and E. Machery (2019), "No Luck for Moral Luck," *Cognition*, 182: 331–48.
Knobe, J. (2010), "Person as Scientist, Person as Moralist," *Behavioral and Brain Sciences*, 33 (4): 315.
Kominsky, J. F., J. Phillips, T. Gerstenberg, D. A. Lagnado, and J. Knobe (2015), "Causal Superseding," *Cognition*, 137: 196–209.
Lagnado, D. A., T. Gerstenberg, and R. I. Zultan (2013), "Causal Responsibility and Counterfactuals," *Cognitive Science*, 37 (6): 1036–73.
Landy, J. F. and E. B. Royzman (2018), "The Moral Myopia Model," in G. Pennycook (ed.), *The New Reflectionism in Cognitive Psychology: Why Reason Matters*, 70–92, New York: Routeledge.
Lench, H. C., D. Domsky, R. Smallman, and K. E. Darbor (2015), "Beliefs in Moral Luck: When and Why Blame Hinges on Luck," *British Journal of Psychology*, 106 (2): 272–87.
Malle, B. F., S. Guglielmo, and A. E. Monroe (2014), "A Theory of Blame," *Psychological Inquiry*, 25 (2): 147–86.
Markman, K. D., N. Mizoguchi, and M. N. McMullen (2008), "It Would Have Been Worse Under Saddam," *Journal of Experimental Social Psychology*, 44 (3): 650–4.
Martin, J. W. and F. Cushman (2016a), "Why We Forgive What Can't Be Controlled," *Cognition*, 147: 133–43.
Martin, J. W. and F. A. Cushman (2016b), "The Adaptive Logic of Moral Luck," in J. Sytsma and W. Buckwalter (eds.), *The Blackwell Companion to Experimental Philosophy*, 190–202, Oxford: Wiley Blackwell.
McCloy, R. and R. M. Byrne (2000), "Counterfactual Thinking About Controllable Events," *Memory & Cognition*, 28 (6): 1071–8.
McCloy, R. and R. M. Byrne (2002), "Semifactual 'Even If' Thinking," *Thinking & Reasoning*, 8 (1): 41–67.
McEleney, A. and R. M. J. Byrne (2006), "Spontaneous Causal and Counterfactual Thoughts," *Thinking and Reasoning*, 12 (2): 235–55.
Mikhail, J. (2007), "Universal Moral Grammar," *Trends in Cognitive Sciences*, 11 (4): 143–52.
Moreno-Rios, S., J. A. Garcia-Madruga, and R. M. Byrne (2008), "Inferences from Semifactual 'Even If' Conditionals," *Acta Psychologica*, 128 (2): 197–209.
Oeberst, A. and I. Goeckenjan (2016), "When Being Wise After the Event Results in Injustice: Evidence for Hindsight Bias in Judges' Negligence Assessments," *Psychology, Public Policy, and Law*, 22 (3): 271.

Parkinson, M. and R. M. J. Byrne (2017), "Counterfactual and Semifactual Thoughts in Moral Judgments About Failed Attempts to Harm," *Thinking and Reasoning*, 23 (4): 409–48.
Phillips, J., J. B. Luguri, and J. Knobe (2015), "Unifying Morality's Influence on Non-moral Judgments," *Cognition*, 145: 30–42.
Pohling, R. and R. Diessner (2016), "Moral Elevation and Moral Beauty: A Review of the Empirical Literature," *Review of General Psychology*, 20 (4): 412–25. https://doi.org/10.1037/gpr0000089.
Roese, N. J. (1997), "Counterfactual Thinking," *Psychological Bulletin*, 121 (1): 133–48.
Roese, N. J. and K. Epstude (2017), "The Functional Theory of Counterfactual Thinking," *Advances in Experimental Social Psychology*, 56: 1–79.
Roese, N. J. and K. D. Vohs (2012), "Hindsight Bias," *Perspectives on Psychological Science*, 7 (5): 411–26.
Rozin, P. and E. B. Royzman (2001), "Negativity Bias, Negativity Dominance, and Contagion," *Personality and Social Psychology Review*, 5 (4): 296–320.
Sanna, L. J. and K. J. Turley (1996), "Antecedents to Spontaneous Counterfactual Thinking: Effects of Expectancy Violation and Outcome Valence," *Personality and Social Psychology Bulletin*, 22 (9): 906–19.
Sarin, A., D. A. Lagnado, and P. W. Burgess (2017), "The Intention-Outcome Asymmetry Effect," *Experimental Psychology*, 64 (2): 124–41.
Schein, C. and K. Gray (2018), "The Theory of Dyadic Morality: Reinventing Moral Judgment by Redefining Harm," *Personality and Social Psychology Review*, 22 (1): 32–70.
Schmeichel, B. J., K. D. Vohs, and R. F. Baumeister (2003), "Intellectual Performance and Ego Depletion: Role of the Self in Logical Reasoning and Other Information Processing," *Journal of Personality and Social Psychology*, 85 (1): 33.
Schnall, S. and J. Roper (2012), "Elevation Puts Moral Values into Action," *Social Psychological and Personality Science*, 3 (3): 373–8.
Schnall, S., J. Roper, and D. M. Fessler (2010), "Elevation Leads to Altruistic Behavior," *Psychological Science*, 21 (3): 315–20.
Siegel, J. Z., M. J. Crockett, and R. J. Dolan (2017), "Inferences About Moral Character Moderate the Impact of Consequences on Blame and Praise," *Cognition*, 167: 201–11.
Smallman, R. (2013), "It's What's Inside that Counts: The Role of Counterfactual Content in Intention Formation," *Journal of Experimental Social Psychology*, 49 (5): 842–51.
Smallman, R. and K. C. McCulloch (2012), "Learning from Yesterday's Mistakes to Fix Tomorrow's Problems: When Functional Counterfactual Thinking and Psychological Distance Collide," *European Journal of Social Psychology*, 42 (3): 383–90.
Smallman, R. and N. J. Roese (2009), "Counterfactual Thinking Facilitates Behavioral Intentions," *Journal of Experimental Social Psychology*, 45 (4): 845–52.
Timmons, S. and R. M. J. Byrne (2019), "Moral Fatigue: The Effects of Cognitive Fatigue on Moral Reasoning," *Quarterly Journal of Experimental Psychology*, 72 (4): 943–54.
Timmons, S., E. Gubbins, T. Almeida, and R. M. Byrne (2021), "Imagined Alternatives to Episodic Memories of Morally Good Acts," *Journal of Positive Psychology*, 16 (2): 178–97.
Van Baaren, R. B., R. W. Holland, K. Kawakami, and A. Van Knippenberg (2004), "Mimicry and Prosocial Behavior," *Psychological Science*, 15 (1): 71–4.
Walsh, C. R. and R. M. J. Byrne (2007), "How People Think 'If Only...' About Reasons for Actions," *Thinking & Reasoning*, 13 (4): 461–83.

Yao, Z. and R. Enright (2018), "The Role of Consequences of Moral Action in Maximizing Moral Elevation," *Journal of Moral Education*, 1–15. https://doi.org/10.1080/03057240.2018.1428540.

Young, L. and M. Koenigs (2007), "Investigating Emotion in Moral Cognition: A Review of Evidence from Functional Neuroimaging and Neuropsychology," *British Medical Bulletin*, 84 (1): 69–79.

Young, L., S. Nichols, and R. Saxe (2010), "Investigating the Neural and Cognitive Basis of Moral Luck," *Review of Philosophy and Psychology*, 1 (3): 333–49.

12

Why Idealized Agency Gets Animal (and Human) Agency Wrong[1]

Caroline T. Arruda and Daniel J. Povinelli

In recent years, the question of nonhuman animal agency has been the subject of direct philosophical inquiry in philosophy of action, philosophy of mind, and ethics.[2] This subject presents a set of difficult philosophical hurdles. Nonhuman animals are clearly capable of some forms of agency (e.g., purposive action), but whether they possess other forms of agency such as the capacity to act for reasons or engage in long-term planning depends on settling controversial questions about the nature of nonhuman animal minds and reasoning (e.g., Arruda and Povinelli 2016; Boeckle et al. 2020; de Mahy, Esteve, and Santariello 2021; Murray 2020). Notwithstanding this relatively new, independent interest in nonhuman animal agency, it has frequently served as an implicit *comparison case* for understanding human agency. For example, many explanations of the relationship between practical deliberation and intentional action in the human case rely on an implicit contrast drawn with putatively less complex reasoning (say, of the purely perceptual sort) in nonhuman animals.

Some might find this to be a relatively straightforward and uncontroversial approach. After all, nonhuman animals, even ones characterized in the literature as cognitively sophisticated, are assumed not to possess certain advanced capacities for agency that we are able to exercise. Moreover, such comparisons may, at first, seem quite fitting. Scholars often appeal to arguments by analogy to explain complex phenomena in nature (here, human agency) by referring to cases that express the same characteristic features as the phenomenon in question but in evolutionarily less complex forms (here, nonhuman animal agency). But just as arguments by analogy depend on the propriety of the analogy being drawn (e.g., the assumption that the relevant features in question are indeed analogous), we can ask whether comparisons between human and nonhuman animal agency are as explanatorily efficacious as they initially appear to be.[3] In what follows, we argue that these comparisons are typically flawed, and thus do not serve their explanatory aims. What's more, they simultaneously undercut the complexity of nonhuman animal agency, on the one hand, and fail to explain actual (as opposed to idealized) human agency on the other.

In this regard, we have two overall aims in this chapter: (1) to show that comparisons between human and nonhuman animal agency undermine our understanding of human agency, particularly with regard to understanding its range of expressions; (2) to show that these same comparisons also affect our understanding of nonhuman animal agency, particularly with regard to our ability to appreciate its complexity. In service of these aims, we begin by sketching two ways that comparison cases can be used in this context, which we dub the Simple Comparison Approach (SCA) and the Wholesale Approach (WA), respectively (Section 12.1). After outlining these approaches and their problems, we then show how the approaches affect (often implicitly) the way in which scientific protocols are designed to investigate nonhuman animal cognition, wherein the question of animals' agency is often, although not always, a vague presumption subordinated to other topics of scientific inquiry (Section 12.2). We conclude, in Section 12.3, by considering whether we might get more theoretical traction on the question of animal agency if we understood core questions in the philosophy of action as concerning *species-specific* theories of agency.

12.1 Two Ways of Drawing Comparisons between Human and Nonhuman Animal Agents (and Why They Are Flawed)

The idea that drawing comparisons between human and nonhuman animal agents is explanatorily efficacious is widespread, albeit oftentimes implicit. The most (in)famous example shows up in moral theory. In that context, Kant (2012) argued that we owe only indirect duties to nonhuman animals because they are not capable of the autonomous self-government of which human agents are capable. Setting aside the moral claims Kant makes, we can see the fingerprint of this human-animal comparison in his justification for these claims—namely, in the claim that nonhuman animal agents deserve less moral consideration because they do not express the form of agency characteristic of human agents. Perhaps more directly to the point, however, is Kant's claim that "[n]ature has willed that the human being should produce everything that goes beyond the mechanical arrangement of his animal existence entirely out of himself, and participate in no other happiness or perfection than that which he has procured for himself free from instinct through his own reason" (2007: 110). Setting aside whether this argument works for a theory of moral standing, it is the descriptive comparison that interests us. Comparisons like this populate the philosophical literature, albeit often implicitly (e.g., Bermúdez 2006: 137;[4] Bratman 1999;[5] Burge 2009;[6] Dennett 1989;[7] Dretske 2006;[8] Hurley 2006: 166;[9] Korsgaard 2009; 98–9, 159–76;[10] 2014, 2018;[11] Marcus 2021;[12] Millikan 2006: 119; Shepherd 2021;[13] Walden 2018: 85;[14] contrast with Butterfill and Apperly 2013; Hyman 2015: 53; Sterelny 2006: esp. 305; see Steward 2009 for a helpful gloss[15]). Despite our explicit efforts to avoid this trap, some may believe even we have fallen prey to it (Arruda and Povinelli 2016).

While these comparisons are implicitly present in much of the writing on agency, our aim in what follows is to draw out how they function and what commitments they would entail *if they were made explicit*. In the service of this end, we systematize the ways that comparisons of this type can get drawn: the SCA and the WA (Sections 12.1.2–12.1.3). We then evaluate the propriety of these types of comparisons, arguing that they are almost always structurally flawed and thus do not serve the end of understanding either human or nonhuman animal agency (Sections 12.1.2.1–12.1.3.1).

12.1.1 Preliminaries

Before turning to the ways the comparisons get drawn, let's briefly consider two (complementary) assumptions that might motivate someone to draw these types of comparisons:

> **The Idealizing Assumption:** The best way to explain human agency is to identify its necessary and sufficient capacities in their idealized forms.
> **The Complexity Assumption:** Nonhuman animal agency is less complex in all ways relative to human agency.

Consider the Idealizing Assumption (which concerns human agency). For the comparisons between human and nonhuman animals to have purchase, it is necessary to assume that the aim of a theory of human agency is to specify its necessary and sufficient (or merely sufficient) conditions. These take the form of the relevant individual capacities (e.g., the capacity to form intentions in light of reasons) that are deployed when acting in a full-blooded fashion. It is common for the target here to be the capacity of agents to consider their reasons in that capacity's most ideal, most-full-blooded form, rather than the everyday and frequently limited capacity for agents to fully consider their reasons.

The Idealizing Assumption does not immediately appear to be problematic insofar as it treats the aim of theories of agency to be to provide the benchmark for full-blooded human agency, while also leaving room for its everyday, less-than-ideal expressions. It is, however, problematic when married to the types of comparisons under consideration in this chapter. This is because defaulting to this assumption in the service of making comparisons between human and nonhuman animal agents skews the nature of the comparison being drawn (as we discuss in detail in Sections 12.1.2–12.1.3).

Now let us consider the Complexity Assumption, which concerns nonhuman animal agency. Again, for either of the explanatory comparisons in question to have purchase, we must assume that the agency to which human agents are being compared is *sufficiently similar* for us to learn something about the capacity in question by drawing the comparison. It also requires making a background assumption (often implicitly) that the thing being compared is either: (1) simpler or less complex relative to the explanandum, or (2) more complex and more sophisticated relative to the explanandum. In the context of comparisons between human and nonhuman animal agents, scholars typically assume (although they need not) that nonhuman animal agency is less developed in all ways relative to human agency.[16] And, for this reason, any comparison with nonhuman animal agents is thought to provide a simpler, clearer context within which to understand and explain human agency.

So how do these assumptions translate into types of ways one might compare human and nonhuman animal agency? There are two ways that they can be drawn:

Explanatory comparison #1 (Explaining human agency): We can appeal to *nonhuman animal agency* in order to (partially) explain *human agency* (either with regard to one or more of its component capacities or with regard to its necessary and sufficient conditions).

Explanatory comparison #2 (Explaining nonhuman animal agency): We can appeal to *human agency* in order to (partially) explain *nonhuman animal agency* (either with regard to one or more of its component capacities or with regard to its necessary and sufficient conditions).

We will show that both types of explanatory comparisons suffer from problems. Let's now turn to considering the specific, systematic ways that the explanatory comparisons can be drawn.

12.1.2 The Simple Comparison Approach

The Simple Comparison Approach (SCA) represents the most flat-footed version of the types of comparisons under consideration. It treats the comparison being drawn as applying *both* to human agency in general *and* to its individually necessary and sufficient capacities.

To illustrate how this approach works, imagine we want to better understand the role that our capacity to reason about, say, the truth of a belief (and the value of a resultant practical aim) plays in the ways we exercise that agency. We might gain some traction, per this approach, by drawing a comparison with chimpanzees' more limited (or potentially nonexistent) capacity for higher-order thought (and this capacity's application in practical reasoning). How does drawing this contrast help explain human agency? Consider an example. When Megan (the chimpanzee) chooses a higher-value food item (a rotten banana) over a lower-value food item (a fresh banana),[17] she does not need to reason about the nature of her preferences and whether the choice of the former conforms to those preferences. In this regard, Megan decides which food item to choose in light of her wants and not in light of any complex, value-laden comparisons. By contrast, when Angela (the adult human) reasons about whether to buy pasta or steak for dinner, she can draw a number of different kinds of complex, value-laden comparisons between the two. Perhaps she prefers steak to pasta but also judges that she prefers to eat a meal that has a lower carbon footprint and thus decides in favor of the pasta. Here, though Angela *could* deliberate in the much more limited fashion exemplified by Megan's choice, Angela *could also* gain more deliberative traction by consulting her preferences, which include some complex value-laden comparisons, and asking which choice conforms to them. Although Angela need not deliberate in this latter fashion, we gain a richer understanding of the scope of her deliberative powers (and thereby her broader exercise of her capacity for agency) by noting that she could. This conclusion is strengthened by the fact that Angela's choice of the pasta (notwithstanding her stronger desire for steak) expresses her more complex deliberative powers. We can see this, in part, by comparing what Angela is able to do with the capacities Megan displays. Noting that Angela's exercise of her agency could exceed that which Megan (could) display(s) helps us to more fully explain the upper limits of Angela's deliberative powers and, thereby, the upper limits of her capacity for agency. To underscore this point, consider that while Megan is surely able to choose a lower-value food item (the fresh banana) because she fears that Apollo, another chimp, will attack her if she takes the rotten banana, she does not deliberate in terms of the concept of making a trade-off among her stronger preferences in light of the value she places on avoiding being attacked. Though this is functionally the same as Angela's deliberation, Angela has the capacity to frame her deliberative choices in light of this type of trade-off whereas Megan may not be able to do so.

Before discussing the problems with this approach, let's probe the reaction that, on the basis of the example above, there seems to be no problem with the SCA. It seems well-suited for understanding the nature of human agency insofar as drawing a contrast with a less cognitively sophisticated creature points in the direction of the upper limits of the capacities necessary and sufficient for human agency. And a justification for this approach could easily be conjured in the form of claims of continuity in evolutionary theory. To put the point more formally, one might justify the use of the SCA in the following way:

1. If one accepts evolutionary theory, one must also accept the idea of mental continuity (e.g., the cognitive capacities associated with acting) among species *whose behaviors resemble each other in ways that are as similar as humans and chimpanzees.*
2. The claim that humans possess mental systems that chimpanzees do not possess is a claim of discontinuity.
   --
3. Therefore, the claim that humans possess mental systems that chimpanzees do not possess is a kind of discontinuity claim that is at odds with evolutionary theory, and thus one should reject it.

One might think that rejecting the SCA requires rejecting the intuitive pull of this argument. After all, it could seem that abandoning the SCA is tantamount to denying the kind of mental continuity described above, whereas accepting the SCA embraces it. There are, however, serious problems with this argument, most notably the ambiguity of "similar" in the case of human and chimpanzee behaviors, respectively.[18] And if there are problems with this argument, then there are problems with any approaches (e.g., the SCA) that depend on it for this plausibility.

It is not our purpose here to present a detailed, knock-down argument to support the above claim (this has been done elsewhere: see note 18). And even in the face of such arguments, one might think the SCA is intuitively plausible without respect to debates about evolution and mental continuity. After all, it seems reasonable to draw some kinds of comparisons between human agents and nonhuman animal agents. This impression notwithstanding, we argue that the SCA is a mistaken approach. It has structural problems that affect its explanatory purchase, to which we now turn.

12.1.2.1 The SCA's Structural Problems: SCA and the Complexity Assumption

First, SCA gets off the ground only if we treat nonhuman animal agency as necessarily less complex in all ways relative to human agency, as laid out in the Complexity Assumption. This is a problem for three reasons:

(a) The SCA treats nonhuman animals' actions as *necessarily* less complex relative to human action on the grounds that the former's overall capacity for agency is generally more minimal than human agency.
(b) The SCA assumes this complexity globalizes to all the relevant component capacities just because it applies to nonhuman animal agency in general.
(c) The SCA downplays the empirically well-established complexity of nonhuman animal action.

To begin, (a) is a problem because it does not follow that any one instance of nonhuman animals' action is less complex relative to the same action-type when performed by human agents *just because* nonhuman animals' overall capacity for agency is generally less complex than humans' capacity for agency. As a somewhat counterintuitive example, in any given instance both chimpanzees and humans might respond appropriately to the gaze direction of others *without explicitly representing their visual (mental) perspective* (chimpanzees because they perhaps cannot do so, humans because it is not necessary to do so in that specific instance). In any such limited comparison, it does not follow that the chimpanzee's resulting expression of agency is less complex that the human's resulting expression of agency. The (non-mentalistic) representations that are initially formed by the two species could be highly similar (or, at least, sufficiently or functionally similar), and thus any expressions of agency that follow could be highly similar as well.

Relatedly, (b) is a problem because it commits the fallacy of composition. Just because nonhuman animal agency is more minimal than human agency *overall* does not entail that the former's component capacities are also necessarily more minimal.

Finally, (c) is a problem in light of what empirical research on nonhuman animal actions reveals about the complexity of their actions. Regardless of how controversial empirical claims about the capacity for higher-order thinking in animals are settled, there is little debate that animals and humans do differ in at least some very important ways in this regard. Some scholars claim that experimental procedures have revealed at least some components of higher-order thinking in animals (Tomasello 2022). Other scholars have attempted to show why none of the existing protocols can say anything one way or the other about the presence of such mental abilities (e.g., Povinelli 2020). But regardless of which position turns out to be empirically correct, all scholars would be forced to acknowledge that any uniquely human forms of higher-order thinking reside alongside capacities shared with other animals (higher-order or not) and thus provide room for humans to reinterpret their actions in a larger number of ways than animals. Likewise, while animals will dramatically overlap with humans in the kinds of interpretations they can place on their actions, there will be other ways in which their interpretations differ. An excellent example is Tomasello's (2022) view that while chimpanzees can reason about (some) mental states, they "do not understand their world in terms of the contrast between subjective points of view and objective reality; they simply experience the world as it appears to them and act accordingly" (14). This, in turn, prompts him to ask, "So how is it that humans have come to view the world in terms of a contrast between subjective and objective perspectives?" (14). This illustrates the point that even the most cognitively liberal interpretations of animals leave ample room for substantial differences in human and animal agency.

12.1.2.2 SCA and the Idealizing Assumption

By forcing us to think of human agency in "scaled up" terms, the SCA inadvertently licenses an overly idealized conception of human agency and action, as represented by what we have called the Idealizing Assumption. Considering agency in "scaled up" terms could suggest a working definition which describes human agency in its most idealized form, where each of its necessary and sufficient capacities is conceptualized in their most developed, most fully expressed, most error-free forms.

Why is this a problem? To begin, it is clear that actual human agents frequently do not fully exercise core aspects of their capacity for agency in this idealized way, even when they are acting as relatively full-blooded agents. Examples include standard mistakes associated with evaluating risk, forming inconsistent intentions and failing to drop one, and falling prey to weakness of will, among others. These "failures" are instances of various types of less-than-ideal agency, where human agents count as acting as agents but exercise at least one of its component capacities in a less-than-full-blooded fashion. Examples notwithstanding, we suggest that the SCA works only if we think that human agency is best understood in its idealized form. But what these examples show is that this approach misses what actual human agency looks like and the various ways that agency can be expressed. Moreover, it sets an unreasonable standard for what constitutes genuine human agency (let alone agency more generally).

12.1.3 The Wholesale Approach

In light of these problems with SCA, particularly its susceptibility to the fallacy of composition, one might think that a natural solution is to modify the sense in which this approach is "simple"—viz., by drawing contrasts both between human agency and nonhuman animal agency *and* between select individual capacities necessary for agency. One might tinker with this overly permissive approach by limiting the kinds of things to which the contrast is supposed to apply. Here, one might think that the relevant contrast to be drawn is between full-blooded human agency, treated as a *set* of necessary and sufficient capacities, and the *set* of capacities nonhuman animals deploy when acting. Let us call this the Wholesale Approach (WA).

Put concretely, rather than trying to understand human agents' capacity for, say, rational deliberation by appealing to nonhuman animal agents' limitations with regard to higher-order thought, we would instead try to explain how human agents deploy this capacity *when acting as agents* by comparing it to the way nonhuman animals deploy a putatively analogous capacity *when acting as agents*. Here, the target is understanding and explaining the scope of the capacity for agency, where explaining its component capacities is done in the service of this broader aim and only in the context of how the capacities are deployed in action.[19]

This may seem like a small shift from the capacities necessary and sufficient for agency *treated individually* (in the SCA) to the capacities necessary and sufficient for agency *treated as an integrated whole* (in the WA). But this impression is mistaken. First, it avoids the fallacy of composition. It does so because it does not license comparisons between characteristics true of agency as a whole (say, that it is less complex) and any one of its component capacities (say, the capacity to act for reasons). Rather, the comparisons are only between the capacity for agency generally, as possessed by human and nonhuman animal agents. Second, it treats agency as the explanandum and, thereby, evaluates its component capacities (e.g., the capacity for rational deliberation) *only in the context of* how they are deployed when agents act. By contrast, SCA assumes that you can learn something about both agency and its component capacities (considered on their own) by drawing the comparisons in question.

12.1.3.1 What Goes Wrong with the WA

While intuitively appealing, the WA suffers from different problems than the SCA. While the Idealizing and Complexity Assumptions play an explicit role in the SCA, they are relevant for the WA in a different, less explicit way. To see how these assumptions, when married with the WA, produce problems, it is necessary to consider the claims to which their conjunction commits one:

> **Commitment 1:** All capacities necessary and sufficient for agency, when treated as an integrated set, are equally complex (or full-blooded) and step up or down together.[20]
> **Commitment 2:** Agency is an integrated set of capacities for which the relevant set of comparisons can be drawn between one set of capacities as possessed by one type of agent, on the one hand, and an identical set of capacities (in some lower-level form) by another type of agent.

Let's begin by explaining what each requires in practice. Consider Commitment (1). Whereas the SCA suffered from the fallacy of composition, the WA does not. Using the WA requires one to accept the following claim: if one capacity necessary for agency (say, the capacity for rational deliberation) is complex in way y, then another capacity necessary for agency (say, instrumental reasoning) is complex in a parallel, stepwise manner. This does not require, like the SCA did, that we draw inferences from the whole (viz., the capacity for agency) to its parts (viz., the capacities individually necessary for agency). Rather, it requires that we treat all the component capacities as equally full-blooded and as equally developed or complex insofar as they constitute the whole that is the capacity for agency.

By contrast, consider Commitment (2). Here the idea is that agency is a set of capacities for which any overall evaluation of whether, and the extent to which, a creature is an agent depends not just on the individual capacities that are possessed, but also how they are integrated and deployed in conjunction with one another.

But are these commitments true? First, let's consider problems they both share. The way that each capacity individually necessary for agency is deployed differs in important ways from our understanding of how the overall capacity for agency is deployed. Moreover, the ways in which *single* capacities are expressed in less-than-ideal ways in these contexts says nothing about the creature's overall capacity for agency. It also works the other way around. A creature's overall capacity for agency says nothing about how individual capacities might be expressed in less-than-ideal cases.

To illustrate the point, consider some examples. One involves habitual actions. In these instances, the overall capacity for agency is deployed in a more minimal fashion while the way we exercise our capacity for, say, bodily control may be comparable to the way that we exercise this capacity in instances of full-blooded agency. A second involves cases of weakness of will. In these cases, agents exercise fairly developed forms of agency notwithstanding the fact that they are falling prey to a very basic form of irrationality.

But, in addition to these counterexamples, these commitments suffer from a more general problem. That is, we cannot treat the capacity for agency (reliably at least) as an *integrated* whole, which is what the WA requires. Put more precisely, the two commitments claim that agential capacities are structured in this integrated way (by necessity). Thus, they run roughshod over the ways its component capacities might come in different strengths or degrees in any one instance of (either human or nonhuman animal) action. Sometimes agency is a "disintegrated whole" for lack of a better phrase. It is "disintegrated" in the sense that while the capacity for agency as a whole might be quite complex, some of the ways its component capacities are expressed are not comparably complex in the context of certain kinds of actions. That is precisely what cases like weakness of will and, perhaps to a lesser degree, habitual action illustrate. Weakness of will is not a case where human agents are, generally, expressing less complex forms of agency overall; rather, they are acting as deliberative agents but their capacity to respond appropriately to what they think is the best course of action by their own lights is expressed in a much more minimal form (if it is expressed at all in this instance). Similarly, human agents acting habitually are not, overall, less complex agents even though this particular instance of agency is, itself, less complex. This challenge undermines *both* commitments, albeit in different ways, and, thereby it holds as grounds for rejecting the WA. Let's now consider the problems that affect each commitment in turn.

In the case of Commitment (1), it is clear that the capacities for agency are not structured in a parallel, step-wise fashion, nor is agency uniformly scalar. This affects how we draw comparisons among nonhuman animals, on the one hand, and human animals, on the other. If agency is not structured in a parallel, step-wise fashion, this means that any comparisons between different types of agents will potentially draw inaccurate conclusions about whether (and, if so, what form of) agency is being expressed. This is because the comparison assumes that as we conceptually move away from *agency-of-a-more-developed-type* (i.e., as it becomes less complex overall), it becomes less complex across all its component capacities. But this is clearly false, as the earlier examples illustrate. And even if it were true for one particular kind of agent or one class of actions, it would not follow that we can infer that a similar, step-wise structure applies to other forms of agency.

Commitment (1) suffers from an additional problem. Different types of agency are not structured or organized in ways that are necessarily analogous to each other even if the types of agency look, on the surface, to be similar. So, *full-blooded* human agency is (arguably) structured around rational deliberation and the capacity to form intentions in light of such deliberation, while agency in other species might not have these same capacities at their core. Here, there is a question about what "structured around" is supposed to pick out. For the moment, let's use the following working definition: there are core capacities without which agency, as possessed by the creature in question, would not be expressed in its canonical (or at least most recognizable) form. These capacities are jointly sufficient for bringing about an instance of agency. A weaker working definition would take the capacities *necessary* for bringing about an instance of agency to be those around which agency is structured. We reject this weaker working definition because what "structured around" is supposed to pick out as the capacities that make agency *distinctive* as a capacity and not merely those capacities that are necessary (but not sufficient) for its realization.

With this stronger working definition in mind, we can apply it to better understand the problems with Commitment (1). It is arguably true that human agency would not be expressed in its most recognizable form if it lacked some form of rational deliberation at its core. If this is right, then comparisons between human and nonhuman animal agency cannot rely on the assumption that they are *comparably structured*, where "structured" picks out the idea specified in the aforementioned working definition. This will hold even if it turns out to be false that rational deliberation is the core capacity around which human agency is structured. The problem with this Commitment is not *which capacity* it proposes is at the core of human agency; rather, it is that it takes there to be a core capacity around which it, and all forms of agency, are structured. And, as we have shown, this is false.

Commitment (2) suffers from a related set of problems. The challenges to Commitment (1) focused on the claim that different forms of agency are *similarly structured or integrated*. The challenges to Commitment (2) derive from the idea that different forms of agency can be what we have called "disintegrated" in comparable ways. Here "disintegrated" simply means that some expressions of the capacity for agency might be full-blooded while some of its component capacities might be less-than-full-blooded. We gave a number of examples of this phenomenon above; however, here we focus on the various ways that agency might be disintegrated such that two forms of disintegrated agency might not be relevantly comparable.

Agency may be disintegrated in different ways. First, it can be disintegrated *overall*. Imagine one agent for whom one capacity is comparatively "over-developed" and another for whom it is comparatively "under-developed." Let's further assume that the way they are expressed together makes agency look non-uniform across its component capacities. As an example, consider a professional musician, whose capacity to sight-read music quickly as she plays far outstrips her ability to fully reflect on what she is doing and why she is doing it as she is playing. Her capacity to sight-read music is "over-developed," while her ability to fully reflect on her reasons for what she does as she plays is comparatively "under-developed." In this case, her capacity for agency is not an "integrated" whole in that the capacities are expressed in different kinds of ways and in differing strengths. If agency can be disintegrated overall, then comparisons *between* agents will be potentially cases of non-comparability given that the *ways* it can be disintegrated might not be reflected in the general comparison between two types of agents for whom the overall capacity for agency looks roughly analogous.

Second, agency can also be "disintegrated" in the context of one particular expression of the overall capacity for agency, as in the case of weakness of will noted earlier. These are cases of what one of us (CTA, *ms*) has elsewhere dubbed "agential failure"—namely, cases where agency is expressed in a less-than-ideal form. Whether these are cases of "failure" properly understood, or simply cases of less-than-ideal agency is not important here. This matters for our purposes because any overall comparisons between types of agents (in order to understand something about their overall capacities for agency) will be based on the presumption that the capacities in question are always fully integrated. But if they are not necessarily always fully integrated, then this raises the question of whether *how* they are integrated depends on the specific contexts in which they are expressed. And if that is true, then it is possible that no overall model for the capacities, considered as a set, will capture this feature of actual agency. Thus, any comparisons between types of agents will be drawn on the basis of the wrong kind of picture of what those capacities, considered as whole (viz., the capacity for agency broadly understood), are like.

12.2 An Empirical Case Study

12.2.1 Analyzing the SCA and WA in the Empirical Literature

Given that researchers rarely make their assumptions regarding the SCA and the WA explicit, it is difficult to analyze how these approaches are deployed in the service of larger experimental projects in the animal cognition literature. That being said, at least two strategies are possible. One strategy would gather published empirical studies that bear on the question of animal agency and then examine researchers' indirect comments or experimental design choices that articulate with the questions we have focused on in the previous sections of this chapter. An obvious difficulty with this approach is that, given there are few researchers (if any) that have framed their empirical studies in terms of agency per se, our analysis of such research projects could be seen as uncharitable. Of course, a defense could be mounted for such an approach: namely, the fact that a researcher does not explicitly frame a given research projects in terms of assumptions about agency in no way implies that such assumptions are absent.

The second approach (which we adopt here) is to carefully describe a single (unpublished) experimental project bearing on the question of agency that was designed and carried out by one of us (DJP), and then share an emic perspective on how assumptions relevant to the SCA and WA were made without explicit recognition and, perhaps more importantly, how these assumptions crippled the project from the get-go. The study in question was designed to compare how chimpanzees reason about their own causative role in a simple event: namely, a light turning on. The study was designed to compare conditions in which (a) a light turned on only when the subject pressed a button, (b) the light turned on *all by itself* (that is, prior to the subject being close enough to reach and press the button) or (c) the light turned on after the subject began to reach to press the button, *but before the subject made contact with the button* (see details below). Importantly, the reason the study in question remains unpublished is because certain background assumptions about the ease of training the animals in some initial discriminations turned out to be mistaken. In fact, we encountered formidable difficulties in training the animals to make the initial discrimination between (a) and (b), and this blocked the path to testing them on critical variants of condition (c). We contend that the unstated assumptions of this protocol map onto aspects of both the SCA and WA and help to reveal the complex nature of their deployment.[21]

12.2.2 Case Study: Protocol for Studying Chimpanzees' Judgments of Self-Caused Events

Consider a simple apparatus consisting of two food reward compartments, one on the left and one on the right, each with a door that can be opened by a subject when searching for a reward. These compartments are hereafter referred to as LEFT and RIGHT. In the middle of the apparatus, equidistant between the two food compartments, we affixed a large, depressible button that sat against an indicator panel that could either be OFF (dark) or ON (flashing bright red). On all trials, the doors to both compartments were locked until the light came ON.

In the *self-cause* condition, the chimpanzee had to push the button in order for the panel to illuminate. Once the chimpanzees pressed the button, they were free to search for food, either LEFT or RIGHT. However, the (arbitrary) relation in this condition was that the food was always LEFT.[22] In a second condition, the light illuminated when the chimpanzee first entered the testing room (*other-cause* condition). In this case, the food was on the RIGHT. The protocol called for each subject to be trained to robustly discriminate between these two conditions before testing commenced. In testing, the protocol called for infrequent probe trials to be interspersed into a background of the *self-* and *other-cause* conditions. As described above, on these probe trials the light illuminated after the chimpanzee had started to reach for the button, but before the subject's hand made contact with it (*cause-at-a-distance-cause* condition). This *cause-at-a-distance* testing condition was designed with several variants, each corresponding to progressively closer distances between the hand and the button before the panel illuminates.[23]

Thus, the rough logic of the study was to first train the chimpanzees to learn to search LEFT if the light came on when they pressed the button, and to search RIGHT if they entered the room and the light illuminated on its own (before they approached the apparatus). Having established this robust discrimination, we assumed that if the chimpanzees possessed an explicit recognition of their own agency in their actions, this training would allow them to parse the two experimental conditions in terms of reasons for why the light comes on:

- *Self-cause* reasoning: <When I make the light come on, the food will be LEFT.>
- *Other-cause* reasoning: <When the light comes on by itself, the food will be RIGHT.>

Thus, after training, the stage would be set to ask where the chimpanzees would search on test (probe) trials when the light came on *after they launched a reach, but before they made contact with the button*. If they did frame the training in terms of *self-* versus *other-causes*, would they attribute the light coming on during the test trials as self-caused (and thus search LEFT), or other-caused (and thus search RIGHT)? And would the timing of the light illumination relative to the phase of the reach (initial, mid-way, almost to the button) systematically influence their searches? [24]

To dispense with the punchline up front, we were never successful in training our chimpanzees to make the basic *self-* versus *other-cause* discrimination when trials of two conditions were intermixed within a single training session. This was not due to disorganized behavior on their part. Indeed, in sessions where all trials were *self-cause*, the subjects rapidly learned to search LEFT after pressing the button (thus making the light come ON). Likewise, in sessions where all trials were *other-cause* (the light came ON by itself), the animals quickly learned to always search RIGHT. But when the trial types were randomly mixed together, their behavior declined to chance; that is, they choose LEFT or RIGHT at random (or, in some cases, defaulted to always choosing LEFT or always choosing RIGHT). This was a not momentary difficulty. Despite extensive efforts, including direct prompting by the experiments (gradually faded out), and many additional trials, the subjects never learned to flexibly deploy their behavior *as if* they were tracking *reasons related to their agency* for why the light was coming on. Thus, we were never able to establish an experimental context in which we could observe how they reacted to ambiguous cases of the deployment of their agency (i.e., the test trials; see note 23).

12.2.3 Background Assumptions

Here, we wish to focus not on the logic of the (unconducted) test trials, but rather on the background assumptions of the training phase. It is clear we never fully considered the possibility that we might not be able to easily train our chimpanzees to cope with mixed sessions of the basic self- versus other-cause trials. This raises the important question of what we were assuming about chimpanzee versus human agency in the training context.

To begin, we believe the training protocol reveals the fingerprint of the WA, deployed at an implicit level. First, recall that WA relies on the idea that one can draw fruitful comparisons between the general capacity for agency as possessed by human agents and the general capacity for agency as possessed by nonhuman animal agents. In this case, the WA is lurking in the background of the protocol's design—namely, that chimpanzees should have been able to learn the preliminary training discriminations easily *in the context of assessing their role as causal agents* precisely because we think human agents can easily make the relevant background distinction between self- and other-caused events. The fact that chimps were unable to do so easily does not necessarily imply that they are less complex agents. Rather, it is possible that the ways in which they are able to exercise their capacity for agency might not map onto all the ways that humans can do so in similar contexts.[25] Nonetheless, the protocol assumed the initial training would be relatively easy for both humans and chimpanzees without ever explicitly stating why. In retrospect, there was an operative background idea that there was a minimal, shared capacity for agency that both humans and chimpanzees would express by learning the initial discrimination "easily."[26]

Aside from the fingerprint of the general WA, there are other ways in which aspects of the WA show up in this protocol. For example, consider what we dubbed Commitment (2):

> Agency is an *integrated* set of capacities for which the relevant set of comparisons can be drawn between one set of capacities as possessed by one type of agent, on the one hand, and an identical set of capacities (in some lower-level form) by another type of agent.

The assumption that chimpanzees would be able to learn the training discrimination as easily as humans seems implicitly based on the idea that their capacity for agency is structured around some form of rational deliberation *much like* that which humans possess (albeit in a less developed form). In this regard, the assumptions explicitly detailed in Commitment (2), and the attendant WA, were again lurking in the background of the protocol design.

But, of course, the chimpanzees struggled with what we assumed would be easy training. But why did they struggle and what can we make of that fact? Again, we can see the role of Commitment (2) in the limitations it places on the available interpretations of this fact. If Commitment (2) and the WA are true, then we ought to conclude that chimpanzees do not, even in a very minimal form, possess the relevant capacities that humans possess for acting for reasons. But we know this is false (e.g., Arruda and Povinelli 2016, 2018). Thus, we have reason to reject both Commitment (2) and the WA.

To see further the limitations that these approaches put on our interpretative frameworks, consider a counterfactual. Imagine that the chimpanzees had been able to successfully complete the aforementioned training (and surely, with enough effort, they might have been able to do so). There is a question about whether that would vindicate using the WA and the attendant Commitment (2). We think it does not. After all, even if they had succeeded on the initial training, there is no guarantee that they would have been deploying higher-order reasoning of the type: "In this case *I made the light come on*," and, "But oh look, in this other case, I didn't make the light come on, *it came on all by itself.*" They could, just as easily, have learned to relate to where their body was when the light came on, and used that to distinguish the cases in question. Note that if something like the latter were the case, the WA and Commitment (2) would both be suspect: there would be no reason to think the chimpanzees were deploying a comparable, but watered-down, capacity for human agency. Instead, it opens the door for them to have been reasoning about the contingency in a way unrelated to what we think of as the recruitment of *self-related reasons* to explain the events in question.[27]

12.3 Conclusions

In one sense, it may seem as though our argument leaves us with very few resources to explain nonhuman animal agency. If we cannot draw comparisons with human agency, which is clearly a robust form of the capacity in question, how are we to determine whether agency is present in other species? By way of conclusion, we propose that we may get more theoretical traction on the question of nonhuman animal agency if we understood the questions about agency as *species-specific*.

What, in a very general form, would this look like? And can we ever draw any fruitful comparisons between agents of different types?

We suggest that theories of agency ought to aim to spell out what constitutes being an agent in the context of a theory of the capacities the specific creature in question possesses.[28] In this regard, there may be no universal set of capacities that are necessary and sufficient for a creature to be an agent; rather, all we can hope for is a set of sufficient conditions for agency for creatures of a given type. But it follows then that *the form of agency* is equally *species-specific*. So, say, human-specific agency may take a form that looks like quite different from, say, a cetacean-specific account. That is, it differs both in its upper bounds for what constitutes agency in its most developed form (or full-blooded agency) and also in the capacities that are sufficient for agency.

A *species-specific* account of agency has the advantage of leaving space for building a theory of nonhuman animal agency without requiring that we settle difficult questions about the possibility of nonconceptual content,[29] nonhuman animals' theory of mind,[30] and nonhuman animals' capacity to reason.[31] We take this to be an advantage. But what, then, of comparisons with human agents? We propose that the route to accomplishing this in the case of human-specific agency lies in the choice of *exemplars*. While it is natural to use human exemplars to build this kind of account, nonhuman primate *exemplars* of agency are essential complements to such a view because they provide a natural route to accounting for variability in the human-specific case. Nonhuman primate agency will have a lower upper boundary for full-blooded agency in comparison to the human case, and some forms of nonhuman primate agency will exemplify roughly isomorphic capacities to those involved in human agency.

Notes

1 We thank the editors of this volume for their helpful comments on earlier drafts.
2 See, for example, Andrew 2000; Arruda and Povinelli 2016, 2018; Bermúdez 2003, 2006; Dennett 1987; DeGrazia 2009; Dreckmann 1999; Glock 2009; Hurley 2003a,

2003b; Hyman 2015; Lurz 2003; Rowlands 2006; Saidel 2009; Shepherd 2021; Steward 2009.

3 Elsewhere, one of us (DJP) has explored in extended detail the challenges in using the overt behavioral similarities between human and nonhuman behavior to sort out the kinds of psychological processes that support them (see e.g., Povinelli and Giambrone 1999). The difficulties emerge from two directions. First, the fact that higher-order representations sometimes attend specific goal-directed actions in humans does not mean that they always do. Second, the fact that, in humans, such higher-order representations sometimes both attend *and causally interact with* the behaviors in question does not mean that such higher-order mental states are present in animals—even when they engage in highly similar goal-directed behaviors. In the present context, this means: (1) the quality of human agency can be quite variable with respect to the same behavior emitted at different time-points; (2) animals may express robust forms of agency that overlap with some, but not all, forms of human agency. See also notes 16 and 18 and Section 12.1.2.1.

4 Notwithstanding the fact the Bermúdez (2006) is vindicating the sense in which nonhuman animals can reason about concepts even though they lack a language of thought, he, too, draws comparisons of the type above.

5 Bratman (1999: 59) too acknowledges that "[n]ot all purposive agents are planning agents," citing nonhuman animals as examples of purposive agents that lack the planning capabilities that he associates with more developed forms of agency.

6 Burge (2009: 256) writes, "Action theory in philosophy, over the last half-century, has been almost as hyper-intellectualized as perception theory. Usually discussion begins with cases involving desire, intention, will, and then focuses on sub-cases of intentional action. There is nothing in itself wrong with this focus, of course. But often it is assumed that such approaches encompass all action. Animal action begins earlier. Much of it is pre-intentional, even pre-representational. Even representational agency precedes intention and belief."

7 Dennett is widely regarded as vindicating nonhuman animal agency. Still, consider the choice between the three interpretative stances for explaining a creature's behavior (viz., the intentional stance, the design stance, and the physical stance). These stances lay on a scale, moving from less complex (the physical stance) to more complex (the intentional stance). Although the choice of which stance to apply depends on their explanatory purchase with regard to the observed behavior, the point here is that choosing the intentional stance depends on a standard for rational action that is modeled on human agency. In this regard, regardless of which stance we choose to explain nonhuman animals' behavior, we are nonetheless relying on a picture of human agency to understand their capacity for agency (we discuss this point more fully elsewhere: Arruda and Povinelli 2016).

8 Although he is discussing different forms of rationality, Dretske (2006: 109) articulates the difference between animal and human rationality in terms of its application to reasoning about actions: "You or I don't have to think behavior B is rational, it doesn't have to accord with our picture of what it makes sense to do, or what it would be best to do, in order for it to be minimally rational. This, indeed, is why I think minimal rationality is a useful concept in thinking about animal rationality[. . .] Why should a chimpanzee or a crow have to be doing what you and I think is rational in order to be doing exactly the same sort of thing (doing something for reasons) you and I are doing when we do what we think is rational? [. . .] If we are going to investigate animal rationality, why not *first* identify minimal rationality in animals, and then, after we are

sure what is being done is being *for* reasons, ask whether the reasons for which it is being done make it a reasonable thing to do?"

9   Hurley (2006), like Bermúdez (2006), is interested in vindicating the sense in which animals are rational agents of a kind. Nonetheless, she models animals' capacity for this kind of agency on what functionally similar capacities they might be able to deploy even though they lack the robust rational capacities humans possess, with the caveat that we ought not simply treat them as "substandard." She writes, "The alieness of nonhuman animals is part of what makes it so interesting to consider whether they can sometimes be understood as rational agents, without simply projecting substandard humanity onto them. In particular, it is interesting to try to understand rational agency in the absence of its distinctively human concomitants such as conceptual and mind-reading abilities."

10 Korsgaard (2009) appeals to the idea of "defective action" to explain lower forms of agency (in both human and nonhuman agents).

11 Korsgaard (2018: 35) writes, "the difference between human beings and the other animals is not that the other animals do not have self-consciousness or selves. It is that we human beings play a particularly active and responsible role in constituting our selves, our own minds and identities."

12 Marcus (2021) writes, "[O]nly rational creatures have practical knowledge in virtue of exercising a power to determine what ends are worth pursuing. Practical thought in humans is the exercise of such a power. It's not that humans do and animals don't act knowingly. It's that what it comes to for the human to act knowingly is different from what it comes to for the animal to act knowingly, on account of the difference in the power the exercise of which constitutes the relevant species of practical knowledge."

13 Shepherd (2021: 100) writes, "It is not my aim here to articulate the metaphorical ladder of agency in any fine-grained way, but it is worth mentioning that we seem to find psychological activity in some animals that approximates practical reasoning, without really qualifying as such. There is a level of psychological complexity in between that of rigid behavioral profiles in characteristic circumstances, and full-blown reasoning of the sort humans sometimes use well."

14 Walden (2018: 85) writes, "Distinguish two kinds of agency. Animal agency consists in an ability to act on the basis of one's intentional attitudes in whatever the distinctive way required for genuine action is. Reflective agency involves animal agency plus successful reflection on the attitudes that produce action."

15 Steward explains the role of these kinds of comparisons in justifying the use of Morgan's Canon in explaining animal action: "As I have already explained, Morgan was operating with a basically tripartite understanding of the psychic 'faculties' which might underlie animal behavior —instinct, intelligence and reason—though he seems to have been perfectly aware that this division was strictly pro tem and likely ultimately to be superseded by a more complex set of divisions, particularly within the vast category that he calls 'intelligence.' Undoubtedly, Morgan's own suggestion that these powers can be arranged hierarchically was underwritten, and perhaps made to seem more obvious than it really is, by assumptions which are false, in particular, the assumption that evolution 'always marches from simple to complex,' as Sober puts it, and the vestiges of the linear conception of a scale of nature which Darwinism refuted, according to which every species can be ranked as 'higher,' 'lower,' or 'equal to' each of the others. In particular, we must suspect Morgan of having taken for granted the thought that 'higher' implies 'more characteristic of, or closer to, distinctively human behavior' and hence the assumption that man is the measure of all things

cognitive. From a less anthropocentric view point, one might indeed be tempted to claim, as Sober suggests at one point, that 'it makes no sense to ask whether the ant's use of pheromones is higher or lower than the plover's use of deception. Both have their place in life's diversity.'"

16 A highly relevant case study is the question of whether chimpanzees (and/or other species) reason about their own and other's mental states *qua* mental states (i.e., whether they possess a "theory of mind") (e.g., Andrews 2020; Tomasello 2022). The results from any number of experimental investigations over the past two decades have convinced many (if not most) scholars that chimpanzees form explicit representations such mental states (e.g., Hare et al. 2000, Hare, Call, and Tomasello 2001; Call et al. 2004; Melis, Call, and Tomasello 2006; Bräuer, Call, and Tomasello 2007; Kaminski, Call, and Tomasello 2008; Grueneisen et al. 2017; Lurz et al. 2018 Krupenye et al. 2016; Kano et al. 2019). To be sure, a (vociferous) minority argument disputes this view and claims that all of the relevant experimental designs fall within a definable genre whose core characteristics render them unable to diagnose the presence of such higher-order reasoning (e.g., Povinelli and Vonk 2004; Povinelli 2020; Povinelli and Henley 2020). Nonetheless, it is important to note that even scholars who are convinced by such experiments still argue for socio-cognitive limitations in nonhuman animals (relative to humans). They claim, for example, that animals do not represent all kinds of mental states (e.g., belief states) or that the lack of language prevents them from sharing their beliefs with others—in either case constraining their expression of agency (see Tomasello et al. 2005; Tomasello 2022). The most general point for our purposes is that in the case of theory of mind (and by extension other domains of cognition such as causal reasoning, tool use, planning, etc.), researchers generally present the capacities of animals as both very much like humans, but also constrained (or "watered-down") relative to humans. In practice, this ascription of more limited forms of social understanding in animals creates ample room for scholars to develop theories that explain how human agency is more powerful/elaborated/complex than even that of our closest living relatives (i.e., chimpanzees; see Tomasello 2022).

17 As a preliminary (and not all that important) part of a protocol for studying chimpanzee social cognition, we once presented our chimpanzees with a choice between a rotten banana and a fresh banana. We prepared the rotten bananas by leaving them in a black plastic bag outdoors in the Louisiana summer for a week. To our surprise, most of the apes (consistently) preferred the rotten bananas—a fact we should have anticipated given that rotten bananas are considerably sweeter.

18 Detailed eviscerations of this argument have been laid out elsewhere (see Povinelli and Giambrone 1999; Povinelli 2004, 2012). In brief, it seems indisputable that *different* mental states may be able to casually modulate the same behavior in humans at different points in time. Sometimes these mental states will be of the higher-order type. On other occasions, they will not be. As a simple case study, sometimes that act of following another's agent's gaze direction might be attended by the mental state of wondering what they <see>. In other cases, it might not be. If higher-order mental states turn out to be uniquely human (i.e., capacities that evolved after the evolutionary split between the human and chimpanzee lineages), then similar (even homologous) behaviors (say, "behavior x") in chimpanzees would (by definition) never be attended by higher-order mental states. This would in no way contradict evolutionary theory. It would simply describe a case in which "behavior *x*" evolved (and was in functional operation) long before humans evolved additional ways of

understanding the behavior. This would set the stage for humans to learn new ways to put the behavior to use. (We note that all of this depends on settling the far more tricky problem of isolating what constitutes a *comparable behavior*; see Povinelli and Giambrone 1999, for a case study involving the social behavior of "gaze-following" and the detection of attention; see Povinelli 2020 for other case studies.)

19 We tried to do so in Arruda and Povinelli (2016).
20 CTA is grateful to Luciana Garbayo and John Symons for pointing out this problem as it applied to an argument made about agency in a related paper in progress.
21 Importantly, we are not interested in whether results from this experimental design could offer reliable information about any particular aspect of chimpanzee agency. Our purpose here is strictly to examine how the SCA and WA are deployed in service of generating experiments.
22 For experimental reasons, the contingencies were counterbalanced across subjects. So, for half of the animals the self-cause condition was yoked to food being on the LEFT; for the other half, the food was on the RIGHT.
23 The protocol defined three distances of the hand from the button that correlated with the light turning ON: 40 cm, 20 cm, and 5 cm. These distances roughly correspond to (1) the earliest phase of a reach, (2) the midpoint of a reach, and (3) almost touching the button. The light was controlled by an infrared beam that closed a circuit when interrupted (thus causing the light to turn ON).
24 To reiterate, there are complex unresolved conceptual issues undergirding this framing of the experiment; in particular, issues surrounding mere actions (intentional, goal-directed behavior) and acting for (or in light of) reasons. Settling these disputes is not important here. We merely wish to show how, in the one context of one experimental design, the SCA and WA are deployed.
25 A slightly different, but complementary, conclusion can also be drawn. The chimpanzees' failure could be understood as an indication that they lack the higher-order interpretative abilities to distinguish between self- and other-causation, which informs and affects the way they are able to express their agential capacities.
26 Another excellent example of this kind of unstated (but clearly operative) assumption can be found in our tests of chimpanzees reasoning about object weight (see Povinelli 2012: ch. 4). Here we assumed, again quite incorrectly, that an initial training phase with young children and chimpanzees would be easy for both species, and would let us then ask more complex questions. The training proved extremely difficult for the chimpanzees and revealed some striking assumptions we had made about the possession and deployment of both species' basic agential capacities.
27 While not spelled out in detail here, part of the broader issue is whether, most of the time, humans exercise their "most recognizable" form of agency (acting in light of reasons). From the standpoint of the reinterpretation hypothesis, there is ample reason to think they do not (see notes 2, 17–18).
28 This approach stands in contrast to the more traditional approach to agency, with the notable exceptions of views such as Davidson's (2001a [1963]) and Dennett's (1987, 1996), according to which we determine first the capacities necessary and sufficient conditions for agency and then determine who or what possesses them.
29 Some arguments, such as those advanced by Carruthers (1996; but compare with Carruthers 2013), Stich (1979), Davidson (2001b, 2001c), Dreckmann (1999), McDowell (2007a: 343, 2007b), and, to some degree, Fodor (1975, but compare with 1990: 152–3), suggest that we need language or other unique cognitive abilities (see Clark 2005) to have concepts, concepts to have propositional attitudes, and

finally, propositional attitudes to form intentions. Of course, other arguments, such as those advanced by Andrews (2000), Bermúdez (2003, 2006, 2009), Beisecker (1999), Carruthers (2005: 92–4), DeGrazia (2009), Dennett (1987, 1996), Dretske (1998), Dreyfus (2007), Glock (2010), Hurley (2003a), Lurz (2003), Pacherie (2011), Rowlands (2006), and Saidel (2009), deny this claim and its consequent.

30 See Andrews 2000; Butterfill and Apperly (2013); Tomasello and Call (2008).
31 We provide such an account in Arruda and Povinelli (2016).

References

Andrews, K. (2000), "Our Understanding of Other Minds: Theory of Mind and the Intentional Stance," *Journal of Consciousness Studies*, 7 (7): 12–24.

Andrews, K. (2020), *The Animal Mind: An Introduction to the Philosophy of Animal Cognition*, London: Routledge.

Arruda, C. T. and D. J. Povinelli (2016), "Chimps as Secret Agents," *Synthese*, 193 (7): 2129–58.

Arruda, C. T. and D. J. Povinelli (2018), "Two Ways of Relating to (and Acting for) Reasons," *Mind & Language*, 33 (5): 441–59.

Beisecker, D. (1999), "The Importance of Being Erroneous: Prospects for Animal Intentionality," *Philosophical Topics*, 27 (1): 281–308.

Bermúdez, J. L. (2003), "The Domain of Folk Psychology," *Royal Institute of Philosophy Supplements*, 53: 25–48.

Bermúdez, J. L. (2006), "Animal Reasoning and Proto-logic," in S. Hurley and M. Nudds (eds.), *Rational Animals?*, 127–37, New York: Oxford University Press.

Bermúdez, J. L. (2009), "Mindreading in the Animal Kingdom," in R. W. Lurz (ed.), *The Philosophy of Animal Minds*, 145–64, New York: Oxford University Press.

Boeckle, M., M. Schiestl, A. Frohnwieser, R. Gruber, R. Miller, T. Suddendorf, R. D. Gray, A. H. Taylor, and N. S. Clayton (1938), "202 'New Caledonian Crows Plan for Specific Future Tool Use,'" *Proceedings of the Royal Society, Series B*, 287: 20201490.

Bratman, M. (1999), "Toxin, Temptation, and the Stability of Intention," in *Faces of Intention*, 58–92, Cambridge: Cambridge University Press.

Bräuer, J., J. Call, and M. Tomasello (2007), "Chimpanzees Really Know What Others Can See in a Competitive Situation," *Animal Cognition*, 10 (4): 439–48.

Burge, T. (2009), "Primitive Agency and Natural Norms," *Philosophy and Phenomenological Research*, 79 (2): 251–78.

Butterfill, S. A. and I. A. Apperly (2013), "How to Construct a Minimal Theory of Mind," *Mind & Language*, 28 (5): 606–37.

Call, J., B. Hare, M. Carpenter, and M. Tomasello (2004), "'Unwilling' Versus 'Unable': Chimpanzees' Understanding of Human Intentional Action," *Developmental Science*, 7 (4): 488–98.

Carruthers, P. (1996), *Language, Thought and Consciousness: An Essay in Philosophical Psychology*, Cambridge: Cambridge University Press.

Carruthers, P. (2013), "Animal Minds Are Real, (distinctively) Human Minds Are Not," *American Philosophical Quarterly*, 50 (3): 233–48.

Carruthers, P. (2005), "Why the Question of Animal Consciousness Might not Matter Very Much," *Philosophical Psychology*, 18 (1): 83–102.

Clark, A. (2005), "Word, Niche and Super-Niche: How Language Makes Minds Matter More," *Theoria. Revista de Teoría, Historia y Fundamentos de la Ciencia*, 203: 255–68.

Davidson, D. (1999), "The Emergence of Thought," *Erkenntnis*, 51 (1): 511–21.
Davidson, D. (2001a), "Actions, Reasons, and Causes," in D. Davidson, *Essays on Actions and Events*, 3–19, Oxford: Clarendon.
Davidson, D. (2001b), "Agency," in D. Davidson, *Essays on Actions and Events*, 43–62, Oxford: Clarendon.
Davidson, D. (2001c), "Freedom to Act," in D. Davidson, *Essays on Actions and Events*, 63–82, Oxford: Clarendon.
Davidson, D. (2001d), "Rational Animals," in D. Davidson, *Subjective, Intersubjective, Objective*, 95–106, Oxford: Clarendon.
de Mahy, D., N. A. Esteve, and A. Santariello (2021), "New Test, Old Problems: Comment on 'New Caledonian Crows Plan for Specific Future Tool Use,'" *Proceedings of the Royal Society, Series B*, 288: 1958, 20210186.
DeGrazia, D. (2009), "Self-Awareness in Animals," in R. W. Lurz (ed.), *The Philosophy of Animal Minds*, 201–17, New York: Oxford University Press.
Dennett, D. (1987), *The Intentional Stance*, Cambridge, MA: MIT Press.
Dennett, D. (1989), "Cognitive Ethology: Hunting for Bargains or a Wild Goose Chase?," in A. Montefiore and D. Noble (eds.), *Goals, No-Goals, and Own Goals: A Debate on Goal-Directed and Intentional Behaviour*, 101–16, London: Unwin Hyman.
Dennett, D. (1996), *Kinds of Minds: Toward an Understanding of Consciousness*, New York: Basic Books.
Dreckmann, F. (1999), "Animal Beliefs and Their Contents," *Erkenntnis*, 51 (1): 597–615.
Dretske, F. (1998), "Minds, Machines, and Money: What Really Explains Behavior," in J. Bransen (ed.), *Human Action, Deliberation and Causation*, 157–73, Dordrecht: Springer.
Dretske, F. (2006), "Minimal Rationality," in S. Hurley and M. Nudds (eds.), *Rational Animals?*, 107–16, New York: Oxford University Press.
Dreyfus, H. L. (2007), "The Return of the Myth of the Mental," *Inquiry*, 50 (4): 352–65.
Fodor, J. A. (1975), *The Language of Thought*, Cambridge, MA: Harvard University Press.
Fodor, J. A. (1990), "Making Mind Matter More," in J. A. Fodor, *A Theory of Content and Other Essays*, Cambridge, MA: MIT Press.
Glock, H. J. (2009), "Can Animals Act for Reasons?," *Inquiry*, 52 (3): 232–54.
Glock, H. J. (2010), "Can Animals Judge?," *Dialectica*, 64 (1): 11–33.
Grueneisen, S., S. Duguid, H. Saur, and M. Tomasello (2017), "Children, Chimpanzees, and Bonobos Adjust the Visibility of Their Actions for Cooperators and Competitors," *Scientific Reports*, 7 (1): 1–10.
Hare, B., J. Call, B. Agnetta, and M. Tomasello (2000), "Chimpanzees Know What Conspecifics Do and Do Not See," *Animal Behaviour*, 59 (4): 771–85.
Hare, B., J. Call, and M. Tomasello (2001), "Do Chimpanzees Know What Conspecifics Know?," *Animal Behaviour*, 61 (1): 139–51.
Hurley, S. (2003a), "Animal Action in the Space of Reasons," *Mind & Language*, 18 (3): 231–57.
Hurley, S. (2003b), "Making Sense of Animals: Interpretation vs. Architecture," *Mind & Language*, 18 (3): 272–80.
Hurley, S. (2006), "Making Sense of Animals," in S. Hurley and M. Nudds (eds.), *Rational Animals?*, 139–74, New York: Oxford University Press.
Hyman, J. (2015), *Action, Knowledge, and Will*, New York: Oxford University Press.
Kaminski, J., J. Call, and M. Tomasello (2008), "Chimpanzees Know What Others Know, but Not What They Believe," *Cognition*, 109 (2): 224–34.
Kano, F., C. Krupenye, S. Hirata, M. Tomonaga, and J. Call (2019), "Great Apes Use Self-experience to Anticipate an Agent's Action in a False-Belief Test," *Proceedings of the National Academy of Sciences*, 116 (42): 20904–9.

Kant, I. (2012), *Groundwork of the Metaphysics of Morals*, Cambridge: Cambridge University Press.
Kant, I. (2007), *Anthropology, History, and Education*, Cambridge: Cambridge University Press.
Korsgaard, C. (2009), *Self-constitution: Agency, Identity, and Integrity*, New York: Oxford University Press.
Korsgaard, C. (2014), "On Having a Good," *Philosophy*, 89 (3): 405–29.
Korsgaard, C. (2018), *Fellow Creatures: Our Obligations to the Other Animals*, New York: Oxford University Press.
Krupenye, C., F. Kano, S. Hirata, J. Call, and M. Tomasello (2016), "Great Apes Anticipate that Other Individuals Will Act According to False Beliefs," *Science*, 354 (6308): 110–14.
Lurz, R. W. (2003), "Neither HOT nor COLD," *Psyche*, 9: 01.
Lurz, R. W., C. Krachun, L. Mahovetz, M. J. Wilson, and W. Hopkins (2018), "Chimpanzees Gesture to Humans in Mirrors: Using Reflection to Dissociate Seeing from Line of Gaze," *Animal Behaviour*, 135: 239–49.
Marcus, E. (2021), "Anscombe and the Difference Rationality Makes," in *The Anscombean Mind*, 241–52, London: Routledge.
McDowell, J. (2007a), "What Myth?," *Inquiry*, 50 (4): 338–51.
McDowell, J. (2007b), "Reply to Dreyfus," *Inquiry*, 50 (4): 366–70.
Melis, A. P., J. Call, and M. Tomasello (2006), "Chimpanzees (*Pan troglodytes*) Conceal Visual and Auditory Information from Others," *Journal of Comparative Psychology*, 120 (2): 154–62.
Millikan, R. G. (2006), "Styles of Rationality," in S. Hurley and M. Nudds (eds.), *Rational Animals?*, 117–26, New York: Oxford University Press.
Murray, S. (2020), "A Case for Conservatism About Animal Consciousness," *Journal of Consciousness Studies*, 27 (9–10): 163–85.
Pacherie, E. (2011), "Nonconceptual Representations for Action and the Limits of Intentional Control," *Social Psychology*, 42 (1): 67–73.
Povinelli, D. J. (2004), "Behind the Ape's Appearance: Escaping Anthropomorhism in the Study of Other Minds," *Dædalus: Journal of the American Academy of Arts and Sciences*, Winter: 29–41.
Povinelli, D. J. (2012), *World Without Weight: Perspectives on an Alien Mind*, New York: Oxford University Press.
Povinelli, D. J. (2020), "Can Comparative Psychology Crack Its Toughest Nut," *Animal Behavior and Cognition*, 7 (4): 589–652.
Povinelli, D. J. and S. Giambrone (1999), "Inferring Other Minds: Failure of the Argument by Analogy," *Philosophical Topics*, 27 (1): 167–201.
Povinelli, D. J. and T. Henley (2020), "More Rope Tricks Reveal Why More Task Variants Will Never Lead to Strong Inferences About Higher-Order Causal Reasoning in Chimpanzees," *Animal Behavior and Cognition*, 7 (3): 392–418.
Povinelli, D. J. and J. Vonk (2004), "We Don't Need a Microscope to Explore the Chimpanzee's Mind," *Mind & Language*, 19 (1): 1–28.
Rowlands, M. (2006), "The Normativity of Action," *Philosophical Psychology*, 19 (3): 401–16.
Saidel, E. (2009), "Attributing Mental Representations to Animals," in R. W. Lurz (ed.), *The Philosophy of Animal Minds*, 35–51, New York: Oxford University Press.
Shepherd, J. (2021), *The Shape of Agency: Control, Action, Skill, Knowledge*, New York: Oxford University Press.

Sterelny, K. (2006), "Folk Logic and Animal Rationality," in S. Hurley and M. Nudds (eds.), *Rational Animals?*, 293–311, New York: Oxford University Press.

Steward, H. (2009), "Sub-Intentional Actions and the Over-Mentalization of Agency," in Constantine Sandis (ed.), *New Essays on the Explanation of Action*. Palgrave Macmillan.

Stich, S. P. (1979), "Do Animals Have Beliefs?," *Australasian Journal of Philosophy*, 57 (1): 15–28.

Tomasello, M. (2022), "What is it Like to Be a Chimpanzee?," *Synthese*, 200 (2): 1–24.

Tomasello, M. and J. Call (2008), "Assessing the Validity of Ape-Human Comparisons: A Reply to Boesch (2007)," *Journal of Comparative Psychology*, 122 (4): 449–52. https://doi.org/10.1037/0735-7036.122.4.449.

Tomasello, M., M. Carpenter, J. Call, T. Behne, and H. Moll (2005), "Understanding and Sharing Intentions: The Origins of Cultural Cognition," *Behavioral and Brain Sciences*, 28 (5): 675–91.

Walden, K. (2018), "Morality, Agency, and Other People," *Ergo: An Open Access Journal of Philosophy*, 5 (3): 69–101.

Index

action
   causation and   1
   experimental method and   4–5
   explanation puzzles of   139–42, 144
   skilled   33–5, 44
   theories of   1
agency cues   173, 175, 201
agency model of free will attribution   172–3, 175, 181
assertion   113, 117, 127, 129
   factive accounts of   116, 121, 130
   knowledge-rule hypothesis of   114–15
   normative status of   123, 127, 130

belief   136–7, 141, 146, 172, 173, 175
blame   3, 116–17, 123, 129, 157, 183, 209
   excuse validation and   126–8
   intentionality and   160, 175
   pro-blame bias   159, 161, 182–3

causal judgment   175–6, 217
   action and   1
   deviance and   2
communication   114
complexity assumption about human agency   231, 234
consciousness   3, 35–7, 82, 112, 153
   concepts of   14–16
   free will and   13
   metacognition and   44
   phenomenal   13–15, 20–2
control   13, 23, 80, 172
   cognitive control   36–8, 56, 64
   ego depletion and   53
   expected value of   57–60
   metacognition and   39–40
   principle of   191
   self-control   51, 66, 156–7, 160, 162
   skilled action and   35
counterfactual thinking   152–4, 162, 213
   additive and subtractive   214
   causality and   153–5
   morally good action and   210, 216, 223–4
   semi-factual statements and   217–18

deliberation   3, 82, 153, 155, 193, 238, 242
delusions   87–90
desire   136–7, 141–2, 146, 172, 173, 175
dual-process theory of moral judgment   194–5, 197–8, 200, 203

free will   151, 157, 159, 162
   the courtroom approach to   171
   the experimental-philosophical approach to   183
   folk theory of   182
   perception of   174, 181
   the perceptual approach to   172, 184

goals   42, 135, 138, 140, 143, 172

hindsight bias   193, 203, 211, 218, 220, 224

idealizing assumption about human agency   231, 235
information agency   156
intentionality   158, 173
   causal judgment and   4, 218
   intention and   172, 194, 212
   irrationality and   76–7
intentional stance   135–6, 138
irrationality   100–1

knowledge   115, 139, 183

mental continuity of animal and human agency   233
mental models   220–2
mental simulation   152, 155–7, 162, 211

mindreading 171
Model Penal Code 197
   sexual assault in the 197–9
moral luck 191–3, 228

negligence 193, 202–3

problem of causal deviance 2
prospection, *see* mental simulation
punishment 157, 162, 172, 183, 193, 199, 201
   consequentialist aims of 192, 194–6
   criminal 194, 196–7
   intentionality and 216

reputation 158
responsibility 152, 158, 160, 172, 182
   avoidance of 160–1

free will and 158–62
moral luck and 192
split-brain patients and 82–4

species-specific approach to agency 243–4
structure of agency 238

teleological principle of rational action 135–7
trade-off reasoning 232–3

unlucky falsehoods 128

vigilance 60–3

wholesale approach to human agency 235–7, 239

www.ingramcontent.com/pod-product-compliance
Lightning Source LLC
Chambersburg PA
CBHW071818300426
44116CB00009B/1354